English Legal System

Catherine Elliott
and Frances Quinn

LONGMAN

LONDON AND NEW YORK

Addison Wesley Longman Ltd
Edinburgh Gate
Harlow, Essex, CM20 2JE, England
and Associated Companies throughout the world.

Published in the United States of America
by Addison Wesley Longman Inc., New York.

First published 1996
Fourth impression 1997

ISBN 0 582 23868.4 PPR

British Library Cataloguing-in-Publication Data
A catalogue record of this book is available from the
British Library

Library of Congress Cataloging-in-Publication Data
Elliott, Catherine.
  English legal system / Catherine Elliott and Frances Quinn.
    p. cm.
  Includes bibliographical references and index.
  ISBN 0–582–23868–4 (pbk.)
  1. Law—Great Britain. 2. Justice. Administration of—Great
Britain. 3. Courts—Great Britain. I. Quinn, Frances. II. Title.
KD662.E45 1996
349.42—dc20
[344.2]
                                              96–12689
                                                  CIP

Set by 35 in Baskerville
Produced by Longman Asia Ltd, Hong Kong
EPC/04

Contents

Preface

This book is designed to provide a clear explanation of the English legal system and how it works in practice today. As ever, the legal system and its operation are currently the subject of heated public debate, and we hope that the material here will allow you to enter into some of that debate and develop your own views as to how the system should develop.

One of our priorities in writing this book has been to explain the material clearly, so that it is easy to understand, without lowering the quality of the content. Too often, law is avoided as a difficult subject, when the real difficulty is the vocabulary and style of legal textbooks. For that reason, we have aimed to use 'plain English' as far as possible, and explain the more complex legal terminology where it arises. There is also a glossary of difficult words at the back of the book. In addition, chapters are structured so that material is in a systematic order for the purposes of both learning and revision, and clear subheadings make specific points easy to locate.

Although we hope that many readers will use this book to satisfy a general interest in law and the legal system, we recognize that the majority will be those who have to sit an examination on the subject. Therefore, each chapter features typical examination questions, with detailed guidance on answering them, using the material in the book. This is obviously useful at revision time, but we recommend that when first reading the book, you take the opportunity offered by the questions sections to think through the material that you have just read and look at it from different angles. This will help you both understand and remember it. You will also find a section at the end of the book which gives useful general advice on answering exam questions on the English legal system.

This book is part of a series that has been written by the same authors. The other books in the series are *Criminal Law*, *Contract Law* and *Tort Law*. We have endeavoured to state the law as at 1 January 1996.

Catherine Elliott
and Frances Quinn
London 1996

Acknowledgements

We are indebted to the following examination boards for permission to reproduce questions which have appeared in their examination papers.

The Associated Examination Board (*AEB*)

Northern Examinations and Assessment Board (*NEAB*)

Oxford and Cambridge Examinations Council (responsible for examinations previously conducted by OCSEB, UCLES and UODLE) (*Oxford*)

University of London Examinations and Assessment Council (*London*)

Welsh Joint Education Committee (*WJEC*)

The examination boards are not responsible for the suggested answers to the questions. Full responsibility for these is accepted by the authors.

Table of Statutes

Cases, Law Reports and Case References: A Guide

In order to understand the table of cases and the reference to cases in this book generally you need to know about the naming of cases, law reports and case references.

▶ Case names

Each legal case that is taken to court is given a name. The name of the case is usually based on the family name of the parties involved. Where there are more than two parties on each side, the case name will usually be shortened to just include one name for each side. In essays the name of the case should normally be put into italics or underlined, though in this book we have chosen to put them in bold. The exact case names in civil law and criminal law are slightly different so we will consider each in turn.

Criminal law case names

If Ms Smith steals Mr Brown's car then a criminal action is likely to be brought by the state against her. The written name of the case would then be **R *v* Smith**. The letter 'R' stands for the latin *Rex* (King) or *Regina* (Queen) depending on whether there was a king or queen in office at the time of the decision. Occasionally the full latin terms are used rather than the simple abbreviation R, so that the case **R *v* Smith** if brought in 1996 while Queen Elizabeth is in office could also be called **Regina *v* Smith**. The idea is that the action is ultimately being brought by the state against Ms Smith.

The 'v' separating the two parties names is short for 'versus', in the same way as one might write Nottingham Forest Football Club v Arsenal Football Club when the two teams are going to play a match against each other. When speaking, instead of saying 'R versus Smith' one should really say 'The Crown against Smith'.

If Ms Smith is only 13, and therefore still a minor, the courts cannot reveal the identity of the child to the public and therefore the case will be referred by her initial rather than her full name: **R *v* S**.

Occasionally criminal prosecutions are brought by the Government's law officers. If an action was brought by the Attorney-General against Ms

Smith it would be called **A-G** *v* **Smith**. If it was brought by the Director of Public Prosecutions it would be called **DPP** *v* **Smith**. Should the state fail to bring an action at all, Mr Brown might choose to bring a private prosecution himself and the case would then be called **Brown** *v* **Smith**.

Civil law case names

In civil law if Mr Brown is in a neighbour dispute with Ms Smith and decides to bring an action against Ms Smith the name of the case will be **Brown** *v* **Smith**. This is orally expressed as 'Brown and Smith', rather than 'Brown versus Smith'. At the original trial, the first name used is the name of the person bringing the action (the plaintiff) and the second name used is that of the defendant. If there is an appeal against the original decision, then the first name will usually be the name of the appellant and the second name that of the respondent, though there are some exceptions to this.

In civil law the state can have an interest in what are described as judicial review cases. For example, Mr Brown may be unhappy with his local council, Hardfordshire City Council, for failing to take action against his neighbour. He may bring an action against the Council and the action would be called **R** *v* **Hardfordshire City Council ex parte Brown**.

In certain family and property actions a slightly different format may be used. For example, if Ms Smith's child, James Smith is out of control and needs to be taken into care, a resulting legal action might be called **Re Smith** or **In re Smith**. 'Re' is latin and simply means 'in the matter of' or 'concerning'. So the name **Re Smith** really means in the matter of James Smith.

As with civil cases there is sometimes a need to prevent the public from knowing the name of the parties, particularly where children are involved. The initials of the child are then used rather than their full name. So the above case might be called **Re S** rather than **Re Smith** to protect James.

▶ The Law Reports

Because some cases lay down important legal principles, over 2,000 each year are published in law reports. Some of these law reports date back over 700 years. Perhaps the most respected series of law reports are those called *The Law Reports,* because before publication the report of each case included in them is checked for accuracy by the judge who tried it. It is this series that should be cited before a court in preference to any other. The series is divided into several sub-series depending on the court which heard the case, as follows:

Appeal Cases (containing decisions of the Court of Appeal, the House of Lords and the Privy Council)

Chancery Division (containing decisions of the Chancery Division of the High Court and their appeals to the Court of Appeal)
Family Division (containing decisions of the Family Division of the High Court and their appeals to the Court of Appeal)
Queen's Bench (containing decisions of the Queen's Bench Division of the High Court and their appeals to the Court of Appeal)

Case reference

ach case is given a reference(s) to explain exactly where it can be found in a law report(s). This reference consists of a series of letters and numbers that follow the case name. The pattern of this reference varies depending on the law report being referred. The usual format is to follow the name of the case by:

A year. Where the date reference tells you the year in which the case was decided, the date is normally enclosed in round brackets. If the date is the year in which the case is reported, it is given in square brackets. The most common law reports tend to use square brackets.
A volume number. Not all law reports have a volume number, sometimes they simply identify their volumes by year.
The law report abbreviation. Each series of law reports have an abbreviation for their title so that the whole name does not need to be written out in full. The main law reports and their abbreviations are as follows:

All England Law Reports	(All ER)
Appeal Cases	(AC)
Chancery Division	(Ch D)
Criminal Appeal Reports	(Cr App R)
Family Division	(Fam)
King's Bench	(KB)
Queen's Bench Division	(QB)
Weekly Law Reports	(WLR)

A page number. This is the page at which the report of the case commences.

For example, **Cozens** *v* **Brutus** [1973] AC 854 means that the case was reported in the Appeal Cases law report in 1973 at page 854; **DPP** *v* **Hawkins** [1988] 1 WLR 1166 means that the case was reported in the first volume of the Weekly Law Report of 1988 at page 1166; and **R** *v* **Angel** (1968) 52 Cr App R 280 means that the case was reported in the 52nd volume of the Criminal Appeal Reports at page 280.

These references can be used to go and find and read the case in a law library which stocks the relevant law reports. This is important as a text book can only provide a summary of the case and has no legal status in itself, it is the actual case which contains the law.

Table of Cases

Introduction

•••••••••••••

This book examines the legal system of England and Wales, looking at how our law is made and applied. However, before you study the institutions involved in these processes, and the processes themselves, it is important to know something about the background against which they operate: the constitution. A constitution is a set of rules which details a country's system of government; in most cases it will be a written document, but in some countries, including Britain, the constitution cannot be found written down in one document, and is known as an unwritten constitution.

Constitutions essentially set out broad principles concerning who makes law and how, and the allocation of power between the main institutions of the state – government, parliament and the judiciary. They may also indicate the basic values on which the country should expect to be governed, such as the idea that citizens should not be punished unless they have broken the law, or that certain rights and freedoms should be guaranteed, and the state prevented from overriding them.

Although constitutional law is a branch of law that is studied in its own right, you will see as you read through this book that the constitutional issues discussed here are extremely important in some areas of debate about the English legal system. You may find it useful to refer back to this introduction at these points.

▶ The unwritten constitution

Britain is very unusual in not having a written constitution – almost every major Western democracy has one. In many cases, the document was written after a major political change, such as a revolution or securing independence from a colonial power.

However, the fact that our constitution is not to be found in a specific document does not mean that we do not have a constitution: if a country has rules about who holds the power to govern, what they can and cannot do with that power, and how that power is to be passed on or transferred, it has a constitution, regardless of the fact that there is no one constitutional

1

document In our constitution, for example, it is established that the Government is formed by the political party which wins a general election, and that power is transferred from that party when they lose an election.

Having said that, the exact details of some areas of our constitution are subject to debate. This is because the sources of the constitution include not only Acts of Parliament and judicial decisions, which are of course written down (although not together in one document), but also what are known as conventions. Conventions are not law, but are long-established traditions which tend to be followed, not because there would be any legal sanction if they were not, but because they have simply become the right way to behave. In this respect they are a bit like the kind of social rules that most people follow – for example, it is not against the law to pick your nose in public, but doing so usually invites social disapproval, so we generally avoid it. In the same way, failing to observe a constitutional convention is not against the law, but provokes so much political disapproval that conventions generally are followed, and most people concerned would see them as binding. Some well-established examples of conventions are that the Queen does not refuse to give her consent to Acts of Parliament; that judges should not undertake activities associated with a political party; and that the Speaker of the House of Commons does his or her job impartially, despite being a member of one of the parties represented in the House. There are, however, a number of conventions about which constitutional experts disagree. For example, there is a convention that when a government loses an election, and a rival party secures a majority in that election, the Queen invites the leader of that rival party to form a government. However, if the election results in no party having an overall majority, it is not clear who the Queen should invite to form a government. In practice, when this has happened, two parties have combined together and agreed on an overall leader (this is called a coalition government), but because the conventions are unwritten, we have no way of knowing what should happen if this were not done.

Because conventions are not law, they are not enforced by the courts; however, someone who has broken a convention may end up being forced to resign from their post as a result of the disapproval it causes.

The separation of powers

One of the basic principles underlying our constitution is that of the separation of powers. According to this principle, developed by the eighteenth-century French philosopher Montesquieu, all state power can be divided into three types: executive, legislative and judicial. The executive represents what we would call the government, and its servants, such as the police and the army; the legislative is Parliament; and the judicial is of course judges.

The basis of Montesquieu's theory was that these three types of power should not be concentrated in the hands of one person or group, since this would give them absolute control, with no one to check that the power was exercised for the good of the country. Instead, Montesquieu argued, each type of power should be exercised by a different body, so that they can each keep an eye on the activities of the other and make sure that they do not behave unacceptably.

Montesquieu believed that England at the time when he was writing was an excellent example of this principle being applied in practice. Whether that was true even then is debatable, and there are certainly areas of weakness now, as we shall see in later chapters.

The supremacy of parliament

A second fundamental principle in our constitution is the supremacy of Parliament. This basically means that Parliament is the highest source of law in the country: it can make whatever law it wants, and the courts must apply that law. So if, for example, Parliament passed a law tomorrow announcing that all newborn babies had to be killed, or that all dog-owners had to keep a cat as well, there might well be huge controversy and public anger, but the laws would still be valid and the courts would, in theory at least, be obliged to apply them.

This position contrasts with that in countries which have what is known as a Bill of Rights. This is a statement of the basic rights which citizens can expect to have protected from state interference; it may be part of a written constitution, or a separate document. In such countries, the courts can refuse to apply legislation which conflicts with the protected rights.

The rule of law

The third basic principle of our constitution is known as the rule of law. It is developed from the writings of the nineteenth-century writer Dicey. According to Dicey, the rule of law had three elements. First, that there should be no sanction without breach, meaning that nobody should be punished by the state unless they had broken a law. Secondly, that one law should govern everyone, including both ordinary citizens and state officials. Thirdly, that the rights of the individual were not secured by a written constitution, but by the decisions of judges in ordinary law.

The real importance of the rule of law today lies in the basic idea underlying all three of Dicey's points (but especially the first) that the state should use its power according to agreed rules, and not arbitrarily. The issue has arisen frequently in the context of the troubles in Northern Ireland. For example, opposition to an alleged shoot to kill policy by the armed forces against suspected terrorists was based on the principle that

suspected criminals should be fairly tried, according to the law, and punished only if convicted.

A written constitution?

There has been much debate in recent years about whether the UK
should have a written constitution. The main reasons put forward in
favour of this are that it would clear up some of the grey areas concerning conventions, make the constitution accessible to citizens, and, some
argue, provide greater protection of basic rights and liberties, such as
freedom of speech.

Written constitutions can be changed, but usually only by means of a
special procedure, more difficult than that for changing ordinary law. It
may, for example, be necessary to hold a referendum on the proposed
change, or gain a larger than usual majority in Parliament, or both. This
contrasts with our unwritten constitution, which can be changed by an
ordinary piece of legislation. For example, some people have argued that
the right of people suspected of crime to remain silent when questioned,
without this being taken as evidence of guilt, was part of our constitution;
nevertheless, that right was essentially abolished by the Criminal Justice
and Public Order Act 1994. If the United Kingdom had had a written
constitution then this right would probably have been contained in it and
a special procedure would have had to be followed to change the constitution to remove that right.

Those in favour of our unwritten constitution argue that it is the
product of centuries of gradual development, and that it is part of our
cultural heritage that it would be wrong to destroy. They also point out
that the lack of any special procedural requirements for changing it
allows flexibility, so that the constitution develops along with the changing needs of society.

1 Sources of law

The word source can mean several different things with regard to law, but for our purposes it primarily describes the means by which the law comes into existence.

English law stems from seven main sources, though these vary a great deal in importance. The basis of our law today is case law, a mass of judge-made decisions which lays down rules to be followed in future cases. For many centuries it was the main form of law and it is still very important today. However, the most important form of law, in the sense that it prevails over most of the others, is statute, or Acts of Parliament, which today is the source of most major changes in the law. As well as being a source of law in their own right, statutes contribute to case law, since the courts occasionally have to interpret statutory provisions, and such decisions lay down new precedents. Delegated legislation is a related source, laying down detailed rules made to implement the broader provisions of statutes.

An increasingly important source of law is the legislation of the European Communities, which is the only type of law that can take precedence over statutes in the UK, and is increasingly influencing the decisions of the courts in interpreting statutes. Finally, custom, equity and obligations relating to international treaties are minor sources of law, though Britain's obligations under the European Convention on Human Rights have produced notable contributions to law reform.

CASE LAW

Before the Norman conquest, different areas of England were governed by different systems of law, often adapted from those of the various invaders who had settled there; roughly speaking, Dane law applied in the north, Mercian law around the midlands, and Wessex law in the south and west. Each was based largely on local custom, and even within the larger areas, these customs, and hence the law, varied from place to place. The king had little control over the country as a whole, and there was no effective central government.

When William the Conqueror gained the English throne in 1066, he established a strong central government and began, among other things, to standardize the law. Representatives of the king were sent out to the countryside to check local administration, and were given the job of adjudicating in local disputes, according to local law.

When these 'itinerant justices' returned to Westminster, they were able to discuss the various customs of different parts of the country, and by a process of sifting, reject unreasonable ones and accept those that seemed rational, to form a consistent body of rules. During this process – which went on for around two centuries – the principle of *stare decisis* ('let the decision stand') grew up. Whenever a new problem of law came to be decided, the decision formed a rule to be followed in all similar cases, making the law more predictable.

The result of all this was that by about 1250, a 'common law' had been produced, that ruled the whole country, would be applied consistently and could be used to predict what the courts might decide in a particular case. It contained many of what are now basic points of English law – the fact that murder is a crime, for example.

The principles of this common law are used today in creating case law. Since all cases are different, judges fairly frequently meet situations which are, or appear to be, significantly different from those already brought before the courts, and they must decide how the law applies to them – whether the law in question comes from the general body of rules of common law, from statute, a combination of the two, or any other source.

Obviously, it would be undesirable for judges simply to make their own interpretation; there would be no consistency, uniformity or predictability; similar cases might be treated quite differently. It was on this basis that the principle of *stare decisis* was established, and as the number and complexity of cases grew, and the modern hierarchy of courts became established, a system of judicial precedent was built up, under which judges in lower courts followed the decisions of the higher ones. This process was made easier by the establishment of a regular system of publication of reports of cases in the higher courts. The body of decisions made by the higher courts, which the lower ones must respect, is known as case law.

▶ Making case law

Case law comes from the decisions made by judges in the cases they try (the verdicts of juries never make case law). The judges listen to the evidence and the legal argument and then prepare a written decision as to which party wins, based on what they believe the facts were, and how the law applies to them. This decision is known as the judgment, and is usually long, containing quite a lot of comment which is not strictly relevant to the case, as well as an explanation of the legal principles on which the judge has made a decision. The explanation of the legal principles on which the decision is made is called the *ratio decidendi* – Latin for the 'reason for deciding'. It is this part of the judgment, known as binding precedent, which forms case law.

All the parts of the judgment which do not form part of the *ratio decidendi* of the case are called *obiter dicta* – which is Latin for 'things said by the way'. These are often discussions of hypothetical situations: for example, the judge might say 'Jones did this, but if she had done that, my decision would have been . . .' None of the *obiter dicta* forms part of the case law, though judges in later cases may be influenced by it, and it is said to be a persuasive precedent.

▶ Judicial precedent

In deciding a case, a judge must follow any decision that has been made by a higher court in a case with similar facts. The rules concerning which courts are bound by which are known as the rules of judicial precedent, or *stare decisis*. As well as being bound by the decisions of courts above them, some courts must also follow their own previous decisions; they are said to be bound by themselves.

▶ The hierarchy of the courts

The European Court of Justice

Decisions of the European Court of Justice (ECJ) on interpretation of the Treaties, validity of the acts of Community institutions and interpretation of the statutes of Council bodies are binding on all English courts. It appears not to be bound by its own decisions.

The House of Lords

Apart from cases concerning European law, this is the highest appeal court on civil and criminal matters, and all other English courts are bound by it. It was traditionally bound by its own decisions, but in 1966, the Lord Chancellor issued a practice statement saying that the House of Lords was no longer to be bound by its previous decisions. However, it overrules previous decisions only rarely. An example was the decision in **R** *v* **R** (1991), that rape within marriage is a crime, which overturned a legal principle that had stood for centuries.

The Court of Appeal

This is split into civil and criminal divisions; they do not bind each other. Both are bound by the House of Lords.

In **Young** *v* **Bristol Aeroplane Co Ltd** (1944), it was held that the civil division is usually bound by its own decisions, but that there were three exceptions:

1 Where the previous decision was made in ignorance of a relevant law (it is said to have been made *per incuriam*).
2 Where there are two previous conflicting decisions.
3 Where there is a later, conflicting House of Lords' decision.

In the criminal division, the results of cases heard may decide whether or not an individual goes to prison, so the criminal division takes a more flexible approach to its previous decisions, and does not follow them where doing so could cause injustice.

The High Court

This court is divided between the Divisional Courts and the ordinary High Court. All are bound by the Court of Appeal and the House of Lords.

The Divisional Courts are the Queen's Bench Division, which deals with criminal appeals and judicial review, and the Chancery Division and the Family Division which both deal with civil appeals. The two civil Divisional Courts are bound by their previous decisions, but the Divisional Court of the Queen's Bench is more flexible about this, for the same reason as the criminal division of the Court of Appeal. The Divisional Courts bind the ordinary High Court.

The ordinary High Court is not bound by its own previous decisions. It can produce precedents for courts below it, but these are of a lower status than those produced by the Court of Appeal or the House of Lords.

Crown Court

The Crown Court is bound by all the courts above it. Its decisions do not form binding precedents, though when High Court judges sit in the Crown Court, their judgments form persuasive precedents, which must be given serious consideration in successive cases, though it is not obligatory to follow them. When a circuit or district judge is sitting no precedents are formed. Since the Crown Court cannot form binding precedents, it is obviously not bound by its own decisions.

Magistrates' and county courts

These are called the inferior courts. They are bound by the High Court, Court of Appeal and House of Lords. Their own decisions are not reported, and cannot produce binding precedents, or even persuasive ones; like the Crown Court, they are therefore not bound by their own decisions.

▶ **How judicial precedent works**

When faced with a case on which there appears to be a relevant earlier decision, either by that court (if bound by itself), or a higher one, the judges can do any of the following:

Follow. If the facts are sufficiently similar, the precedent set by the earlier case is followed, and the law applied in the same way to produce a decision.

Distinguish. Where the facts of the case before the judge are significantly different from those of the earlier one, then the judge distinguishes the two cases and need not follow the earlier one.

Overrule. Where the earlier decision was made in a lower court, the judges can overrule that earlier decision if they disagree with the lower court's statement of the law. The outcome of the earlier decision remains the same, but will not be followed. The power to overrule cases is only used sparingly because it weakens the authority and respect of the lower courts.

Reverse. If the decision of a lower court is appealed to a higher one, the higher court may change it if they feel the lower court has wrongly interpreted the law. Clearly when a decision is reversed, the higher court is usually also overruling the lower court's statement of the law.

In practice the process is rather more complicated than this, since decisions are not always made on the basis of only one previous case; there are usually several different cases offered in support of each side's view of the question.

▶ **How do judges really decide cases?**

The independence of the judiciary was ensured by the Act of Settlement 1700, which transferred the power to sack judges from the Crown to Parliament. Consequently, judges should theoretically make their decisions based purely on the logical deductions of precedent, uninfluenced by political or career considerations.

The eighteenth-century legal commentator, William Blackstone, introduced the declaratory theory of law, stating that judges do not make law, but merely, by the rules of precedent, discover and declare the law that has always been: '[the judge] being sworn to determine, not according to his private sentiments . . . not according to his own private judgment, but according to the known laws and customs of the land: not delegated to pronounce a new law, but to maintain and expound the old one.' Blackstone does not accept that precedent ever offers a choice between two or more interpretations of the law; where a bad decision is made, he states, the new one that reverses or overrules it is not a new law, nor a statement that the old decision was bad law, but a declaration that the previous decision was 'not law', in other words that it was the wrong answer. His view presupposes that there is always one right answer, to be deduced from an objective study of precedent.

Today, however, this position is considered somewhat unrealistic. If the operation of precedent is the precise science Blackstone suggests, a large majority of cases in the higher courts would never come to court at all. The lawyers concerned could simply look up the relevant case law and predict what the decision would be, then advise whichever of the clients would be bound to lose not to bother bringing or fighting the case. In a civil case, or any appeal case, no good lawyer would advise a client to bring or defend a case that they had no chance of winning. Therefore, where such a case is contested, it can be assumed that unless one of the lawyers has made a mistake, it could go either way, and still be in accordance with the law. Further evidence of this is provided by the fact that one can read a judgment of the Court of Appeal, argued as though it were the only possible decision in the light of the cases that had gone before, and then discover that this apparently inevitable decision has promptly been reversed by the House of Lords.

In practice, then, judges' decisions may not be as neutral as Blackstone's declaratory theory suggests; they have to make choices which are by no means spelt out by precedents. Yet, rather than openly stating that they are choosing between two or more equally relevant precedents, the courts find ways to avoid awkward ones, which give the impression that the precedents they do choose to follow are the only ones that could possibly apply. In theory, only the House of Lords, which can overrule its own decisions as well as those of other courts, can depart from precedent; all the other courts must follow the precedent that applies in a particular case, however much they dislike it. In fact, there are a number of ways in which judges may avoid awkward precedents that at first sight might appear binding:

- By distinguishing the awkward precedent on its facts – arguing that the facts of the case under consideration are different in some important way from those of the previous case, and therefore the rule laid down does not apply to them. Since the facts are unlikely to be identical, this is the simplest way to avoid an awkward precedent, and the courts have made some extremely narrow distinctions in this way.

- By distinguishing the point of law – arguing that the legal question answered by the precedent is not the same as that asked in the present case.
- By stating that the precedent has been superseded by more recent decisions, and is therefore outdated.
- By giving the precedent a very narrow *ratio decidendi.* The only part of a decision that forms binding precedent is the *ratio,* the legal principle on which the decision is based. Since judges never state 'this is the *ratio decidendi*', it is possible to argue at some length about which bits of the judgment actually form the *ratio* and therefore bind courts in later cases. Judges wishing to avoid an awkward precedent may reason that those parts of the judgment which seem to apply to their case are not part of the *ratio,* and are only *obiter dicta,* which they are not obliged to follow.
- By arguing that the precedent has no clear *ratio decidendi.* There are usually three judges sitting in Court of Appeal cases, and five in the House of Lords; where each judge in the former case has given a different reason for coming to the same decision, or where, for example, two judges of the House of Lords take one view, two more another, and the fifth agrees with none of them, it can be argued that there is no one clear *ratio decidendi* for the decision.
- By claiming that the precedent is inconsistent with a later decision of a higher court, and has been overruled by implication.
- By stating that the previous decision was made *per incuriam,* meaning that the court failed to consider some relevant statute or precedent. This method is used only rarely, since it clearly undermines the status of the court below.
- By arguing that the precedent is outdated, and no longer in step with modern thinking – this is the approach taken by the House of Lords in **R** *v* **R** (1991), the case which changed the law on marital rape.

We can see that there is considerable room for manoeuvre within the doctrine of precedent, so what factors guide judicial decisions, and to what extent? The following are some of the answers that have been suggested.

Dworkin: a seamless web of principles

Ronald Dworkin argues that judges have no **real** discretion in making case law. He sees law as a seamless web of principles, which supply a right answer – and only one – to every possible problem. Dworkin reasons that although stated legal rules may 'run out' (in the sense of not being directly applicable to a new case) legal principles never do, and therefore judges never need to use their own discretion.

In his book *Law's Empire*, Professor Dworkin claims that judges first look at previous cases, and from those deduce which principles could be said to apply to the case before them. Then they consult their own sense of justice as to which apply, and also consider what the community's view of justice dictates. Where the judge's view and that of the community coincide, there is no problem, but if they conflict, the judges then ask themselves whether or not it would be fair to impose their own sense of justice over that of the community. Dworkin calls this the interpretive approach, and although it may appear to involve a series of choices, considers that the legal principles underlying the decisions mean that in the end only one result could possibly surface from any one case.

Dworkin's approach has been heavily criticized as being unrealistic; opponents believe that judges do not consider principles of justice but take a much more pragmatic approach, looking at the facts of the case, not the principles.

Critical theorists: precedent as legitimation

Critical legal theorists, such as David Kairys take a quite different view. They argue that judges have considerable freedom within the doctrine of precedent. Kairys suggests that there is no such thing as legal reasoning, in the sense of a logical, neutral method of determining rules and results from what has gone before. He states that judicial decisions are actually based on 'a complex mixture of social, political, institutional, experiential and personal factors', and simply legitimated, or justified, by reference to previous cases. The law provides 'a wide and conflicting variety' of such justifications 'from which courts pick and choose'.

The process is not necessarily as cynical as it sounds. Kairys points out that he is not saying that judges actually make the decision and then consider which precedents they can pick to justify it; rather their own beliefs and prejudices naturally lead them to give more weight to precedents which support those views. Nevertheless, for critical legal theorists, all such decisions can be seen as reflecting social and political judgments, rather than objective, purely logical deductions.

Critical theory argues that the neutral appearance of so-called 'legal reasoning' disguises the true nature of legal decisions which, by the choices made, uphold existing power relations within society, tending to favour, for example, employers over employees, property owners over those without, women over men, and rich developed countries over poor undeveloped ones.

Griffith: political choices

In similar vein, Griffith argues that judges make their decisions based on what they see as the public interest, but that their view of this interest is coloured by their background and their position in society. He suggests that the narrow social background – usually public school and Oxbridge – of the highest judges (see p. 89), combined with their position as part of established authority, leads them to believe that it is in the public interest that the established order should be maintained: in other words, that those who are in charge – whether of the country or, for example, in the workplace – should stay in charge, and that traditional values should be maintained. This leads them to 'a tenderness for private property and dislike of trade unions, strong adherence to the maintenance of order, distaste for minority opinions, demonstrations and protests, the avoidance of conflict with Government policy even where it is manifestly oppressive of the most vulnerable, support of governmental secrecy, concern for the preservation of the moral and social behaviour [to which they are] accustomed'.

As Griffith points out, the judges' view of public interest assumes that the interests of all the members of society are roughly the same, ignoring the fact that within society, different groups – employers and employees, men and women, rich and poor – may have interests which are diametrically opposed. What appears to be acting in the public interest will usually mean in the interest of one group over another, and therefore cannot be seen as neutral.

Waldron: political choices, but why not?

In his book, *The Law*, Waldron agrees that judges do exercise discretion, and that they are influenced in those choices by political and ideological considerations, but argues that this is not necessarily a bad thing. He contends that while it would be wrong for judges to be biased towards one side in a case, or to make decisions based on political factors in the hope of promotion, it is unrealistic to expect a judge to be 'a political neuter – emasculated of all values and principled commitments.'

Waldron points out that to be a judge at all means a commitment to the values surrounding the legal system: recognition of Parliament as supreme, the importance of precedent, fairness, certainty, the public interest. He argues that this alone is a political choice, and further choices are made when judges have to balance these values against one another where they conflict. The responsible thing to do, according to Waldron, is to think through such conflicts in advance, and to decide which might generally be expected to give way to which. These will inevitably be political and ideological decisions. Waldron argues that since such decisions have to be made 'the thing to do is not to try to hide them, but to be as explicit as possible'. Rather than hiding such judgments behind 'smoke-screens of legal mystery... if judges have developed particular theories of morals, politics and society, they should say so up front, and incorporate them explicitly into their decision-making.'

Waldron suggests that where judges feel uncomfortable about doing this, it may be a useful indication that they should re-examine their bias, and see whether it is an appropriate consideration to be influenced by. In addition, if the public know the reasoning behind judicial decisions 'we can evaluate them and see whether we want to rely on reasons like that for the future'.

The judiciary: neutral decision-making

Judges themselves still cling to the image of themselves as neutral decision-makers, even thought they admit that there are choices to be made. In a 1972 lecture Lord Reid agreed that the declaratory theory was something of a 'fairytale', but argued that:

> Everyone agrees that impartiality is the first essential in any judge. And that means not only that he must not appear to favour either party. It also means that he must not take sides on political issues. When public opinion is sharply divided on any question – whether or not the division is on party lines – no judge ought in my view to lean to one side or the other if that can possibly be avoided. But sometimes we get a case where that is very difficult to avoid. Then I think we must play safe. We must decide the case on the preponderance of existing authority.

The caution extended even where there was 'some freedom to go in one or other direction'; in these cases 'we should have regard to common sense, legal principle and public policy in that order'.

Lord Reid made it clear that the first two criteria were unlikely to leave much room for the application of the third, but his reasoning fails to take into account the fact that common sense is by no means a fixed quality – it may be common sense to an employer, for example, that pickets should not be allowed to disturb those employees who want to work, and equally common sense to those pickets that they should be able to protect their jobs in any peaceful way possible. Common sense may be as much a value judgment as public interest.

▶ Do judges make law?

Although judges have traditionally seen themselves as declaring or finding rather than creating law, and frequently state that making law is the prerogative of Parliament, there are several areas in which they clearly do make law.

In the first place, historically, a great deal of our law is and always has been case law, made by judicial decisions. Contract and tort law are still largely judge-made, and many of the most important developments – for example, the development of negligence as a tort – have had profound effects. And even though statutes have later been passed on these subjects, and occasionally Parliament has attempted to embody whole areas of common law in statutory form, these still embody the original principles created by the judges.

Secondly, the application of law, whether case law or statute, to a particular case is not usually an automatic matter. Terminology may be vague or ambiguous, new developments in social life have to be accommodated, and the procedure requires interpretation as well as application. As we have suggested, judicial precedent does not always make a particular decision obvious and obligatory – there may be conflicting precedents, their implications may be unclear, and there are ways of getting round a precedent that would otherwise produce an undesirable decision. If it is accepted that Blackstone's declaratory theory does not apply in practice, then clearly the judges do make law, rather than explaining the law that is already there. The theories advanced by Kairys, Griffith and Waldron all accept that judges do have discretion, and therefore they do to some extent make law.

Where precedents do not spell out what should be done in a case before them, judges nevertheless have to make a decision. They cannot simply say that the law is not clear and refer it back to Parliament, even though in some cases they point out that the decision before them would be more appropriately decided by those who have been elected to make decisions on changes in the law. This was the case in **Airedale NHS** *v* **Bland** (1993), where the House of Lords considered the fate of Tony Bland, the football supporter left in a coma after the Hillsborough stadium disaster. The court had to decide whether it was lawful to stop supplying the drugs and artificial feeding that were keeping Mr Bland alive, even though it was known that doing so would mean his death soon afterwards. Several Law Lords made it plain that they felt that cases raising 'wholly new moral and social issues' should be decided by Parliament, the judges' role being to 'apply the principles which society, through the democratic process, adopts, not to impose their standards on society'. Nevertheless, the courts had no option but to make a decision one way or the other, and they decided that the action was lawful in the circumstances, because it was in the patient's best interests.

Thirdly, our judges have been left to define their own role, and the role of the courts generally in the political system, more or less as they please. They have, for example, given themselves the power to review decisions of any public body, even when Parliament has said those decisions are not to be reviewed. And despite their frequent pronouncements that it is not for them to interfere in Parliament's law-making role, the judges have made it plain that they will not, unless forced by very explicit wording, interpret statutes as encroaching on common law rights or judge-made law (see p. 31). They also control the operation of case law without reference to Parliament: an obvious example is that the practice direction announcing that the House of Lords would no longer be bound by its own decisions, which made case law more flexible and thereby gave the judges more power, was made on the court's own authority, without needing permission from Parliament or any other authority.

▶ When should judges make law?

Again, this is a subject about which there are different views, not least among the judiciary.

Adapting to social change

In 1952, Lord Denning gave a lecture called 'The Need for a New Equity', arguing that judges had become too timid about adapting the law to the changing conditions of society. They were, he felt, leaving this role too much to Parliament, which was too slow and cumbersome to do the job well (by 1984, he felt that judges had taken up the task again).

Lord Scarman, in **Mcloughlin** *v* **O'Brian** (1982), stated that the courts' function is to adjudicate according to principle, and if the results are socially unacceptable Parliament can legislate to overrule them. He felt that the risk was not that case law might develop too far, but that it stood still and did not therefore adapt to the changing needs of society.

Paterson's survey of nineteen Law Lords active between 1967 and 1973 found that at least twelve thought that the Law Lords had a duty to develop the common law in response to changing social conditions.

Types of law

Lord Reid has suggested that the basic areas of common law were appropriate for judge-made law, but that the judges should respect the need for certainty in property and contract law, and that criminal law, except for the issue of *mens rea*, was best left to Parliament.

Consensus law-making

Lord Devlin has distinguished between activist law-making and dynamic law-making. He saw new ideas within society as going through a long process of acceptance. At first society will be divided about them, and there will be controversy, but eventually such ideas may come to be accepted by most members of society, or most members will at least become prepared to put up with them. At this second stage we can say there is a consensus. We can see this process in the way that views have changed in this century on subjects such as homosexuality and sex before marriage.

Law-making which takes one side or another while an issue is still controversial is what Devlin called dynamic law-making, and he believed judges should not take part in it because it endangered their reputation for independence and impartiality. Their role is in activist law-making, concerning areas where there is a consensus. The problem with Devlin's view is that in practice the judges sometimes have no choice but to embark on dynamic law-making. In **Gillick** *v* **West Norfolk and Wisbech Area Health Authority** (1985), the House of Lords was asked to consider whether a girl under sixteen needed her parents' consent before she could be given contraceptive services. It was an issue on which there was by no means a consensus, with one side claiming that teenage pregnancies would increase if the courts ruled that parental consent was necessary, and the other claiming that the judges would be encouraging under-age sex if they did not. The House of Lords held, by a majority of three to two, that a girl under sixteen did not have to have parental consent if she was mature enough to make up her own mind. But the decision did not end the controversy, and it was widely suggested that the judges were not the right people to make the choice. However, since Parliament had given no lead, they had no option but to make a decision one way or the other, and were therefore forced to indulge in what Devlin would call dynamic law-making.

Respecting parliamentary opinion

It is often stated that judges should not make law where there is reason to believe Parliament does not support such changes. In **President of India** (1984), the House of Lords felt that there was a strong case for over-ruling a nineteenth-century decision that a party could receive no interest on a contract debt, but they noted that the Law Commission had recommended that this rule should be abolished and the legislators specifically decided not to do so. Lord Brandon said that to make new law in these circumstances would be an 'unjustifiable usurpation of the function which properly belongs to Parliament'.

Similarly, it is sometimes argued that judges should avoid making law in areas of public interest which Parliament is considering at the time. Lord Radcliffe suggested that in such areas, judges should be cautious 'not because the principles adopted by Parliament are more satisfactory or more enlightened, but because it is unacceptable constitutionally that there should be two independent sources of law-making at work at the same time'.

Protecting individual rights

In a 1992 lecture, Anthony Lester QC argued that while judges must have regard to precedent, they could still use their discretion within the system of precedent more effectively. He argued that in the past, judges have abdicated responsibility for law-making by surrounding themselves with self-made rules (such as the pre-1966 rule that the House of Lords was bound by its own decisions). Since the 1960s, however, he feels that this tendency has gradually been reduced, with judges taking on more responsibility for developing the common law in accordance with contemporary values, and being more willing to arbitrate fairly between the citizen and the state. Lester praises this development, arguing that the judges can establish protection for the individual against misuse of power, where Parliament refuses to do so.

▶ Should judges behave like law-makers?

Bearing in mind that, despite their protests, judges clearly do make law, some scholars have suggested that judges should decide hard cases on policy grounds – weighing social consequences, choosing the best option for the future, in the way we expect a legislator to do. Hart, for example, thinks it an advantage of the open texture of legal language that it leaves room for the flexible adaptation of policy in this way. Others, however, have expressed doubts about whether judges are the right people to produce policy-based legislation, even in hard cases. There are obvious reasons for caution: judges have neither the competence nor the accountability to deal adequately with considerations of policy; and the adversarial environment of the courtroom may not be the best forum for addressing the needs of society as a whole.

▶ Advantages of case law and judicial precedent

Certainty

Judicial precedent means litigants can assume that like cases will be treated alike, rather than judges making their own random decisions, which nobody could predict. This helps people plan their affairs.

Detailed practical rules

Case law is a response to real situations, as opposed to statutes, which may be more heavily based on theory and logic. Case law shows the detailed application of the law to various circumstances, and this gives more information than statute.

Free market in legal ideas

The right-wing philosopher Hayek has argued that there should be as little legislation as possible, with case law becoming the main source of law. He sees case law as developing in line with market forces; if the *ratio* of a case is seen not to work, it will be abandoned, if it works it will be followed. In this way the law can develop in response to demand. Hayek sees statute law as imposed by social planners, forcing their views on society whether they like it or not, and threatening the liberty of the individual.

Flexibility

Law needs to be flexible to meet the needs of a changing society, and case law can make changes far more quickly than Parliament. The most obvious signs of this are the radical changes the House of Lords has made in the field of criminal law, since announcing in 1966 that they would no longer be bound by their own decisions.

▶ Disadvantages of case law

Complexity and volume

There are hundreds of thousands of decided cases, comprising several thousand volumes of law reports, and more are added all the time. Judgments themselves are long, with many judges making no attempts at readability, and *ratio decidendi* of a case may be buried in a sea of irrelevant material. This can make it very difficult to pinpoint appropriate principles.

Rigidity

The rules of judicial precedent mean that judges must follow a binding precedent even where they think it is bad law, or inappropriate. This can mean that bad judicial decisions are perpetuated for a long time before they come before a court high enough to have the power to overrule them.

Illogical distinctions

The fact that binding precedents must be followed unless the facts of the case are significantly different can lead to judges making minute distinctions between the facts of a previous case and the case before them, so that they can distinguish a precedent which they consider inappropriate.

This in turn leads to a mass of cases all establishing different precedents in very similar circumstances, and further complicates the law.

Unpredictability

The advantages of certainty can be lost if too many of the kind of illogical distinctions referred to above are made, and it may be impossible to work out which precedents will be applied to a new case.

Dependence on chance

Case law changes only in response to those cases brought before it, so important changes may not be made unless someone has the money and determination to push a case far enough through the appeal system to allow a new precedent to be created.

Unsystematic

Case law develops according to the facts of each case and so does not provide a comprehensive code. A whole series of rules can be built on one case, and if this is overruled the whole structure can collapse.

Lack of research

When making case law the judges are only presented with the facts of the case and the legal arguments, and their task is to decide on the outcome of that particular dispute. Technically, they are not concerned with the social and economic implications of their decisions, and so they cannot commission research or consult experts as to these implications, as Parliament can when changing the law. In the USA the litigants are allowed to present written arguments containing socio-economic material, and Lord Simon has recommended that a law officer should be sent to the court in certain cases to present such arguments objectively. However, Lord Devlin considered that allowing such information would encourage the judges to go too far in making law.

Retrospective

Changes made by case law apply to events which happened before the case came to court, unlike legislation, which usually only applies to events after it comes into force. This may be considered unfair, since if a case changes the law, the parties concerned in that case could not have known what the law was before they acted. US courts sometimes get round the problems by deciding the case before them according to the old law, while declaring that in future the new law will prevail: or they may determine with what degree of retroactivity a new rule is to be enforced.

Undemocratic

Lord Scarman pointed out in **Stock** *v* **Jones** (1978) that the judge cannot match the experience and vision of the legislator; and that unlike the legislator the judge is not answerable to the people. Theories, like Griffith's, which suggest that precedent can actually give judges a good deal of discretion, and allow them to decide cases on grounds of political and social policy, raise the question of whether judges, who are unelected, should have such freedom.

• •
ANSWERING QUESTIONS

1 **To what extent does the doctrine of precedent curb judicial creativity?** *WJEC*
The first thing to note here is that the words 'judicial creativity' really mean the judges' ability to create or make law. Your introduction should briefly describe what precedent is. A summary of the material contained under the headings 'judicial precedent' and 'how judicial precedent works' would be sufficient here.

Your essay should essentially put forward two opposing sets of arguments: on the one hand, the ways in which precedent curbs judges' freedom to make law; and on the other hand, the arguments that have been put forward that judges do actually have quite a bit of freedom. To illustrate the first set of arguments, you could discuss the role of the *ratio decidendi*, and the need for consistency and certainty in the law. When dealing with the opposing argument, you might discuss the three main points under the heading 'Do judges make law' in this chapter: the sheer amount of case law in our system (especially in contract and tort); the point that applying the law is not usually an automatic matter; and the fact that judges have been left to define their own role in the system. You should finish with a conclusion, drawing on the points you have made, that states how far you think precedent does curb judicial creativity.

2 **In what ways does legal reasoning both bind and free the judiciary in deciding particular cases?** *WJEC*
The first thing to note is that 'legal reasoning' in this context simply means the process by which judges work out how the rules laid down in previous cases apply to later ones – in other words, the creation of case law. You could tackle this question in two sections: how does this legal reasoning bind the judiciary; and in what circumstances does it allow freedom in making decisions?

For the first part, you need to explain the principle of judicial precedent, and outline the situations in which judges are bound by previous decisions. You could bring in here the declaratory theory of law.

In the second part, you can describe the ways in which judges can avoid awkward precedents, and bring in some of the theories about how judges really decide cases. You could also discuss the effects of the 1966 House of Lords Practice Direction.

Your conclusion might state whether you think that legal reasoning strikes the right balance between binding the judges and allowing them freedom, giving reasons for your view.

3 **What would be the effect on English law of the abolition of the doctrine of binding precedent?** *London*

You first need to describe the doctrine of binding precedent, but do not spend too much time on this, as pure description is not what the question is asking for.

You should then consider what the law would lose if precedent were abandoned – the material on the advantages of precedent is relevant here. Then talk about the disadvantages of the system of precedent, and what might be gained by abolishing it. You could bring in the effects of the 1966 House of Lords Practice Direction as an example of the relaxation of precedent, and talk about whether you feel it has benefitted the law or not, mentioning appropriate cases.

You might mention innovations which would lessen the role of precedent, such as codification, and say whether you feel they would be desirable and why.

Your conclusion could state whether or not you feel precedent serves a useful role, and outline any changes which you feel should be made to its operation.

4 **To what extent does the doctrine of precedent allow judges to make law?** *WJEC*

Here again, you need to start by defining judicial precedent. You can then go on to describe the ways in which it prevents judges from making new law, and the declaratory theory. Follow this with a discussion of the ways in which judges can avoid awkward precedents, and whether this means that they make law. You might use some examples of judges making law, such as R v R. You can use the material on how judges really decide cases, and on whether judges make law to debate how far judges are allowed by precedent to make law. You should make the point that theorists such as Kairys and Griffith who argue that precedent allows a great deal of discretion are arguing that judges do make law.

You might also introduce some of the ideas about when judges ought to make law, pointing out that some argue that they should actually be more active lawmakers than they are – Anthony Lester's arguments are relevant here.

As a conclusion, you could suggest whether the present system strikes the right balance in the extent to which it allows judges to make law, giving reasons for your views and suggesting any changes you think should be made.

STATUTE LAW

Statutes are made by Parliament, which consists of the House of Commons, the House of Lords and the Monarch. In Britain, Parliament is sovereign, which has traditionally meant that the law it makes takes precedence over that from any other source, though as we shall see, membership of the EC has compromised this principle. EC law aside, Parliament can make or cancel any law it chooses, and the courts must enforce it. In other countries, such as the USA, the courts can declare such legislation unconstitutional, but our courts may not do that.

Making an Act of Parliament

Bills

All statutes begin as a Bill, which is a proposal for a piece of legislation. There are three types of Bill:

Public Bills. These are prepared by the Cabinet and change the general law of the whole country. They are often preceded by a Green Paper, a consultation document putting forward tentative proposals, which interested parties may consult and give their views on.

Private Members' Bills. These are prepared by an individual back bench MP (someone who is not a member of the Cabinet). MPs wanting to put forward a Bill have to enter a ballot to win the right to do so, and then persuade the Government to allow enough parliamentary time for the Bill to go through. Consequently very few such Bills become Acts, and they tend to function more as a way of drawing attention to particular issues. Some, however, have made important contributions to legislation, an example being the 1967 Abortion Act which stemmed from a Private Members' Bill put forward by David Steele.

Private Bills. These are usually proposed by a local authority, public corporation or large public company, and usually only affect that sponsor. An example might be a local authority seeking the right to build a bridge or road.

The actual preparation of Bills is done by expert draftsmen known as Parliamentary Counsel.

First reading

The title of the prepared Bill is read to the House of Commons. This is called the first reading, and acts as a notification of the proposed measure.

Second reading

At the second reading, the proposals are debated fully, and may be amended, and members vote on whether the legislation should proceed. In practice, the whip system (party officials whose job is to make sure MPs vote with their party) means that a Government with a reasonable majority can almost always get its legislation through at this and subsequent stages.

Committee stage

The Bill is then referred to a committee of the House of Commons for detailed examination, bearing in mind the points made during the debate. At this point further amendments to the Bill may be made.

Report stage

The committee then reports back to the House, and any proposed amendments are debated and voted upon.

Third reading

The Bill is re-presented to the House. There may be a short debate, and a vote on whether to accept or reject the legislation as it stands.

House of Lords

The Bill then goes to the House of Lords, where it goes through a similar process of three readings. If the House of Lords alters anything, the Bill returns to the Commons for further consideration. The Commons then responds with agreement, reasons for disagreement, or proposals for alternative changes.

At one time legislation could not be passed without the agreement of both houses, which meant that the unelected House of Lords could block legislation put forward by the elected House of Commons. The Parliament Acts of 1911–1949 lay down special procedures by which proposed legislation can go for Royal Assent without the approval of the House of Lords after specified periods of time. In fact these procedures are almost never used, as the House of Lords usually drops objections that are resisted by the Commons.

Royal assent

In the vast majority of cases, agreement between Lords and Commons is reached, and the Bill is then presented for Royal Assent. Technically, the Queen must give her consent to all legislation before it can become law, but in practice that consent is never refused.

The Bill is then an Act of Parliament, and becomes law, though most do not take effect from the moment the Queen gives her consent, but on a specified date in the near future.

In the case of legislation about which there is no controversy, the procedure may be simplified, with the first three readings in the Lords, then three in the Commons, with the Bill passing back to the Lords only if there is disagreement. Private Bills technically go through the above procedure, and are examined to make sure that adequate warning has been given to anyone affected by the provisions, but there is little debate on them. Consolidating Acts, which simply bring together all the existing law on one topic also go through an accelerated procedure, with no debate, because they do not change the law; codification bills on the other hand, go through the normal process (see p. 72).

▶ Statutory interpretation

Although Parliament makes legislation, it is left to the courts to apply it. The general public imagine that this is simply a case of looking up the relevant law and ruling accordingly, but the reality is not so simple. Despite the fact that Acts of Parliament are carefully drawn up by expert draftsmen, there are many occasions in which the courts find that the implications of a statute for the case before them are not at all clear.

Bennion (1990) has identified a number of factors that may cause this uncertainty:

- a word is left out because the draftsman thought it was automatically implied. For example, a draftsman writing a statute banning men with facial hair from parks might write that 'men with beards or moustaches are prohibited from parks'. Does this mean that a man who has a beard **and** a moustache would be allowed in? If the words and/or were used it would be clear, but the draftsman may have thought this was automatically implied.
- a broad term was used, leaving it to the user to decide what it includes. Where a statute bans vehicles from the park, this obviously includes cars and lorries, but the courts would have to decide whether it also prohibited skateboards, bikes, or roller skates, for example.

- an ambiguous word or phrase was used on purpose, perhaps because the provision is politically contentious. The European Communities Act 1972 was ambiguous about the position of UK legislation.
- the events of the case before the court were not foreseen when the legislation was produced. In the example given above regarding vehicles, skateboards might not have been invented when the statute was drafted, so it would be impossible for Parliament to say whether they should be included in the term 'vehicles'.
- the wording is inadequate because of a printing, drafting or other error.

In any of these cases, the courts must try to discover how Parliament intended the law to apply to the case before them. Once this is done, the interpretation given to a statute, or part of one, becomes part of case law in just the same way as any other judicial decision, and subject to the same rules of precedent – lower courts must interpret the statute in the same way, while higher ones may decide that the interpretation is wrong, and reverse the decision if it is appealed, or overrule it in a later case.

How are statutes interpreted?

Parliament has given the courts two main sources of guidance on statutory interpretation. The Interpretation Act 1978 provides certain standard definitions of common provisions, such as the rule that the singular includes the plural and 'he' includes 'she', while interpretation sections at the end of most modern Acts define some of the words used within them – the Police and Criminal Evidence Act 1984 contains such a section.

Apart from this very limited assistance, it has been left to the courts to decide what method to use to interpret statutes, and three basic approaches have developed, in conjunction with certain aids to interpretation.

Rules of interpretation

The literal rule

This rule gives all the words in a statute their ordinary and natural meaning, on the principle that the best way to interpret the will of Parliament is to follow the literal meaning of the words they have used. Under this rule, the literal meaning must be followed, even if the result is silly: Lord Esher stated, in **R** *v* **Judge of the City of London Court** (1982): 'If the words of an Act are clear, you must follow them, even though they lead to a manifest absurdity. The court has nothing to do with the question of whether the legislature has committed an absurdity'.

Examples of the literal rule in use are:

Whitely *v* **Chapell** (1868). A statute aimed at preventing electoral malpractice made it an offence to impersonate 'any person entitled to vote' at an election. The accused was acquitted because he impersonated a dead person and a dead person was clearly not entitled to vote!

London and North Eastern Railway Co *v* **Berriman** (1946). A railway worker was knocked down and killed by a train, and his widow attempted to claim damages. The relevant statute provided that this was available to employees killed while engaging in 'relaying or repairing' tracks; the dead man had been doing routine maintenance and oiling, which the court held did not come within the meaning of 'relaying and repairing'.

Fisher *v* **Bell** (1961). After several violent incidents in which the weapon used was a flick-knife, Parliament decided that these knives should be banned. The Restriction of Offensive Weapons Act 1959 consequently made it an offence to 'sell or offer for sale' any flick-knife. The defendant had flick-knives in his shop window and was charged with offering these for sale. The courts held that 'offers for sale' must be given its ordinary meaning in law, and that in contract law this was not an offer for sale but only an invitation to people to make an offer to buy. The defendant was therefore not guilty of a crime under the Act, despite the fact that this was obviously just the sort of behaviour that Act was set up to prevent.

Advantages of the literal rule It respects parliamentary sovereignty, giving the courts a restricted role and leaving law-making to those elected for the job.

Disadvantages of the literal rule Where use of the literal rule does lead to an absurd or obviously unjust conclusion, it can hardly be said to be enacting the will of Parliament, since Parliament is unlikely to have intended absurdity and injustice. The case of **London and North Eastern Railway Co** *v* **Berriman** (above) is an example of literal interpretation creating injustice where Parliament probably never intended any – the difference in the type of work being done does not change the degree of danger to which the workers were exposed.

In addition, the literal rule is useless where the answer to a problem simply cannot be found in the words of the statute. As Hart has pointed out, some terms have a core of certainty and a penumbra of doubt: the example above of an imaginary law banning 'vehicles' from the park clearly illustrates this. Where such a broad term is used, the answer is simply not there in the words of the statute, and the courts have to use some other method.

The Law Commission in 1969 pointed out that interpretation based only on literal meanings 'assumes unattainable perfection in draftsmanship'; even the most talented and experienced draftsmen cannot predict every situation to which legislation may have to be applied. As

Ingman notes, it also expects too much of words in general, which are at best 'an imperfect means of communication'. The same word may mean different things to different people, and words also shift their meanings over time.

Zander, in his book *The Law-Making Process*, describes the literal approach as 'mechanical, divorced both from the realities of the use of language and from the expectations and aspirations of the human beings concerned . . . in that sense it is irresponsible'.

The golden rule
This provides that if the literal rule gives an absurd result, which Parliament could not have intended, then (and only then) the judge can substitute a reasonable meaning in the light of the statute as a whole. It was defined by Lord Wensleydale in **Grey *v* Pearson** (1857): 'the grammatical and ordinary sense of the word is to be adhered to, unless that would lead to some absurdity, or some repugnance or inconsistency with the rest of the instrument, in which case the grammatical and ordinary sense of the words may be modified so as to avoid that absurdity and inconsistency, but no further'.

Examples of the golden rule in use are:

R *v* Allen (1872). S. 57 of the Offences Against the Person Act 1861 stated that 'Whosoever being married shall marry any other person during the life of the former husband or wife . . . shall be guilty of bigamy'. It was pointed out that it was impossible for a person already married to 'marry' someone else – they might go through a marriage ceremony, but would not actually be married; using the literal rule would make the statute useless. The courts therefore held that 'shall marry' should be interpreted to mean 'shall go through a marriage ceremony'.

Maddox *v* Storer (1963). Under the Road Traffic Act 1960, it was an offence to drive at more than 30 mph in a vehicle 'adapted to carry more than seven passengers'. The vehicle in the case was a minibus made to carry eleven passengers, rather than altered to do so, and the court held that 'adapted to' could be taken to mean 'suitable for'.

Adler *v* George (1964). The defendant was charged under s. 3 of the Official Secrets Act 1920, with obstructing a member of the armed forces 'in the vicinity of any prohibited place'. He argued that the natural meaning of 'in the vicinity of' meant near to, whereas the obstruction had actually occurred in the prohibited place itself, an air force station. The court held that while in many circumstances 'in the vicinity' could indeed only be interpreted as meaning near to, in this context it was reasonable to construe it as including being within the prohibited place.

Advantages of the golden rule The golden rule can prevent the absurdity and injustice caused by the literal rule, and help the courts put into practice what Parliament really means.

Disadvantages of the golden rule The Law Commission noted in 1969 that the 'rule' provided no clear meaning of an 'absurd result'. As in practice that was judged by reference to whether a particular interpretation was irreconcilable with the general policy of the legislature, the golden rule turns out to be a less explicit form of the mischief rule (discussed below).

The mischief rule

This rule was laid down in the case of **Heydon** in the sixteenth century, and provides that judges should consider three factors:

- what the law was before the statute was passed;
- what problem, or 'mischief', the statute was trying to remedy;
- what remedy Parliament was trying to provide.

The judge should then interpret the statute in such a way as to put a stop to the problem that Parliament was addressing.

Examples of the mischief rule in use are:

Smith *v* Hughes (1960). The Street Offences Act 1958 made it a criminal offence for a prostitute to solicit potential customers in a street or public place. In this case, the prostitute was not actually in the street, but was sitting in a house, on the first floor, and tapping on the window to attract the attention of the men walking by. The judge decided that the aim of the Act was to enable people to walk along the streets without being solicited, and since the soliciting in question was aimed at people in the street, even though the prostitute was not in the street herself, the Act should be interpreted to include this activity.

Elliott *v* Grey (1960). The Road Traffic Act 1930 provided that it was an offence for an uninsured car to be 'used on the road'. The car in this case was on the road, but jacked up, with its battery removed, but the court held that as it was nevertheless a hazard of the type which the statute was designed to prevent, it was covered by the phrase 'used on the road'.

Royal College of Nursing *v* DHSS (1981). the 1967 Abortion Act stated that terminations of pregnancy were legal only if performed by a 'registered medical practitioner'. By 1972, surgical abortions were largely being replaced by drug-induced ones, in which the second stage of the process (attaching the patient to a drip), was carried out by nurses, under the instructions of a doctor. The House of Lords ruled that the mischief which the Act sought to remedy was the uncertain state of the previous law, which drove many women to dangerous back-street abortionists. It sought to do this by widening the grounds on which abortions could be obtained, and ensuring that they were carried out with proper skill in hygienic conditions, and the procedure in question promoted this aim, and was not unlawful. It was a controversial decision, with Lords Wilberforce and Edmund Davies claiming that the House was not interpreting legislation but rewriting it.

Advantages of the mischief rule The mischief rule helps avoid absurdity and injustice, and promotes flexibility. It was described by the Law Commission in 1969 as a 'rather more satisfactory approach' than the other two established rules.

Disadvantages of the mischief rule **Heydon**'s case was the product of a time when statutes were a minor source of law, compared to the common law. Drafting was by no means as exact a process as it is today, and the supremacy of Parliament was not really established. At that time too, what statutes there were tended to include a lengthy preamble, which more or less spelt out the 'mischief' with which the Act was intended to deal. Judges of the time were very well qualified to decide what the previous law was and what problems a statute was intended to remedy, since they had usually drafted statutes on behalf of the king, and Parliament only rubber-stamped them. Such a rule may be less appropriate now that the legislative situation is so different.

Aids to interpretation

Whichever approach the judges take to statutory interpretation, they have at their disposal a range of material to help. Some of these aids may be found within the piece of legislation itself, or in certain rules of language commonly applied in statutory texts – these are called internal aids. Others, outside the piece of legislation, are called external aids.

Internal aids
The literary rule and the golden rule both direct the judge to internal aids, though they are taken into account whatever the approach.

The statute itself To decide what a provision of the Act means the judge may draw a comparison with provisions elsewhere in the statute. Clues may also be provided by the long title of the Act or the subheadings within it.

Rules of language Developed by lawyers over time, these rules are really little more than common sense, despite their intimidating names. As with the rules of interpretation, they are not always precisely applied. Examples include:

Ejusdem generis General words which follow specific ones are taken to include only things of the same kind. For example, if an Act used the phrase 'dogs, cats and other animals' the phrase 'and other animals' would probably include other domestic animals, but not wild ones.

Expressio unius est exclusio alterius Express mention of one thing implies the exclusion of another. If an Act specifically mentioned 'Persian cats', the term would not include other breeds of cat.

Noscitur a sociis A word draws meaning from the other words around it. If a statute mentioned 'cat baskets, toy mice and food', it would be reasonable to assume that 'food' meant cat food, and dog food was not covered by the relevant provision.

Presumptions The courts assume that certain points are implied in all legislation. These presumptions include the following:

- statutes do not change the common law;
- the legislature does not intend to remove any matters from the jurisdiction of the courts;
- existing rights are not to be interfered with;
- laws which create crimes should be interpreted in favour of the citizen where there is ambiguity;
- legislation does not operate retrospectively: its provisions operate from the day it comes into force, and are not backdated;
- statutes do not affect the monarch.

It is always open to Parliament to go against these presumptions if it sees fit – for example, the European Communities Act 1972 makes it clear that some of its provisions are to be applied retrospectively. But unless the wording of a statute makes it absolutely clear that Parliament has chosen to go against one or more of the presumptions, the courts will assume that the presumptions apply.

In its 1969 report on statutory interpretation, the Law Commission pointed out that there was no established order of precedence in the case of conflict between the different presumptions; and that the individual presumptions were often imprecise in scope.

There is also room for debate as to why certain values are selected for protection and not others, and as to why there is disagreement among the judges as to the strength of the protection that ought to be accorded. For example, the presumption that existing rights are not to be interfered with serves to protect the existing property or money of individuals, but there is no presumption in favour of people claiming state benefits.

External aids
The mischief rule directs the judge to external aids, including the following.

Historical setting A judge may consider the historical setting of the provision that is being interpreted, as well as other statutes dealing with the same subjects.

Dictionaries and textbooks These may be consulted to find the meaning of a word, or to gather information about the views of legal academics on a point of law.

Reports Legislation may be preceded by a report of a Royal Commission, the Law Commission or some other official advisory committee (see p. 74). The House of Lords stated in **Black-Clawson International Ltd** (1975) official reports may be considered as evidence of the pre-existing state of the law and the mischief that the legislation was intended to deal with.

Treaties Treaties and international conventions can be considered when following the presumption that Parliament does not legislate in such a way that the UK would be in breach of its international obligations.

Previous practice General practice and commercial usage in the field covered by the legislation may shed light on the meaning of a statutory term.

Hansard This is the official daily report of parliamentary debates, and therefore a record of what was said during the introduction of legislation. For over 100 years, the judiciary held that such documents could not be consulted for the purpose of statutory interpretation. During his career, Lord Denning made strenuous efforts to do away with this rule, and in **Davis** *v* **Johnson** (1978), justified his interpretation of the Domestic Violence Act 1976 by reference to the parliamentary debates during its introduction. The House of Lords however rebuked him for doing so, and maintained that the rule should stand.

In 1993, the case of **Pepper** *v* **Hart** overturned the rule against consulting Hansard, and it appears that such consultation is now allowed – though unfortunately too late for Lord Denning, now retired. The case was between teachers at a fee-paying school (Malvern College) and the Inland Revenue, and concerned the tax which employees should have to pay on perks, benefits related to their job. Malvern College allowed its teachers to send their sons there for one-fifth of the usual fee, if places were available. Tax law requires employees to pay tax on perks, and the amount of tax is based on the cost to the employer of providing the benefit, which is usually taken to mean any extra cost that the employer would not otherwise incur. The amount paid by Malvern teachers for their sons' places covered the extra cost to the school of having the child there (in books, food and so on), but did not cover the school's fixed costs, for paying teachers, maintaining buildings and so on, which would have been the same whether the teachers' children were there or not. Therefore the perk cost the school little or nothing, and so the teachers maintained that they should not have to pay tax on it. The Inland Revenue disagreed, arguing that the perk should be taxed on the basis of the amount it saved the teachers on the real cost of sending their children to the school.

The reason why the issue of consulting parliamentary debates arose was that during the passing of the Finance Act which laid down the tax rules in question, the then Secretary to the Treasury, Robert Sheldon, had specifically mentioned the kind of situation that arose in **Pepper** *v* **Hart**. He had stated that where the cost to an employer of a perk was minimal, employees should not have to pay tax on the full cost of it. The question was, could the judges take into account what the Minister had said? The House of Lords convened a special court of seven judges, which decided that they could look at Hansard to see what the Minister has said, and that his remarks could be used to decide what Parliament had intended.

Although **Pepper** *v* **Hart** makes it clear that parliamentary debates can be used as evidence of parliamentary intention, there is still much debate as to how useful they can be, and whether they really can be considered to be good evidence of what Parliament intended. The following are some of the arguments for use of these sources:

Usefulness. Lord Denning's argument, advanced in **Davis** *v* **Johnson** (1978), was that to ignore them would be to 'grope in the dark for the meaning of an Act without switching on the light'. When such an obvious source of enlightenment was available, it was ridiculous to ignore it – in fact Lord Denning said after the case that he intended to continue to consult Hansard, but simply not say he was doing so.

Other jurisdictions. Legislative materials are used in many foreign jurisdictions, including the USA and many other European countries. In such countries, these materials tend to be more accessible and concise than Hansard – it is difficult to judge whether they are consulted because of this quality, or whether the fact that they are consulted has encouraged those who produce them to make them more readable. It is argued that the latter might be a useful side-effect of allowing the judges to consult parliamentary materials.

Media reports. Parliamentary proceedings are reported in newspapers and on radio and television. Since judges are as exposed to these as anyone else, it seems ridiculous to blinker themselves in court, or to pretend that they are blinkered.

The arguments against the use of these sources are:

Lack of clarity. The House of Lords, admonishing Lord Denning for his behaviour in **Davis** *v* **Johnson**, and directing that parliamentary debates were not to be consulted, stated that the evidence provided by the parliamentary debates might not be reliable; what was said in the cut and thrust of public debate was not 'conducive to a clear and unbiased explanation of the meaning of statutory language'.

Time and expense. Their Lordships also suggested that if debates were to be used, there was a danger that the lawyers arguing a case would devote too much time and attention to ministerial statements and so on, at the expense of considering the language used in the Act itself.

> It would add greatly to the time and expense involved in preparing cases involving the construction of a statute if counsel were expected to read all the debates in Hansard, and it would often be impracticable for counsel to get access to at least the older reports of debates in select committees in the House of Commons; moreover, in a very large proportion of cases such a search, even if practicable would throw no light on the question before the court . . .

Parliamentary intention. The nature of parliamentary intention is difficult, if not impossible, to pin down (see below). Parliamentary debates usually reveal the views of only a few members, and even then, those words may need interpretation too.

What is parliamentary intention?

Does parliamentary intention mean the intention of every individual member? Obviously not, since not every member will have voted for a particular Bill. The intention of all those who did vote for the Bill is no more easy to define: support of a Bill, whether by speaking or just by voting for it, may reflect loyalty to the party whip, rather than approval or even genuine understanding of the measure. Even among all the MPs who genuinely support a Bill, there may be many different opinions as to its purpose. If parliamentary intention is taken to mean the intention of Parliament as a whole, how is that to be judged? Conducting an opinion poll every time a statutory provision proves difficult to interpret is hardly a practical proposition.

In fact, the people who will have paid most attention to the wording and purpose of a statute are the Ministers who seek to get them through Parliament, the civil servants who advise the Ministers, and the draftsmen who draw up the legislation. They can hardly be said to amount to Parliament.

As Glanville Williams has pointed out, the fact is that if the courts are having trouble deciding how a statutory provision applies in a particular situation, the chances are that that situation was never foreseen by Parliament. In that case the idea of parliamentary intention with regard to that situation is a fiction.

In view of all this, as Lord Reid has pointed out, judges are not really searching for the intention of Parliament, but for 'the meaning of the words which Parliament used. We are seeking not what Parliament meant, but the true meaning of what they said.'

How do judges really interpret statutes?

This question has much in common with the discussion of case law and the operation of precedent (p. 9); in both cases, discussion of rules conceals a certain amount of flexibility. The so-called 'rules of interpretation' are not rules at all, but different approaches. Judges do not methodically apply these rules to every case, and in any case, the fact that they can conflict with each other and produce different results necessarily implies some choice as to which is used. There is choice too in the relative weight given to internal and external aids, and rules of language, and approaches have varied over the years.

During the nineteenth century, a very literal approach came into favour, modified only slightly by use of the golden rule. In 1969, the Law Commission reported that literalism was being given undue emphasis, and since the 1970s, the judiciary, and the House of Lords in particular, have stressed that words should not be interpreted too literally, but in accordance with their broader context. There is still argument, however, as to how far this can go.

During his judicial career, Lord Denning was in the forefront of moves to establish a more purposive approach, aiming to produce decisions that put into practice the spirit of the law, even if that meant paying less than usual regard to the letter of the law, the actual words of the statute. He felt that the mischief rule could be interpreted broadly, so that it would not just allow the court to look at the history of the case, but it would also allow the court to carry out the intention of Parliament, however imperfectly this might have been expressed in the words used. The court in the case of **Heydon** suggested that the mischief rule could be used in this broader sense.

Denning stated his view in **Magor and St Mellors *v* Newport Corporation** (1952): 'We do not sit here to pull the language of Parliament to pieces and make nonsense of it . . . we sit here to find out the intention of Parliament and carry it out, and we do this better by filling in the gaps and making sense of the enactment than by opening it up to destructive analysis'.

This approach was roundly criticized by the House of Lords, with Lord Simonds describing 'filling in the gaps' as 'a naked usurpation of the judicial function, under the guise of interpretation . . . If a gap is disclosed, the remedy lies in an amending Act.'

Denning's views nevertheless contributed to the growth of a more purposive approach which has gained ground in the last 20 years, with courts seeking to interpret statutes in ways which will promote the general purpose of the legislation. However, the courts still maintain that this cannot be taken too far. Lord Diplock stated in **Duport Steels Ltd *v* Sirs** (1980) that there was no place for the mischief rule where a statute was not ambiguous, even if a literal interpretation would give an absurd result:

> Where the meaning of the statutory words is plain and unambiguous, it is not for the judges to invent fancied ambiguities as an excuse for failing to give effect to its plain meaning because they themselves consider that the consequences of doing so would be inexpedient, or even unjust or immoral. In controversial matters . . . there is room for differences of opinion as to what is expedient, what is just, and what is morally justifiable. Under our constitution it is Parliament's opinion on these matters that is paramount.

Even where there was ambiguity, Lord Diplock felt that the mischief rule could only be used within tightly limited circumstances, which he defined in **Jones *v* Wrothram Park Settled Estates** (1980), stating that the mischief rule should only be applied where:

- it was possible to determine from consideration of the Act alone the precise mischief that the Act was to remedy; and
- it was an accident that the mischief had not been resolved by the Act's literal meaning; and
- it was possible to state with certainty what were the additional words that would have been inserted by the draftsman, and approved by Parliament, had the omission been drawn to their attention.

This approach clearly contrasts with that of Denning, who felt that the mischief rule should be used even where the wording was clear, if following that wording would lead to an absurd or obviously unjust result, and did not need to be used as tightly as suggested by Lord Diplock.

As with case law, there are various theories about the way in which judges use the discretion they have in statutory interpretation.

Dworkin: fitting in with principles

Dworkin (1986) claims that in approaching a case, the job of judges is to develop a theory about how the particular measure they are dealing with fits with the rest of the law as a whole. If there are two possible interpretations of 'economic' or 'vehicle' (or whatever the term is) the judge should favour the one that allows the provision to sit most comfortably with the purpose of the rest of the law and with the principles and ideals of law and legality in general. This should be done, not for any mechanical reason, but because a body of law which is coherent and unified is, just for that reason, a body of law more entitled to the respect and allegiance of its citizens.

Cross: a contextual approach

Cross suggests that the courts take a 'contextual' approach in which, rather than choosing between different rules, they conduct a progressive analysis, considering first the ordinary meaning of the words in the context of the statute (taking a broad view of context), and then moving on to consider other possibilities if this provides an absurd result. Cross suggests that the courts can read in words that are necessarily implied, and have a limited power to add to, alter or ignore words that would otherwise make a provision unintelligible, absurd, totally unreasonable, unworkable or completely inconsistent with the rest of the Act.

Willis: the just result

John Willis's influential article 'Statute Interpretation in a Nutshell' was cynical about the use of the three 'rules'. He points out that a statute is often capable of several different interpretations, each in line with one of the rules. Despite the emphasis placed on literal interpretation, Willis suggests that the courts view all three rules as equally valid. He claims they use whichever rule will produce the result that they themselves believe to be just.

Griffith: political choices

As with case law (see p. 13), Griffith claims that where there is ambiguity, the judiciary choose the interpretation that best suits their view of policy. An example of this was the 'Fares Fair' case, **Bromley London Borough Council *v* Greater London Council** (1983). The Labour-controlled GLC had enacted a policy – which was part of their election manifesto – to lower the cost of public transport in London, by subsidizing it from the money paid in rates. This meant higher rates. Conservative-controlled Bromley Council challenged the GLC's right to do this.

The powers of local authorities (which then included the GLC) are defined entirely by statute, and there is an assumption that if a power has not been granted to a local authority by Parliament, then it is not a power the authority is entitled to exercise. The judges' job then was to discover what powers Parliament had granted the GLC, and to determine whether their action on fares and rates was within those powers.

Section 1 of the Transport (London) Act (1969) states: 'It shall be the general duty of the Greater London Council to develop policies, and to encourage, organize and where appropriate, carry out measures which

will promote the provision of integrated, efficient and economic transport facilities and services in Greater London.' The key word here was
'economic', with each side taking a different view of its meaning.

The GLC said 'economic' meant 'cost-effective', in other words, giving good value for money. They stated that good value covered any of the
policy goals that transport services could promote: efficient movement of
passengers, reduction of pollution and congestion, possibly even social
redistribution. Bromley Council, on the other hand, said that 'economic'
meant 'breaking even': covering the expenses of its operation out of the
fares charged to the passengers and not requiring a subsidy.

It is not difficult to see that both sides had a point – the word 'economic' could cover either meaning, making the literal rule more or less
useless. Because of this, Lord Scarman refused to consult a dictionary,
stating that 'The dictionary may tell us the several meanings the word can
have but the word will always take its specific meaning (or meanings)
from its surroundings.' Lord Scarman stressed that those surroundings
meant not just the statute as a whole, but also the general duties of the
GLC to ratepayers; that duty must co-exist with the duty to the users of
public transport.

Lord Scarman concluded:

'Economic' in s. 1 must, therefore, be construed widely enough to
embrace both duties. Accordingly, I conclude that in s. 1(1) of the
Act 'economic' covers not only the requirement that transport
services be cost-effective but also the requirement that they be
provided so as to avoid or diminish the burden on the ratepayers
so far as it is practicable to do so.

Griffith has argued that the idea of a 'duty' to ratepayers as explained
in the case is entirely judge-made, and that the Law Lords ruling that the
interests of transport users had been preferred over those of rate-payers
is interfering with the role of elected authorities. He suggests that 'public
expenditure can always be criticised on the ground that it is excessive or
wrongly directed', but that it is the role of elected bodies to make such
decisions, and if the public does not like them 'the remedy lies in their
hands at the next election'.

It is certainly odd that when the judges make so much play of the fact
that Parliament should legislate because it is elected and accountable,
they do not consider themselves bound to respect decisions made in
fulfilment of an elected body's manifesto. What the Lords were doing,
argues Griffith, was making a choice between two interpretations based
not on any real sense of what Parliament intended, but 'primarily [on]
the Law Lords' strong preference for the principles of the market economy
with a dislike of heavy subsidisation for social purposes' – in other words
a political choice.

The judiciary would argue against this proposition, but it is certainly difficult to see where any of the 'rules of interpretation' fitted into

this case; none of the rules of interpretation or the aids to interpretation forced the judges to favour Bromley Council's interpretation of the law over that of the GLC. They could have chosen either interpretation and still been within the law, so that choice must have been based on something other than the law.

▶ Interpretation of European legislation

Under Article 177 of the Treaty of Rome, the European Court is the supreme tribunal for the interpretation of European Community law. Section 3(1) of the European Communities Act 1972 states that questions as to the validity, meaning or effect of Community legislation are to be decided in accordance with the principles laid down by the European Court.

In the light of these provisions, Lord Denning stated that when interpreting European law, English courts should take the same approach as the European Court would:

> No longer must they examine the words in meticulous detail. No longer must they argue about the precise grammatical sense. They must look to the purpose or intent. To quote the words of the European Court in the **Da Costa** case they must deduce from the wording and the spirit of the Treaty the meaning of the Community rules . . . They must divine the spirit of the Treaty and gain inspiration from it. If they find a gap, they must fill it as best they can. They must do what the framers of the instrument would have done if they had thought about it. So we must do the same. (**Bulmer** *v* **Bollinger** (1974)).

In other words, he was saying that rather than using the literal rule, the courts should apply a broadly-interpreted mischief rule – which was of course, the same approach that he felt should be applied to domestic legislation.

If the English courts are uncertain as to how a piece of European legislation should be interpreted they can, and sometimes must, refer it to the European Court of Justice for interpretation (see p. 52). In such circumstances the case is adjourned, until the European Court directs the English one on how to interpret the European legislation. The English court then re-opens the case in England and applies this interpretation.

Effect of the EEC on the interpretation of UK law

Section 2(4) of the European Communities Act 1972 provides that all parliamentary legislation (whether passed before or after the European

Communities Act) must be construed and applied in accordance with Community law. The case of **R *v* Secretary of State for Transport ex parte Factortame** (1990) makes it clear that the English courts must apply EC law which is directly effective even if it conflicts with English law, including statute law (these issues are discussed more fully in the section on European law).

▶ Reform of statutory interpretation

The Law Commission examined the interpretation of statutes in 1967 and had 'little hesitation in suggesting that this is a field not suitable for codification'. Instead, it proposed certain improvements within the present system.

* More liberal use should be made of internal and external aids.
* In the event of ambiguity, the construction which best promoted the 'general legislative purpose' should be adopted. This could be seen as supporting Denning's approach.
* The advantages and disadvantages of allowing references to parliamentary debates were considered but no firm recommendation made.

The Renton Committee on the Preparation of Legislation produced its report in 1975, making many proposals for improving the procedure for making and drafting statutes, including the following:

* Acts could begin with a statement of purpose in the same way that older statutes used to have preambles.
* There should be a move towards including less detail in the legislation, introducing the simpler style used in countries such as France.
* More use could be made in statutes of examples showing the courts how an Act was intended to work in particular situations.
* Long, un-paragraphed sentences should be avoided.
* Statutes should be arranged to suit the convenience of the ultimate users.
* There should be more consolidation of legislation.

In 1978, Sir David Renton, in a speech entitled 'Failure to Implement the Renton Report' noted that there had been a small increase in the number of draftsmen and increased momentum in the consolidation process, but that Parliament had continued to pass a huge amount of legislation, with no reduction in the amount of detail and scarcely any use of statements of purpose.

ANSWERING QUESTIONS

1 'Some may say ... that judges should not pay any attention to what is said in Parliament. They should grope about in the dark for the meaning of an Act without switching on the light.' (Lord Denning MR, in Davis v Johnson (1978)). Discuss with reference to statutory interpretation. *Oxford*
Your introduction should outline the issues Lord Denning is referring to: the fact that the sovereignty of Parliament requires judges to interpret legislation in the way in which Parliament intended, and the difficulties of ascertaining that intention. If you know the case referred to, it helps to say a little about it, but if not, do not worry – it is more important to understand the issues raised by the quote.

You could then go on to point out that the specific point discussed in **Davis v Johnson** was whether Hansard should be consulted as evidence of parliamentary intention, and outline the rule prior to **Hart v Pepper**, and the changes made by that case.

Then you need to discuss whether consulting Hansard really does help judges understand parliamentary intention, using the arguments for and against.

If you have time, you might discuss other issues concerning statutory interpretation, particularly the debate between the more purposive approach promoted by Lord Denning, and the more literal style of his opponents, focusing on which approach best enables the judges to apply parliamentary intention.

Your conclusion might state whether you think judges should be able to consult Hansard, and how far you think it helps them decide on parliamentary intention; you might mention any other way in which you think they could better apply this intention, perhaps including some of the suggestions for reform.

2 A statute states that 'It is an offence to loiter or solicit in a street for the purposes of prostitution.'

Mary, a known prostitute, sits in a large bay window on the first floor of a house overlooking a busy street. She taps the window to attract the attention of men on the pavement. She invites John upstairs by beckoning and pointing to the door. He accepts her invitation.

Jane, a known prostitute, who is unable to speak, stands on a street corner and waits for men in cars to stop. She is observed getting into a car and handing Peter, the driver, a card which he reads. He then drives off immediately, without Jane.

Have any offences been committed? Discuss the rules of statutory interpretation which guide you to your answer. *WJEC*
You might start your answer by briefly describing the three rules of interpretation, and pointing out that there is no strict procedure dictating

which should be applied, even though they can lead to different interpretations of the same statute.

You then need to take each person in turn, starting with Mary. The first thing to note is that it appears the offence can be committed in two ways: by either loitering in the street, or soliciting in the street, each for the purposes of prostitution. Taking a literal approach first, can Mary be said to be loitering in the street or soliciting in the street? Since she is not physically in the street, it seems unlikely that she could be described as loitering there. She is clearly soliciting, but can she be said to be doing so 'in the street'? She may not be in the street, but her soliciting appears to be taking effect in the street, so do you think the term can be interpreted to cover her behaviour? You could then point out that since there appears to be some ambiguity, the golden rule should be applied, allowing you to modify the sense of the words in order to resolve the ambiguity – point out that in a real case, you would want to look at the rest of the statute to help you do this.

If the golden rule is unhelpful, you could apply the mischief rule – again, in real life, you would want to consult the rest of the statute, and probably other materials too, to establish the purpose of the statute, so that you could interpret the provision in line with that purpose. Using this rule, whether Mary had committed an offence would depend on what the purpose of the statute was: if it was to stop men in the street being harassed by prostitutes, you might feel that the provision should be interpreted to make Mary guilty of an offence; alternatively, if, for example, the purpose was to keep prostitution within brothels, you might find that Mary had not committed an offence.

You also need to consider the issue of whether Mary's behaviour is 'for the purposes of prostitution'; there does seem to be evidence of this, but on the facts as we have them here, it is only evidence which the jury or magistrates will consider, rather than definite proof.

Moving on to Jane, you can see that on a literal interpretation, she is loitering in the street, but is she doing so for the purposes of prostitution? Here again, you might point out that you would need to know more about the facts (particularly what is on the card), but if there is evidence that she is acting for the purposes of prostitution, an offence may have been committed since she is clearly loitering in the street. The statute appears not to require that the accused should both loiter and solicit, so even though soliciting in the normal sense of the word would seem to require some sort of verbal communication, the fact that she has not spoken to the man does not mean she cannot have committed the offence. Since the literal rule does not give rise to ambiguity or absurdity, it appears not to be necessary to apply the golden or mischief rules.

You should conclude by pointing out that to make a firm decision on whether an offence has been committed, you would need to consider both internal and external aids to interpretation. You might also point out that there is a presumption that statutes which impose a criminal penalty should be interpreted in favour of the citizen where there is ambiguity, which might mean that in Mary's case the ambiguity could mean that she has committed no offence.

3 Examine the role of the judiciary in the interpretation of legislation.
Your introduction should define what legislation is, and why the judiciary should need to interpret it. Then go on to explain why the role of the judiciary in statutory interpretation is so important: the constitutional issues of parliamentary sovereignty; and the fact that judges are not elected, and are technically supposed to be declaring the intention of Parliament rather than making law themselves.

You can then go on to discuss the problems of deciding what parliamentary intention actually is, and the ways in which the courts attempt to ascertain and apply the intention of Parliament when interpreting legislation – the three rules, external and internal aids (including the changes made by **Pepper v Hart** and the usefulness or otherwise of consulting Hansard).

You then need to address the question of whether the role of the judges involves making law: whether it should do so, and if so how far. You should make use of the material on how judges really interpret statutes, contrasting it with the 'official' view.

Your conclusion could state whether you feel the role currently played by judges in interpreting legislation is the right one, and why, or if you feel that the judges go too far making law, you might suggest how this could be curbed.

•
DELEGATED LEGISLATION

In many cases, the statutes passed by Parliament lay down a basic framework of the law, with creation of the detailed rules delegated to Government departments, local authorities, or public or nationalized bodies; the statute is known as the enabling Act. There are three main forms of delegated legislation:

Statutory instruments. These are made by Government departments.
Bye-laws. These are made by local authorities, public and nationalized bodies, such as British Rail. Byelaws have to be approved by central government.
Orders in council. These are made by Government in times of emergency. They are drafted by the Government department, approved by the Privy Council and signed by the Queen.

On an everyday basis, delegated legislation is an extremely important source of law. The output of delegated legislation far exceeds that of Acts of Parliament, and its provisions include rules that can substantially affect the day-to-day lives of huge numbers of people – safety laws for industry, road traffic regulations, and rules relating to state education, for example.

Why is delegated legislation necessary?

Delegated legislation is necessary for a number of reasons:

Insufficient parliamentary time. Parliament does not have the time to debate every detailed rule necessary for efficient government.

Speed. It allows rules to be made more quickly than they could by Parliament. Parliament does not sit all the time, and its procedure is slow and cumbersome; delegated legislation often has to be made in response to emergencies and urgent problems.

Technicality of the subject matter. Modern legislation often needs to include detailed, technical provisions – those in building regulations or safety at work rules for example. MPs do not usually have the technical knowledge required, whereas delegated legislation can use experts who are familiar with the relevant areas.

Need for local knowledge. Local bye-laws in particular can only be made effectively with awareness of the locality.

Flexibility. Statutes require cumbersome procedures for enactment, and can only be revoked or amended by another statute. Delegated legislation, however, can be put into action quickly, and easily revoked if it proves problematic.

Future needs. Parliament cannot hope to foresee every problem that might arise as a result of a statute, especially concerning areas such as health provision or welfare benefits. Delegated legislation can be put in place as and when such problems arise.

Control of delegated legislation

Consultation

Those who make delegated legislation often consult experts within the relevant field, and those bodies who are likely to be affected by it. In the case of road traffic regulations for example, ministers are likely to seek the advice of police, motoring organizations, vehicle manufacturers and local authorities before making the rules. Often the relevant statute makes such consultation obligatory and names the bodies who should be consulted. Under the National Insurance Act 1946, for example, draft regulations must be submitted to the National Insurance Advisory Committee, and any minister proposing to make rules of procedure for a tribunal within a department is required by the Tribunals and Inquiries Act 1971 to consult the Council on Tribunals. In other cases there may be a general statutory requirement for 'such consultation as the minister thinks appropriate with such organizations as appear to him to represent the interest concerned'.

Publication

All delegated legislation is public, and therefore available for public scrutiny.

Supervision by Parliament

- Parliamentary sovereignty means that Parliament can at any time revoke a piece of delegated legislation itself, or pass legislation on the same subject as the delegated legislation.
- Enabling Acts dealing with subjects of special, often constitutional, importance may require Parliament to vote its approval of the delegated legislation. This is called the affirmative resolution procedure, whereby delegated legislation is laid before one or both Houses (sometimes in draft), and becomes law only if a motion approving it is passed within a specified time (usually 28 or 40 days). Since a vote has to be taken, the procedure means that the Government must find parliamentary time for debate, and opposition parties have an opportunity to raise any objections. In practice, though, it is very rare for Government not to achieve a majority when such votes are taken.
- Much delegated legislation is put before Parliament for MPs under the negative resolution procedure. Within a specified time (usually 40 days), any member may put down a motion to annul it. An annulment motion put down by a backbencher is not guaranteed to be dealt with, but one put down by the Official Opposition usually will be. If, after debate, either House passes an annulment motion, the delegated legislation is cancelled.
- A parliamentary committee watches over the making of delegated legislation, and reports to each House on any delegated legislation which requires special consideration, including any regulations made under an Act that prohibits challenge by the courts, or which seem to make unusual or unexpected use of the powers granted by the enabling Act. However, the Committee may not consider the merits of any instrument.
- MPs can ask ministers questions about delegated legislation at question time, or raise them in debates.
- Although the House of Lords cannot veto proposed Acts, the same

does not apply to delegated legislation. In 1968 the House of Lords rejected an order imposing sanctions against the Rhodesian Government made under the Southern Rhodesia Act 1965.

Control by the courts: judicial review

While the validity of a statute can never be challenged by the courts because of parliamentary sovereignty, delegated legislation can. It may be challenged on any of the following grounds under the procedure for judicial review.

Procedural *ultra vires*. Here the complainant claims that the procedures laid down in the enabling act for producing delegated legislation have not been followed. In **Agricultural, Horticultural and Forestry Training Board** *v* **Aylesbury Mushrooms Ltd** (1972), an order was declared invalid because the requirement to consult with interested parties before making it had not been properly complied with.

Substantive *ultra vires*. This is usually based on a claim that the measure under review goes beyond the powers Parliament granted under the enabling Act. In **Commissioners of Customs and Excise** *v* **Cure and Deeley Ltd** (1962), the powers of the Commissioners to make delegated legislation under the Finance (No. 2) Act 1940 was challenged. The Act empowered them to produce regulations 'for any matter for which provision appears to them necessary for the purpose of giving effect to the Act'. The Commissioners held that this included allowing them to make a regulation giving them the power to determine the amount of tax due where a tax return was submitted late. The High Court invalidated the regulation on the grounds that the Commissioners had given themselves powers far beyond what Parliament had intended; they were empowered only to collect such tax as was due by law, not to decide what amount they thought fit.

Unreasonableness. If rules are manifestly unjust, have been made in bad faith (for example by someone with a financial interest in their operation) or are otherwise so perverse that no reasonable official could have made them, the courts can declare them invalid.

Criticism of delegated legislation

- It is undemocratic because it is often made by civil servants rather than elected representatives. Delegation of detailed administrative rules may be acceptable, but it is argued that matters of principle should be decided by Parliament.

- There is too much of it.
- There is sub-delegation, with delegated legislation being made by people other than those who were given the original power to make it.
- There are problems with the system of controls.
- Publicity is of limited value as a control if few people know where to find out about delegated legislation, or are unaware of on what grounds it can be challenged and how to go about doing so.
- Although the affirmative resolution procedure usually ensures that parliamentary attention is drawn to important delegated legislation, it is rarely possible to prevent such legislation being passed.
- The Parliamentary Committee that oversees delegated legislation is not allowed to consider its merits, and its report on such legislation has no binding effect, though it may draw parliamentary attention to it.
- Judicial review is a haphazard means of control, relying on individual challenges being put before the courts. Such a challenge depends on individual resources and energy and may not be made until years after the enactment of delegated legislation, when it finally affects someone prepared and able to challenge it. Where a piece of delegated legislation largely affects individuals who are not given to questioning rules, are unaware of their rights, or lack the finances to go to court, it will go completely unchallenged.
- In some cases enabling acts confer extremely wide discretionary powers on ministers, along the lines that the minister 'may make such regulations as he thinks fit for the purpose of bringing the Act into operation'. This means that almost nothing can be considered *ultra vires*, and judicial review is effectively frustrated.
- The public are frequently unaware of its existence.

●
ANSWERING QUESTIONS

Evaluate the various controls over delegated legislation. *London*
Your introduction should explain what delegated legislation is. You should then go on to explain why it needs to be controlled – the main reason being the fact that it is not made by Parliament. Describe the controls that exist, and then go through the problems with those controls (the section on judicial review, p. 314, provides extra material which will be useful here). Your conclusion should state whether you feel the controls are adequate, and if not, whether you feel anything could be done to improve them.

• • • • • • • • • • • • • • • • • •
EUROPEAN LAW

The European Community currently comprises fifteen Western European countries. The original members – France, West Germany, Belgium, Luxembourg, Italy and The Netherlands – founded the community in 1951, when they created the European Coal and Steel Community (ECSC). Six years later, they signed the Treaties of Rome, creating the European Economic Community (EEC) and the European Atomic Energy Community (Euratom). The original six were joined by the UK, Ireland and Denmark in 1973, Greece in 1981 and Spain and Portugal in 1986, and in the same year, the member countries signed the Single European Act, which laid the foundation for free movement of goods and people within the Community (the single market), and for greater political unity. Finland, Austria and Sweden joined in 1995.

▶ The aims of the European Communities

The original aim of the first treaty signed, the Treaty of Paris, was to create political unity within Europe and prevent another world war. The ECSC placed the production of steel and coal in all the member states under the authority of a single community organisation, with the object of indirectly controlling the manufacture of arms and therefore helping to prevent war between member states. Euratom was designed to produce cooperative nuclear research, and the EEC to improve Europe's economic strength.

Though all three communities still exist, it is the EEC (now the EC) that has the most significance, particularly for law. Its object now is to weld Europe into a single prosperous area by abolishing all restrictions affecting the movement of people, of goods and money between member states, producing a single market of over 350,000,000 people, available to all producers in the member states. This, it is hoped, will help Europe to compete economically with Japan and the United States, the member states being stronger as a block than they could possibly be on their own. The 1986 Single European Act was a major step towards this goal, setting a target of 1992 for the abolition of trade barriers between member states. The practical effect of this is that, for example, a company manufacturing rivets in Leeds, with an order from a company in Barcelona, can send the rivets all the way there by lorry, without the driver having to fill in customs forms as he or she crosses every border. The rivets will be made to a common EC standard, so the Spanish firm will know exactly what they are going to receive, while any trademarks or other rights over the design of the rivets will be protected throughout the member states.

Just as goods can now move freely throughout the Community, so can workers; for example, a designer from Paris can go and work in London, or Milan, or Dublin, with no need for a work permit and no problem with immigration controls.

Along with these closer economic ties, it is intended that there should be increasing political unity, though there is some disagreement – particularly, though not exclusively, in Britain – as to how far this should go. The Treaty of Maastricht, signed in 1992, is the latest move in this direction; it outlines the aims of a single currency, joint defence and foreign policies, and inter-governmental cooperation on justice and home affairs, but when and how far these aims will be achieved is still a matter of debate. Further decisions are likely to be taken at the inter-governmental conference in 1996.

▶ The institutions of the European Communities

By 1960, all three communities were covered by unified governing bodies: the Council, the Commission, the European Parliament and the Court of Justice of the European Communities. The rest of our discussion looks at their role in the EC alone.

The Commission

The Commission is composed of twenty members, called Commissioners, who are each appointed for four years by general agreement with the member states. They must be nationals of a member state, and in practice there tends to be two each from the largest states – France, Germany, Italy, Spain and the UK – and one from the rest. However, the Commissioners do not represent their own countries; they are independent, and answerable as a group to the European Parliament. The idea is that the Commission's commitment to furthering overall Community interests balances the Council of Ministers, whose members represent national interests. Only the European Parliament can dismiss Commissioners before the end of their four-year term.

The Commission's role includes formulating proposals for new Community policies, which are put forward to the Council for turning into legislation; almost all EC legislation begins with proposals from the Commission. It is also responsible for ensuring that EC legislation is carried out, and will investigate alleged breaches by member states, and where necessary bring them before the European Court. In some circumstances it has its own law-making powers, delegated by the Council. It is assisted in all these functions by an administrative staff, which has a similar role to that of the civil service in the UK.

The Council of Ministers

The Council of Ministers has traditionally been the supreme legislative body in the EC, and its role is to take the broad policies of the Treaties and formulate them into more concrete rules. The Council does not have a permanent membership – in each meeting, the members, one from each country, are chosen according to the subject under discussion (so, for example, a discussion of matters relating to farming would usually be attended by the Minister of Agriculture of each country). Presidency of the Council rotates among the member states every six months.

Although it is the Council which has most legislative power, generally it cannot act on its own initiative but must wait for proposals from the Commission. The Treaties lay down different voting arrangements for different kinds of Council decisions. The most important areas require a unanimous vote, but most decisions are passed on a 'qualified majority'. In this system, each country has a certain number of votes: France, Germany, Italy, and the United Kingdom have ten; Spain has eight; Belgium, Greece, Portugal and The Netherlands have five; Denmark, Ireland and Finland three; Luxembourg two. A decision requiring a qualified majority can only be taken with the support of a specified number of votes (which varies according to the type of decision being made), and this number is calculated to ensure that the larger states cannot force decisions on the smaller ones.

The Council may be questioned by the European Parliament, but the chief control is exercised by member states' own national governments over their ministers who attend the Council.

The European Council

Heads of State or Government and Foreign Ministers of member states evolved an informal convention of twice-yearly summit meetings to discuss important issues. Much of the high-profile EEC business tended to be done at these meetings, which have now been recognized and formalized as the European Council by Article 2 of the Single European Act 1986. They are now required to take place twice a year and, when discussing Community matters, have the same powers as the Council of Ministers, though the two are technically separate.

The European Parliament

The Parliament is composed of 518 members (MEPs), who are directly elected in their own countries. In Britain they are elected in the same way as MPs, and each represent a geographical area, though these are much larger than those of MPs, since there are only 81 MEPs for the whole country. Elections are held every five years.

The individual member countries are each allocated a number of seats, roughly according to population, though on this basis the smaller countries are over-represented. Members sit in political groupings rather than with others from their own country.

The European Parliament examines Commission proposals before they are discussed by the Council, and in many important matters the Council consults with the Parliament before enacting any legislation. Under the original EEC Treaty, its role in this process was merely advisory and supervisory, and the Council could pass legislation regardless of objections from the Parliament. However, the Single European Act and the Maastricht Treaty increased the powers of the Parliament, so that it can now veto legislation in certain areas, including environmental protection, health, education, consumer protection and transport. In addition, a 'Cooperation procedure', which applies particularly to legislation concerning the harmonization needed for the single market, allows the Parliament to give a 'second reading' to Council proposals, and requires more formal communication between them.

There is also another area in which the Parliament is given a greater say: the Community budget. The Council places the draft proposals for the budget before the Parliament which has power, acting by majority vote, to reject it.

The European Court of Justice (ECJ)

The ECJ has the task of supervising the uniform application of Community law throughout the member states. It is important not to confuse it with the European Court of Human Rights, which deals with alleged breaches of human rights by countries who are signatories to the European Convention on Human Rights. It is completely separate, and not an institution of the European Community.

The ECJ, which sits in Luxembourg, has fifteen judges, appointed by agreement among member states, for a period of six years (which may be renewed). The judges are assisted by eight advocates-general, who produce opinions on the cases assigned to them, indicating the issues raised and suggesting conclusions. These are not binding, but are nevertheless usually followed by the Court. Both judges and advocates-general are chosen from those who are eligible for the highest judicial posts in their own countries.

Most cases are heard in plenary session, that is with all the judges sitting together. Only one judgment will be delivered, giving no indication of the extent of agreement between the judges, and these often consist of fairly brief propositions, from which it can be difficult to discern any *ratio decidendi*. Consequently, lawyers seeking precedents often turn to the opinions written by the advocates-general. Since September 1989 the full ECJ has been assisted by a new Court of First Instance to deal with specialist economic law cases. Parties in such cases may appeal to the full ECJ on a point of law.

The majority of cases heard by the ECJ are brought by member states and institutions of the Community, or are referred to it by national courts. It has only limited power to deal with cases brought by individual citizens, and such cases are rarely heard.

The ECJ has two separate functions: a judicial role, deciding cases of dispute; and a supervisory role.

The judicial role of the ECJ

The ECJ hears cases of dispute between parties, which fall into two categories: proceedings against member states, and proceedings against EC institutions.

Proceedings against member states may be brought by the Commission, or by other member states, and involve alleged breaches of Community law by the country in question. In **Re Tachographs: EC Commission *v* UK** (1979), the ECJ upheld a complaint against the UK for failing to implement an EEC regulation making it compulsory for lorries used to carry dangerous goods to be fitted with tachographs (devices used to record the speed and distance travelled, with the aim of preventing lorry drivers from speeding, or from driving for longer than the permitted number of hours). The Commission usually gives the member state the opportunity to put things right before bringing the case to the ECJ.

Proceedings against EC institutions may be brought by member states, other EC institutions and in certain circumstances, by individual citizens or organizations. The procedure can be used to review the legality of EC regulations, directives or decisions, on the grounds that proper procedures have not been followed, the provisions infringe the Treaty or any rule relating to its application, or powers have been misused.

Decisions made in these kinds of cases cannot be questioned in UK courts.

The supervisory role of the ECJ

Article 177 of the Treaty of Rome provides that any court or tribunal in a member state may refer a question on EC law to the ECJ if it considers that 'a decision on that question is necessary to enable it to give judgment'. The object of this referral system is to make sure that the law is interpreted in the same way throughout the Community.

A reference must be made if the national court is one from which there is no further appeal – so in Britain, the House of Lords must refer such questions, while the lower courts usually have some discretion about whether or not to do so; the Article 177 procedure is expensive and time consuming, often delaying a decision on the case for a long time, and so lower courts have been discouraged from using it. Consequently attempts have been made to set down guidelines by which a court could determine when a decision would or would not be necessary.

In **Bulmer** *v* **Bollinger** (1974), the Court of Appeal was asked to review a judge's exercise of discretion to refer a question under Article 177. They pointed out that the European Court could not interfere with the exercise of a judge's discretion to refer, and Lord Denning set down guidelines on the points which should be taken into account in considering whether a reference was necessary. He stated that no reference should be made:

- where it would not be conclusive of the case, and other matters would remain to be decided;
- where there had been a previous ruling on the same point;
- where the court considers that point to be reasonably clear and free from doubt;
- where the facts of the case had not yet been decided.

Denning's guidelines are narrower than those issued by the ECJ and have probably been the reason why fewer references are made under Article 177 from the UK than from any other member state. The further up the English court system a case has to go before it is submitted for a ruling, the less likely it is that it will ever be submitted, since few litigants have the resources to pursue a case that far. Where referral is requested by a party in the case and refused, that party cannot appeal to the ECJ, only to a higher English court.

Where a case is submitted, proceedings will be suspended in the national court until the ECJ has given its verdict. This verdict does not tell the national court how to decide the case, but simply explains what the Community law on the matter is. The national court then has the duty of making its decision in the light of this.

Regardless of which national court submitted the point for consideration, a ruling from the ECJ should be followed by all other courts in the Community – so theoretically, a point raised by a county court in England may result in a ruling that the highest courts in all the member states are to follow. Where a ruling reveals that national legislation conflicts with Community law, the national government usually enacts new legislation to put the matter right.

The court's decisions can be changed only by its own subsequent decision or by an amendment of the Treaty, which would require the unanimous approval of member states through their own Parliaments. Decisions of the European Court cannot be questioned in English courts. This principle has limited the jurisdiction of the House of Lords as a final appellate court.

An illustration of the use of Article 177 is the case of **Marshall** *v* **Southampton Area Health Authority** (1986). Miss Marshall, a dietician, was compulsorily retired by the Authority from her job when she was 62, although she wished to continue to 65. It was the Authority's policy that the normal retiring age for its employees was the age at which state retirement pensions became payable; for women this was 60, though the

Authority had waived the rule for two years in Miss Marshall's case. She claimed that the Authority was discriminating against women by adopting a policy that employees should retire at state pension age, hence requiring women to retire before men. This policy appeared to be legal under the relevant English legislation but was argued to be contrary to a Council directive providing for equal treatment of men and women. The national court made a reference to the ECJ asking for directions on the meaning of the directive. The ECJ found that there was a conflict with United Kingdom law, and the UK later changed its legislation to conform.

It is important to note that the ECJ is **not** an appeal court from decisions made in the member states. It does not substitute its own decisions for those of a lower court (except those of its own Court of First Instance). It will assist a national court at any level in reaching a decision, but the actual decision remains the responsibility of the national court. When parties in an English case talk of taking the case to Europe, the only way they can do this is to get an English court to make a referral for an Article 177 ruling, and they may have to take their case all the way to the House of Lords to ensure this.

Each member state enforces the judgments of the European Court through its own enforcement system, and the European Court has no machinery for the enforcement of its judgments in or against member states.

The Court of Justice in its advisory capacity may also give its opinion as to whether proposed agreements between the Community and non-member states or international organizations are likely to violate the Treaties.

▶ Sources of European law

The European Communities Act 1972 provided that from 1 January 1973 the UK had new sources of law: the European Communities Treaties themselves, plus the various types of legislation made by the EEC. Rulings of the ECJ also affect English law (see above).

These are sources of law only in the areas in which the EC is concerned, which currently comprise agriculture and fishing, companies, competition, free movement of workers and goods, education, consumer policy, health, and the environment.

Treaties

These are the highest source of EC law, and as well as laying down the general aims of the Communities, they themselves create some rights and obligations. Any provision in an EC Treaty which clearly creates rights or imposes obligations on individuals, business and governments can be relied on and used in argument just as if they were UK statutes. For example, Article 119 of the EEC Treaty provides that 'men and women shall receive equal pay for equal work'. In **Macarthys** *v* **Smith** (1979), Article 119 was held to give a woman in the UK the right to claim the same wages as were paid to the male predecessor in her job, even though she had no such right under the UK equal pay legislation passed in 1970, before the UK joined the Communities.

Other Treaty provisions which can be used in this way include the prohibition on discriminations between workers which restrict their free movement between member states; the right to set up in business in another state under the conditions laid down for nationals of that state; and the right of equal pay for equal work.

These provisions give citizens of member states rights against governments (described as the provision having vertical effect), and against other citizens and organizations (described as having horizontal effect). They take precedence over any inconsistent UK law.

Treaty provisions which are merely statements of intent or policy, rather than establishing clear rights or duties, require detailed legislation to be made before they can be enforced in the member states.

Regulations

A regulation is the nearest Community law comes to an English Act of Parliament. Regulations apply throughout the Community, usually to people in general, and they become part of the law of each member nation as soon as they come into force, without the need for each country to make its own legislation.

Regulations must be applied even if the member state has already passed legislation which conflicts with them. In **Leonesio** *v* **Italian Ministry of Agriculture** (1973), a regulation to encourage reduced dairy production stated that a cash premium should be payable to farmers who slaughtered cows and agreed not to produce milk for five years. Leonesio had fulfilled this requirement, but was refused payment because the Italian constitution required legislation to authorize government expenditure. The ECJ said that once Leonesio had satisfied the conditions, he was entitled to the payment; the Italian government could not use its own laws to block that right.

Directives

Directives set out objectives to be achieved by member states, leaving the states themselves to implement the objectives by making their own national legislation. If member states fail to do this within a specified time limit, the directive can be directly applied either by national courts or by the ECJ.

This means that in general, directives do not create individual rights until translated into domestic legislation. However, several cases have made inroads into this principle. First, it was held in **Marshall** *v* **Southampton Area Health Authority** (see p. 53) that directives may have vertical direct effect (meaning direct effect against governments) where the directive creates individual rights, and the content of the rights can be clearly ascertained from it.

In such cases, directives can be used against not just governments themselves, but institutions of governments, to establish rights where directives have not been implemented at all, or where legislation is in conflict with them. Organs of the state include those made responsible by the state for pursuing public functions under state control, of which health authorities were considered to be one; had Miss Marshall's employer been a private company, she would not have been able to rely on the directive in the same way.

In **Van Duyn** *v* **Home Office** (1974), the Home Office refused Van Duyn permission to enter the UK, because she was a member of a religious group, the Scientologists, which the Government wanted to exclude from the country at the time. Van Duyn argued that her exclusion was contrary to provisions in the Treaty of Rome on freedom of movement. The Government responded by pointing out that the Treaty allowed exceptions on public policy grounds, but Van Duyn then relied on a later directive which said that public policy could only be invoked on the basis of personal conduct, and Van Duyn herself had done nothing to justify exclusion. The case was referred to the ECJ, which found that the obligation conferred on the Government was clear and unconditional, and so created enforceable rights.

The reasoning behind this approach was explained in **Publico Ministerio** *v* **Ratti** (1980), where the ECJ pointed out that member states could not be allowed to rely on their own wrongful failure to implement directives as a means of denying individual rights.

Directives have no horizontal direct effect (so they do not give individuals rights against each other). However, where UK legislation is in conflict with a directive, a complainant cannot simply invoke the directive in court, but can apply for judicial review against the relevant minister. If successful, the offending UK legislation will be ineffective. In addition, the case of **Italy** *v* **Francovich** (1992) established that where a government fails to implement a directive within the specified time limit, a person who is caused loss by that failure can sue for damages. The directive with which the case was concerned required states to set up a scheme to ensure that employees received outstanding wages if their employer became insolvent. The Italian Government failed to set up such a scheme, and when Francovich's employer went bust, he lost wages, and there was no scheme to compensate him. In this case, the directive did not have direct horizontal effect because it was not clear and unconditional, but the ECJ held that even so, Francovich had a right to damages from the Italian Government. Such damages would, it said, be payable wherever the purpose of a directive is to confer rights on individuals, those rights can be identified from the words of the directive, and there is a causal link between the member state's failure to implement the directive, and the citizen's loss.

It is possible that the same rule may apply where a government appears to implement a directive, but in fact misinterprets its purpose, so that the domestic legislation does not implement it properly, though no case on this point has arisen.

A further development in this area is the case of **Marleasing SA** *v* **La Comercial Internacional de Alimentation SA** (1992), where the ECJ held that national courts should, so far as possible, interpret national legislation so that it conforms with directives. In **Webb** *v* **EMO Air Cargo** (1993), the House of Lords pointed out that this had to be done 'without distorting the meaning of the domestic legislation', and that an interpretation consistent with a directive could only be made where the words of the domestic legislation could support it, but this still means that there may be cases where individuals may be able to horizontally enforce rights contained in a directive even before it has been implemented by legislation.

Decisions

A decision may be addressed to a state, a person or a company and is binding only on the recipient. For example, the EC might make a decision requiring British Rail to increase the number of trains it runs through the channel tunnel, and that decision would affect only BR.

Recommendations and opinions

The Council and the Commission may issue recommendations and opinions which, although not to be disregarded, are not binding law.

▶ How does EC law affect the UK?

Membership of the EC has had a number of effects on UK law and our legal system.

New sources of law

Joining the EEC created new sources of law for the UK, and very important ones. Section 2(4) of the European Communities Act provides that English law should be interpreted and have effect subject to the principle that EC law is supreme; this means that EC law now takes precedence

over all domestic sources of law. As a result, it has had a profound effect
on the rights of citizens in this country, and in particular, on the rights
of employees and of women. For example, in **R** *v* **Secretary of State for
Employment ex parte Equal Opportunities Commission** (1994), the House
of Lords found that parts of the Employment Protection (Consolidation)
Act 1978 were incompatible with EC law on equal treatment for male and
female employees, because the Act gave part-time workers fewer rights
than full-timers. Since most part-time workers were women, this was held
to discriminate on the basis of sex, and the UK Government was forced
to change the law, and greatly improve the rights of part-time workers.

The role of the courts

Because EC law takes precedence over domestic legislation, the role of
the courts has changed as a result of membership of the Community.
Before the UK joined the EEC, statutes were the highest form of law, and
judges had no power to refuse to apply them. Now however, they can –
in fact they should – refuse to apply statutes which are in conflict with
directly effective EC law.

The leading case in this area is **R** *v* **Secretary of State for Transport
ex parte Factortame** (1990). It arose from the fishing policy decided by
member states in 1983, which allowed member states to limit fishing
within twelve miles of their own shores to boats from their own country,
and left the remainder of the seas around the Community open to fishing
boats from any member state. In addition, to preserve stocks of fish, each
state was allocated a quota of fish, and required not to exceed it. Soon
after the new rules were in place, the UK Government became concerned that Spanish fishing boats were registering as British vessels, so
that their catches counted against the British quota rather than the Spanish, and genuine British fisherman were therefore getting a smaller share.
The Government therefore passed the Merchant Shipping Act 1988, which
contained provisions to prevent the Spanish trawlers taking advantage of
the British quota.

Spanish boat owners challenged the Act, claiming it was in conflict
with EC law on the freedom to set up business anywhere in the Community, and the House of Lords agreed. They stated that s. 2(4) of the
European Communities Act 'has precisely the same effect as if a section
were incorporated in . . . [the 1988 Act, saying] that the provisions with
respect to registration of British fishing vessels were to be without prejudice to the directly enforceable Community rights of nationals of any
member state . . .'.

The decision was criticized as compromising the rights of the UK
Parliament to make law for this country, but the House of Lords was firm
in dismissing such complaints, pointing out that it was very clear before
the UK joined the Community that doing so would mean giving up some

degree of sovereignty over our own law, and that this was accepted voluntarily when the UK joined the Community. 'Under . . . the Act of 1972, it has always been clear that it was the duty of a United Kingdom court, when delivering final judgment, to override any rule of national law found to be in conflict with any directly enforceable rule of Community law . . .'.

The role of the courts is also affected by the principle stated in **Marleasing**, that they should, wherever possible, interpret statutes in accordance with directives (which as we have seen, do not generally have direct effect). This means that the courts now have a new external aid to consider when interpreting statutes, and should take notice of it wherever they can do so without straining the words of the statute.

The operation of the UK courts is also affected by the supervisory jurisdiction of the ECJ, as explained above, and this gives a further source of law, since the courts of all member states are bound by ECJ decisions on the interpretation and application of EC law.

The future

One view of the influence of United Kingdom membership of the EEC on our national law was given by Lord Denning, in poetic mood, in **Bulmer v Bollinger**: 'The Treaty is like an incoming tide. It flows into the estuaries and up the rivers. It cannot be held back.' Lord Scarman, obviously in an equally lyrical frame of mind, commented:

> For the moment, to adopt Lord Denning's imagery, the incoming tide has not yet mingled with the home waters of the common law: but it is inconceivable that, like the Rhone and the Arve where those two streams meet at Geneva, they should move on, side by side, one grey with the melted snows and ice of the distant mountains of our legal history, the other clear blue and clean, reflecting modern opinion. If we stay in the Common Market, I would expect to see its principles of legislation and statutory interpretation, and its conception of an activist court whose role is to strengthen and fulfil the purpose of statute law, replace the traditional attitudes of English judges and lawyers to statute law and the current complex style of statutory drafting.

What Lord Scarman was referring to was the difference in approach between the English legal system and those in mainland Europe. When drafting statutes, for example, English law has tended towards tightly written, very precise rules, whereas the continental style is looser, setting out broad principles to be followed. As a result, the continental style of statutory interpretation takes a very purposive approach, paying most attention to putting into practice the spirit of the legislation, and filling in any gaps in the wording if necessary, as opposed to the more literal style traditionally associated with English judges. The ECJ tends to take the continental approach, and it has been suggested that as time goes on, this will influence our own judges more and more, leading to more creative judicial decision making, with corresponding changes in the drafting of statutes.

It has also been suggested that once our legal system becomes accustomed to judges setting aside Acts of Parliament because they do not conform to EC law, some of the objections to establishing a Bill of Rights (see p. 348) might also disappear, since allowing judges to set aside statutes in conflict with it would no longer seem such a big step.

ANSWERING QUESTIONS

1 **(a) Examine the jurisdiction of the Court of Justice of the European Communities and explain and illustrate the relationship between that court and courts in the United Kingdom** *(12 marks)*
(b) Discuss the legislation of the European Communities and examine its effect on law in the United Kingdom *(13 marks) AEB*

Part (a): The ECJ has two separate types of jurisdiction, judicial and supervisory, so you should discuss each of them in turn, explaining the kinds of cases dealt with, and who can bring them. Give examples of cases from each type. In explaining the relationship between the ECJ and the UK courts, you should point out that the ECJ is not an appeal court for the UK, but that its decisions under the Article 177 procedure do create precedents for the UK courts.

Part (b): here you should explain the different types of EC legislation, and discuss the principle of direct effect, distinguishing between horizontal and vertical direct effect. Explain the effect of each type of EC legislation in turn, citing cases which illustrate your points. Discuss the supremacy of EC law over domestic law, and the case of **Factortame**, the changes to the role of the courts in interpreting domestic legislation, and the possible impact for the future. You should point out that, so far at least, EC legislation only covers a limited number of areas.

CUSTOM

As we have seen, the basis of the common law was custom. The itinerant justices sent out by William the Conqueror (see p. 6) examined the different local practices of dealing with disputes and crime, filtered out the less practical and reasonable ones, and ended up with a set of laws that were to be applied uniformly throughout the country. As Sir Henry Maine, a nineteenth-century scholar who studied the evolution of legal systems has pointed out, this did not mean that custom itself was ever law – the law was created by the decisions of judges in recognizing some customs and not others.

Custom still plays a part in modern law, but a very small one. Its main use is in cases where a traditional local practice – such as fishermen being allowed to dry their nets on a particular piece of land, or villagers holding a fair in a certain place – is being challenged. Custom was defined in the **Tanistry** Case (1608) as 'such usage as has obtained the force of law', and in these cases, those whose practices are being challenged assert that the custom has existed for so long that it should be given the force of law, even though it may conflict with the general common law.

▶ When can custom be a source of law?

To be regarded as conferring legally enforceable rights, a custom must fulfil several criteria.

'Time immemorial'

It must have existed since 'time immemorial'. This was fixed by a statute in 1275 as meaning 'since at least 1189'. In practice today claimants usually seek to prove the custom has existed as far back as living memory can go, often by calling the oldest local inhabitant as a witness. However, this may not always be sufficient. In a dispute over a right to use local land in some way, for example, if the other side could prove that the land in question was under water until the seventeenth or eighteenth century, the right could therefore not have existed since 1189. In **Simpson** *v* **Wells** (1872), a charge of obstructing the public footway by setting up a refreshment stall was challenged by a claim that there was a customary right to do so derived from 'statute sessions', ancient fairs held for the purpose of hiring servants. It was then proved that statute sessions were first authorized by the Statutes of Labourers in the fourteenth century, so the right could not have existed since 1189.

Reasonableness

A legally enforceable custom cannot conflict with fundamental principles of right and wrong, so a customary right to commit a crime, for example, could never be accepted. In **Wolstanton Ltd** *v* **Newcastle-under-Lyme Borough Council** (1940) the lord of a manor claimed a customary right to take minerals from under a tenant's land, without paying compensation for any damage caused to buildings on the land. It was held that this was unreasonable.

Certainty and clarity

It must be certain and clear. The locality in which the custom operates must be defined, along with the people to whom rights are granted (local fishermen, for example, or tenants of a particular estate) and the extent of those rights. In **Wilson** *v* **Willes** (1806) the tenants of a manor claimed the customary right to take as much turf as they needed for their lawns from the manorial commons. This was held to be too vague, since there appeared to be no limit to the amount of turf which could be taken.

Locality

It must be specific to a particular geographic area. Where a custom is recognized as granting a right, it grants that right only to those specified – a custom giving fishermen in Lowestoft the right to dry their nets on someone else's land would not give the same right to fishermen in Grimsby. Custom is only ever a source of local law.

Continuity

It must have existed continuously. The rights granted by customs do not have to have been exercised continuously since 1189, but it must have been possible to exercise them at all times since then. In **Wyld** *v* **Silver** (1963), a landowner wishing to build on land where the local inhabitants claimed a customary right to hold an annual fair, argued that the right had not been exercised within living memory. The court nevertheless granted an injunction preventing the building.

Exercised as of right

It must have been exercised peaceably, openly and as of right. Customs cannot create legal rights if they are exercised only by permission of someone else. In **Mills** *v* **Corporation of Colchester** (1867) it was held that a customary right to fish had no legal force where the right had always depended on the granting of a licence, even though such licences had traditionally been granted to local people on request.

Consistency

It must be consistent with other local customs. For example, if a custom is alleged to give the inhabitants of one farm the right to fish in a lake, it cannot also give the inhabitants of another the right to drain the lake. The usual course where a conflict arises is to deny that the opposing custom has any force, though this is not possible if it has already been recognized by a court.

Obligatory

Where a custom imposes a specific duty, that duty must be obligatory – a custom cannot provide that the lord of a manor grants villagers a right of way over his land only if he likes them, or happens not to mind people on his land that day.

Conformity with statute

Custom cannot conflict with statute law, which will always prevail.

ANSWERING QUESTIONS

Examination questions are rarely, if ever, devoted to custom alone; however, you should revise it if you are thinking of answering a question on sources of law generally.

EQUITY

In ordinary language, equity simply means fairness, but in law it applies to a specific set of legal principles, which add to those provided in the common law. It was originally inspired by ideas of fairness and natural justice, but is now no more than a particular branch of English law. Lawyers often contrast 'law' and equity, but it is important to know that when they do this, they are using 'law' to mean common law. Equity and common law may be different, but both are law. Equity is an area of law which can only be understood in the light of its historical development.

▶ How equity began

As we have seen, the common law was developed after the Norman Conquest through the 'itinerant justices' travelling around the country and sorting out disputes. By about the twelfth century, common law courts had developed which applied this common law. Civil actions in these courts had to be started by a writ, which set out the cause of the action or the grounds for the claim made, and there grew up different types of writ. Early on, new writs were created to suit new circumstances, but in the thirteenth century this was stopped. Litigants had to fit their circumstances to one of the available types of writ; if the case did not fall within one of those types, there was no way of bringing the case to the common law court. At the same time, the common law was itself becoming increasingly rigid, and offered only one remedy, damages, which was not always an adequate solution to every problem – if a litigant had been promised the chance to buy a particular piece of land, for example, and the seller then went back on the agreement, damages might not be an adequate remedy since the buyer really wanted the land, and may have made arrangements on the basis that it would be acquired.

Consequently, many people were unable to seek redress for wrongs through the common law courts. Many of these dissatisfied parties petitioned the king, who was thought of as the 'fountain of justice'. These petitions were commonly passed to the Chancellor, the king's chief minister, as the king did not want to spend time considering them. The Chancellor was usually a member of the clergy, and was thought of as 'keeper of the king's conscience'. Soon litigants began to petition the Chancellor himself, and by 1474, the Chancellor had begun to make decisions on the cases on his own authority, rather than as a substitute for the king. This was the beginning of the Court of Chancery.

Litigants appeared before the Chancellor, who would question them, and then deliver a verdict based on his own moral view of the question. The Court could insist that relevant documents be disclosed, as well as questioning the parties in person, unlike the common law courts which did not admit oral evidence until the sixteenth century, and had no way of extracting the truth from litigants. Because the Court followed no binding rules, relying entirely on the Chancellor's view of right and wrong, it could enforce rights not recognized by the common law, which, hidebound by precedent, was failing to adapt to new circumstances. The Court of Chancery could provide whatever remedy best suited the case – the decree of specific performance, for example, would have meant that the seller of land referred to above could be forced to honour the promise. This type of justice came to be known as equity.

▶ Common law and equity

Not surprisingly, the Court of Chancery became popular, and caused some resentment among common lawyers, who argued that the quality of decisions varied with the length of the Chancellor's foot – in other words, that it depended on the qualities of the individual Chancellor. Because precedents were not followed and each case was considered purely on its merits, justice could appear arbitrary, and nobody could predict what a decision might be.

On the other hand this very flexibility was seen as the great advantage of equity – where any rules are laid down, there will always be situations in which those rules produce injustice. The more general the rule, the more likely this is, yet it is impossible to foresee and lay down all the specific exceptions in which it should not apply. Equity dealt with these situations by applying notions of good sense and fairness, but in doing so laid itself open to the charge that fairness is a subjective quality.

The common lawyers particularly resented the way in which equity could be used to restrict their own jurisdiction. Where the common law gave a litigant a right which, in the circumstances, it would be unjust to exercise, the Court of Chancery could issue a common injunction, preventing the exercise of the common law right. An example might be where a litigant had made a mistake in drawing up a document. Under common law the other party could enforce the document anyway, even if they were aware of the mistake but failed to draw attention to it. This was considered inequitable, and a common injunction would prevent the document being enforced.

Matters came to a head in 1615 in the Case of **The Earl of Oxford**, where conflicting judgments of the common law courts and the Court of Chancery were referred to the king for a decision; he advised that where there was conflict, equity should prevail. Had this decision not been made, equity would have been worthless – it could not fulfil its role of filling in the gaps of the common law unless it was dominant.

Nevertheless, the rivalry continued for some time, but gradually abated as equity too began to be ruled by precedent and standard principles, a development related to the fact that it was becoming established practice to appoint lawyers rather than clergy to the office of Lord Chancellor. By the nineteenth century, equity had a developed case law and recognizable principles, and was no less rigid than the common law.

▶ The Judicature Acts

Once equity became a body of law, rather than an arbitrary exercise of conscience, there was no reason why it needed its own courts. Consequently the Judicature Acts of 1873–75, which established the basis of the court structure we have today, provided that equity and common law could both be administered by all courts, and that there would no longer be different procedures for seeking equitable and common law remedies. Although the Court of Chancery remained as a division of the High Court, like all other courts it can now apply both common law and equity.

▶ Equity today

It is important to note that the Judicature Acts did not fuse common law and equity, only their administration. There is still a body of rules of equity which is distinct from common law rules, and acts as an addition to it. Although they are implemented by the same court, the two branches of the law are separated in the following ways. Where there is conflict, equity still prevails.

Equitable maxims

Although both the common law and equity lay down rules developed from precedents, equity also created maxims which had to be satisfied before equitable rules could be applied. These maxims were designed to ensure that decisions were morally fair. The following are some of them.

'He who comes to equity must come with clean hands'

This means that plaintiffs who have themselves been in the wrong in some way will not be granted an equitable remedy. In **D & C Builders** *v* **Rees** (1966) a small building firm did some work on the house of a couple named Rees. The bill came to £732, of which the Rees had already paid £250. When the builders asked for the balance of £482, the Rees announced that the work was defective, and they were only prepared to pay £300. As the builders were in serious financial difficulties (as the Rees knew), they reluctantly accepted the £300 'in completion of the account'. The decision to accept the money would not normally be binding in contract law, and afterwards the builders sued the Rees for the outstanding amount. The Rees claimed that the court should apply the doctrine of equitable estoppel, which can make promises binding when they would normally not be. However, Lord Denning refused to apply the doctrine, on the grounds that the Rees had taken unfair advantage of the builders' financial difficulties, and therefore had not come 'with clean hands'.

'He who seeks equity must do equity'

Anyone who seeks equitable relief must be prepared to act fairly towards their opponent. In **Chappell** *v* **Times Newspapers Ltd** (1975), newspaper employees who had been threatened that they would be sacked unless they stopped their strike action applied for an injunction to prevent their employers from carrying out the threat. The court held that in order to be awarded the remedy, the strikers should undertake that they would withdraw their strike action if the injunction was granted. Since they refused to do this, the injunction was refused.

'Delay defeats equities'

Where a plaintiff takes an unreasonably long time to bring an action, equitable remedies will not be available. The unreasonableness of any delay will be a matter of fact to be assessed in view of the circumstances in each case. In **Leaf** *v* **International Galleries** (1950) the plaintiff bought a painting of Salisbury Cathedral described (innocently) by the seller as a genuine Constable. Five years later, the buyer discovered that it was nothing of the sort, and claimed the equitable remedy of rescission, but the court held that the delay had been too long.

These maxims (there are several others) mean that where a plaintiff's case relies on a rule of equity, rather than a rule of common law, that rule can only be applied if the maxims are satisfied – unlike common law rules which have no such limitations.

Equitable remedies

Equity substantially increased the number of remedies available to a wronged party. The following are the most important:

Injunction. This orders the defendants to do or not to do something.
Specific performance. This compels a party to fulfil a previous agreement.
Rectification. This order alters the words of a document which does not express the true intentions of the parties to it.
Rescission. This restores parties to a contract to the position they were in before the contract was signed.

Equitable remedies are discretionary. A plaintiff who wins the case is awarded the common law remedy of damages as of right, but the courts may choose whether or not to award equitable remedies. They are very much an addition to common law remedies, and usually only available if common law remedies are plainly inadequate.

Equitable principles have had their greatest impact in the development of the law of property and contract, and remain important in these areas today. The two best-known contributions come from property law, and are the developments of the law of trusts, and the basis of the rules which today govern mortgages. The creation of alternative remedies has also been extremely important.

▶ Equity tomorrow

Equity has shown itself capable of adapting and expanding to meet new needs, and so creating law reform. During the 1950s and 1960s, it responded to increasing marital breakdown by stating that a deserted wife could acquire an equitable interest in the family home, providing an interim solution to a growing problem until legislation could be passed in the form of the Matrimonial Homes Act 1967. And in the 1970s, two important new remedies were created by extending the scope of injunctions: the Anton Piller order, by which the court can order defendants to allow their premises to be searched and relevant documents to be removed, and the Mareva injunction, a court order to a third party, such as a bank, to freeze the assets of a party to a dispute where there is a danger that they may be removed from the court's jurisdiction (by being taken out of the country, for example, and therefore made unavailable if damages were ordered by the court).

However, more recent attempts to extend equitable jurisdiction, notably in **Scandinavian Trading Tanker Co AB** *v* **Flota Petrolera Ecuatoriana** (1983), and **Sport International Bussum BV** *v* **Inter-Footwear Ltd** (1984), have been firmly resisted by the House of Lords.

The availability of discretionary remedies means it still fulfils the traditional function of supplementing the common law, providing just and practical remedies where the common law alone is not enough, but restricting itself to cases where those remedies are felt to be genuinely and justly deserved.

• •
ANSWERING QUESTIONS

'Equity was, and in many ways still is, common law's safety valve.'
(Denham) Does this accurately describe the role of equity, both past and present? *Oxford*
It would be a good idea to divide this essay into two parts, dealing first with the role of equity in the past, and then in the present. On the historical side, you can start by explaining how it was that common law came to need a 'safety valve', and whether equity fulfilled this role, explaining both its initial success, and then the way in which equity too became rigid, limiting its success as a 'safety valve'.

Then move on to equity's present day role, pointing out the extra remedies which equity provides, which might be seen as a safety valve where common law remedies are insufficient. You could point out that the equitable maxims may act as a check on the role of a safety valve, since they limit the cases in which equity will intervene. You should discuss some of the cases referred to above, and the areas of law in which equity is important today. You might finish with some of the material under the heading of 'equity tomorrow'.

• • • • • • • • • •
TREATIES

When the United Kingdom enters into treaties with other countries, it undertakes to implement domestic laws that are in accordance with the provisions of those treaties. For the purposes of the legal system, probably the most important treaty signed by the UK Government is the European Convention on Human Rights, which is discussed on p. 342.

▶ Implementation of treaties

In many countries, treaties automatically become part of domestic law when the country signs them. However, in the UK, the position is that signing treaties usually does not instantly make them law, so citizens cannot rely on them in proceedings brought in UK courts. Only when Parliament produces legislation to enact its treaty commitments do those commitments become law – the Taking of Hostages Act 1982 is an example of legislation incorporating the provisions of international treaties. Until such legislation is produced, individuals cannot usually take advantage of the protections envisaged by treaties.

However, there are some treaties which do not precisely follow this rule. Parts of the treaties setting up the European Communities are directly applicable in British courts, and can be relied on to create rights and duties just like an English statute (this subject is discussed in the section on European law).

• •

ANSWERING QUESTIONS

An examination question on the European Convention on Human Rights can be found at the end of the section on civil liberties.

2 Law reform

A n effective legal system cannot stand still. Both procedures and substantive law must adapt to social change if they are to retain the respect of at least most of society, without which they cannot survive. Many laws which were made even as short a time ago as the nineteenth century simply do not fit the way we see society today – until the early part of this century, for example, married women were legally considered the property of their husbands, while, not much earlier, employees could be imprisoned for breaking their employment contracts.

Most legislation in this country stands until it is repealed – the fact that it may be completely out-of-date does not mean it technically ceases to apply. The offences of challenging to fight, eavesdropping and being a common scold for example, which long ago dropped out of use, nevertheless remained on the statute book until they were abolished by the Criminal Law Act 1967. In practice, of course, many such provisions simply cease to be used, but where it becomes clear that the law may be out of step with social conditions, or simply ineffective, there are a range of ways of bringing about change.

▶ Judicial change

Case law can bring about some reform – one of the most notable recent examples was the decision in **R** *v* **R** (1991), in which the House of Lords declared that a husband who has sexual intercourse with his wife without her consent may be guilty of rape. Before this decision, the law on rape within marriage was based on an assertion by the eighteenth century jurist Sir Matthew Hale, that 'by marrying a man, a women consents to sexual intercourse with him, and may not retract that consent.' This position had been found offensive for many years before **R** *v* **R**. In 1976, Parliament considered it during a debate on the Sexual Offences Act, but decided not to make changes at that time, and it was not until 1991 that the Court of Appeal and then the House of Lords held that rape within marriage should be considered an offence.

Lord Keith stated that Hale's assertion reflected the status of women within marriage in his time, but since then both the status of women, and the marriage relationship had completely changed. The modern view of husband and wife as equal partners meant that a wife could no longer be considered to have given irrevocable consent to sex with her husband; the common law was capable of evolving to reflect such changes in society, and it was the duty of the court to help it do so.

In practice, however, major reforms like this are rarely produced by the courts, and would not be adequate as the sole agency of reform. Norman Marsh's book *Law Reform in the United Kingdom* puts forward the following reasons for this:

- As we saw in the chapter on case law, there is no systematic, state-funded process for bringing points of law in need of reform to the higher courts. The courts can only deal with such points as they arise in the cases before them, and this depends on the parties involved having sufficient finance, determination and interest to take their case up through the courts. Consequently, judge-made reform proceeds not on the basis of which areas of law need changes most, but on a haphazard presentation of cases.
- Judges have to make the decision based on the way the issues are presented to them by the parties concerned. They cannot commission research, or consult with interested bodies to find out the possible effects of a decision on individuals and organizations other than those in the case before them – yet their decision will apply to future cases.
- Judges have to recognize the doctrine of precedent, and for much of the time this prohibits any really radical reforms.
- The reforming decision may be unjust to the losing party. Law reforms made by Parliament are prospective – they come into force on a specified date, and we are not usually expected to abide by them until after that date. Judicial decisions, on the other hand, are retrospective, affecting something that happened before the judges decided what the law was. The more reformatory such a decision is, the less the likelihood that the losing party could have abided by the law, even if they wanted to.
- Judges are not elected, and therefore feel they should not make decisions which change the law in areas of great social or moral controversy. In such cases they will often point out to Parliament the need for it to make reforms, as happened in the **Bland** case concerning the Hillsborough stadium disaster victim (see p. 15).

The majority of law reform is therefore carried out by Parliament. It is done in four ways:

- **Repeal** of old and/or obsolete laws.
- **Creation** of completely new law, or adaptation of existing provisions,

to meet new needs. The creation of the offence of insider dealing
(where stockbrokers, for example, make money by using
information gained by virtue of a privileged position) in the
Companies Act 1980 was a response to public concern about 'sharp
practice' in the city.

- **Consolidation**. When a new statute is created, problems with it may
  become apparent over time, in which case further legislation may
  be enacted to amend it. Consolidation brings together successive
  statutes on a particular subject and puts them into one statute. For
  example, the legislation in relation to companies was consolidated
  in 1985.

- **Codification**. Where a particular area of the law has developed over
  time to produce a large body of both case law and statute, a new
  statute may be created to bring together all the rules on that
  subject (case law and statute) in one place. That statute then
  becomes the starting point for cases concerning that area of the
  law, and case law, in time, builds up around it. The Criminal
  Attempts Act 1981 and the Police and Criminal Evidence Act 1984
  are examples of codifying statutes. Codification is thought to be
  most suitable for areas of law where the principles are well worked
  out; areas that are still developing, such as tort, are less suitable for
  codifying.

These types of reform often happen together – the Public Order Act
1986, for example, created new public order offences designed to deal
with specific problems of the time, such as football hooliganism, and at
the same time, repealed out of date public order offences.

Some significant law reforms have come about as a result of Private
Members' Bills (see p. 23) – an example is the 1967 Abortion Act which
resulted from a Private Members' Bill put forward by David Steele.

▶ Pressures for reform

The inspiration for reform may come from a variety of sources, alone or
in combination. As well as encouraging Parliament to consider particular
issues in the first place, they may have an influence during the consultation stage of legislation, by commenting on the Green Paper (see
p. 23).

Pressure groups

Groups concerned with particular subjects may press for law reform in
those areas – examples include charities such as Shelter, Help the Aged
and the Child Poverty Action Group; professional organizations such as

the Law Society and the British Medical Association; business representatives such as the Confederation of British Industry. Justice is a pressure group specifically concerned with promoting law reform in general.

Pressure groups use a variety of tactics, including lobbying MPs, gaining as much publicity as possible for their cause, organizing petitions, and encouraging people to write to their own MP and/or relevant Ministers. Some groups are more effective than others: size obviously helps, but sheer persistence and a knack for grabbing headlines can be just as productive – the anti-porn campaigner Mary Whitehouse almost singlehandedly pressurized the Government to create the Protection of Children Act 1978, which sought to prevent child pornography. The amount of power wielded by the members of a pressure group is also extremely important – organizations involved with big business tend to be particularly effective in influencing legislation.

Political parties

Some of the most high-profile legislation is that passed in order to implement the Government party's election manifesto, or its general ideology – examples include the privatizations of gas and water and the creation of the Poll Tax by the Conservative Government which began in 1979.

The civil service

Although technically neutral, the civil service nevertheless has a great effect on legislation in general. It may not have party political goals, but various departments will have their own views as to what type of legislation enables them to achieve departmental goals most efficiently – which strategies might help the Home Office control the prison population, for example, or the Department of Health make the NHS more efficient. Ministers rely heavily on senior civil servants for advice and information on the issues of the day, and few would consistently turn down their suggestions.

Treaty obligations

The UK's obligations under the treaties establishing the European Community and the European Convention on Human Rights both influence changes in British law (see pp. 54 and 342).

Public opinion and media pressure

As well as taking part in campaigns organized by pressure groups, members of the public make their feelings known by writing to their MPs, to ministers and to newspapers. This is most likely to lead to reform where the ruling party has a small majority. Public opinion and media pressure interact; the media often claims to reflect public opinion, but it can also whip it up. What appears to be a major epidemic of a particular crime may in fact be no more than a reflection of the fact that once one interesting example of it hits the news, newspapers and broadcasting organizations are more likely to report others. An example of this is the rash of stories during 1993 about parents going on holiday and leaving their children alone, inspired by the film 'Home Alone'. Leaving children alone like this may have been common practice for years, or it may be something done by a tiny minority of parents, but the media's selection of stories gives the impression of a sudden epidemic of parental negligence that, without any research into the extent of the problem, could easily whip up sufficient public concern to prompt legislation.

▶ Agencies of law reform

Much law reform happens as a direct response to pressure from one or more of the above sources, but there are also a number of agencies set up to consider the need for reform in areas referred to them by the Government. Often problems are referred to them as a result of the kind of pressures listed above – the Royal Commission on Criminal Justice 1993 was set up as a result of public concern and media pressure about high-profile miscarriages of justice, such as the Birmingham Six and the Guildford Four.

The Law Commission

Established in 1965 (along with another for Scotland), the Law Commission is a permanent body, comprising five people drawn from the judiciary, the legal profession and legal academics. In practice, the chairman tends to be a High Court judge, and the other four members to include a QC experienced in criminal law, a solicitor with experience of land law and equity, and two legal academics. They are assisted by legally-qualified civil servants.

The Commission's task is 'to take and keep under review all the law with which [it is] concerned with a view to its systematic development and reform, including in particular the codification of such law, the elimination of anomalies, the repeal of obsolete and unnecessary enactments, the reduction of the number of separate enactments and generally the simplification and modernisation of the law' (Law Commissions Act 1965).

The Commission works on topics referred to it by the Lord Chancellor, and also general reform programmes agreed from time to time by Parliament. Its job also includes advising other bodies concerned with law reform.

Where the Commission is working on substantive law reform, it produces a 'working paper', detailing the present law on the relevant subject, criticisms of it, and options for change, with a provisional view of the options it prefers. This is circulated to a wide range of interested parties (though unlike the Australian Law Reform Commission, it tends not to hold public meetings), and their views are sought. Following this, a final report is produced, with a draft Bill (prepared by parliamentary draftsmen temporarily transferred to the Commission).

There is some chance of proposals from the Commission becoming legislation if the subject concerned comes within the jurisdiction of the Lord Chancellor's Department; there is less chance if they concern other departments, particularly the Home Office and the Department of the Environment.

The Law Reform Committee

This part-time body, set up in 1952, comprises judges, lawyers and academics, as well as civil service assistance. It considers problems of civil law which are referred to it by the Lord Chancellor.

The Criminal Law Revision Committee

The CLRC is the criminal law counterpart to the Law Reform Committee, responsible to the Home Secretary rather than the Lord Chancellor, and includes the Director of Public Prosecutions (DPP) as well as judges and academics. For its 1984 report on sexual offences, it was advised by a policy advisory committee, which included probation officers, a consultant psychiatrist, a social worker and a sociologist.

Royal Commissions

These are set up to study particular areas of law reform, usually as a result of criticism and concern about the area concerned. They are made up of a wide cross-section of people: most have some expertise in the area concerned, but usually only a minority are legally qualified. The Commissions are supposed to be independent and non-political.

A Royal Commission can commission research, and also take submissions from interested parties. It produces a final report detailing its recommendations, which the Government can then choose to act upon or not. Usually a majority of proposals are acted upon, sometimes in amended form.

The most recent Royal Commissions are the 1979 Royal Commission on Legal Services, the 1981 Royal Commission on Criminal Procedure, and the Royal Commission on Criminal Justice, which reported in 1993.

Public enquiries

Where a particular problem or incident is causing social concern, the Government may set up a one-off, temporary committee to examine possible options for dealing with it. Major disasters, such as the Hillsborough football stadium disaster and the sinking of the ferry *Herald of Free Enterprise*; events such as the Brixton Riots; and advances in technology, especially medical technology, such as the ability to fertilize human eggs outside the body and produce 'test tube babies' may all be investigated by bodies set up especially for the job. These usually comprise individuals who are independent of Government, often with expertise in the particular area. Academics are frequent choices, as are judges – Lord Scarman headed the enquiry into the Brixton riots.

Public enquiries consult interested groups, and attempt to reach a consensus between them, conducting their investigation as far as possible in a non-political way. In the case of disasters and other events, they may try to discover the causes, as well as making recommendations on legislation to avoid a repeat.

Other temporary committees

From time to time, various Government departments set up temporary committees to investigate specific areas of law. One of the most important recent examples is the Civil Justice Review, many of whose recommendations formed the basis for the Courts and Legal Services Act 1990 (see pp. 208 and 211).

▶ Performance of the law reform bodies

The Law Commission

One of the principal tasks of the Commission at its inception was codification, and this programme has not on the whole been a success. The Commission's programme was ambitious: in 1965 it announced that it would begin codifying family law, contract, landlord and tenant, and evidence. Attempts in the first three were abandoned – family in 1970, contract in 1973 and landlord and tenant in 1978. Evidence was never begun.

Zander (1988) suggests the reasons for the failure are 'a mixture of conservatism and a realisation on the part of draftsmen, legislators and even judges that it simply did not fit the English style of lawmaking'. The draftsmen were not keen on the idea that codes would have to be drawn up in a broader manner than was normal for traditional statutes. Legislators were doubtful of the concept of a huge Bill which would attempt to state the law in a vast area such as landlord and tenant. The judges objected to the vision promoted by Lord Scarman, the Commission's first chairman, of the code coming down like an iron curtain making all pre-code law irrelevant. As Zander explains, this appeared to the judges like 'throwing the baby out with the bathwater – losing the priceless heritage of the past and wasting the fruits of legislation and litigation on numerous points which would still be relevant to interpret the new code'.

The only real progress on codification has been in the criminal law. From 1968–74, the Commission produced a series of working papers, but in 1980 announced that its shortage of resources would not allow it to continue, and appealed for help with the task. The Society of Public Teachers of Law responded, and set up a four-person committee which by 1985 had produced a draft code. Compared to the attempts at codification in other areas this is real progress, but even here there has been no legislative result as yet.

However, opinions are mixed on whether codification would prove to be of very great value even if it ever becomes possible. Supporters say it would provide accessibility, comprehensibility, consistency and certainty. A code allows people to see their rights and liabilities more clearly than a mixture of case law and separate statutes could, and should encourage judges and others who use it to look for and expect to find answers within it. Lord Hailsham has said that a good codification would save a great deal of judicial time and so reduce costs, and Glanville Williams makes the point that criminal law is not like the law of procedure, meant for lawyers only, but is addressed to all classes of society, and so the greater accessibility and clarity of a code should be particularly welcomed in this area.

However, critics say a very detailed codification could make the law too rigid, losing the flexibility of the common law. And if it were insufficiently detailed, as Zander points out, it would need to be interpreted by the courts, so creating a new body of case law around it which would defeat the object of codification and make the law neither more accessible nor more certain. It may be that the Law Commission's failure to codify the law signifies a problem with codification, not with the Law Commission.

Instead of proceeding with large-scale codification, the Law Commission chose to clarify areas of law piece by piece, with the aim of eventual codification if possible. Family law in particular has been significantly reformed in this way, even if the results are, as Zander points out, a 'jumble of disconnected statutes rather than a spanking new code'.

As far as general law reform is concerned, the Commission has made over 100 proposals for major reforms, around 70 per cent of which have been adopted, though not always without amendment. As well as the major family law reforms, the Commission has rationalized tort law in the area of interference with goods, and radically changed contract law by recommending control of exclusion clauses. Its report, *Conspiracy and Criminal Law Reform*, helped shape the Criminal Law Act 1977 and its working paper, *Offences Against Public Order*, was instrumental in creating the Public Order Act 1986.

Stephen Cretney, a legal academic who has been a Law Commissioner, suggests that one of its most important contributions has simply been getting law reform under discussion and examination, and drawing attention to the needs of various areas.

Criminal Law Revision Committee

The Theft Acts 1968 and 1978 are generally thought of as the CLRC's greatest achievement. The legislation effectively codified the previous law in this area, aiming for a fundamental reconsideration of the principles underlying this branch of the law to be embodied in a modern statute. Unfortunately this was not a complete success; as Smith and Hogan point out, one offence (that of obtaining a pecuniary advantage by deception) proved so troublesome that it had to be completely reviewed in the 1978 Act, and 'in some other respects cracks are beginning to show through . . . The legislation would benefit from a review.' Reported appeals in the first ten years of the Theft Act were more than double the number made in the ten years before.

The CLRC was also responsible for a report into the criminal justice system, which stated that the system had shifted much too far in favour of defendants' rights. It recommended a string of measures designed to tip the balance back in favour of the prosecution, including abolishing the right to silence, on the grounds that 'it is as much in the public interest that a guilty person should be convicted as that an innocent person should be acquitted.' As Zander points out, this contravenes the traditional belief that it is better that ten guilty people go free than that one innocent one is convicted – the reasoning behind our system's insistence on a suspect being innocent until proven guilty.

The report caused a storm of opposition, not only from civil liberties campaigners but from members of both Houses of Parliament, lawyers and judges, and none of it was implemented. History seems to suggest that the Committee's assessment was badly mistaken. The report was delivered in 1972; two years later, the Birmingham Six were wrongly convicted, followed in 1975 by the Guildford Four and in 1976 by the Maguire Seven. A whole string of other miscarriages of justice also date from this period. It is difficult to see these as the work of a system too heavily weighted towards defendants' rights.

The Committee works only when summoned by the Home Secretary and this has not been done since 1985.

The Law Reform Committee

In practice, the Law Reform Committee largely considers fairly narrow issues requiring technical solutions rather than radical changes. Its contributions to law reform include proposals implemented in the Occupiers' Liability Act (1984), and a report on limitation periods which led to the Latent Damage Act 1986.

Royal Commissions

These have had mixed success. The 1978 Royal Commission on Civil Liability and Compensation for Personal Injury produced a report that won neither public nor Government support, and few of its proposals were implemented.

The Royal Commission on Criminal Procedure has most of its recommendations implemented by the Police and Criminal Evidence Act 1984 (PACE), but subsequent criticisms of PACE mean this is less of a success than it appears. The Royal Commission stated that the aim behind its proposals was to secure a balance between the rights of individuals suspected of crime, and the need to bring guilty people to justice. PACE has however been criticized by the police as leaning too far towards suspects' rights, and by civil liberties campaigners as not leaning far enough.

Perhaps the most successful Royal Commission in recent years has been the Royal Commission on Assizes and Quarter Sessions, which reported in 1969. Its proposals for the reorganization of criminal courts were speedily implemented.

As regards the 1993 Royal Commission on Criminal Justice, this has met with mixed success. Some of its recommendations have been introduced in the Criminal Justice and Public Order Act 1994, and others are likely to reach the statute book in the near future, such as amendments to the criminal appeal system. On the other hand the Government has ignored some of its proposals and has proceeded to introduce changes that it was specifically opposed to, for example the abolition of the right to silence.

Public enquiries and other temporary committees

These rely to a great extent on political will, and the best committees in the world may be ineffective if they propose changes that a government dislikes. Lord Scarman's investigation into the Brixton riots is seen as a particularly effective public enquiry, getting to the root of the problem by going out to ask the people involved what caused it (his Lordship, then retired, shocked his previous colleagues by taking to the streets of Brixton and being shown on television chatting to residents and cuddling their babies). His proposals produced some of the steps towards police accountability in PACE. The Civil Justice Review was also instrumental in bringing about reform, though views on the success of the changes are mixed (see p. 28).

▶ Problems with law reform agencies

- There is no obligation for Government to consult the permanent law reform bodies, or to set up Royal Commissions or other committees when considering major law reforms. Mrs Thatcher set up no Royal Commissions during her terms of office, despite the fact that important and controversial legislation – such as that abolishing the GLC – was being passed.
- Governments also have no obligation to follow recommendations, and perfectly well thought out proposals may be rejected on the grounds that they do not fit in with a government's political position. An example was the recommendation of the Law Commission in 1978 that changes be made to the rule that interest is not payable on a contract debt unless the parties agreed otherwise. The idea was supported by the House of Lords in **President of India** (1984), but the Government was persuaded not to implement the proposals after lobbying from the CBI and consumer organizations.

  Even where general suggestions for areas of new legislation are implemented, the detailed proposals may be radically altered. The recommendations of law reform agencies may act as justification for introducing new legislation, yet as Zander points out, often when the Bill is published it becomes clear that the carefully constructed package put together by the law reform agency 'has been unstitched and a new and different package has been constructed'.
- Where proposals are implemented, ideas that are effective in themselves may be weakened if they are insufficiently funded when put into practice – a matter on which law reform bodies can have little or no influence. The 1981 Royal Commission on Criminal Procedure's recommendations were largely implemented in the Police and Criminal Evidence Act 1984, and one of them was that suspects questioned in a police station should have the right to free legal advice, leading to the setting up of the duty solicitor scheme. While the idea of the scheme was seen as a good one, underfunding by the Legal Aid Board has brought it close to collapse, and meant that in practice relatively small numbers of suspects actually get advice from qualified, experienced solicitors within a reasonable waiting time. This has clearly frustrated the aims of the Royal Commission's recommendation.

- Royal Commissions and temporary committees have the advantage of drawing members from wide backgrounds, with a good spread of experience and expertise. However, in some cases this can result in proposals that try too hard to represent a compromise. The result can be a lack of political support and little chance of implementation. It is generally agreed that this was the problem with the Pearson Report, the report of the Royal Commission on Civil Liability and Compensation for Personal Injury.
- Where temporary law reform committees have a high proportion of non-lawyers, the result can be more innovative, imaginative ideas than might come from legally-trained people who, however open-minded, are within 'the system' and accustomed to seeing the problems in a particular framework. However, this benefit is heavily diluted by the fact that the strong influence of the legal profession on any type of reform can defeat such proposals even before they reach an official report.

    An example was the suggestion of the Civil Justice Review in its consultation paper that the county courts and High Court might merge, with some High Court judges being stationed in the provinces to deal with the more complex cases there. Despite a warm welcome from consumer groups and the National Association of Citizens Advice Bureaux, the proposals were effectively shot down by the outcry from senior judges who were concerned that their status and way of life might be adversely affected, and the Bar, which was worried that it might lose too much work to solicitors. In the event the proposal was not included in the final report.

- Royal Commissions and temporary committees are disbanded after producing their report, and take no part in the rest of the law-making process. This is in many ways a waste of the expertise they have built up.
- There is no single ministry responsible for law reform so that often no Minister makes it their priority.

ANSWERING QUESTIONS

1 'It shall be the duty of the Commissions to take and keep under review all the law with which they are respectively concerned, with a view to its systematic development and reform, including in particular the codification of such law . . .' (S. 3, Law Commissions Act 1965). Should the Law Commission concentrate on codification, or are there more suitable ways of reforming the law? *Oxford*

You could start by defining what codification is, and mention the plans for codification which the Law Commission had when it was created, and what happened to them. Then go on to discuss the advantages and disadvantages of codification, and whether you feel that the Law Commission should still concentrate on it.

You could then move on to look at the other ways of reforming the law. As well as examining the successful work which the Law Commission has done, you could look at other ways of law reform – such as the way in which public enquiries and temporary committees examine specific problems, using advisors who are not necessarily lawyers, but may have experience in the relevant field – do you think this is an approach the Law Commission should consider?

Your conclusion should sum up what you think the Commission's priorities should be and why.

2 **'The Law Commission has provided an important impetus to the process of law reform in England and Wales'. Discuss.** *WJEC*
Here you are basically being asked how well the Law Commission has done its job. Your introduction might state what the Commission was set up to do, and then the rest of your essay can consider whether it has fulfilled that function and thereby given an important impetus to law reform.

You might want to consider the successes of the Law Commission first, and then go on to talk about codification, pointing out that the Commission has not provided much of an impetus in this area, but discussing the arguments on whether codification would actually be beneficial anyway. Finish by summing up what you think the Commission's contribution has been.

3 **Critically evaluate the role of the law reform bodies.** *Oxford*
Note that this question can apply not only to the official bodies such as the Law Commission, but also to informal ones such as pressure groups, and you need to discuss both types. It may be a good idea to divide your answer into official and unofficial law reform bodies: taking each in turn, you can describe how they operate and assess their effectiveness, pointing out any problems in the way they work. Don't forget that what is needed is a **critical** account – just listing the bodies and what they do will get you very few marks. What the examiners want to know is not just what the bodies do, but how well they do it. Your conclusion might generally sum up the effect of these multiple bodies, saying whether, taken together, you feel they do an adequate job in reforming the law.

3 The judiciary

The judicial hierarchy

At the head of the judiciary is the Lord Chancellor, who effectively appoints all the other judges. He is President of the Supreme Court (comprising the High Court, the Crown Court and the Court of Appeal), and officially President of the Chancery Division, though in practice the vice-chancellor fulfils this role. When the Lord Chancellor sits as a judge it is in the House of Lords or the Privy Council, but most Lord Chancellors do so only rarely; in recent years the only Chancellors to sit at all regularly have been Lords McKay and Hailsham.

The appointment is a political one; the Lord Chancellor is normally a cabinet minister, and speaker of the House of Lords. Although technically appointed by the Queen, he is chosen by the Prime Minister, and goes out of office when that party loses an election, as well as being eligible for removal by the Prime Minister like any other minister.

As well as controlling judicial appointments, the Lord Chancellor has powers to give directions about the business of the courts, and responsibility for the Law Commission and the legal aid and advice scheme. There are no formal qualifications for the post, but all previous Lord Chancellors have been barristers; Lord McKay is the first not to come from the English Bar.

There are eleven Lords of Appeal in Ordinary, also known as the Law Lords. They sit in the House of Lords and the Privy Council. Thirty-one Lord Justices of Appeal currently sit in the Court of Appeal. The civil division of the Court of Appeal is presided over by the Master of the Rolls; the criminal division by the Lord Chief Justice. Lord Woolf has recommended that a senior judge should also be appointed to be the head of the whole civil justice system.

High Court judges are also known as puisne judges (pronounced puny), meaning junior judges. They are knighted on appointment and as well as sitting in the High Court also hear the most serious criminal law cases in the Crown Court. In 1995 there were 99 such judges. Circuit judges traditionally sit in the county court and in the middle-ranking Crown Court cases, but since a reform in the Criminal Justice and Public Order Act

1994 they can now also occasionally act as judges in the criminal division of the Court of Appeal. District judges hear the minor cases in the county court. Recorders – there are about 500 of them altogether – are part-time Crown Court judges hearing the least serious of the criminal cases tried in that court. The period of working as a recorder is often treated as an apprenticeship before being made a circuit judge. Because of the number of minor Crown Court cases, there are now assistant recorders as well, and retired judges may also be called upon to help out. Stipendiary magistrates are full-time professional magistrates working mainly in larger cities.

Tribunal cases are heard by tribunal members. The chairperson is often an academic or practising lawyer, while the rest of the panel are usually not legally qualified, but have experience in a relevant area.

▶ Appointments to the judiciary

The 1990 Courts and Legal Services Act has widened entry to the judiciary, reflecting the proposed changes in rights of audience (see p. 111), and opening up the higher reaches of the profession to solicitors as well as barristers. To be appointed as a Lord of Appeal in Ordinary a person must either have held judicial office for two years or have a right of audience in the Supreme Court. Usually they will have been judges in the Court of Appeal before being appointed to the House of Lords. The qualification for appointment as a Lord Justice of Appeal is either that they were a judge in the High Court or they have had a right of audience in the High Court for ten years. To be appointed as a puisne judge it is also necessary to have had a right of audience for ten years in the High Court. Circuit judges, recorders or assistant recorders can now be appointed from anyone who has had general rights of audience in the Crown Court or county courts for ten years. Anyone who has been a district judge for at least three years is also eligible for appointment as a circuit judge, and the requirement that solicitors serve three years as a recorder before appointment as a circuit judge has been removed.

The Lord Chancellor, the Lords of Appeal in Ordinary and the Lord Justices of Appeal are appointed by the Queen on the advice of the Prime Minister who in turn is advised by the Lord Chancellor. High Court judges, circuit judges and recorders are all appointed by the Queen on the advice of the Lord Chancellor.

The selection process of judges in the High Court and above was explained in a pamphlet issued by the Lord Chancellor's office in May 1986. This states that the Lord Chancellor's Department gathers information about potential candidates over a period of time by making informal inquiries from leading barristers and judges. No single person's view about the suitability of a particular candidate should be decisive. Although facts obtained about potential candidates are normally available to the candidates on request so that they can ensure that they are correct, opinions given in confidence will not be revealed on the grounds that this would make people less willing to assist the Lord Chancellor by giving their frank opinions. One does not apply for such judicial office, but waits to be invited. Selected candidates are interviewed, and the final decision is formally taken by the Lord Chancellor.

Over the years there has been considerable criticism of the method in which judges were appointed. The Lord Chancellor is essentially a political appointment and both the Prime Minister and the Lord Chancellor could be swayed by political factors in the selection of judges. The Lord Chancellor usually presents the Prime Minister with a shortlist of two or three names listing them in the order of his own preference. Mrs Thatcher is known to have selected Lord Hailsham's second choice on one occasion. A partial, but probably inadequate response to this criticism was made in 1995 when the procedure for the appointment of circuit and district judges was reformed. Such posts are advertised in newspapers, and interviews are carried out by a panel including one lay member. The interview panel will then make a recommendation but the Lord Chancellor is not bound by this and has stated that the opinions of leading judges and lawyers will continue to be sought and have considerable weight in reaching the final decision. The Lord Chancellor has said that appointments are to be made regardless of gender, race, religion and sexual orientation – in the past homosexuality could act as a bar to judicial office. The new procedure is to be extended to all judges below the High Court.

Those appointed are normally in their fifties, and technical brilliance as a lawyer is not regarded as a vital precondition, although greater emphasis is placed on legal ability when appointments to the Chancery Division or to the appellate courts are considered.

Judicial selection in other countries

In civil law systems, such as France, there is normally a career judiciary. Individuals opt to become judges at an early stage, and are specifically trained for the job, rather than becoming lawyers first as they do here. The judiciary is organized on a hierarchical basis, and judges start in junior posts, dealing with least serious cases, and work up through the system as they gain experience. One drawback is that they can be viewed as part of the civil service, rather than as independent of Government.

In the United States there are two basic methods of selection, appointment and election, although a compromise between the two methods is often made. All federal judges are appointed by the President, subject to confirmation by the Senate, which may include examining a prospective judge's character and past life, as the confirmation of Clarence Thomas, the judge accused of sexual harassment, did recently. Most state and local judges are elected, although genuine competition for a post is rare. In a number of states elections are used to confirm in office judges who have been in their posts for a limited period.

The Bill of Rights leads Americans to favour single-issue pressure groups which mount legal campaigns – most famously in the case of the 1954 decision to end racial segregation in schools – to achieve political aims. These groups realize the vital importance of the person who decides such cases and therefore spend a lot of time and money researching potential candidates to see if their views fit, and if not, whether there is any damaging information which could be used to prevent their appointment. There are also associations which are interested simply in enhancing the reputation of the court, so that the American Bar Association, in particular, launches extensive inquiries of every nominee involving hundreds of interviews with judges, academics and commissioning studies of a candidate's opinions.

Although most US judicial nominations are confirmed, 20 per cent of nominees are rejected and, more importantly, presidents are discouraged from proposing people who might fall at this hurdle. The knowledge that one will have to submit oneself to such public examination might affect the way in which judges behave earlier in their careers.

Training

Judges are appointed in middle life after having acquired years of experience as a barrister or sometimes as a solicitor, but aside from the training they have undergone for their profession, they receive only a short period of *ad hoc* additional training arranged by the Judicial Studies Board. This has increased recently: the advent of the Children Act 1989 has prompted input to judicial training from social workers, psychiatrists and paediatricians, and the new Ethnic Minorities Advisory Boards has been advising new judges on race issues. However, the Judicial Studies Board has made it clear that increased resources will be needed if its activities are to be developed further.

Pay

Judges are paid large salaries, which are not subject to an annual vote in Parliament: the Lord Chief Justice receives £124,138; Lords of Appeal £114,874; and High Court judges £98,957. The official justification for this is the need to attract an adequate supply of candidates of sufficient calibre for appointment to judicial office, and in fact top barristers can earn more by staying in practice. In the past, for many the security of a pensionable position after years of self-employment made up for a slight cut in salary, but the 1993 Judicial Pensions and Retirement Act requires twenty years of judicial service rather than fifteen before full pension rights are obtained. With the earlier retirement age (see below), few judges will currently satisfy this requirement and the change has been very unpopular being described as the equivalent of a 7.5 per cent cut in salary. The Bar Council is urging the Government to pay salaries at different rates depending on the area of law, for example tax and commercial law judges would receive more.

Promotion

The traditional view has been that there is no system of promotion of judges, on the grounds that holders of judicial office might allow their promotion prospects to affect their decision-making. In practice, judges are promoted from lower courts to higher courts: potential recorders generally have to have proved themselves as assistant recorders; circuit judges as recorders. Those appointed to the High Court have usually served as a recorder or deputy High Court judge. The process appears to be much the same as that for initial appointments, being based on confidential soundings from those within the system.

Termination of appointment

There are four ways in which a judge may leave office:

Dismissal. Apart from the Lord Chancellor, judges of the High Court and above are covered by the Act of Settlement 1700, which provides that they may only be removed from office by the Queen on the petition of both Houses of Parliament. The machinery for dismissal has been used successfully only once, when in 1830 Sir Jonah Barrington, a judge of the High Court of Admiralty in Ireland, was charged with appropriating £922 to his own use. Proceedings against the judge were conducted in each House and each passed a resolution against the judge calling for his dismissal, which was then confirmed by the king. No judge has been removed by petition of Parliament this century.

Under the Courts Act 1971, circuit judges, district judges and stipendiary magistrates can be dismissed by the Lord Chancellor for 'inability or misbehaviour'. In fact this has occurred only once since the passing of the Act: Judge Bruce Campbell (a circuit judge) was sacked in 1983 after being convicted of smuggling spirits, cigarettes and tobacco into England in his yacht. In July 1994 the Lord Chancellor made it clear that 'misbehaviour' could include a conviction for drink-driving or any offence involving violence, dishonesty or moral turpitude. It would also include any behaviour likely to cause offence, particularly on religious or racial grounds or behaviour that amounted to sexual harassment.

In addition to dismissal, there is of course, also the power not to re-appoint those who have been appointed for a limited period only.

Resignation. In practice, serious misbehaviour is dealt with not by dismissal, but by the Lord Chancellor suggesting to the judge that he or she should resign.

Retirement. The Lord Chancellor has recently reduced the retirement age to 70.

Removal due to infirmity. The Lord Chancellor has powers to remove a judge who is disabled by permanent infirmity from the performance of his or her duties and who is incapacitated from resigning his or her post.

Discipline and criticism

In practice the mechanisms for disciplining judges who misbehave are more significant than those for removal, which is generally a last resort. Judges may be criticized in Parliament, or rebuked in the appellate courts, and are often censured in the press. There may be complaints from barristers, solicitors or litigants, made either in court or in private to the judge personally. 'Scurrilous abuse' of a judge may, however, be punished as contempt of court.

Independence of the judiciary

In our legal system great importance is attached to the idea that judges should be independent. In addition to the common sense view that they should be independent of pressure from the Government and political and other groups, and therefore able to decide cases impartially, judicial independence is required by the constitutional doctrine known as the separation of powers. First put forward by the eighteenth-century French political theorist Montesquieu, this doctrine states that the only way to safeguard individual liberties is to ensure that the power of the state is divided between three separate and independent arms: the judiciary, comprising the judges; the legislature who make the laws, in our case Parliament; and the executive, the Government of the day. The idea is that each arm of the state should operate independently, so that each one is checked and balanced by the other two, and none becomes all-powerful; Montesquieu stated that if all the powers were concentrated in the hands of one group, the result would be tyranny.

Therefore the doctrine requires that the individuals should not occupy a position in more than one of the three arms of the state – judiciary, legislature and executive; that each should exercise its functions independently of any control or interference from the others, and that one arm of the state should not exercise the functions of either of the others.

The way in which the separation of powers works can be seen, for example, in judicial review, where the courts can scrutinize the behaviour of the executive, and in some cases declare it illegal. Other safeguards include the security of tenure given to judges, which ensures they cannot be removed at the whim of one of the other branches; the fact that their salaries are not subject to a parliamentary vote; and the rule that they cannot be sued for anything done while acting in their judicial capacity. Independence in decision-making is provided through the fact that judges are only accountable to higher judges in appellate courts.

However, there are a number of problems with the idea of the judiciary as independent (see p. 91).

Criticisms of the judiciary

Background, ethnic origin, sex and age
Judges are overwhelmingly white, male and middle to upper class, and frequently elderly, leading to accusations that they are unrepresentative of, and distanced from the majority of society. In 1995, 80 per cent of Lords of Appeal, Heads of Division, Lord Justices of Appeal and High Court judges were educated at Oxford or Cambridge. Over 50 per cent of the middle-ranking circuit judges went to Oxbridge but only 12 per cent of the lower-ranking district judges did. In a study carried out in 1994 by Labour Research it was found that of 641 judges, 80 per cent had been to public school. Sir Thomas Legg, the permanent secretary at the Lord Chancellor's Department, answered criticism over the Oxbridge domination of the higher courts from MPs, by insisting: 'It is not the function of the professional judiciary to be representative of the community.'

Chris Mullin, a Labour MP, has commented that the only woman judge in the Court of Appeal happened to be the sister of a previous Lord Chancellor and the daughter of a Lord of Appeal. There are only six female High Court judges and just 29 of the 540 circuit judges are women. Law Society research conducted in 1991 suggested that male barristers were nearly twice as likely to obtain judicial appointment as women in practice for the same length of time. Ethnic minorities are even more scarcely represented; no members of the ethnic minorities have been appointed to the higher courts, and of all judges fewer than 30 were known to be from ethnic minorities. Lord Lane the 76-year-old former Lord Chief Justice, said after his retirement that his regret at being forced off the bench was due, at least partly, to the fact that his colleagues were 'a jolly nice bunch of chaps'. This remark reinforces the view of many that the judiciary is actually a sort of rarefied gentlemen's club.

The age of the full-time judiciary has remained constant over many years: the average on appointment is about 52 or 53. Inevitably, given the system of promotion, the average age is higher in the higher courts, thus the average age of a district judge was 54.3 and that of a Law Lord was 66.5 in 1995. Even the recently reduced retirement age is still five years older than that for most other occupations – Lord Denning retired at 83. It can be no surprise that Lord Denning, now in his nineties, does not agree with the changes to the retirement age. 'You can often do good work after 75; I think I did some of my best work, gave some of my judgments of greatest value, after 75,' he was reported as saying. The Labour Party has argued that the retirement age should be even lower, at about 65. David Pannick has written in his book, *Judges*, that 'a judiciary composed predominantly of senior citizens cannot hope to apply contemporary standards or to understand contemporary concerns'.

Before the Courts and Legal Services Act 1990, judges were almost exclusively selected from practising barristers. Since it is difficult for anyone without a private income to survive the first years of practice, successful barristers have tended to come from reasonably well-to-do families, who are of course more likely to send their sons or daughters to public schools and then to Oxford or Cambridge. Although the background of the Bar is gradually changing, the age at which judges are appointed mean that it will be some years before this is reflected in the ranks of the judiciary.

The new opportunities provided for solicitors to join the judiciary, provided by the Courts and Legal Services Act 1990 may in time alter the traditional judicial background, since this branch of the profession provides wider opportunities for women, members of the ethnic minorities and those from less privileged backgrounds.

Selection and appointment

The present system of selection has been criticized, by the constitutional reform organization Charter 88 among others, as being secretive and lacking clearly defined selection criteria. The process is handled by a small group of civil servants who, although they consult widely with judges and senior barristers, nevertheless wield a great deal of power. With no formal network or mechanism for obtaining information, the danger is that too much reliance is placed on a collection of anecdotal reports from fellow lawyers, with candidates given no opportunity to challenge damning things said about them.

The fact that those who advise on appointments are already well established within the system could make it unlikely that they will encourage appointment from a wider base: Lord Bridge, the retired Law Lord, commented in a 1992 television programme that they tend to look for 'chaps like ourselves'. As Helena Kennedy QC has put it 'the potential for cloning is overwhelming', and the outlook for potential female judges and those from the ethnic minorities not promising. The reforms introduced in 1995 seem to be merely window dressing as the Lord Chancellor has admitted that the process of obtaining 'soundings' will remain important.

The fact that appointments are effectively in the hands of a Government minister is also seen as a problem, and although in theory the Lord Chancellor is accountable through Parliament for his appointments, in practice this means very little. The same arguments apply to the system of promotion.

However, in his book *The Judge*, Lord Devlin says that, while it would be good to open up the legal profession, so that it could get the very best candidates from all walks of life, the nature of the job means that judges will still be the same type of people whether they come from public schools and Oxbridge or not, namely those 'who do not seriously question the status quo'.

Training
Considering the importance of their work, judges receive very little training. They may be experienced as lawyers, but the skills needed by a good lawyer are not identical to those required by a good judge. Unlike the career judge system seen on the continent, where judges cut their judicial teeth in the lower courts, and gain experience as they move up to more serious cases, our judges often begin their judicial careers with cases that may involve substantial loss of liberty for the individual. Nor are they required to have shown expertise in the areas of law they will be required to consider: it is perfectly possible for a High Court judge to try a serious criminal case, and possibly pass a sentence of a long term of imprisonment, without ever having done a criminal case as a lawyer in practice.

The most serious cases of all in the civil courts are not being heard by High Court judges but by deputy High Court judges. These deputies are circuit judges spending a few days in London or, more likely, barristers filling time between cases. The only thing to be said about this system is that it is cheaper for the Treasury.

Procedures for criticism and dismissal
Over the years there have been a few judges whose conduct has been frequently criticized, but who have nevertheless remained on the Bench, and the lack of a formal machinery for complaints is seen as protecting incompetent judges. However, this has to be balanced against the protection that security of tenure gives to judicial independence.

Problems with judicial independence
Despite the emphasis placed on the independence of the English judiciary, a number of factors compromise it.

- Apart from where European law is involved, it is never possible for the courts to question the validity of existing Acts of Parliament. In the United Kingdom all Acts of Parliament are treated as absolutely binding by the courts, until such time as any particular Act is repealed or altered by Parliament itself in another statute. The judiciary are therefore ultimately subordinate to the will of Parliament – unlike, for example, judges in the USA, who may declare legislation unconstitutional. Dworkin has argued that if judges had the power to set aside legislation as unconstitutional, judicial appointments would become undesirably political, and judges would be seen as politicians themselves. He points to the political character of high judicial appointments in America.

- The position of the Lord Chancellor as a member of the judiciary, the executive and the legislature clearly goes against the idea that no individual should be part of all three arms of the state, and his role ultimately means that all judicial appointments are made by the Government. Politically, the most important judicial appointment is that of Master of the Rolls; as president of the Court of Appeal his or her view on the proper relationship between the executive government and the individual is crucial. The appointment of Lord Donaldson, successor to Lord Denning, in 1982, was seen as a strongly political appointment and one which the Prime Minister favoured: he had been a Conservative councillor, and was not promoted during the years of the previous Labour Government, 1974–79. There was some publicity concerning Lord Donaldson's political views at the time of the GCHQ case, and as a result, his Lordship declined to preside over the Court of Appeal when it considered the Government's appeal in that case.

   Those barristers retained to represent the Government in court actions in which the government are involved – called Treasury counsel – are very likely to be offered High Court judgeships in due course.

   Lords of Appeal in Ordinary are also members of more than one arm of the state, since they take part in the legislative business in the House of Lords. However, they tend not to get involved in political controversy or ally themselves with a particular party, confining their contributions to technical questions of a legal nature. They rarely sit in legislative debates and by the same token, the political members of the Lords do not participate in judicial hearings.

- Judges also get involved in non-judicial areas with political implications, such as chairing enquiries into events such as Bloody Sunday in Londonderry, the Brixton riots or the Zeebrugge ferry disaster. Most recently Lord Justice Scott has been chairing the high profile inquiry into the arms-to-Iraq affair. This function can often be seen to undermine the political neutrality of the judiciary – in the early 1970s, for example, Lord Diplock headed an inquiry into the administration of justice in Northern Ireland, the report of which led to the abolition of jury trials for terrorist offences in

Northern Ireland. To this day such hearings are known as Diplock courts, which does nothing to uphold the reputation for independence of the judiciary.

- In his book *Straight from the Bench*, the retired circuit judge James Pickles alleges that judges who are ambitious cannot be truly independent because they have to be careful not to offend the Lord Chancellor or his officials – this leads, he says, to 'cringing conformity'. The fact that the Lord Chancellor is a Government minister lends further weight to the idea that the system of appointment and promotion compromises judicial independence. A recent illustration of this may be the case of Mr Justice Wood. He was president of the Employment Appeal Tribunal who had refused to deal with some cases in the more economical way that the Lord Chancellor wanted. He received a letter from the Lord Chancellor asking him to 'consider his position' as president of the tribunal. When questioned about this by legal peers in the House of Lords, Lord McKay denied that he was suggesting that Wood should resign. Mr Justice Wood did in fact retire shortly afterwards though he said that he had planned to do so even before the incident occurred. The legal peers accused the Lord Chancellor, Lord McKay, of acting unconstitutionally in apparently pressuring a judge to adopt cost-cutting procedures or resign. The incident reflected general concern that pressures from the Treasury to contain the costs of the legal system were threatening judicial independence.
- Although judges generally refrain from airing their political views, they are sometimes forced to make political decisions, affecting the balance between individuals and the state, the allocation of resources, and the relative powers of local and national government. Despite the official view of judges as apolitical, the fact that these decisions have political ramifications cannot be avoided; judges do not have the option of refusing to decide a case because it has political implications, and have to make a choice one way or the other.

However, concerns have been expressed that too often such decisions defend the interests of the Government of the day, sometimes at the expense of individual liberties. In the wartime case of **Liversidge** *v* **Anderson** (1942), Lord Atkin voiced concern about the decision by a majority of judges in the House of Lords that the Home Secretary was not required to give reasons to justify the detention of a citizen, commenting that the judges had shown themselves 'more executive minded than the executive'.

Recent cases have borne out this concern. In **McIlkenny** *v* **Chief Constable West Midlands** (1980), Lord Denning dismissed allegations of police brutality against the six men accused of the Birmingham pub bombings with the words:

Just consider the course of events if this action were to go to trial . . . If the six men fail, it will mean that much time and money and worry will have been expended by many people for no good purpose. If the six men win, it will mean that the police were guilty of perjury, that they were guilty of violence and threats, that the confessions were involuntary and were improperly admitted in evidence: and that the convictions were erroneous. That would mean that the Home Secretary would have either to recommend they be pardoned or he would have to remit the case to the Court of Appeal under section 17 of the Criminal Appeal Act 1968. This is such an appalling vista that every sensible person in the land would say: it cannot be right that these actions should go any further. They should be struck out.

In **R** *v* **Ponting** (1985), the civil servant Clive Ponting was accused of leaking documents revealing that the Government had covered up the circumstances in which the Argentine ship the General Belgrano was sunk during the Falklands war. Ponting argued that he had acted 'in the interests of the state' (a defence laid down in the Official Secrets Act at the time), but Mr Justice McGowan directed the jury that 'interests of the state' meant nothing more or less than the policies of the government of the day. Nevertheless the jury acquitted Ponting (see p. 132).

Right wing bias

In addition to their alleged readiness to support the Government of the day, the judiciary have been accused of being particularly biased towards the interests traditionally represented by the right wing of the political spectrum. In his influential book *The Politics of the Judiciary*, Griffith states that: 'in every major social issue which has come before the courts in the last thirty years – concerning industrial relations, political protest, race relations, government secrecy, police powers, moral behaviour – the judges have supported the conventional, settled and established interests.'

Among the cases he cites in support of this theory is **London Borough of Bromley** *v* **Greater London Council** (1982). In this case the Labour-run GLC had won election on a promise to cut bus and tube fares by 25 per cent. The move necessitated an increase in the rates, levied on the London boroughs, and one of those boroughs, Conservative-controlled Bromley, challenged the GLC's right to do this. The challenge failed in the High Court, but succeeded on appeal. The Court of Appeal judges condemned the fare reduction as 'a crude abuse of power', and quashed the supplementary rate that the GLC had levied on the London boroughs to pay for it. The House of Lords agreed, the Law Lords holding unanimously that the GLC was bound by a statute requiring it to 'promote the provision of integrated, efficient and economic transport facilities and services in Greater London', which they interpreted to mean that the bus and tube system must be run according to 'ordinary business principles' of cost-effectiveness. The decision represented a political defeat for the Labour leaders of the GLC and a victory for the Conservative councillors of Bromley.

Other cases cited by Griffith include **Council of Civil Service Unions** *v* **Minister for the Civil Service** (1984) – the 'GCHQ' case in which the House of Lords supported the withdrawal of certain civil servants' rights to belong to a trade union; **Attorney-General** *v* **Guardian Newspapers Ltd** (1987), which banned publication of *Spycatcher*, a book on the security services, even though it was generally available in America and Australia; and several cases arising out of the 1984 miners' strike, such as **Thomas** *v* **NUM (South Wales Area)** (1985), in which injunctions were sought to prevent protesters collecting at pit gates and shouting abuse at those going to work. The judge, according to Griffith, had some difficulty in finding the conduct illegal, but eventually decided that it amounted to 'a species of private nuisance, namely unreasonable interference with the victim's right to use the highway'; Griffith describes the decision as 'judicial creativity at its most blatant'.

Commentators have also noted that the great advances in judicial review in the 1960s and 1970s came almost entirely at the expense of Labour policies, and that judicial reluctance to review the decision of the executive is most likely to be decisive in cases where the executive has a Conservative cast to it. However, the past few years have seen a shift; the Conservative Home Secretary Michael Howard's decisions have several times been found illegal by the courts. Legal journalist and writer, Joshua Rozenberg argued that the bias at least in favour of the establishment has broken down. He has written:

> Much of the responsibility for the rift between judiciary and government must fall on the shoulders of the Lord Chancellor. By shaking up the legal profession and paving the way for solicitors – and probably, before long, Crown Prosecution Service lawyers – to appear in the higher courts, and by his lack of support for judges on the key issues of pay, hours and pensions, Lord Mckay has fashioned a fundamental shift in the natural order: a judiciary which can no longer be relied on to support the establishment.
> (*The Guardian*, Tuesday 12 April 1994.)

Bias against women

In her book *Eve was Framed*, Helena Kennedy argues that the attitude of many judges to women is outdated, and sometimes prejudiced. The problems are particularly apparent in cases involving sexual offences; Kennedy cites the comments of judge Harold Cassell in 1990, that a man who had unlawful intercourse with his twelve-year-old stepdaughter was understandably driven to it by his pregnant wife's loss of interest in sex, and the direction of Judge Wild in a 1982 rape case: 'women who say no do not always mean no . . . if she doesn't want it, she only has to keep her legs shut and she will not get it without force'. Similar words were used by Judge Dean in a 1990 case.

Kennedy alleges that women are judged according to how well they fit traditional female stereotypes. Because crime is seen as stepping outside the feminine role, women are more severely punished than men, and women who do not fit traditional stereotypes are treated most harshly. She points out that three times as many women as men go to prison for a first offence (though this may be affected by their lack of financial resources, making financial penalties unsuitable). According to a report by the National Association for the Care and Resettlement of Offenders (NACRO) in 1990, 53 per cent of women have two or fewer convictions when they first go to prison compared to 22 per cent of men.

Research by the sociologist Pat Carlen into what affects the decision to send a woman to prison received the following answers from members of the judiciary:

- 'Women who live more ordered lives don't commit crime because with a husband and children to look after, they don't have time.'
- 'It may not be necessary to send her to prison if she has a husband. He may tell her to stop it.'
- 'If they have left their husbands and their children are in care it may seem a very good idea to send them to prison for three months.'
- 'If she's a good mother, we don't want to take her away. If she's not a good mother it doesn't really matter.'

Lack of specialization

The centralized nature of our system is striking when we compare it with systems in other countries. In France, for example, each region has its own court structure, and there are hundreds of judges of the same status and none with the pre-eminent status of our elite. Our centralist tradition has inhibited the creation of a specialist court like the Conseil d'Etat, and it is argued that the development of our administrative law has suffered as a result.

This centralized model with judges of universal competence is coming under increasing pressure, with some areas of law seen as so specialist in nature that they are thought to require specialist courts to handle them, known as tribunals. Each tribunal has its own specialist judges. There has also been a call for greater informality which has led to the increased use of tribunals and to the use of mediation systems as an alternative to using the court system. Lord Woolf in his interim report has recommended that High Court and circuit judges should concentrate on fewer areas of work without becoming single subject specialists. At the moment district judges who wish to become circuit judges have to sit as recorders first and hear criminal cases, as a type of apprenticeship. Lord Woolf has recommended that this should no longer be necessary.

However it can also be argued that the system as a whole has gained by the overview provided by our elite judges and from the fact that they have the opportunity to develop the principles of the common law through the full range of cases, be they criminal, civil or administrative.

Shortage of time

There is a growing concern that judges currently have insufficient time allocated for them to read the papers for a case. Court of Appeal judges are only allocated four reading days a month when they can do legal research. The rest of the time they are expected to be sitting hearing court cases. This is in striking contrast with some appellate judges in the United States who only hear cases four days per month.

▶ Reform of the judiciary

Appointments and promotion

Several different ways of opening up the process of appointment and promotion to public scrutiny and accountability have been suggested. In 1972 the law reform group Justice recommended that the Lord Chancellor should be assisted by a small advisory committee, which could comprise representatives of the Bar, the Law Society, academic lawyers, the judiciary and possibly some lay members with skills in personnel matters and selection procedures. Interested bodies could propose names to the committee and individuals wishing to be considered could put their own names forward. The Lord Chancellor himself could likewise put names to the committee, but he would not be permitted to make appointments without having first secured the committee's view.

The constitutional reform group Charter 88 want to see the setting up of a Judicial Appointments Commission, comprising judges, lawyers, academics and lay members, appointed by a Select Committee and answerable to Parliament. Younger lawyers, academics, and more solicitors should be eligible, and they also recommend positive discrimination in favour of female and ethnic minority applicants, and the introduction of part-time appointments and a proper career structure to help women. This has been done in both the Netherlands and France, where near parity between the sexes now exists. In the long term, say Charter 88, it is important to improve access to the legal profession as a whole and provide better funding for training, so that students from all backgrounds could apply.

It has also been suggested that the elevation of judges from circuit to High Court and from High Court to the Court of Appeal should all be in the hands of the independent Judicial Commission, with the usual way of becoming a High Court judge from the Circuit Bench.

The Labour Party has suggested that more judicial appointments should be made of people from an academic background. The first academic to be appointed as a judge was Professor Brenda Hoggett, who became Mrs Justice Hale of the High Court at the beginning of 1994. Before becoming a University lecturer she had practised as a barrister and had become a QC.

Dismissal and discipline

From time to time the suggestion has been made that the system of dismissal would be improved if there were some form of fair hearing for judges before they were dismissed and if the allegations against them were sifted by some form of tribunal or special commission. Justice, in its 1972 report on the judiciary, recommended that there should be a three-man judicial commission to which the Lord Chancellor should have to refer any case in which he thought there were grounds for dismissing a judge of the High Court or above. The commission would inquire into the matter and recommend whether the question should be referred to the Judicial Committee of the Privy Council, which would then advise the Queen whether the judge should be dismissed. Any other judge dismissed by the Lord Chancellor should have the right of appeal to the judicial committee, which would appoint a judicial commission to apply the same procedure. A similar mechanism already exists in Scotland.

The Labour Party has produced a policy document in 1995 suggesting that complaints against judges could be made to a commission and details of such complaints could be published in the form of league tables with judges being named. League tables would show the number of times a particular judge had been referred to the commission and the number of complaints upheld. A party spokesperson is reported to have said that if a judge had been complained about six times, and five of the complaints had been upheld 'it would be inconceivable' that the judge would continue to work in the same field.

Training

It has been widely suggested that judges should receive more training, not just at the beginning of their careers, but at frequent intervals throughout. Helena Kennedy suggests that judges might also benefit from sabbaticals, in which they could study the practices of other jurisdictions, and the work of social agencies and reform groups.

Judge Pickles has put forward the view that the judiciary needs more training in sociology, psychology, penology and criminology, and to learn more about how criminals are dealt with in other systems Lord Scarman has put forward similar views. Lord Woolf has proposed that judges should receive training in information technology so that they can make greater use of computers in their work.

•
ANSWERING QUESTIONS

Questions about the judiciary generally focus on their independence, but as this is closely related to appointments, background and selection, you need to know more than just the information under the heading of independence of the judiciary, as the following example shows.

1 Can true judicial independence ever be achieved under the present method of appointment? *Oxford*
Your introduction should explain why judicial independence is important. Then look at each aspect of judicial appointment and consider how it effects the independence of the judiciary; points to raise are the position of the Lord Chancellor, the secretive nature of the appointment procedure, and the role of the civil servants. You might then consider the background of the judges, as a result of the selection procedure, and whether this affects independence, giving examples (the material on right-wing and executive bias is relevant here). You might want to compare our system with those of other countries, and the independence of the judiciary there. Then look at suggested reforms, and finally conclude with your view on whether the judiciary can be sufficiently independent under our system, and if not, which reforms should be made.

2 'For nearly 300 years, the English judge has been guaranteed his independence.' How far is this true? In your opinion, can the decisions of our judges be regarded as satisfactory to all members of society?
Your introduction should place the reference to 300 years by mentioning the provisions of the Act of Settlement (p. 9). After that the question seems to need answering in two parts: has the English judge been guaranteed independence, and in the light of the answer, can his or her judgments properly be regarded as satisfactory to all members of society?

In the first part, you should look at the factors that are supposed to guarantee the independence of the judiciary: security of tenure, separation of powers, salaries not subject to a parliamentary vote and so on (see p. 88). Then go on to examine the problems with independence, that suggest it is not guaranteed.

In the second part of your answer, you can give examples of cases where the lack of judicial independence has resulted in decisions that are not satisfactory to certain members of society – again, the material on right-wing and executive bias is useful here.

If you have time you could add that the lack of independence is not the only reason that their decisions are not satisfactory to all members of society, and bring in the material about the background of judges and their alleged bias against women. If you have time you could add suggestions for reform, perhaps briefly in your conclusion.

NB If you happen to have swotted up on judges, you will naturally be looking for a question in which you can show off this knowledge, but beware: questions which at first sight look as though they concern the judiciary may actually be about statutory interpretation and the law-making role of judges – the following are examples:
Explain and critically examine the approaches adopted by judges to the interpretation of statutes. *AEB*
and
Explain and illustrate the following statement: 'There was never a more sterile controversy than that upon the question of whether a judge makes law. Of course he does. How can he help it? (Radcliffe) *London*

The material for answering this kind of question can be found in chapter 1: Sources of law.

4 Barristers and solicitors

The British legal profession, unlike that of most other countries, includes two separate branches: barristers and solicitors (the term 'lawyer' is a general one which covers both branches). They each do the same type of work – advocacy, which means representing clients in court, and paper work, including drafting legal documents and giving written advice – but the proportions differ, with barristers generally spending more time in court.

In addition, some types of work have traditionally been available to only one branch (conveyancing to solicitors, and advocacy in the higher courts to barristers, for example), and barristers cannot usually be hired directly by clients – their first point of contact will usually be a solicitor, who then engages a barrister on their behalf if it proves necessary. As we shall see though, these divisions are beginning to break down.

▶ Solicitors

There are around 70,000 solicitors. Their governing body is the Law Society, which supervises training and discipline, as well as acting on behalf of the profession as a whole.

Work

Solicitors have traditionally been able to do advocacy work in the magistrates' court and the county court, but not generally in the higher courts. This situation was changed in the Courts and Legal Services Act, and now suitably qualifed solictors can secure rights of audience in any court (see p. 113). Even those solicitors who do not have full rights of audience can appear in the High Court in bankruptcy proceedings, or to read out a formal, unchallenged statement; and in the Crown Court if the case is an appeal from the magistrates' court, or has been committed to the Crown Court for sentence, and they appeared in the same case in the magistrates' court. They can also appear before a single judge of the Court of Appeal, and in High Court proceedings held in chambers.

In general, an individual solicitor will usually do much less advocacy work than a barrister, and many none at all – though there are exceptions, and as more and more solicitors gain full rights of audience, these exceptions may increase. In any case, solicitors as a group do more advocacy than barristers, simply because 98 per cent of criminal cases are tried in the magistrates' court, where the advocate is usually a solicitor. The amount of advocacy done by solicitors is also likely to grow as a result of the removal of many contract and tort cases from the High Court to the county court, one of the provisions of the Courts and Legal Services Act 1990.

For most solicitors, paper work takes up the majority of their time. It includes conveyancing (legal aspects of the buying and selling of houses and other property), drawing up wills, and so on, as well as giving written and oral legal advice. A survey commissioned by the Law Society in 1985 showed that solicitors' gross income fees came from the following sources: domestic conveyancing 29 per cent; company and commercial 25 per cent; probate and wills 9 per cent; matrimonial 7 per cent; crime 5 per cent; other areas 25 per cent.

Until 1985, solicitors were the only people allowed to do conveyancing work, but this is no longer the case – people from different occupations can qualify as licensed conveyancers, and the service is often offered by banks and building societies. Probate work can now also be done by banks, building societies, insurance companies and legal executives, and consequently the proportions of work done by solicitors are changing.

Clients approach the solicitor of their choice directly, and the solicitor can choose whether or not to take on the case. Organizations such as the Solicitors' Family Law Association keep lists of solicitors who specialize in particular areas, and voluntary bodies such as the Citizens Advice Bureaux also advise clients on who to see locally.

Solicitors can, and usually do, form partnerships, with other solicitors. They work in ordinary offices, with, in general, the same support staff as any office-based business, and have offices all over England and Wales and in all towns. Practices range from huge London-based firms dealing only with large corporations, to small partnerships or individual solicitors, dealing with the conveyancing, wills, divorces and minor crime of a country town. Some solicitors work in Law Centres and other advice agencies, government departments, private industry and education rather than in private practice.

Qualifications and training

Almost all solicitors begin with a degree. Although no minimum degree classification is laid down, increased competition for entry to the profession means that most successful applicants now have an upper second class degree, and very few get in with less than a lower second.

Students whose degree is not in law have to take the one-year course leading to the Common Professional Examination (CPE). It is possible for non-graduate mature students, who have demonstrated some professional or business achievements, to enter the profession with a two-year, wider CPE course, but only a handful do so, and it is not a route the Law Society encourages – they suggest that for most people, it is worth putting in the extra year to do a law degree and enter in the conventional manner, especially bearing in mind that many universities and colleges now offer mature students law degrees which can be studied part-time, so that students do not have to give up paid employment.

The next step, for law graduates and those who have passed the CPE, is a one-year Legal Practice course, designed to provide practical skills, including advocacy, as well as legal and procedural knowledge. Both the CPE and the Legal Practice course are eligible only for discretionary LEA grants, and are not covered by the Government's student loan scheme. The Law Society provides a very small number of bursaries, and has also negotiated a loans scheme with certain high street banks, which offers up to £5,000, which students do not begin paying back until they have finished studying. The vast majority of students are obliged to fund themselves or rely on loans.

After passing the legal practice exams, the prospective solicitor must find a place, usually in a firm, to serve a two-year apprenticeship; there can be intense competition for these places, especially in times of economic difficulty when firms are reluctant to invest in training. Formally known as articles, the two-year period is now called a training contract, and includes a 20-day practical skills course, building on subjects studied during the Legal Practice course. Trainee solicitors (or articled clerks as they were traditionally known) are paid, and the Law Society currently lays down a minimum wage of £12,150 in inner London, and £10,850 in the provinces. With fewer places available due to the economic climate, the Law Society considered abolishing the minimum wage in 1993, in the hope that lower costs might encourage firms to take on more trainees. That idea was rejected, but the minimum wage was frozen in 1993, and the extra allowance for trainees working in outer London firms abolished – they now receive the same as their counterparts in the provinces.

It is possible to become a solicitor without a degree, by completing the one-year Solicitors First Examination Course, and the Legal Practice course, and spending five years in articles. Legal executives (see p. 118) sometimes go on to qualify this way.

Both stages of solicitors' training have been changed recently, with more emphasis being placed on practical skills in general, and advocacy in particular. These changes have been made in response to recommendations by the Royal Commission on Legal Services 1979 and the Ormrod Committee.

The majority of solicitors qualifying each year are still law graduates

– in 1992, 3,067 of the 4,697 admitted to the Law Society Roll had a law degree, with only 632 graduates in subjects other than law. However, the Law Society say that the non-law degree and CPE route is becoming more popular, with a third of places on Legal Practice courses currently being taken by people aiming to qualify this way. Legal academics have expressed some concern about this, but the Law Society point out that in some years, pass rates for non-law graduates in Solicitors' Finals have been higher than those for law graduates.

Though still a small proportion of those qualifying, Fellows of the Institute of Legal Executives (see p. 118) are entering the profession in increasing numbers – only 47 were admitted in 1989, but this had risen to 139 by 1992 (making up the rest of the total were applicants from overseas, solicitors transferring from Scotland or Northern Ireland, and ex-barristers).

All solicitors who have been admitted since 1982 are now required to participate in continuing education throughout their careers, and in 1998, this scheme will be extended to include all solicitors, regardless of how long ago they qualified. They are required to do sixteen hours a year, with the subjects covered depending on each individual's areas of interest or need. Records must be kept of courses attended.

Complaints

Complaints are first made to the Solicitors Complaints Bureau, an independent body which tries to conciliate the client and the solicitor. If this is unsuccessful, the complaint may be referred to the Disciplinary Tribunal, which can, among other things, give clients their fees back. The 1990 Courts and Legal Services Act (CLSA) set up a Legal Services Ombudsman to deal with complaints against both solicitors and barristers. Solicitors can also be sued for negligent work.

In 1994, a National Consumer Council report criticized the Solicitors Complaints Bureau for delay and operational problems.

Promotion to the judiciary

Until recently, solicitors were only eligible to become circuit judges, but the Courts and Legal Services Act 1990 has opened the way for them to become judges in the higher courts (see chapter 3: The judiciary).

▶ Barristers

There are around 7,000 barristers, known collectively as the Bar. Their governing body is the Bar Council, which, like the Law Society, acts as a kind of trade union, safeguarding the interests of barristers, and also as a watchdog, regulating barristers' training and activities.

Work

Advocacy is the main function of barristers, and much of their time will be spent in court or preparing for it. Until the changes made under the CLSA, barristers were, with a few exceptions, the only people allowed to advocate in the superior courts – the House of Lords, the Court of Appeal, the High Court, the Crown Court and the Employment Appeal Tribunal. Barristers also do some paper work, drafting legal documents and giving written opinions on legal problems.

Barristers are usually engaged by a solicitor on behalf of a client, and work on what is called the 'cab rank' rule – technically, this means that if they are not already committed for the time in question, they must accept any case which falls within their claimed area of specialization and for which a reasonable fee is offered (in practice, barristers' clerks, who take their bookings, may manipulate the rule to ensure that barristers are able to avoid cases they do not want to take). Barristers may also be directly hired by certain professionals, such as accountants.

Barristers must be self-employed and under Bar rules, cannot form partnerships, but they usually share offices, called chambers, with other barristers. All the barristers in a particular chambers share a clerk, who is a type of business manager, arranging meetings with the client and the solicitor and also negotiating the barristers' fees. Around 70 per cent of practising barristers are based in London chambers, though they may travel to courts in the provinces; the rest are based in the other big cities.

Not all qualified barristers work as advocates at the Bar. Like solicitors, some are employed by law centres and other advice agencies, government departments or private industry, and some teach. Some go into these jobs after practising at the Bar for a time, others never practise at the Bar.

Qualifications and training

The starting point is (at least) an upper second class degree. If this degree is not in law, applicants must do the one-year course leading to the Common Professional Examination (the same course taken by would-be solicitors with degrees in subjects other than law). Mature students may be accepted without a degree, but applications are subject to very stringent consideration, and this is not a likely route to the Bar.

All students then have to join one of the four Inns of Court: Inner Temple, Middle Temple, Gray's Inn and Lincoln's Inn, all of which are in London, and study for a year at the Inns of Court School of Law. The course includes oral exercises, and tuition in interviewing skills and negotiating skills, and as with solicitors' training, more emphasis has been laid on these practical aspects in recent years. Only discretionary Local Education Authority grants are available for this year and the CPE, and neither are covered by the Student Loan Scheme. Until recently, scholarships and loans were offered by the Bar Council and the Inns, but these have been discontinued.

During this time, students must also dine at their Inn 18 times (until recently 24 times). This rather old-fashioned custom stems from the idea that students would benefit from the wisdom and experience of their elders if they sat among them at mealtimes. Although it may be of little educational value these days, and does nothing to promote a modern image of the profession either, the Bar has been reluctant to give up its tradition.

After this, the applicant is called to the Bar, and must then find a place in a chambers to serve his or her pupillage. This is a one-year apprenticeship in which pupils assist a qualified barrister, who is known as their pupil master. Competition for pupillage places can be fierce, and this is aggravated by the fact that pupillage is usually done in two six-month blocks, with different pupil masters and usually in different chambers, so there are in effect two places to be found. Since 1992, pupils have been required to take a further advocacy course before the end of pupillage, as part of the increased emphasis on practical skills.

Around half the 900 pupils each year receive funding of £6,000 for their twelve-month pupillage from their chambers, but for the rest, finance can be a big problem unless their parents are able to help out. As well as general living expenses, pupils need to find money for smart clothes for court, a wig and gown, books and travelling expenses. Pupils may take on cases in their second six months, but the fees for that work are generally not high, and do not come in until some time after the work is done.

Pupillage completed, the newly-qualified barrister must find a permanent place in a chambers, known as a tenancy. This can be the most difficult part, and some are forced to 'squat' – remaining in their pupillage chambers for as long as they are allowed, without becoming a full member – until they find a permanent place.

After ten years in practice, a barrister may apply to become a Queen's Counsel, or QC (sometimes called a silk, as they wear gowns made of silk). This usually means they will be offered higher-paid cases, and need do less preliminary paper work. They may apply several times before being accepted. Not all barristers attempt or manage to become QCs – those that do not are called juniors, even up to retirement age. Juniors may assist QCs in big cases, as well as working alone.

The Bar is considering plans for further compulsory education during the first three years of independent practice, and possibly even afterwards, and the Royal Commission on Criminal Justice 1993 felt this should be adopted.

Complaints

Barristers cannot be sued for negligent conduct of a case in court, nor for negligent preparation at the pre-trial stage – this principle was laid down in **Rondel** *v* **Worsley** (1969). For a client who is dissatisfied, the only initial option is to make a complaint to the Bar Council; it can take disciplinary action against the barrister, though this does not directly help the client.

The Legal Services Ombudsman can investigate grievances about the Bar Council's treatment of a particular complaint, and recommend discipline or compensation. If the Bar Council does not follow this recommendation it must publicize the reason why it has not done so.

Promotion to the judiciary

Suitably experienced barristers are eligible for appointment to all judicial posts, and the majority of current judges have practised at the bar (for details of appointments, see chapter 3: The judiciary).

▶ Background of barristers and solicitors

Class

Both lawyers and law students come predominantly from middle-class homes – evidence presented to the Royal Commission on Legal Services in 1979 suggested that over 60 per cent of law students' parents were either professional or managerial, and only 8 per cent were in manual work.

Part of the reason for this has been the lack of funding for legal training, which has made it very difficult for students without well-off parents to qualify, especially as barristers. In recent years the difficulties have worsened, as shortage of funds has meant that Local Educational Authorities have become more reluctant to award discretionary grants even to cover fees, let alone for living expenses. A survey by the Law Society in 1992 found that of the 102 LEAs who replied, only six would consider giving discretionary grants to students on the CPE course, and 57 to students on the Legal Practice course. Even these did not undertake to give grants to everyone who applied, and where grants were given, they rarely covered more than a percentage of tuition fees – a grant of £749 towards tuition fees of £3,500 was typical. Maintenance grants were given in exceptional circumstances, but again, would usually only cover a percentage of living expenses. Early estimates of current figures suggest the picture is becoming even bleaker – several of the LEAs which did consider allowing grants in 1992 were no longer doing so.

Sex

Women have only entered the legal profession in significant numbers in the last 25 years, and remain under-represented, especially at higher levels: in 1989–90 only 18 per cent of practising barristers and 23 per cent of practising solicitors were women. As far as intake is concerned, the position is improving: nearly half of new barristers, and more than half of new solicitors, are women. However, a 1994 report by the Bar Council and the Lord Chancellor's department, '*Without Prejudice*', found that there was still discrimination at every other stage, including earnings and field of work. In both branches, women tend to earn less and finish their careers at a lower level than men. Law Society figures for 1991 showed that only 28 per cent of female solicitors were partners in their firms, compared to 62 per cent of men, while at the Bar, less than 6 per cent of QCs are women, and there have only ever been a handful of female heads of chambers.

The situation is changing, with the Law Society in particular investigating the possibilities for career breaks and part-time work for both men and women with families, though problems for female barristers, who must be self-employed, are more difficult to tackle.

Race

The Royal Commission on Legal Services 1979 reported that ethnic minorities are not adequately represented in the legal profession. In 1989, ethnic minorities formed 5 per cent of the Bar, which it believes compares favourably with other professions, but were badly represented at the upper end of the profession, with only a handful of QCs. The proportions are slightly better among solicitors, yet white Europeans still comprised 81 per cent of the students enrolling with the Law Society in 1989–90.

Both the Law Society and the Bar Council have announced they are taking steps to prevent racial discrimination, but the success or otherwise of this may be seen by the regular news stories of black candidates doing less well in legal examinations than whites, particularly at the Bar. There are also reports that black candidates find it very difficult to obtain articles.

Clearly the background of the legal profession is largely white, middle-class and male. This is changing slowly, but until selection is much wider, it will continue to cause problems, both for the profession, which is often seen as unapproachable, and so discourages some clients from seeking help (see the discussion on unmet legal need, p. 179); and within the judiciary – its members come from the legal profession, and unless lawyers are drawn from a wide range of the population, judges cannot be either, and will continue to be seen, sometimes justifiably, as remote and out of touch with ordinary people's lives.

▶ Performance of the legal professions

A survey of lawyers' services carried out for the 1979 Royal Commission on Legal Services found that 84 per cent of clients were satisfied with the work done, and only 13 per cent dissatisfied, which was interpreted as a vote of confidence for the profession. The Commission concluded that 'Most legal work is transacted well and efficiently. Most clients are satisfied with the service they receive'. However, as Zander (1988) points out, their research method was not entirely reliable, since lay individuals are unlikely to have enough knowledge and experience to make an informed assessment of the work; significantly, a similar survey involving corporate clients more likely to use lawyers frequently reported a higher level of dissatisfaction.

The rosy view of the 1979 Royal Commission was not shared by everyone, either before or since, and a few highly publicized evaluations from inside the professions have painted a more worrying picture. In 1976, solicitor Michael Joseph published a book denouncing conveyancing as 'a racket', paying solicitors huge amounts for a small amount of work that lay people could do as well, or better, for themselves. He followed this in 1984 with *Lawyers Can Seriously Damage Your Health*, describing in detail three personal injury cases revealing gross incompetence on the part of both solicitors and barristers.

Nor does the performance of lawyers in criminal cases win universal approval. In 1979 the barrister and legal journalist Marcel Berlins conducted a small, informal study of criminal advocacy, and described 'poor, sometimes inexcusable standards of presentation', with barristers forgetting vital details, including the charge, and apparently unaware of key legal details.

Berlins's views have been backed up by criticism from the 1993 Royal Commission on Criminal Justice. It found that defence cases were often inadequately prepared, usually because such work was delegated to clerks and given too little supervision, and there were problems with inadequate advocacy, on the part of both barristers and solicitors. The Commission suggested that inadequate training might be at the root of the problems with advocacy, and expressed particular concern at the practice of allowing pupil barristers to take on cases in their second six months, and at the lack of detailed assessment of the experience gained by individual pupils during pupillage. It recognized that both branches of the profession were already strengthening advocacy training, but felt there was still room for improvement.

A further problem highlighted by the Commission was that lawyers appeared to be failing to advise convicted clients about the possibility of appeal. Research commissioned by the Royal Commission and carried out by Plotnikoff and Wilson discovered that the provision and quality of advice was uneven, and many lawyers seriously misunderstood the powers of the Court of Appeal. Some 9 per cent of prisoner respondents to the study said they had not been visited by their lawyer at the end of the case, while 23 per cent had had contact with their lawyers but no mention had been made of the possibility of appealing. Almost 90 per cent of the solicitors and barristers in the study had not given their client any written information about appeals. Although these problems were felt to be partly due to defects in the guidance documents on the subject provided by the Court of Appeal, the Law Society and the Bar Council, bad practice on the part of the professions was also to blame.

The Courts and Legal Services Act 1990 sets up a Lord Chancellor's advisory committee which will consider, among other things, the education of solicitors and barristers.

▶ Do we need legal professionals?

In many areas, non-legally qualified people do the work of lawyers as well as professionals could, and sometimes more effectively – an obvious example is the large number of volunteer and employed lay advisers in the Citizens Advice Bureaux who provide an accessible, economic and uncomplicated service to deal with legal and other queries. Legal executives often become so well experienced in particular areas that they need no supervision from their legally qualified colleagues, and take on much of the work that the general public assumes only solicitors can do. Some work may even be better done by clients themselves, as Joseph's study of conveyancing seemed to show. So why should we need a profession (or two), and why should that profession be allowed sole access to certain types of work?

There are many reasons why a legal profession might be considered desirable, but two broad theories shed some interesting light on the reasons why we maintain it. The first, functionalism, emphasizes the importance of keeping society together, and it sees one important way of doing this as maintaining the status quo, keeping the structure of society the same.

Functionalists believe professions in general contribute to this process. They say those within a profession will share certain values, put public service before profit, and use expert knowledge for the good of society – the implication is that professionals have higher moral standards than ordinary people. They are supposed to believe in 'public service' and 'shared professional ethics', while plumbers, car manufacturers and shop-keepers, for example, are only interested in money. This is used to justify the fact that they are the only people to have access to certain types of work.

It is difficult to reconcile this view with the fact that many lawyers compete to work for the big legal firms, working for the most powerful members of society – not because the work is interesting or socially useful, but because it pays so well.

A second theory, that of market control, has a very different view of the role played by professionals. It takes as its starting point the market place, where different suppliers compete with each other to get consumers to buy their goods and services. Economic theory reasons that at any given level of quality, consumers will choose the cheapest goods or services, so those offering good quality services cheaply will sell a lot, and the rest will go bust.

This may be good news for consumers, but tough for producers, who must be constantly striving to provide a better product for less money, while looking over their shoulder to make sure that someone else is not providing it cheaper or better than they can. Consequently, producers try get round this competitive situation, and they can do so in a number of different ways – by forming monopolies and cartels, or by controlling the raw materials or the patents to a manufacturing process, for example.

Market control theory suggests that having professions is just one of those ways of escaping uncontrolled competition. Professions restrict access to their market by controlling who enters the profession, saying that only those with complicated qualifications can offer services in this area; they control the way in which professionals offer their services, for example by stopping members of the profession using aggressive advertising to compete with each other; and they keep their own special area of expertise as complex and as obscure as they can.

One of the leading proponents of this point of view is Richard Abel, Professor of Law at the University of California. His book on the legal profession in England and Wales describes in great detail how solicitors and barristers have controlled who becomes lawyers, how they operate and what they sell. He suggests that they have done this in their own interests, to keep the price of legal services high. A recent example of this process is the fact that now the difficult economic situation has increased competition for jobs, the Bar Council has raised its entry requirement for initial training from a second class to an upper second class degree. Similarly, Abel has shown that the pass rate in Law Society exams goes up when there is a shortage of jobs, and down when there is a shortage of recruits.

▶ Moves towards fusion?

The divided legal profession dates from the nineteenth century, when the Bar agreed to give all conveyancing work and all direct access to clients to the solicitors, in return for sole rights of audience in the higher courts and the sole rights to become senior judges for barristers. However, since the late 1960s, there have been a series of moves towards breaking down the division.

1969. In its submission to the Royal Commission on Assizes and Quarter Sessions, the Law Society argued for rights of audience in the Crown Court, but the Commission's report (the Beeching report) recommended only that solicitors should be allowed to advocate in areas where there were insufficient numbers of barristers. The Lord Chancellor was given powers to allow solicitors extended rights of audience in such circumstances.

1972. A Practice Direction from the Lord Chancellor's Department stated that solicitors could appear in appeals or committals for sentencing from the magistrates' to the Crown Court, where they had appeared for that client in the magistrates' court.

1979. The Law Society lobbied the Royal Commission on Legal Services for Crown Court rights of audience in either way offences, and for limited rights in the High Court. The Bar Council opposed the proposals, and the Commission recommended no change in rights of audience – though its decision was made only by an eight to seven majority. Complete fusion was unanimously rejected.

1985. In **Abse** *v* **Smith**, the then MP Cyril Smith challenged a judge's ruling that his solicitor could not read out a seven-line statement in the High Court. The judge's ruling was upheld, but later a Practice Direction from the Lord Chancellor's Department permitted solicitors to appear in the Supreme Court in formal or unopposed proceedings, and when judgment is given in open court.

1986. The Law Society document *Lawyers and the Courts: Time for Some Changes* proposed that all lawyers should undergo the same training, work two or three years in 'general practice', and then choose to go on to train as barristers if they wanted to and were competent – rather as doctors choose, after preliminary training, to become GPs or to specialize and train further. While in 'general practice', lawyers would have rights of audience in the lower courts and tribunals; after that three years, they would be under no restrictions other than to act within their competence, and the Bar would therefore become a body of specialist advocates. The Bar Council's response to the document rejected this idea.

In the same year, the Legal Aid Scrutiny Report suggested allowing solicitors to appear for guilty pleas in the Crown Court. It estimated that this would save the Legal Aid fund around £1m a year.

1987. The Government's White Paper on Legal Aid rejected the Scrutiny Report's proposal.

1988. The Marre Committee was set up by the Bar Council and the Law Society to look, among other things, at whether any changes were needed in the structure of the profession. It largely advocated maintaining the status quo, but did recommend that rights of audience in the Crown Court be extended to solicitors recommended by a Rights of Audience Board, and that barristers should be allowed to take instructions directly from professions other than solicitors.

1990. The Courts and Legal Services Act makes the following provisions.
- Direct access to barristers by certain professional clients;
- Access to the higher levels of the judiciary for solicitors;
- Multi-disciplinary partnerships to be allowed, subject to the agreement of the professions' ruling bodies. Traditionally neither solicitors nor barristers were allowed to form partnerships with members of other professions; the Act provides that there should be no legal obstacle to them doing so, but that there was equally nothing to stop the Law Society and/or the Bar Council making their own rules to prevent such partnerships. So far neither branch has relaxed its rules, and multi-disciplinary partnerships are still not allowed – the Bar is particularly opposed to the idea.
- Rights of audience in all courts should be extended to 'suitably qualified' persons, not necessarily barristers or solicitors. The Act does not itself define 'suitably qualified'; applications by professional groups to be recognized as such are considered by the Lord Chancellor's Advisory Committee, and then have to be approved by the Lord Chancellor and four judges. The Act states that the general objective is that there should be a wider choice of people providing legal services, and that rights of audience and litigation should only be determined by reference to education, training and membership of a professional body with an effective set of rules. It is thought that accountants, property surveyors and tax specialists might be some of the groups who could be awarded rights of audience in the courts.

1992. The Committee recommended that experienced solicitors should be given extended rights of audience after a short training course. They would then be given an advocacy certificate, allowing them to appear for either party in the High Court, and for the defence in the Crown Court. The certificate would be renewed each year, providing a specified number of hours had been spent in court. Solicitors holding advocacy certificates would be required to work on an equivalent basis to the Bar's cab rank rule. The recommendations exclude solicitors employed in industry and other organizations, on the grounds that they were not sufficiently independent, and members of the Crown Prosecution Service, partly because its performance suggested it was not ready for added responsibility, and partly to avoid the danger of creating a 'monolithic' state prosecution service taking all prosecution work.

By mid-1995, over 200 solicitors had won rights of audience in the higher courts, and the numbers are steadily growing. However, winning rights of audience has been one thing; winning acceptance quite another. In one case, when an unrepresented defendant appeared at Sheffield Crown Court, the circuit judge attempted to find counsel to take on the case, but on being informed that a solicitor advocate was present in court, commented 'We don't need to stoop that low, do we?' After a complaint to the presiding circuit judge, he apologized in open court. Some solicitors who have gained rights of audience have said they are unwilling to use them, particularly in the High Court, for fear that judges' prejudice against solicitor advocates may prejudice the chances of the clients they represent.

The future

Not surprisingly, these moves, particularly the changes made by the Courts and Legal Services Act, have led to much discussion about whether the professions will eventually fuse. In the first place, there are suggestions that the Act may be the first step in Government plans to fuse the professions by legislation. Until 1985, the two professions had been largely left alone to carve up access to clients between themselves – as we have seen, the original division was created by the professions themselves, not imposed upon them by Government. The removal of solicitors' exclusive rights to conveyancing was the first major Government interference in the autonomy of the professions, and the Courts and Legal Services Act has been seen as a further step towards regulation by Government rather than the professions themselves.

It has also been suggested that fusion may occur without Government intervention if large numbers of solicitors take up extended rights of audience, because the Bar could simply be squeezed out of business. Solicitors still have exclusive rights to initial contact with most clients, and therefore those who gain advocacy certificates will have the choice of whether or not to pass them on to a barrister, or do all the work on a case themselves.

Even if fusion does not occur, clearly the changes in rights of audience will have an impact on the structure of the profession, and if the Bar does survive it may well be in a shrunken form. There is some debate however, about which areas of the Bar would be worst hit. At the moment, barristers largely fall into two groups: those who specialize in commercial fields, such as company law, tax and patents; and those who have what is called a general common law practice, which means that they deal with a fairly wide range of common legal issues, such as crime, housing and family law.

It has been argued that the specialist commercial lawyers will survive, because they have a specialist knowledge that solicitors cannot provide. However, the major city solicitor firms are already tending to specialize more themselves, and if they begin to combine specialized advice with rights of audience, the commercial Bar will clearly be threatened. In addition, these city firms can offer high incomes, and are therefore able to recruit first-rate students who in the past had been attracted to the more prestigious Bar. As these high-fliers filter through to higher levels within firms, the Bar's traditional claims of expertise at the highest levels of legal analysis will be difficult to sustain.

The chances for common law barristers look more promising. They cater for the needs of the high street solicitor, who is likely to have a wide-ranging practice. Much of their time will be taken up with seeing clients and gathering information about their case, leaving little opportunity to swot up on the finer details of every area of the law with which clients need help; so where specialist legal analysis is needed, they refer the client to a barrister experienced in that particular area. Even if such solicitors do take up the opportunity to advocate in the higher courts – most already do a fair amount in the magistrates' and county courts – they are still likely to use barristers to advocate in cases where detailed legal argument, and so specialized knowledge, are required. In addition to advocacy, high street solicitors often use common law barristers as a source of specialized legal advice, and there seems to be no reason why extending rights of audience should alter this practice.

It has also been suggested that if the rules on multi-disciplinary practices were relaxed with regard to the Bar, many young barristers would be tempted to join solicitors' firms, rather than struggle to establish a sole practice, and that this movement could also lead to the demise or shrinkage of the Bar in its present form.

Arguments against two professions

Expense
With the divided profession a client often has to pay both a solicitor and a barrister, sometimes a solicitor and two barristers, and as Michael Zander puts it 'To have one taxi meter running is less expensive than to have two or three'. The 1986 Legal Aid Scrutiny Report suggested that extending solicitors' rights of audience to guilty pleas alone in the Crown Court would have saved the Legal Aid fund around £1m a year at that time.

Inefficiency
A two-tier system means work may be duplicated unnecessarily, and the solicitor prepares the case with little or no input from the barrister who will have to argue it in court. Barristers are often selected and instructed at the last moment – research by Bottoms and McLean in Sheffield revealed that in 96 per cent of cases where the plea was guilty, and 79 per cent where it was not guilty, clients saw their barrister for the first time on the morning of the trial. In this situation important points may be passed over or misunderstood.

Waste of talent
Prospective lawyers must decide very early on which branch of the profession they wish to enter, and if, having chosen to be a solicitor, the lawyer later discovers a talent for advocacy, they may be denied the chance to use it to the full.

Other countries
All common law countries have bodies of specialist advocates, and possibly need them, but no other country divides its legal profession in two as England does.

Arguments for two professions

Specialization
Two professions can each do their different jobs better than one profession doing both.

Independence
The Bar has traditionally argued that its cab rank principle guarantees this, ensuring that no defendant, however heinous the charges, goes undefended; and that no individual should lack representation because of the wealth or power of the opponent. The fact that barristers operate independently, rather than in partnerships, also contributes. However, the Courts and Legal Services Act does provide for solicitors with advocacy certificates to operate on a cab rank basis, which has somewhat weakened the Bar's argument. In addition, successful barristers do get round the cab rank rule in practice.

Importance of good advocacy
Our adversarial system means that the presentation of oral evidence is important; judges have no investigative powers and must rely on the lawyers to present the case properly.

The 1979 Royal Commission suggested that fusion would lead to a fall in the quality of the advocacy, arguing that although many solicitors were competent to advocate in the magistrates' and county courts, arguing before a jury required different skills and greater expertise, and if rights were extended it was unlikely that many solicitors would get sufficient practice to develop these.

The Bar Council's submission to the Lord Chancellor's Advisory Committee recommended that solicitors would need several months of training to appear in the Crown Court; this too was rejected.

Access to the Bar
Critics of moves towards fusion argued that it may lead to many leading barristers joining the large firms of commercial solicitors, so making their

specialist skills less accessible to the average person. Smaller practices might generate insufficient business to justify partnership with a barrister and find it difficult to secure a barrister of equal standing to the opponent's; they would be reluctant to refer a client to a large firm, for fear of losing them permanently. A major drift towards large firms could worsen the already uneven distribution of solicitors throughout the country.

The judiciary
A reduction in the number of specialist advocates might make it more difficult for the Lord Chancellor to make suitable appointments to the Bench; although the political candidates would increase, they would not be as well known to the Lord Chancellor and his senior advisers. On the other hand this might eventually mean appointments would have to be made on a more open, regulated system, and from a wider social base.

Use of court time
Cases are not given a fixed time, only a date; depending on the progress of previous cases they may appear at any time during a morning or afternoon session, or be held over until another day – the idea behind this is that the clients and their lawyers should wait for courts, rather than the other way round. It has been suggested that barristers are best organized for this, though there seems no reason why, within a united profession, those lawyers who specialize in court work could not organize themselves accordingly.

▶ Other proposals for reform

Wider opportunities

The Charter 88 constitutional reform pressure group has argued that students should be funded throughout their legal training, so helping to open up the profession to the most able candidates, from a wide variety of backgrounds, regardless of means.

The Law Society and the Bar have established a working group studying funding pressures, and representations have been made to the Department of Education, pointing out that training for other professions such as medicine and teaching is paid, and that limiting funding is likely to further narrow the social background of the profession, but so far with no success. One interesting way round the problem is the four-year law degree offered by the University of Northumbria, which incorporates the Legal Practice course within it; as an undergraduate course, it is eligible for the mandatory grant. However the Law Society do not see widespread adoption of this plan as either likely, or an adequate answer to the problem.

In 1995, a Bar working party recommended introducing a 'clearing house' scheme for pupillage applications, which would work rather like that for university applications. All applicants would fill in one form, nominating the chambers in which they would like to work; the form would be designed so that the applicant's name could be detached before the application was considered, so increasing neutrality. However, selection criteria would still be for individual chambers to decide.

Helena Kennedy QC argues that selection for the Bar in particular has always been based too much on 'connections' and financial resources rather than on ability, with both pupillages and scholarships too often given to a narrow class of applicant. As well as recommending public funding for legal education, she suggests that grants for pupillage should be centrally distributed by the Bar, rather than the Inns and chambers, and there should be incentives for chambers to take on less conventional candidates. Selection and scholarship-awarding committees throughout both professions should include women and members of the ethnic minorities. Kennedy also argues that 'ridiculous' practices such as compulsory dining reinforce the middle-class, public school ethos of the bar, and should be abolished.

Better training

Michael Zander argues that both the academic and the vocational stages of training could be improved, with a consequent rise in professional standards. Law degrees should include at least preliminary practical training in areas such as drafting documents and developing interviewing skills. Both pupillage and articles can be 'infinitely variable' in quality, according to Zander, 'ranging from excellent to deplorable' depending on where they are undertaken. He suggests a more integrated training is needed, like that undertaken by medical students, with better links between academic and vocational stages, and cites the Ormrod Committee's suggestion that articles be abolished and replaced with a fully developed practical skills course, followed by three years' supervised practice after qualification.

The Law Society has suggested a form of 'general practice' training (see p. 112).

▶ Other legal personnel

Legal executives

Most firms of solicitors employ legal executives, who do much of the same basic work as solicitors (except advocacy). Their qualifications are supervised by the Institute of Legal Executives, and although technically they are under the supervision of their employers, in practice many experienced executives specialize in particular areas – such as conveyancing – and take almost sole charge of that area. From the firm's point of view, they are obviously a cheaper option than solicitors for getting this work done, and in many cases will be more experienced in their particular area than a solicitor; however, clients are usually unaware that when they pay for a solicitor, they may be receiving the services of a legal executive.

ANSWERING QUESTIONS

1 Do you consider that the current system of legal education and training can provide the lawyers that this country needs?
The first thing to note about this question is that it is not asking what the present system of legal eduction and training is; it wants to know how well that system performs. You do need to show that you are aware of the system, but a detailed description of it will waste time and gain few marks.

Your introduction should point out what you understand by the term lawyers – we suggest that you concentrate on barristers and solicitors in your answer, even though technically judges are also lawyers. Then you need to state what you think are the qualities this country needs in its lawyers – you might mention legal knowledge and practical skills, efficiency, cost-effectiveness, and an ability to use its skills for the benefit of all the members of society, for example.

You can then go on to outline the system of legal education and training but **keep it brief**! There is no point in writing pages of detailed description, because that is not what the question asks for. You need to point out that training for barristers and solicitors is different, and then just mention the stages for each.

The main part of your essay should be concerned with assessing whether the system provides the qualities you have mentioned in your introduction, and we suggest you consider them in turn. The following are points you might like to make:

- the need for legal knowledge and practical skills. You could mention the criticisms made by the 1993 Royal Commission and the studies by Berlins and Joseph, and point out that both professions are moving towards a more practical approach.
- the need for a cost-effective, efficient service. Here you might mention some of the disadvantages of the fact that we train two different types of lawyers to play two different roles – the criticisms of the divided profession in terms of cost and inefficiency are relevant here. You could also put forward the argument that a divided profession is wasteful of talent, especially as it divides so early on.

- the need for lawyers to be accessible to all members of the community. Here you will need to use some of the material on unmet legal need from chapter 8, pointing out that the middle-class image of solicitors puts many people off using them, especially for problems such as social security and employment. You can then point out that the system of training contributes directly to this problem, because it is so difficult for a student without well-off parents to survive financially during training, and so the profession continues its middle-class base.

You might want to bring in the issue of whether we need professional lawyers at all, mentioning the work done by unqualified legal advisers in agencies such as the Citizens Advice Bureaux. You could also discuss here the market control theory which suggests that professions exist not to provide the best services, but as a way of controlling competition – so the emphasis on high academic qualifications can be seen as a way of limiting entry to the market.

It would be a good idea to point out that one of the reasons why this question is so important is that legal education and training provides not only lawyers, but eventually the judiciary – point out for example, that only when the legal profession becomes more mixed in terms of race, class and sex will the judiciary follow suit.

If you have time, you could include any reforms which you feel would improve legal education and training.

Your conclusion should sum up whether you feel legal education does provide the lawyers we need. You might point that the Courts and Legal Services Act sets up a Lord Chancellor's advisory committee which can advise on legal training, so we may see more changes in the future.

2 **How far do the provisions of the Courts and the Legal Services Act 1990 answer the criticisms that have been made of the legal profession in recent years?** *WJEC*

You could begin your answer to this question by outlining the provisions of the CLSA as regards the legal professions: the extension of rights of audience, the relaxing of the rules on multi-disciplinary partnerships, and the changes in jurisdiction of the civil courts (see p. 268). Do not spend too long on this – the question asks you to analyse the results of the Act, so mere description of what it does will only count for a limited number of marks.

You can then discuss the criticisms which have been made of the legal profession: the comments about the class, race and sex of those who enter it; the criticisms of their performance; and the problems of cost and inefficiency associated with a divided profession. Then go on to look at how far the CLSA reforms have addressed these problems – you might mention, for example, that if the CLSA reforms are seen as making fusion more likely, this may reduce the problems associated with a divided profession, and that greater competition, as a result of wider rights of audience, might be seen as potentially improving performance. You should also point out where the CLSA seems to have failed to address the criticisms – it appears to offer little to widen access of candidates to the professions for example. You could then highlight some reforms which you feel would address these criticisms – some suggestions are made in the section on possible reforms in this chapter.

5 The jury system

The jury system

History

The jury system was imported to Britain after the Norman conquest, though its early functions were quite different from those it fulfils today. The first jurors acted as witnesses, providing information about local matters, and were largely used for administrative business – gathering information for the Domesday Book for example. Later, under Henry II, the jury began to take on an important judicial function, moving from reporting on events they knew about, to deliberating on evidence produced by the parties involved in a dispute. Gradually it became accepted that a juror should know as little as possible about the facts of the case before the trial, and this is the case today.

A major milestone in the history of the jury was in the case of **Bushell** (1670). Before this, judges would try to bully juries into convicting the defendant, particularly where the crime had political overtones, but in *Bushell's Case* it was established that the jury were the sole judges of fact, with the right to give a verdict according to their conscience, and could not be penalized for taking a view of the facts opposed to that of the judge. The importance of this power now is that juries may acquit a defendant, even when the law demands a guilty verdict.

Today the jury is considered a fundamental part of the English legal system, though as we shall see, only a minority of cases are tried by jury. The main Act that now governs jury trial is the Juries Act 1974.

The function of the jury

The jury have to weigh up the evidence and decide what are the true facts of the case – what actually happened. The judge directs them as to what is the relevant law, and the jury then have to apply the facts to that law and thereby reach a verdict. If it is a criminal case and the jury have given a verdict of guilty, the judge will then decide on the appropriate sentence. In civil cases the jury decide on how much money should be awarded in damages.

122

▶ When are juries used?

Criminal cases

All cases tried in the Crown Court at first instance have to be tried by a jury. In theory, juries are used for the most important criminal cases – indictable offences and either-way offences when tried in the Crown Court (see p. 220). Yet some serious offences, such as assaulting a police officer or drink-driving are summary only, while even the most trivial theft may be tried by a jury if the defendant so wishes. The Government attempted to deal with this situation in the Criminal Law Bill 1977, with a proposal that thefts involving property worth less than £20 should be summary offences, but this was roundly defeated in Parliament. As it was accepted in the same Bill that criminal damage worth less than £2,000 should be summary only, the reasoning seems to be that any offence that reflects upon a person's honesty should be treated as serious, regardless of the financial value. The 1977 Criminal Law Act also made most driving offences summarily triable only and reflected a move to take more cases away from jury trials.

Despite the symbolic importance of juries in the criminal justice system, they actually decide a tiny minority of cases. Only about 5 per cent of criminal cases are tried in the Crown Court, and in 1993 65 per cent of these defendants pleaded guilty. In some of the remaining cases the judge will have directed an acquittal, or there will have been a change of plea. Jury verdicts therefore account for only around one per cent of criminal cases, some 30,000 cases.

Civil cases

In the past most civil cases were tried by juries, but trial by jury in the civil system is now almost obsolete. The erosion of the use of juries in civil cases was very gradual and appears to have started in the middle of the nineteenth century, when judges were given the right, in certain situations, to refuse to let a case be heard before a jury and insist that it be heard in front of a sole judge instead. Now less than one per cent of civil cases are tried by a jury. Today the Supreme Court Act 1981 gives a qualified right to jury trial of civil cases in four types of cases:

- libel and slander;
- malicious prosecution;
- false imprisonment;
- fraud.

In these cases jury trial is to be granted, unless the court is of the opinion that the trial requires any prolonged examination of documents or accounts, or any scientific or local investigation which cannot conveniently be made with a jury. This right is exercised most frequently in defamation actions.

In all other cases the right to jury trial is at the discretion of the court. In **Ward** *v* **James** (1966) the Court of Appeal stated that in personal injury cases (which constitute the majority of civil actions), trial should be by judge alone unless there were special considerations. In **Singh** *v* **London Underground** (1990) an application for trial by jury of a personal injury claim arising from the King's Cross underground fire of November 1987 was refused on the ground that a case involving such wide issues and technical topics was unsuitable for a jury.

There has been criticism of the distinction drawn between the four types of case which carry a qualified right to trial by jury and other civil cases. The Faulks Committee on Defamation 1975 rejected arguments for the complete abolition of juries in defamation cases, but recommended that in such cases the court should have the same discretion to order jury trial as it does in other civil cases, and that the function of the jury should be limited to deciding issues of liability, leaving the assessment of damages to the judge.

▶ Qualifications for jury service

Before 1972, only those who owned a home which was over a prescribed rateable value were eligible for jury service. The Morris Committee in 1965 estimated that 78 per cent of the names on the electoral register did not qualify for jury service under this criteria, and 95 per cent of women were ineligible. This was either because they lived in rented accommodation or because they were wives or other relatives of the person in whose name the property was held. The Committee recommended that the right to do jury service should correspond with the right to vote. This reform was introduced by the Criminal Justice Act 1972 and the relevant law can now be found in the Juries Act 1974 (as amended). This Act now provides that potential jury members must be:

- aged 18 to 70;
- on the electoral register; and
- resident in the UK, Channel Islands or Isle of Man for at least five years since the age of 13.

From this group, certain categories are excluded or excused.

Disqualification

People who have been sentenced to prison or a young offenders' institute or its equivalent may be disqualified from jury service, depending on how long the sentence was for and how recently it was made. Someone who has received a sentence of probation, for example, is disqualified for ten years.

Ineligibility

Five categories of people are ineligible for jury service:

1 the judiciary.
2 those concerned with the administration of justice, such as barristers, solicitors, prison officers, and police officers and even secretaries working for the Crown Prosecution Service.
3 the clergy. The Runciman Commission saw no logical reason for the existence of this exception and recommended its abolition.
4 people with mental ill health.
5 people on bail in criminal proceedings. This disqualification was introduced by s. 40 of the Criminal Justice and Public Order Act 1994 following a recommendation made by the Runciman Commission.

Excusal as of right

People who have duties that are considered more important than jury service may choose whether or not they wish to serve. These include MPs, members of the House of Lords, members of the armed forces and doctors and nurses. People over 65 can also be excused as of right. Following an extension of the law by s. 42 of the Criminal Justice and Public Order Act 1994 practising members of a religious society or order whose beliefs are incompatible with jury service are excused from performing such service.

Discretionary excusal

Others may be excused at the discretion of the judge if they show good reason, such as childcare problems, holidays booked which would clash with the jury service, personal involvement with the facts of the case, or conscientious objection. Where appropriate jury service may be deferred rather than excused completely.

Discharge

Where there is some doubt about a potential juror's capacity to serve – because of deafness, language problems or infirmity for example – the judge will decide whether to discharge the person concerned. Section 41 of the Criminal Justice and Public Order Act 1994 provides that the judge can discharge a juror if, in his or her opinion, the person is incapable of acting effectively as a juror on account of a physical disability.

▶ Summoning the jury

Computers are used to produce a random list of potential jurors from the electoral register. Summons are sent out (with a form to return confirming that the person does not fall into any of the disqualified or ineligible groups), and from the resulting list the jury panel is produced. This is made public for both sides in forthcoming cases to inspect, though only names and addresses are shown (before 1977 the occupation of the juror was also stated). It is at this stage that jury vetting may take place (see below). Jurors also receive a set of notes which explain a little of the procedure of the jury service and the functions of the juror.

Jury service is compulsory for all those not disqualified, ineligible or excused, and failure to attend on the specified date, or unfitness for service through drink or drugs is contempt of court and can result in a fine.

The jury for a particular case is chosen by random ballot in open court – the clerk has each panel member's name on a card, the cards are shuffled and the first twelve names called out. Unless there are any challenges (see p. 127), these twelve people will be sworn in. In a criminal case there are usually twelve jurors and there must never be fewer than nine. In civil cases in the county court there are eight jurors.

▶ Jury vetting

Jury vetting consists of checking that the potential juror does not hold 'extremist' views which some feel would make them unsuitable for hearing a case. It is done by checking police, Special Branch and security service records.

This controversial practice first came to light in the 1978 'ABC Trial', in which two journalists and a soldier were accused of collecting secret information, in breach of the Official Secrets Act. During the trial it became known that the jury had been vetted to check their 'loyalty', under guidelines laid down by the Attorney-General, and a new trial was ordered.

The ensuing publicity eventually led to the publication of the Attorney-General's guidelines, which it was admitted had been in use since 1974. These guidelines were revised in 1988. They confirm that as a rule, juries should be chosen at random, with people being excluded only under the statutory exceptions, and that the proper way for the prosecution to exclude a juror was challenge for cause in open court (see below). But it was also stated that vetting might be necessary in certain special cases: those involving terrorism, where it was felt a juror's political beliefs might prevent him or her being impartial or lead to undue pressure on other jurors; and those concerning national security, where in addition to the problem of strong political beliefs there was the danger that some jurors might reveal evidence given in camera (i.e. heard in private and not in open court). Jurors could only be 'stood by' (see below) if the vetting revealed a very strong reason for doing so. In order to vet a jury in these cases authorization from the Attorney-General is required, who will be acting on the advice of the Director of Public Prosecutions. Checking whether a person has a criminal record is permissible in a much wider range of cases without special permission.

The legality of vetting was considered by the Court of Appeal in two cases during 1980. In **R *v* Sheffield Crown Court ex parte Brownlow**, the defendants were police officers, and the defence wanted the jury vetted for previous convictions. The prosecution opposed it, but the Crown Court judge ordered that vetting should take place, and this decision was upheld by the Court of Appeal. Lords Denning and Shaw, *obiter dicta*, vigorously condemned vetting in security and terrorist cases as unconstitutional (because it was not provided for in the Juries Act 1974), and an invasion of privacy.

In **R *v* Mason** (1980), a convicted burglar appealed on the grounds that the jury had been vetted for previous convictions, a common practice in the particular court at the time. The Court of Appeal decreed that vetting for previous convictions was necessary in order to ensure that disqualified persons could not serve. In such situations Lord Lawton described vetting as 'just common sense', though it should not be used to gain tactical advantage in minor cases.

Although vetting for previous convictions has clearly been accepted by the courts, vetting for other purposes has only been considered *obiter*, and all vetting remains controversial. Supporters claim that it can promote impartiality by excluding those whose views might bias the other members of the jury, and make them put pressure on others, as well as protecting national security and preventing disqualified persons from serving. Opponents say it infringes the individual's right to privacy, and gives the prosecution an unfair advantage, since it is too expensive for most defendants to undertake, and they do not have access to the same sources of information as the prosecution. Only on very rare occasions has the defence been granted legal aid to make its inquiries into the panel.

The whole process is still not sanctioned by legislation, and despite the publication of the Attorney-General's guidelines, it is impossible to know whether they are being followed – 60 potential jurors were vetted by MI5 for the Clive Ponting case, despite the fact that there was no apparent threat to national security.

Challenges

As members of the jury panel are called, and before they are sworn in, they may be challenged in one of two ways:

Challenge for cause. Either side may challenge for cause, on the grounds of privilege of peerage, disqualification, ineligibility or assumed bias. Jurors cannot be questioned before being challenged to ascertain whether there are grounds for a challenge. A successful challenge for cause is therefore only likely to succeed if the juror is personally known, or if jury vetting has been undertaken. If a challenge for cause is made it is tried by the trial judge.

Stand by. Only the prosecution may ask jurors to stand by for the Crown. Although there are specified grounds for this, in practice no reason need be given, and this is generally how jury vetting is used. The use of the power to stand by has been limited by guidelines issued by the Attorney-General which specifically state that the abolition of the peremptory challenge (see below) means that the power to stand by should only be used in connection with jury vetting or where the juror is manifestly unsuitable and the defence agrees with the exercise of the power.

In addition, the judge may discharge any juror, or even the whole jury, to prevent scandal or the perversion of justice. In one case the fact that a juror was giving the accused a lift in his car to the court each morning was found to be a reason to discharge that juror. In **Bansal** (1985) a case involved an Anti-National-Front demonstration and the trial judge ordered that the jury should be drawn from an area with a large Asian population. However this approach was rejected as wrong in **R** *v* **Ford** (1989). The Court of Appeal held that race could not be taken into account when selecting jurors, and that a judge could not discharge jurors in order to achieve a racially representative jury.

Until 1988 there was a third type of challenge, peremptory challenge, available only to the defence. This meant that the defence could challenge up to three jurors without showing cause, which was equivalent to the prosecution's power to 'stand by' a juror. This was abolished, amid much opposition, on the recommendation of the Roskill Committee on fraud trials, on the grounds that it interfered with the random selection process and allowed defence lawyers to 'pack' the jury with those they thought were likely to be sympathetic. This was felt to be a particular problem when there were several defendants as (theoretically) they could combine their rights to peremptory challenge.

This limited process of challenging the jury should be contrasted with the system in the USA where it can take days to empanel a jury, particularly where the case has received a lot of pre-trial media coverage.

▶ Are juries representative?

The basis of the use of juries in serious criminal cases is that the twelve people are randomly selected, and should therefore comprise a representative sample of the population as a whole. This ideal is closer with the abolition of the property qualification and with the use of computers for the random selection process. Before computers were used an official would pick out names from the electoral list. Research by Baldwin and McConville (*Jury Trials* 1979) suggested that this could lead to discrimination. They found that only 1 per cent of jurors in Birmingham at the time were of Asian or West Indian origin, and 3.6 per cent were of Irish origin while their proportion in the population as a whole was 12 per cent and 10 per cent respectively. This could only partly be explained by language difficulties. They also found that there was a lack of women on the juries. This may be partly accounted for by excusal due to childcare problems, and to the local practice, now discontinued, of summoning twice as many men as women.

In fact, random selection may make a jury less likely to be representative – if, for example, many women are found to be excused through childcare difficulties, summoning twice as many women as men might be a better way to achieve a representative section of the community.

Since Baldwin and McConville's research the gender and racial balance appears to have improved. Research carried out by Zander and Henderson 1993 found that women were only slightly under represented and that non-white jurors constituted 5 per cent of jurors while they made up 5.9 per cent of the national population.

While this is encouraging it has been argued by the Commission for Racial Equality that consideration needs to be given to the racial balance in particular cases. They suggest that where a case has a racial dimension and the defendant reasonably believes that he or she cannot receive a fair trial from an all white jury, then the judge should have the power to order that three of the jurors come from the same ethnic minority as the defendant or the victim. The Runciman Commission gave their endorsement to this proposal.

The Society of Black Lawyers had, in addition, submitted to the Runciman Commission that there should always be a right to a multiracial trial, that peremptory challenges should be reinstated and that certain cases with a black defendant should be tried by courts in areas with high black populations, and panels of black jurors who would be available at short notice should be set up.

One of the problems with the recent Rodney King case in Los Angeles, where a policeman was found not guilty of assaulting a black motorist despite a videotape of the incident showing brutal conduct, was that the case was tried in an area with a very high white population, while the incident itself had occurred in an area with a high black population. However, the decision in **R** *v* **Ford** (1989), that there is no principle that a jury should be racially balanced, still holds.

Peremptory challenge was abolished because it was said to have interfered with the principle of random selection, especially in multi-defendant trials. However, Vennard and Riley's study found that the peremptory challenge was only used in 22 per cent of cases, with no evidence of widespread pooling of challenges, and research for the Crown Prosecution Service in 1987 showed that the use of peremptory challenge had no significant effect on the rate of acquittals.

Peremptory challenge could in fact be used to make juries more balanced in terms of race and sex, and it seems rather unjust that while the defence have had their right to a peremptory challenge removed, the prosecution is still allowed to stand by for the Crown.

A further problem in recent years has been the number of people who have kept their names off the Electoral Register in order to avoid paying the Poll Tax – 1.8 million people have disappeared from the Register since the Poll Tax was established. It remains to be seen whether numbers will go back to normal now that the rating system has been changed.

As Smith and Bailey (1988) point out, the rules of disqualification, ineligibility and excusal as of right and the use of jury vetting mean that a number of people are excluded who might make very good jurors, and these exclusions mean that juries cannot be said to be representative of society as a whole. However, they conclude that the requirement that jurors should be competent to serve outweighs the importance of random selection.

▶ The secrecy of the jury

Once they retire to consider their verdict, jurors are not allowed to communicate with anyone other than the judge and an assigned court official, until after the verdict is delivered. Afterwards they are forbidden by the Contempt of Court Act 1981 from revealing anything that was said or done during their deliberations.

The arguments in favour of secrecy have been stated by Mr Justice McHugh as:

- It ensures freedom of discussion in the jury room;
- It protects jurors from outside influences, and from harassment;
- If the public knew how juries reached their verdict they might respect the decision less;
- Without it citizens would be reluctant to serve as jurors;
- It ensures the finality of the verdict;
- It enables jurors to bring in unpopular verdicts;
- It prevents unreliable disclosures by jurors and misunderstanding of verdicts.

The arguments against secrecy and in favour of disclosure have been stated by the same author as:

- making juries more accountable;
- making it easier to enquire into the reliability of convictions and rectify injustices;
- showing where reform is required;
- educating the public;
- ensuring each juror's freedom of expression.

Research into the work of juries has always been made difficult by the requirement for secrecy. The Runciman Commission has recommended that the Contempt of Court Act 1981 should be amended so that valid research can be carried out into the way juries reach their verdicts.

▶ The verdict

Ideally juries should produce a unanimous verdict, but in 1967 majority verdicts were introduced of ten to two (or nine to one if the jury has been reduced during the trial). This is now provided for in the Juries Act 1974. When the jury withdraw to consider their verdict they must be told by the judge to reach a unanimous verdict. If, however, the jury have failed to reach a unanimous verdict after what the judge considers a reasonable period of deliberation, given the complexity of the case (not less than two hours), the judge can direct them that they may reach a majority verdict. The foreman of the jury must state in open court the numbers of the jurors agreeing and disagreeing with the verdict. Majority verdicts were intended to help prevent jury 'nobbling' (where someone involved in the trial puts pressure on jurors to vote in a particular way, by bribes or threats). It also avoids the problem of one juror with extreme or intractable views holding out against the rest, and should lessen the need for expensive and time-consuming retrials. However, Brown and Neal's 1988 research found that the introduction of majority verdicts has not substantially affected the number of hung juries and consequent re-trials. Freeman (1981) has suggested that majority verdicts dilute the concept of proof beyond reasonable doubt – on the grounds that if one juror is not satisfied, a doubt must exist – and give less protection against the risk of convicting the innocent. This in turn weakens public confidence in the system.

In Scotland the jury consists of fifteen people and a conviction can be based on a simple majority verdict.

▶ Advantages of the jury system

Antiquity
The jury's pre-eminence in the criminal process goes back to the thirteenth century and our whole adversarial trial system is founded upon it.

Public participation

Juries allow the ordinary citizen to take part in the administration of justice, so that verdicts are seen to be those of society rather than of the judicial system, and satisfies the constitutional tradition of judgment by one's peers. Lord Denning describes jury service as giving 'ordinary folk their finest lesson in citizenship'.

However, Ingman points out despite this symbolic importance of juries, the system remains dominated by judges and magistrates. Only a small proportion of cases are tried by juries, and even in these, judges can exert considerable influence.

Certainty

The jury adds certainty to the law, since it gives a general verdict which cannot give rise to misinterpretation. In a criminal case the jury simply states that the accused is guilty or not guilty, and gives no reasons. Consequently the decision is not open to dispute.

Bastion of liberty against the state

The jury is seen as protecting the citizen against the application of oppressive laws, because it has the right to acquit a defendant according to its conscience, even if the law demands a conviction. A celebrated example of a jury using this power is the Clive Ponting case, where the defendant, a civil servant, had passed to an MP documents relating to the sinking of the Argentinian battleship, the *General Belgrano*, by a British submarine during the Falklands war in 1982. These documents were clearly covered by s. 2 of the Official Secrets Act 1911, and the judge directed the jury that under s. 2 Ponting had no authorization to pass them to someone such as the MP, and no other lawful justification for his act. Nevertheless the jury acquitted.

More recently, in 1991 a jury acquitted two men accused of helping the Soviet agent George Blake to escape from Wormwood Scrubs prison in 1966, even though they had admitted the facts and the judge had directed that they had no defence.

However, today this power is to some extent compromised by the fact that some offences which involve the state are summary offences and therefore never reach a jury. These include some of the charges arising out of demonstrations and strikes, and this gave rise to particular concern during the 1984 miners' strike.

This freedom of the jury can in turn lead to reform. In the early nineteenth century all felonies were in theory punishable by death. One of them was theft of goods or money above the value of one shilling, and pressure on the Government to change the law arose because juries would often avoid the imposition of the death penalty by finding the value of the property to be less than one shilling. More recently the offence of causing death by dangerous driving was created because juries were reluctant to convict motorists of manslaughter.

Lack of viable alternatives

All the possible alternatives to juries throw up problems of their own (see p. 138).

▶ Disadvantages of the jury system

The system no longer needs juries

Trial by jury has been virtually eliminated in civil cases without any harmful effects, and as judges are supposed to be independent of the state and other vested interests, it is suggested that the argument for juries has lost much of its force.

However, it might be argued that the issues at stake in criminal trials make juries desirable, and as we saw when we looked at the judiciary, judges are not quite as independent as they appear.

Jurors lack the requisite skills

Jerome Frank has quoted one juror as saying:

> We couldn't make head or tail of the case or follow all the messing about that the lawyers did. None of us believed the witnesses on either side anyway, so we made up our minds to disregard the evidence on both sides and decide the case on its merits.

Lord Denning argued in *What Next in the Law?* that the selection of jurors is too wide, resulting in jurors that are not competent to perform their task. Praising the 'Golden Age' of jury service when only 'responsible heads of household from a select band of the middle classes' were eligible to serve, he claims that the 1972 changes have led to jurors being summoned who are not sufficiently intelligent or educated to perform their task properly. Denning suggests that jurors should be selected in much the same way as magistrates are, with interviews and references required. This throws up several obvious problems: a more complicated selection process would be more time-consuming and costly; finding sufficient people willing to take part might prove difficult; and a jury that is intelligent and educated can still be biased, and may be more likely to be so if drawn from a narrow social group.

Particular concern has been expressed about the average jury's understanding of complex fraud cases. The Roskill Committee concluded that trial by random jury was not a satisfactory way of achieving justice in such cases, with many jurors 'out of their depth', and Ingman points out that through 'inexperience and ignorance', jurors may rely too heavily on what they are told by the lawyers at the expense of the real issues. However, the Roskill Committee was unable to find accurate evidence of a higher proportion of acquittals in complex fraud cases than in any other kind – much of their conclusions was based on research by Baldwin and McConville, yet none of the questionable acquittals reported there was in a complex fraud case. Smith and Bailey point out that the research on the decision-making abilities of juries suggests that they are capable of coming to reasoned and fair verdicts in even complex cases. Evidence of the police to the Runciman Commission stated that the conviction rates for serious fraud, when compared with the overall conviction rate for cases that are considered by a jury, show that in serious fraud trials the jury are actually convicting a slightly higher percentage.

Smith and Bailey (1992) suggest that lawyers should try harder to simplify matters for the jury, and that judges too could pay more attention to this, rather than concentrating on making their summings-up 'appeal-proof'. Levi (1988) concluded that jury performance would be considerably improved if 'greater care were devoted to the instruction of the jury on points of evidence and of the method to be followed when assessing it'. He suggests that intelligent lay persons are at least as competent as lawyers to decide issues of fairness, reasonableness and dishonesty, and their presence can be an antidote to excessive technicality.

Jury verdicts often go against the evidence, particularly in acquittals

Former Metropolitan Police Commissioner, Sir Robert Mark, is among those who have levelled this accusation against juries, claiming that half the defendants tried by juries are acquitted. The Home Office Research and Planning Unit has suggested that juries are twice as likely as magistrates to acquit.

This is a difficult area to research, as the Contempt of Court Act 1981 prohibits asking jurors about the basis on which they reached their decision. The research generally involves comparing actual jury decisions with those reached by legal professionals, or by shadow juries, who sit in on the case and reach their own decision just as the official jurors are asked to do.

A piece of research commissioned by the Roskill Committee on fraud trials concluded that jurors who found difficulty in comprehending the complex issues involved in fraud prosecution were more likely to acquit. They suggested that the jurors characterized their own confusions as a form of 'reasonable doubt' leading them to a decision to acquit.

A study by McCabe and Purves, *The Jury at Work* (1972) looked at 173 acquittals, and concluded that fifteen (9 per cent) defied the evidence, the rest being attributable to weakness of the prosecution case or failure of their witnesses, or the credibility of the accused's explanation. McCabe and Purves viewed the proportion of apparently perverse verdicts as quite small, and from their observations of shadow juries, concluded that jurors did work methodically and rationally through the evidence, and try to put aside their own prejudices.

However, Baldwin and McConville's 1979 study ('Jury Trials') examined 500 cases, both convictions and acquittals, and found up to 25 per cent of acquittals were questionable (as well as 5 per cent of convictions), and concluded that given the serious nature of the cases concerned, this was a problem. They describe trial by jury as 'an arbitrary and unpredictable business'.

Zander (1988) points out that the high rate of acquittals must be seen in the light of the high number of guilty pleas in the Crown Court – 67 per cent in 1986. It must also be noted that many acquittals are directed or ordered by the judge. According to evidence from the Lord Chancellor's Department to the Runciman Commission in 1990–91 40 per cent of all acquittals were ordered by the judge because the prosecution offered no evidence at the start of the trial. A further 16 per cent of the acquittals were directed by the judge after the prosecution had made their case as there was insufficient evidence to leave to the jury. Thus the jury were only responsible for 41 per cent of the acquittals, which was merely 7 per cent of all cases in the Crown Court. Bearing in mind the pressures on defendants to plead guilty, it is not surprising that those who resist tend to be those with the strongest-sounding cases – and of course the standard of proof required is very high. Nor is it beyond the bounds of possibility that part of the difference in conviction rates between magistrates and juries is due to magistrates convicting the innocent rather than juries acquitting the guilty.

Juries are not sufficiently objective

Ingman suggests that juries may be biased for or against certain groups – for example, they may favour attractive members of the opposite sex, or be prejudiced against the police in cases of malicious prosecution or false imprisonment (and of course, some jurors may also be biased towards the police, and other figures of authority such as customs officers).

Bias appears to be a particular problem in libel cases, where juries prejudiced against newspapers award huge damages, apparently using them punitively rather than as compensation for the victim. Examples include the £500,000 awarded to Jeffrey Archer in 1987, and the £300,000 to Koo Stark a year later, as well as **Sutcliffe** *v* **Pressdram Ltd** (1990), in which *Private Eye* was ordered to pay £600,000 to the wife of the Yorkshire

Ripper. In the latter case Lord Donaldson described the award as irrational, and suggested that judges should give more guidance on the amounts to be awarded – not by referring to previous cases or specific amounts, but by asking juries to think about the real value of money (such as what income the capital would produce, or what could be bought with it).

Jury nobbling

This problem led to the suspension of jury trials for terrorist offences in Northern Ireland, and has caused problems in some English trials. In 1982 several Old Bailey trials had to be stopped because of attempted 'nobbling', one after seven months, and the problem became so serious that juries had to sit out of sight of the public gallery, brown paper was stuck over the windows in court doors, and jurors were warned to avoid local pubs and cafes and eat only in their own canteen. In 1984, jurors in the Brinks-Mat trial had to have police protection to and from the court, and their telephone calls intercepted, while in August 1994 a four-month fraud trial at Southwark Crown Court had to be abandoned after the jury had already delivered their verdict on one of the charges.

A new criminal offence was created under the Criminal Justice and Public Order Act 1994 to try and give additional protection to the jury. This provides under s. 51 that it is an offence to intimidate or threaten to harm, either physically or financially, certain people involved in a trial including jurors. Any offence that would have been committed under common law is still retained.

The Criminal Procedure and Investigation Bill has been prepared and presented in the Queen's speech at the end of 1995. If it becomes law (which is likely to happen in 1996) in its current form it proposes a radical reform. Where a person would have been acquitted of an offence and someone is subsequently convicted of interfering with or intimidating jurors or witnesses in the case then the High Court could quash the acquittal and the person could be retried. This would be a wholly exceptional development in the law as the current position is that an acquittal is sacred. The traditional view is that a retrial after acquittal would be a breach of fundamental human rights. An argument in favour of the change is that it might reduce the chance of jury nobbling taking place in the first place.

Appeal is difficult

When judges sit alone their judgment consists of a detailed and explicit finding of fact. When there is a jury it returns an unexplained verdict which simply finds in favour of one party or another. The former is more easily reviewed by appellate courts because the findings and the inferences of the trial judge can be examined. But when the appellate court is faced with a jury's verdict, it must support that verdict if there is any reasonable view of the evidence which leads to it.

Compulsory jury service

Jury service is often unpopular but a refusal to act as juror amounts to a contempt of court. Resentful jurors might make unsatisfactory decisions; in particular, jurors keen to get away as soon as possible are likely to simply go along with what the majority say, whether they agree or not.

Excessive damages

In the past juries in civil cases have awarded very high damages. The Court of Appeal now has the power either to order a new trial on the ground that damages awarded by a jury are excessive or, without the agreement of the parties, to substitute for the sum awarded by the jury such sum as appears to the court to be proper.

Cost and time

While a contested case in a magistrates' court costs around £1,500 and an uncontested case around £500, the equivalent figures for the Crown Court are £13,500 and £2,500.

The jury process is time-consuming for all involved, with juries spending much of their time waiting around to be summoned into court.

According to Lord Denning, some accused people, who qualify for legal aid, exploit the delay arising from opting for jury trial. This can give them many months to dispose of any assets before they are convicted, while the prosecution witnesses' recollection of the relevant events will be weaker. As Denning points out, the delay benefits lawyers too, at the expense of taxpayers. On the other hand, for many of those accused – especially those held on remand – the delay is far from an advantage.

Distress to jury members

Juries trying cases involving serious crimes of violence, particularly rape, murder or child abuse, may have to listen to deeply distressing evidence, and in some cases, to inspect graphic photographs of injuries. This can be extremely upsetting, a fact that was recognized by the criminal justice system in the 1995 trial of serial killer Rosemary West, where jury members were offered professional counselling to help them cope with what they heard and saw during the trial.

For further criticism see also the notes on jury vetting, the non-representative nature of juries, and the termination of peremptory challenges. The material on mode of trial discussed at p. 220 is also relevant.

▶ Replacing the jury

The single judge

This would save time at trial, through not having to explain so many matters to the jury, and reduce the likelihood of verdicts not in accordance with the law. In theory it should also lessen the risk of bias or outside influence – the problem of jury nobbling in Northern Ireland has led to single judges sitting in certain cases, on the recommendation of the Diplock report.

The disadvantages of this option include the lack of community participation, the loss of independence and impartiality of the jury, and the possibility that judges sitting alone would become case-hardened or prosecution-minded. Further, there would be little protection against individual prejudices, and decisions on guilt being taken by one person might be too heavy a burden.

A bench of judges

This could consist of three or five judges, to give a more balanced view. However it would be expensive and there might be problems in recruiting the required number of judges. The nature of the judiciary would be transformed, and it is alleged that a considerable increase in the number of judges would weaken the bench. There would be important implications for the legal profession if a career judiciary became necessary.

The composite tribunal

Some European jurisdictions, especially in the Scandinavian countries, rely heavily on the composite tribunal of lay people and judge, and in this country, a Crown Court judge sits with two lay magistrates on certain appeals from the magistrates' court. Replacing juries with this system would probably mean speedier trials, because the judge would be involved in all discussion, and community participation would be maintained because the lay people involved would be able to outvote the judge.

The Roskill Committee on fraud trials recommended (although there was a dissenting minority) that such a tribunal be established to deal with complex fraud cases, but the government has decided not to implement this proposal.

Possible disadvantages of this scheme might include the judge having too great a say, and the need to train lay people, which could mean that they would no longer be representative of the community.

The special jury

A jury would be selected from non-lawyers and would be trained for the jury service. This would ensure that jurors were capable of doing the job assigned to them, but would lose the benefits of random selection. Though some lay participation would be maintained, the people involved would very probably be drawn from a similarly narrow group to that of magistrates, with all the disadvantages that that entails.

Reform of the jury system

Since none of the alternatives offer the perfect solution, could the jury system be altered to meet some of the criticisms made of it? Aside from tinkering with the selection process, either along the lines suggested by Lord Denning, or in some other way, more emphasis could certainly be put on ensuring that juries understand court procedure and the evidence presented to them. Some steps towards this have been taken recently, with the production of an explanatory video now being shown to all jurors.

It has been suggested that judges should retire with the jury in order to ensure that the case is judged on the evidence. Although this idea probably gives an undesirable amount of influence to the professional judge, at the expense of the jury's freedom, some purpose might be served by allowing a court official to sit in on the jury's deliberations – not to influence or take part in the verdict, but merely to advise on what is and is not proper for the jury to take into account when making their decision.

Other possibilities for reform include removing the issue of damages from the jury, making more offences summary only, and increasing the financial allowances for jurors so that fewer people find compulsory service a burden.

The 1974 Faulks committee recommended that juries should no longer be available as a right in defamation actions. It found that judges were not as remote from real life as popularly supposed. Judges gave reasons whereas juries did not; juries found complex cases difficult, were unpredictable, and were more expensive as jury trials are more time consuming, as explanations have to be geared for them and not a judge.

The Roskill committee recommended that trial by jury in complex criminal fraud cases should be abolished and replaced by a Fraud Trials Tribunal consisting of a judge and two lay members:

> Out of all the citizens who, in the course of any year, find themselves in difficulties with the law only a small portion will be tried by a jury. The underlying logic of this situation we find puzzling in the extreme. If society believes that trial by jury is the fairest form of trial, is it too costly and troublesome to be universally applied? . . . But if jury trial is not inherently fair, given its extra cost and trouble, what are the merits which justify its retention? Society appears to have an attachment to jury trial which is emotional or sentimental rather than logical.

. . . .
ANSWERING QUESTIONS

The majority of questions on the jury system require roughly the same basic material, and the main focus for all exam boards is a critical appraisal of the advantages and disadvantages of the system. We will look first at the simplest type of essay.

1 **Evaluate the importance of the jury system.** *London*
Your introduction should **briefly** outline what the jury is, what it does and when, and how it is selected. You should then work through the advantages of the jury, pointing out how these make the jury important in the legal system. Follow this with a look at the disadvantages of the system. If you have time, run through the alternatives to juries and state whether (and why) you think any of these could provide a partial or complete replacement for juries.

Since the question asks you to **evaluate** the jury system, you should conclude by saying whether you think the advantages outweigh the disadvantages, and perhaps giving your opinion on whether the jury should be abolished, or still has a valuable role to play. If you feel it should be abolished, you might suggest which of the alternatives should replace it, while if you feel it should be retained, you could point out any reforms that you feel should be made.

2 **'We believe that twelve persons selected at random are likely to be a cross-selection of the people as a whole and thus represent the views of the common man.' (Lord Denning MR in R v Sheffield Crown Court ex parte Brownlow (1980)). Do you consider that this statement justifies the use of juries in criminal cases? Is there any other satisfactory justification?**
Here you first need to discuss to what extent juries are representative, mentioning the limitations on random selection imposed by the rules on eligibility, disqualification, jury vetting and so on, and using the material on the representativeness of juries found on p. 128. Having outlined this you should say whether in your opinion this alone justifies trial by jury in criminal cases, and why, using the material on public participation as an advantage of the jury system (p. 132).

Then move on to the other justifications for jury trials in criminal cases, which are of course the advantages listed on p. 131. You should make it clear whether you feel these are alternative justifications to the principle of representing society, or complementary ones. You can then point out that despite these justifications, there are problems with the jury system, and work through the disadvantages we have listed (remember that this question deals with juries in criminal trials only, and leave out irrelevant material such as the problems with damages for libel). Go through the alternatives to the jury system as well if you have time.

Your conclusion should sum up whether you think that the principle of random selection and representativeness and/or any of the other advantages you have discussed outweigh the disadvantages strongly enough to justify the use of juries in criminal trials. If you conclude that the justifications are not sufficient, you should say what you feel should replace the jury system and why.

3 Bill Sykes is charged with manslaughter.
(a) Explain to him the sequence of events that will occur after he is charged, up to and including his trial.
(b) Critically examine the process of selection of the jury for the trial. *Oxford*
The information for answering part (a) will be found in chapter 9: Criminal justice system. For part (b) you should first of all explain what the process of jury selection is, detailing the qualification for jury service, the process of summoning the jury, jury vetting and challenges. As the question asks you to 'critically examine' this process you also need to highlight the strengths and the weaknesses of this process.

Looking first at the strengths, the main point would be that the process of selection allows ordinary people from throughout the community to take part in the administration of justice and this is seen as promoting fairness and acceptance of the criminal legal process in general – the idea of judgment by one's peers.

As regards the weaknesses of the system, you could mention such issues as the problems associated with jury vetting and challenges and discuss the issue of whether juries are truly representative of the community as a whole, as examined in this chapter.

If you are aiming to revise juries for your exam, you should also be prepared for a combined question on the role of lay people in the English legal system – in recent years examination boards have tended to incorporate the jury within such a question, rather than examining it as a single topic, and if you do not have at least some grasp of this additional material, you run a serious risk of wasting your revision on juries. We consider a question on lay participation in chapter 7.

6 Magistrates

THE MAGISTRATES' COURTS

The magistrates' courts used to be run by the Home Office but this function was given to the Lord Chancellor's Department in 1992. The organization of the magistrates' courts has been reformed recently by the Police and Magistrates' Court Act 1994, amending the Justices of the Peace Act 1979.

The country is divided geographically into 105 commissions which are then subdivided into what are known as petty sessional areas or benches of which there are around 600, though they vary considerably in size. Each petty sessional area has its own courthouse and justices' clerk. In the past the courthouses were essentially run by local committees for each commission area, with a maximum membership of 35 magistrates. But this approach was criticized by a Scrutiny Report carried out for the Home Office in 1989. The study concluded that at the time there was no coherent management structure; the justices' clerks were semi-autonomous but their exact managerial role was not clearly defined; they felt that there was an inadequate link between the distribution of resources and the actual work being carried out; performance and efficiency were not being monitored; and that the service was not giving value for money, with insufficient budgetary control. They pointed to evidence that trials in magistrates' courts were becoming more expensive and that there was a backlog in cases to be heard. They proposed that some of these problems could be remedied by the establishment of a centralized 'Magistrates' Court Agency' which would be responsible for running the magistrates' courts service, and directly answerable to the relevant minister.

These proposals were rejected by the Magistrates' Association, an influential body that represents magistrates. They were anxious to protect the independence of the magistrates and also felt that magistrates should continue to have a role in the administration of the courts. Their criticisms were taken into account when the government drew up its White Paper on the topic and the 1994 Police and Magistrates' Courts Act which followed. The Lord Chancellor has been given the power to reduce the number of Commission areas to about half of their current number

142

in order to streamline the system. Now each commission area is administered by a Magistrates' Courts Committee (MCC). These committees will be much smaller than their predecessors, with a maximum of twelve members of which up to two will not be magistrates. The original proposal was that the chair of the MCC would be a nominee of the Lord Chancellor but this was rejected by Parliament because of the fear that this might expose the committee to political pressure. This body appoints justices' clerks and the other court staff and provides the court rooms, equipment, and training for magistrates under the supervision of the Judicial Studies Board.

Each commission area has a justices' chief executive. Their role is to carry out the day-to-day administration of the commission area. They are appointed by their MCC with the approval of the Lord Chancellor, and have performance-related and fixed-term contracts of employment. They must have the same minimum qualifications as a justices' clerk and can, with the Lord Chancellor's approval, be both a justices' clerk and a justices' chief executive at the same time.

If the MCC is failing in its duties without reasonable cause its members can be removed by the Lord Chancellor and replaced for up to three months with the Lord Chancellor's own appointees.

There are new funding arrangements for the courts. Sixty per cent of their funding is now allocated on the basis of their workload, 25 per cent according to their efficiency in fine enforcement, 10 per cent depends on the time taken to deal with cases and the remaining 5 per cent for 'quality of service'. Performance targets have also been introduced. Both arrangements have led to fears that the independence of the courts is threatened.

The Police and Magistrates' Courts Act 1994 creates a new inspectorate of the magistrates' courts, known as 'Her Majesty's Magistrates' Courts Service Inspectorate'. It will inspect the organization and administration of the courts and report back to the Lord Chancellor. In addition magistrates' courts' accounts can now be reviewed by the Audit Commission. The aim of both these measures is to make the magistrates' service more accountable.

THE JUSTICES OF THE PEACE

▶ History

Like juries, lay magistrates have a long history in the English legal system, dating back to the Justices of the Peace Act 1361, which, probably in response to a crime wave, gave judicial powers to appointed lay people. Their main role then, as now, was dealing with criminals, but they also exercised certain administrative functions, and until the nineteenth century the business of local government was largely entrusted to them. A few of these administrative powers remain today.

There are about 30,000 lay magistrates (also called justices of the peace, or JPs), trying over one million criminal cases a year – 95 per cent of all criminal cases, and 20 times the number in the Crown Courts. They are therefore often described as the backbone of the English criminal justice system.

There are about 100 stipendiary magistrates, who are not lay people, and are paid a salary of almost £60,000. On top of the permanent stipendiaries there are also 'acting' stipendiaries who work part-time usually with a view to establishing their competence in order to get a full-time position in the future. They are appointed by the Queen on the recommendation of the Lord Chancellor, and must have a seven-year general advocacy qualification, meaning that they have had a right of audience in at least the lower courts for a minimum of seven years. They act as sole judge in their particular magistrates' courts, and are mostly to be found in the large cities, and in London in particular where 46 are based. Despite their name, they are really part of the professional judiciary, and most of the comments about magistrates in this chapter do not really apply to them.

▶ Selection and appointment

Lay magistrates are appointed by the Lord Chancellor in the name of the Crown, on the advice of local selection committees (for historical reasons, magistrates in Lancashire, Greater Manchester and Merseyside are appointed by the Chancellor of the Duchy of Lancaster in the name of the Crown).

Members of the local committees are appointed by the Lord Chancellor; they are themselves usually drawn from the magistracy, and the Lord Chancellor is supposed to ensure that they have good local knowledge, and represent a balance of political opinion. Their identity was at one time kept secret, but names are now available to the public.

Candidates are usually put forward to the committee by local political parties, voluntary groups, trade unions and other organizations, though individuals may apply in person. In 1966 Lord Gardiner, then Lord Chancellor, caused a stir by directing local committees to take into consideration the political affiliations of candidates.

The only qualifications laid down for appointment to the magistracy are that the applicants must be under 60 and live within 15 miles of the area for which they are to act (Justices of the Peace Act 1979 s. 7), though these qualifications may be dispensed with if the Lord Chancellor considers it to be in the public interest to do so. In practice they must also be able to devote an average of half a day a week to the task, for which usually only expenses and a small loss of earnings allowance are paid. Legal knowledge or experience is not required; nor is any level of academic qualification.

Certain people are excluded from appointment: police officers, traffic wardens and members of the armed forces; people with certain criminal convictions; undischarged bankrupts; and anyone else whose work is considered incompatible with the duties of a magistrate.

Candidates are interviewed by the committee, who then make a recommendation to the Lord Chancellor; this is usually followed.

Removal and retirement

Magistrates usually have to retire at 70, but they may indirectly be compulsorily retired before this, by being moved to the supplemental list, if, because of age or infirmity, they cannot do their job, or if they neglect to do so.

Lay magistrates can also be removed by the Lord Chancellor at any time without being given reasons, but in fact this is really only done where a magistrate is deemed to have misbehaved, or acted in a way that is inconsistent with the office – in 1985, magistrate Kathleen Cripps was dismissed by the Lord Chancellor for taking part in a CND demonstration outside the court where she normally sat because of a case being heard there. Her application to the High Court for judicial review of the decision was unsuccessful. The Lord Chancellor made it clear in 1994 that 'misbehaviour' justifying removal included conviction of a drink-driving offence or any offence involving violence, dishonesty or immoral conduct; or any behaviour that could cause offence particularly on racial or religious grounds or that amounted to sexual harassment.

Background

Class

The 1948 report of the Royal Commission on Justices of the Peace showed that about three quarters of all magistrates came from professional or middle-class occupations, and little seems to have changed since. Skyrne's research in 1977 found that only 8.2 per cent of magistrates were manual workers.

One of the reasons for this may be financial. While employers are required to give an employee who is appointed a magistrate reasonable time off work, not all employers are able or willing to pay wages for the time taken off. To meet this difficulty, in 1968 a loss of earnings allowance was introduced, but this is not overly generous and will usually be less than the employee would have earned.

A further problem is that employees who take up the appointment against the wishes of their employer may find their promotion prospects jeopardized. This means that only those who are self-employed, or sufficiently far up the career ladder to have some power of their own can serve as magistrates without risking damage to their own job prospects. The outcome is that those outside the professional and managerial classes are proportionately under represented on the bench which is still predominantly drawn from the more middle-class occupations.

Lord Mckay has offered a partial solution by allowing appointments among the over-60s, in the hope that working-class people who were prevented from serving during their working lives will do so in retirement, but these measures appear to have had relatively little effect in increasing the number of working class people on the bench.

Age

There are few young magistrates – most are middle-aged or older. The problems concerning employment are likely to have an effect on the age as well as the social class of magistrates; people at the beginning of their careers are most dependent on the goodwill of employers for promotion, and least likely to be able to take regular time off without damaging their career prospects. They are also more likely to be busy bringing up families.

While a certain maturity is obviously a necessity for magistrates, younger justices would bring some understanding of the lifestyles of a younger generation.

Politics

Government figures released in 1995 showed that a high proportion of magistrates were Conservative voters, and few voted Labour. A sample survey of 218 new appointments as magistrates in England and Wales showed that 91 were Conservative voters, 56 Labour, 41 Liberal Democrat, 24 had no political affiliation, and four voted Plaid Cymru. A report analysing the figures for 1992 in *The Independent* compared the proportion of Conservative voters among magistrates to the proportion in their local area: in two Oldham constituencies, 52 per cent of the local people voted Labour, but only 27 per cent of magistrates, and slightly more magistrates than constituents in general voted Conservative. In Bristol, Labour had won 40 per cent of the votes, slightly more than the Tories; of the magistrates, 142 said they were Tory, and only 85 Labour.

Race

The Lord Chancellor's department reported in 1987 that the proportion of black magistrates was almost 2 per cent, as against the proportion of black people in the general population of around 4.69 per cent. The rate of appointment of black people had increased steadily from 1.77 per cent in 1980 to 4.57 per cent in 1986. It was therefore hoped that the number of black lay magistrates would gradually increase but this appears not to have happened as figures for 1992 still show that only 2 per cent of lay magistrates are black.

Sex

The sexes are fairly evenly balanced among lay magistrates with 54 per cent men and 46 per cent women. However stipendiaries are primarily male, 87 being male and 11 female.

▶ Training

Magistrates are not expected to be experts on the law, and the aim of their training is mainly to familiarize them with court procedure, the techniques of chairing, and the theory and practice of sentencing. They undergo a short induction course on appointment, and all magistrates appointed since 1 January 1966 have to undergo basic continuous training comprising twelve hours every three years. Magistrates who sit in juvenile courts or on domestic court panels receive additional training.

Skyrne claims that the money spent on the training and continuing education of magistrates is 'negligible'. He says the amount and quality of the instruction has varied according to the interest and energy of the particular individuals responsible in the area, and in general 'falls far short of what is needed'. Nor do magistrates themselves always play their part: in October 1986, the Lord Chancellor told the annual meeting of the Magistrates' Association that a number of senior magistrates were not bothering to attend the training courses and that if they continued to disregard training requirements, would no longer be allowed to chair benches. The new Magistrates' Commission Committees have now been given responsibility for providing training under the supervision of the Judicial Studies Board.

▶ Criminal jurisdiction

Lay magistrates generally sit in groups of three. In criminal cases, they have four main functions:

- Hearing applications for bail.
- Transfer for trial proceedings (see p. 223).
- Trial. Magistrates mainly try the least serious criminal cases. They are advised on matters of law by a justice's clerk, but they alone decide the facts, the law and the sentence.
- Appeals. In appeals from the magistrates' court to the Crown Court, magistrates sit with a judge.

Magistrates also exercise some control over the investigation of crime, since they deal with applications for bail and for warrants from the police.

The role of magistrates in the criminal justice system has been effectively increased in recent years. Some offences which were previously triable either way have been made summary only, notably in the Criminal Law Act 1977, where most motoring offences, and criminal damage worth less than £2,000 were made summary only (since raised to £5,000 in the Criminal Justice and Public Order Act 1994). The Government proposed at the time that thefts involving small amounts of money should also be made summary offences, but there was great opposition to the idea of removing the right to jury trial for offences which reflected on the accused's honesty. The proposal was dropped, but is still suggested from time to time.

The vast majority of new offences are summary only – there was controversy over the fact that the first offence created to deal with so-called 'joy-riding' was summary, given that the problem appeared to be a serious one, and critics assume that it was made a summary offence in the interests of keeping costs down. Since then, the more serious offence of joyriding known as aggravated vehicle-taking, which occurs when joyriding causes serious personal injury or death, has been reduced to a summary offence by the Criminal Justice and Public Order Act 1994. Other serious offences which are summary only include assaulting a police officer, and many of the offences under the Public Order Act 1986.

The strongest proposals for increasing magistrates' criminal jurisdiction have come from the 1993 Royal Commission on Criminal Justice, which has recommended abolishing the defendant's right to insist on trial by jury for either way offences (see p. 220), though the Government has not yet adopted this proposal.

▶ Civil jurisdiction

Magistrates grant licences to pubs and betting shops, and have jurisdiction over domestic matters such as adoption. When hearing such matters it is known as the family proceedings court. The Child Support Agency has taken over most of the work in relation to fixing child maintenance payments.

The courts' domestic functions overlap considerably with the jurisdiction of the county court and High Court, though some uniformity of approach is encouraged by the fact that appeals from this area of the magistrates' court have to go to the Family Division of the High Court.

The fact that for domestic matters there are different procedures and different substantive law for the different types of court, and cases are generally assigned to the magistrates' court because they fall within certain financial limits, has led to the criticism that there is a second class system of domestic courts for the poor, with the better off using the High Court and county courts where cases are heard by professional and highly qualified judges. Because of this, magistrates sitting in domestic cases must now be drawn from a panel of specially trained magistrates, and the bench must be mixed in terms of sex.

▶ The magistrates' clerk

There are about 250 magistrates' clerks (also known as the clerk to the justices). They are employed by the Magistrates' Courts Committee for their area subject to the approval of the Lord Chancellor. Most must have a five year magistrates' court qualification, that is to say they must have had a right of audience in relation to all proceedings in the magistrates' courts for at least five years, though some hold office by reason of their length of service. In the past there have been problems with recruiting suitably qualified people, partly because the local organization of the courts meant there was no clear career structure. This led many clerks to leave for the Crown Prosecution Service where pay and promotion prospects were better.

As well as having administrative functions clerks advise the magistrates on law and procedure. They are not supposed to take any part in the decision of the bench; legal and procedural advice should be given in open court, and the clerk should not go with the magistrates if they retire to consider their decision. Their independence is guaranteed by s. 78 of the Police and Magistrates' Courts Act 1994 which provides that when advising magistrates they are not to be subject to directions from anyone, including the Justices' Chief Executive and the Magistrates' Courts Committee.

▶ Advantages of the magistracy

Cost

In 1989 the system cost about £20 million a year to run, while it brought in a total income of £269,088,000 in 1989–91 from fines, fees and fixed penalties. Lay magistrates try the vast majority of criminal cases. Paying stipendiary magistrates to deal with such an enormous caseload would be hugely expensive – at least £100m a year in salaries alone, plus the cost of training. It would also take a long time to amass the required number of legally qualified candidates.

Switching to Crown Court trials would be even more expensive. The Home Office Research and Planning Unit has estimated that the average cost of a contested trial in the Crown Court is around £13,500, with guilty pleas costing around £2,500, both including the cost of criminal legal aid. By contrast, the costs of trial by lay magistrates are £1,500 and £500. This is partly a reflection of the greater seriousness of cases tried in the Crown Court, but clearly Crown Court trials are a great deal more expensive overall.

Lay involvement

This is the same point as that quoted in favour of the jury (see p. 131); however, given the restricted social background of magistrates, and their alleged bias towards the police, the true value of this may be doubtful. Magistrates do not have the option, as juries do, of delivering a verdict according to their conscience.

Weight of numbers

The simple fact that magistrates must sit in threes may make a balanced view more likely.

Local knowledge

Magistrates must live within a reasonable distance of the court in which they sit, and therefore may have a more informed picture of local life than judges.

▶ Disadvantages of the magistracy

Inconsistency

There is considerable inconsistency in the decision-making of different benches. This can be seen in the differences in awards of legal aid and in particular in relation to sentencing. The ideas of fairness on which our criminal justice system are based require that similar crimes committed in similar circumstances by offenders with similar backgrounds should receive a similar punishment. In the Crown Court, this consistency is promoted by the trial judge's own knowledge about sentencing patterns, their use of specialist law books on the subject, the fact that the court proceedings are fully recorded and the close control applied by the Criminal Division of the Court of Appeal.

Magistrates on the other hand generally receive little guidance on consistent sentencing – aside from their basic training, all they have is a Home Office booklet on the subject and advice from their clerk. In 1985, a Home Office publication, *Managing Criminal Justice* reported that while benches tried to ensure that their own decisions were consistent, they made little effort to achieve consistency with neighbouring magistrates' courts. The Home Office figures were further analysed by the National Association of Probation Officers, which found that magistrates in urban areas tended to be less punitive than those in rural areas: in 1983, Bristol magistrates imprisoned 14 per cent of males found guilty of indictable offences, while in nearby Weston-super-Mare, magistrates imprisoned 22 per cent (including suspended sentences). It was suggested that magistrates in inner city areas have a better understanding of the causes of crime than their rural colleagues; on the other hand they may simply be more used to it.

There are also marked variations in the granting of bail applications: in 1985, magistrates' courts in Hampshire granted 89 per cent of bail applications, while in Dorset only 63 per cent were allowed.

Bias towards the police

Police officers are frequent witnesses, and become well-known to members of the Bench, and it is alleged that this results in an almost automatic tendency to believe police evidence. One magistrate was incautious enough to admit this: in **R *v* Bingham JJ ex parte Jowitt** (1974), a speeding case where the only evidence was that of the motorist and a police constable, the chairman of the Bench said 'Quite the most unpleasant cases that we have to decide are those where the evidence is a direct conflict between a police officer and a member of the public. My principle in such cases has always been to believe the evidence of the police officer, and therefore we find the case proved.' The conviction was quashed on appeal because of this remark.

Magistrates were particularly criticized in this respect during the 1984 miners' strike, for imposing wide bail conditions which prevented attendance on picket lines, and dispensing what appeared to be conveyor-belt justice.

Background

Despite the recommendations of two Royal Commissions (1910 and 1948), that magistrates should come from varied social backgrounds, magistrates still appear to be predominantly white, middle-class and middle-aged, with a strong Conservative bias.

The lack of representation of ethnic minorities is a particular problem; respondents to a 1988 study by the National Association for the Care and Resettlement of Offenders emphasized their view of courts as a white institution sitting in judgment upon black people, and their consequent lack of confidence in the system. King and May's research in 1985 found evidence of racial prejudice among some members of advisory committees, and concluded that both the selection procedure itself and the criteria applied by the committees discriminated, directly or indirectly, against ethnic minorities. No Afro-Caribbean people and few Asians were members of advisory committees, and while in some areas there had been a significant increase in the number of black magistrates appointed, the proportion on the bench in many areas still fell far short of the proportion of black people in the local community.

The selection process has also been blamed for the general narrowness of magistrates' backgrounds: Elizabeth Burney's 1979 study into selection methods concluded that the process was almost entirely dominated by existing magistrates who over and over again simply appointed people with similar backgrounds to their own.

The effect of their narrow background on the quality and fairness of magistrates' decisions is unclear: Bond and Lemon's 1976 survey of 160 newly appointed magistrates found no significant towards evidence of differences in attitude, due to social class, penal philosophy, sentencing practice, the causes of crime, court procedure and the role of the magistrate. Some differences appeared on the basis of political affiliation, with Conservatives likely to have a more punitive penal philosophy. The research did not show whether particular attitudes are reflected in behaviour on the Bench, although Bond and Lemon speculate that they might be.

Some feel the background of the Bench is not a particular problem: Jackson's *The Machinery of Justice in England* points out that 'Benches do tend to be largely middle to upper class, but that is a characteristic of those set in authority over us, whether in town hall, Whitehall, hospitals and all manner of institutions'.

However, a narrow social and ethnic background does make the Bench unrepresentative of lay people in general, and may weaken confidence in their decisions, on the part of society in general as well as the defendants before them. It might also be suggested that Jackson's argument that those 'set in authority over us' always tend to be middle to upper class is not a good reason for not trying to change things.

▶ Suggested reforms

Stipendiary magistrates

These could either replace lay magistrates, or sit together with them, so providing a legally-qualified input. It would be very expensive, and is unlikely ever to be considered, but the Royal Commission on Criminal Justice did recommend more use of stipendiary magistrates.

The clerks' role

Magistrates' clerks could be appointed to the Bench, becoming legally qualified chairpersons, or could be given the formal power to rule on points of law, while leaving the determination of the facts, as at present, to the lay justices. The Royal Commission on Criminal Justice 1993 has recommended that pre-trial hearings might be chaired by the clerks (see p. 224).

The selection process

Widespread advertising for magistrates, particularly in areas with high ethnic populations, rather than waiting for nominations; better loss of earnings allowances; and creche facilities at courts (to attract young parents) are all ways of attracting a more varied range of candidates.

Legislation preventing employers from discriminating against magistrates would be difficult to enforce, but might at least make employers more wary about being seen to discriminate, and thus encourage more working class and younger applicants.

Local advisory committees could be widened to include members of the ethnic minorities and the working class, perhaps drawn from community organizations and trade unions.

Improvements in consistency

Achieving precise uniformity in sentencing and granting of bail throughout the country is probably impossible, given the number of cases handled by magistrates' courts, but more detailed guidelines, regularly updated, more training, and some supervision by the higher courts could at least curb the wilder variations.

- -
ANSWERING QUESTIONS

As well as the following examples, the role of magistrates may also be considered as part of a question on lay involvement in the criminal justice system generally (see p. 158), and in questions on the criminal justice system itself (see p. 234).

1 'Magistrates' courts are cheap, but it is wrong that matters of vital concern to the citizen should be decided by amateurs.' In your opinion, how far is this statement true?
You need to address the three points made by this question in turn. First, are magistrates cheap? This is covered in the first point under Advantages of magistracy p. 149.

Secondly, can they be fairly described as amateurs? You could mention here that magistrates do not have legal qualifications, but do have some training – you might point out the extra training given to magistrates dealing with family and juvenile cases. You should also mention the role of the clerk, who can guide them on the law.

You then need to point out what matters of vital concern they decide – these will mainly be criminal, and you should point out that some summary and either way offences can be serious, and even those which appear minor, such as driving offences, can have serious consequences for individuals. In civil cases, the magistrates' family jurisdiction can be seen as being of vital importance for the citizen.

The main emphasis in your essay should be on the next part: do you think it is right that amateur magistrates should decide such important cases? Do not be tempted to simply list the advantages and disadvantages of magistrates – although that is the information you will use, you must relate it to the idea of magistrates as amateur. Obvious points to make would be those about inconsistency, and possibly about bias towards the police.

You might then go on to state any advantages of magistrates which could outweigh, or balance out, the problems of being amateurs – their local knowledge, and the fact that they involve the community, for example.

You could then make a brief comparison between trial by magistrates and trial by jury, perhaps pointing out that juries too are amateurs and they too have been accused of providing amateur justice. You could also compare trial by magistrates with the other alternatives – those listed as alternatives to juries (p. 138) are also alternatives to magistrates. You might point out that one of the allegations made against magistrates – that they come from a narrow social background – is even more true of professional judges. If you have time, run through some of the suggested reforms to magistrates, such as better training.

Your conclusion should state your opinion – you might say that magistrates are amateur and should not be given such vital matters to deal with, or that their advantages outweigh their amateur status. You might say that if reforms were made, the position would be improved, or even suggest that amateur status is a positive advantage – it all depends what the rest of your answer has argued – but you should give some opinion.

2 **Recent reforms have increased the powers of magistrates in the criminal justice system. Are their powers now too great – or too small?**
You need to start by outlining the criminal powers of magistrates, and particularly those powers which have come about as a result of recent changes – these are described in the section on criminal jurisdiction in this chapter. You could point out that there are also areas where magistrates have lost powers – the abolition of committal proceedings, and the decreased use of magistrates' warrants (see chapter 9). The main part of your essay should concentrate on whether the powers should be increased or decreased.

You need to go through any reasons why it might be seen as a good idea to increase the powers of magistrates – cost is obviously one, and you might also consider some of the other advantages of magistrates, such as local knowledge or community involvement, which also justify increased powers.

Then consider any reasons why magistrates' powers should not be increased, or should even be decreased. The problems of bias towards the police and inconsistency are obviously relevant here.

If you have time, you could run through any of the relevant reforms mentioned in this chapter, and if you have been arguing that magistrates' powers are too great, say whether you think those powers would be acceptable, or could be increased, if these reforms were carried out.

7 Lay participation in the legal system

A s well as serving as magistrates and jurors, lay people fulfil other functions within the legal system.

▶ Tribunal members

Tribunals are presided over by a panel, which is usually headed by a legally qualified chairperson. Other members of the panel are usually lay people chosen for their knowledge and experience in the relevant area – doctors sit on Medical Appeal Tribunals, for example, and the panel for an Industrial Tribunal will include one lay member drawn from a panel approved by the Confederation of British Industry, and one from a panel approved by the Trade Union Congress.

▶ 'McKenzie friends'

Where a litigant chooses to represent themselves in court, they may take along someone to advise them, though this person may not themselves address the court. They are called a 'McKenzie friend' or 'McKenzie advisor' after the case in which the court made it clear that the attendance of a lay advisor was permissible: **McKenzie** *v* **McKenzie** (1971). Workers from Citizens Advice Bureaux, Law Centres and law students' groups are among those who commonly act as 'McKenzie friends', though anyone requested by the litigant could do so.

'McKenzie friends' may in fact be legally qualified: solicitor Ole Hansen acted in this capacity in a High Court case in 1993; as a solicitor he would not at the time have been allowed to represent a client directly in that court.

▶ Lay assessors and scientific advisors

Under the Supreme Court Act 1981, judges may appoint people with special expertise in a particular area to sit with them in certain cases –

usually those involving scientific or technical evidence. Their role is to hear the evidence and give the judge whatever assistance is needed in interpreting it and forming a judgment, though the judge still makes the final decision. In the event of an appeal, the appeal court may take the reasoning of lay assessors into account when assessing the original court's decision.

In most cases, lay persons are given technical advice from lawyers to make legal decisions – for example the magistrates are advised by the legally qualified magistrates' clerk and the judge sums up the law and the facts for the benefit of the jury.

▶ Advantages of lay participation

* It is cheap.
* It involves the community and promotes public confidence.
* Simplicity of procedure. Lay involvement can help stop the legal procedures becoming too complex – it has been suggested that the only reason why Crown Court procedure has had to remain intelligible to the general public is because it is necessary for the jury to understand the proceedings.

▶ General disadvantages

* 'Amateur justice' – the alleged inconsistency of magistrates and 'perverse' verdicts of juries. The lay panels which heard supplementary benefit appeals in the 1960s and 1970s were a disaster, deciding cases on the basis of who they thought were 'the deserving poor', and had to be replaced by a panel of two lay persons with specialist knowledge of welfare problems and a legally qualified, experienced chairperson.
* Lack of procedure. The simple approach can go too far. As an example, discipline in prisons is in the hands of boards of visitors, the bulk of whose membership is drawn from magistrates; they hold hearings when prisoners are accused of offences against prison discipline, such as rioting, and may impose punishments. The courts had to intervene in the process, in **R** *v* **Board of Visitors of Hull Prison ex parte St Germain** (1979), because boards of visitors were found to be showing complete disregard for the rules of natural justice.
* Ignoring the law. While the jury's right to find a verdict according to its conscience is seen as a strength and a safeguard, the tendency of some lay participants to ignore the law can have the opposite effect. Mental Health Review Tribunals, for example, have

to decide whether to release compulsorily detained mental patients, and must do so if the patient is no longer mentally ill or no longer needs to be detained. In a number of recent cases the tribunals decided not to release patients who fell into one of these categories because they felt that some of them might be dangerous, or unable to survive in the outside world. The High Court has quashed the tribunal decisions as being wholly outside their statutory power.

• Problems with bias. It is suggested that lay people may be less able than professionals to put any personal prejudices aside.

ANSWERING QUESTIONS

1 **Evaluate the use of lay persons in the administration of justice.** *London*
For this question you need to talk about magistrates and juries, and the other lay people mentioned in this chapter. Obviously there is quite a lot of material in this area in the book so you need to be selective. You might say a little about the long history of lay involvement in your introduction, and perhaps mention the more recent changes – the fact that juries are now very rarely used in civil cases and the extension of the magistrates' role in criminal justice.

You are asked to evaluate, so you need to assess the strengths and weaknesses of using lay people in the administration of justice. A good way of structuring your essay would be to deal with strengths common to lay participants in general, such as those listed in this chapter (cheapness, involvement of the community and simplicity), and then any benefits which are specific to particular types of lay involvement, for example the specific background knowledge possessed by some of the industrial tribunal members. You can then follow the same procedure for the weaknesses of lay involvement, looking at the general points made in this chapter (amateurism, lack of procedure, ignoring the law, and problems with bias), and then discussing any weaknesses specific to particular lay participants.

Your conclusion should say how effective and useful you think lay participants are in the legal system, and on the basis of that you may want to say whether you think their role should be increased, reduced or abolished.

2 **'Experience of the performance of juries and lay magistrates tends to confirm that decisions in legal cases should be left to lawyers'.**
(a) Describe the qualifications, appointment and role of jurors and magistrates.
(b) Do you agree with the statement above? *AEB*
Part (a) is self-explanatory – the only point to watch is that you should not spend so long on this part that you leave yourself insufficient time for the

second part. For part (b), you need to outline the evidence concerning the performance of juries and lay magistrates, from within the relevant chapters. Then you need to say whether in your view this evidence does mean that decisions should be left to lawyers, which effectively means professional judges (including stipendiary magistrates). Bring in any reasons which might outweigh these problems – such as cost, or the importance of community involvement.

You should also talk about the alternatives to juries and magistrates, both those involving lawyers only, and those which mix the two – these are detailed in chapter 5: The jury system. You need to assess whether these would be a better alternative. You could also talk about any reforms which you feel would improve the performance of magistrates or juries.

Note that this question is only asking about the lay role in decision making – so McKenzie friends and scientific advisers are not relevant here.

8 Legal aid and advice

Since society requires that all its members keep the law, it follows that all members of society should be not only equally bound by, but equally served by the legal system, regardless of financial means. Legal rights are worthless unless they can be enforced. Yet justice, as one judge has observed, may be open to all, but only 'in the same way as the Ritz Hotel'. The high cost of taking legal action is notorious: evidence collected for the Civil Justice Review suggested that costs in the county courts were, on average, 99 per cent of the damages won, and in the High Court, around 25 per cent. In civil cases, those who lose their case usually have to pay their opponent's costs as well as their own. This means that without financial help, access to justice will be out of reach for many people.

By contrast, the cost of litigation gives the rich three major advantages: they can hire the best representation, and pay for the time to do the job properly; they can afford to take the risk of losing; and they can use their wealth to bully a less well-off opponent, by dragging out the case or making it more complex. Bear in mind that 'the rich' does not just mean the millionaire in the Rolls Royce, but also the employer you might want to sue for unfair dismissal, the company whose products could make you ill, or the builder who left you with a leaky roof, and you can see the problem.

Before the advent of state-funded legal services, it was in many ways true to say that there was one law for the rich and another for the poor – or at least that the law worked in one way for those sufficiently well-off to use it to defend themselves and their property, and quite another for those whose only contact with it came in being punished for breaking it. This is no longer the case, but as we shall see, access to legal services remains far from equitably distributed – and experts increasingly recognize that finance is not the only barrier.

STATE-FUNDED LEGAL AID AND ADVICE SCHEMES

State funding of legal services began in 1949, with the Legal Aid and Advice Act. It is now covered by the Legal Aid Act 1988, and comprises six separate schemes:

- The legal advice and assistance scheme, known as the 'Green Form scheme' (because the application form is green).
- Assistance by way of representation (ABWOR).
- Civil legal aid.
- Criminal legal aid.
- Duty solicitor schemes in police stations.
- Duty solicitor schemes in criminal cases in magistrates' courts.

The cost of the statutory scheme overall was over £1.3 billion in 1994–95, five times higher than in 1979. Part of the reason for the dramatic rise is said to be increases in the rates of divorce, home ownership and car ownership, all of which give rise to more legal cases – and the bigger workloads which produce delays, which further raises costs.

Legal aid is not always free – for civil and criminal legal aid, clients whose income or savings are above a certain limit may be expected to contribute towards their legal costs. And with civil legal aid, it may act more like a loan, since the costs may be deducted from the amount a successful client wins (see below).

The Lord Chancellor is the Government minister responsible for the legal aid scheme, but its day to day administration is undertaken by the Legal Aid Board, through area directors and committees.

Eligibility for some types of legal aid is decided by means and merits tests. A means test assesses eligibility on the basis of the applicant's disposable income, which means the money left each week after paying for certain essential living expenses; and sometimes disposable capital, which effectively means savings. Only those with disposable incomes below the limit laid down for the type of legal aid required will be eligible for help. Merits tests are assessed on the basis of whether the applicant's case is likely to succeed, and whether it is sufficiently important to justify state funding – so, for example, where a merits test is applied, cases where the applicant is suing someone for a very small amount of money would be unlikely to get legal aid. The specific details of the means and merits tests vary according to the type of legal aid, and some impose neither test.

▶ The Green Form scheme

This provides legal advice and assistance in any civil or criminal matter, except conveyancing and drawing up wills (apart from in certain exceptional cases). The assistance given can include drafting letters and other documents, and advising clients who intend to represent themselves in court on what to say, but does not cover representation in court by the solicitor. The solicitor can do up to two hours work (three in divorce cases), and if more is needed, must apply to the area director for an extension.

Eligibility

Applicants must pass a means test, which can be assessed on the spot by the solicitor. Until 1993, around 30 per cent of the population qualified under the means test; of that 30 per cent, the poorest received free help, and the rest had to contribute towards the cost, though nothing like the full amount. But the rising cost of the scheme led the Government to sharply cut back availability; now only those with a disposable income of less than £70 a week are eligible for the scheme. Applicants falling inside this group get free advice, but those earning above are now excluded completely, and the scheme providing assistance for those above the limit for free help, providing that they paid contributions, has been abolished.

▶ Assistance by way of representation (ABWOR)

This is an extension of the Green Form scheme, which provides representation in selected circumstances, which at present comprise the following:

- Most civil proceedings in magistrates' courts; in practice these are usually family matters.
- In urgent cases, in any other magistrates' court or county court proceedings, where the applicant is not receiving (and has not been refused) representation, and the court is satisfied that the hearing should go ahead on the same day and the applicant would otherwise be unrepresented.
- In proceedings before mental health review tribunals.
- In proceedings before a prison board of visitors, if the board of visitors permits.
- For a range of minor criminal proceedings in the magistrates' court, including bail applications. ABWOR also covers giving advice in these situations and helping the client to make an application for subsequent representation.

Eligibility

ABWOR is granted subject to the same means tests as for the Green Form scheme, except in the circumstances listed in the final point above, when it is free to anyone who needs it. Applications for ABWOR in the first, third and fourth categories listed above require authority from the area director, and must pass a merits test by satisfying the area director that there are reasonable grounds for bringing, defending or being a party to the proceedings.

▶ Civil legal aid

This covers all the work involved in bringing or defending a civil case, including representation in court by the solicitor or a barrister.

Where a legally-aided client wins a case, if the costs recovered from the other party (and any contributions made by the legally-aided client) do not cover the amount spent by the legal aid fund, the fund may recover the difference from the damages won (subject to certain restrictions in matrimonial cases). This is called the statutory charge. In such cases civil legal aid acts more like a loan. In some cases, the statutory charge may mean that all the damages are swallowed up by the legal aid fund and the client ends up with no money, and a rather cynical view of the justice system.

Eligibility

There is both a merits and a means test. The merits test asks whether it is reasonable for the claimant to bring or defend the action. The board may refuse funding if the circumstances of the case suggest that it would be unreasonable for the client to receive it; where the client would be likely to gain only trivial advantage from the proceedings; where the proceedings are not the sort in which a solicitor would usually be engaged; or where ABWOR is thought more appropriate. Civil legal aid is not usually allowed for claims worth less than the Small Claims Court limit of £3,000.

The means test for civil legal aid was tightened at the same time as that for the Green Form scheme. In 1992–93, those with a disposable income of £3,060 a year were eligible for free civil legal aid; from 1993, that was reduced to £2,294 – Income Support level. The way in which disposable income is calculated was also changed; in measuring disposable income, the applicant can claim a fixed allowance for a dependant partner or children, and these allowances were reduced, so rendering people ineligible for legal aid even though they were on incomes which had previously been low enough.

In addition to those who qualified for free legal aid, civil legal aid was available to those above £3,060 a year, but below the eligibility limit for civil legal aid, who paid contributions towards their case, the level of which was assessed by the means test. The changes announced in 1992 restricted levels of eligibility with contributions to those with a disposable income of less than £6,800 (£7,500 in personal injury cases). In addition, the contributions payable, and their duration, were increased. Previously, the amount to be contributed would be assessed and set at the beginning of the case, and could be paid in monthly instalments over a year; now contributions must continue to be paid for as long as a case lasts, rather than being a single amount set at the beginning. For example, before the changes were made, a single person earning £11,500 would have been at the top of the scale of eligibility, and would have had to pay the highest contribution: £785. They would, however, know that the sum would be all there was to pay. But since 1993, a person on the same income would have to pay £1,500 a year throughout the duration of the case – so with a personal injury case typically taking two or three years, the bill could end up at £3,000 or more, and the litigant would not know exactly how much they would have to pay before the case started.

▶ Criminal legal aid

Like civil legal aid, this covers the whole range of legal advice, assistance and representation. Because decisions often need to be made more quickly than in civil cases, application is to the courts, rather than the legal aid board.

Eligibility

There are both means and merits tests. The Legal Aid Act 1988 specifies that if the means test is satisfied, legal aid **must** be granted in the following circumstances:

* where the charge is murder;
* where the prosecution is seeking leave to appeal to the House of Lords;
* where a previously unrepresented defendant who has been kept in custody applies for bail and is likely to be refused;
* where a defendant is kept in custody pending pre-sentencing reports.

The courts **may** grant legal aid (where the means test is satisfied) if it appears to be 'in the interests of justice'; if the court is not sure whether this is the case, any doubts should be resolved in favour of the defendant. The Legal Aid Act 1988 lays down certain criteria – originally known as the Widgery criteria – which may suggest that it would be in the interests of justice to grant legal aid:

* where the offence is a serious one, which if proved means defendants are likely to lose their liberty or livelihood, or suffer serious damage to their reputations;
* where the case raises a substantial question of law;
* where defendants are unable to follow the proceedings or state their own case because of language difficulties, mental illness or some other mental or physical illness;
* where the nature of the defence demands the tracing and interviewing of witnesses, or expert cross-examination of a prosecution witness;
* where legal representation is desirable in the interests of someone other than the accused (for example the victim in a child abuse

case, who would clearly suffer from being cross-examined by the defendant in person).

This list is not intended to be complete, and other factors may be taken into account if they are relevant.

▶ Duty solicitor schemes in police stations

These were set up in response to the provisions of the Police and Criminal Evidence Act 1984, which provides a right to legal advice for suspects detained by the police. They are available 24 hours a day in approximately 94 per cent of police stations to give advice and assistance (clients are not obliged to use duty solicitors and may consult their own solicitors privately).

Eligibility

The scheme is available to anyone either arrested and held in custody in a police station, or voluntarily 'helping with enquiries', free of charge. There are no means or merits tests.

▶ Duty solicitor schemes in magistrates' courts

Solicitors on a rota basis are present at the courts to advise unrepresented defendants.

Eligibility

Defendants are not eligible for representation by a duty solicitor in committal proceedings, where their plea is not guilty, or, unless the solicitor considers the case exceptional, in non-imprisonable offences (Green Form advice and full criminal legal aid are available for these proceedings). There is no other merits test, and no means test or contributions.

▶ Criticisms: the statutory scheme as a whole

Eligibility levels

As explained above, eligibility levels for the means-tested schemes have been drastically lowered since 1992. In 1979, 79 per cent of adults were eligible for civil legal aid, including those who would have had to pay contributions, but by 1993 this had dropped to 48 per cent.

The result of this has been that while the very poor may get legal aid, and the rich, as ever, can afford their own legal costs, the vast majority of people on moderate incomes face a choice between incurring severe financial burdens, or simply being unable to assert their legal rights.

As Ole Hansen has pointed out, the situation has been made worse by the fact that legal costs have been rising faster than earnings. Between 1985 and 1990, average earnings rose 38 per cent, and the average legal aid bill rose 60 per cent, and privately-funded cases may well have risen more quickly than that. This means that proportionately more people would find it difficult or impossible to afford legal fees.

Even for those who do still qualify for legal aid, eligibility for free help runs out at an extremely low level, and above that, the contributions payable have long been a significant financial burden, especially for those at the top end of the eligibility scale. In 1989–90, 79 per cent of those granted legal aid were not required to pay contributions, which given the low level of eligibility for this, suggests that many of those who were asked to pay contributions were deterred from taking up legal aid. The fact that contributions are now payable throughout the duration of a case, so that litigants cannot know in advance how much they will be expected to spend, and that they are so much higher, may well discourage people from taking legal action at all.

Ironically, it has been pointed out that as far as personal injury cases are concerned, the cuts in legal aid may cost the state more than they save. The Spinal Injuries Association has highlighted the fact that many people disabled by accidents live on benefits which put them above eligibility for free help, but these benefits are designed to (just) cover daily living expenses, not fund expensive litigation. If those people were eligible for legal aid, they could sue those responsible for the fact that they can no longer work; as it is, they have to be supported by the state, often for life. In most cases the benefits payable, low as they are, cost the state a great deal more than giving the person legal aid would.

What makes this situation worse is that the cuts seem to have been deeper than they needed to be – the legal aid scheme has cost £170 million less than expected over the past couple of years. As a result, the Legal Action Group, which campaigns on legal services, claims that the cuts were made for ideological rather than practical reasons, and that the same applies to the reforms currently proposed by the Lord Chancellor (see p. 179).

Cost

As explained above, the cost of the statutory scheme has increased dramatically over recent years. This fact is said to have been the main reason for the reforms currently planned by the Lord Chancellor.

Funding

Lawyers claim the system is underfunded and some lawyers working within it are badly paid, with the result that many lawyers are not interested in taking part. In an article called '*A Future for Legal Aid?*', Ole Hansen has suggested that the underfunding inevitably results in a second-class service, not necessarily because of lack of quality in the lawyers themselves, but because they simply cannot afford to spend the same amount of time on a case as a privately-funded lawyer. This has particularly important implications in the area of criminal legal aid (see p. 169).

Reliance on private practice

When the legal aid system was set up the Government had a choice between using the existing private practice structures or setting up a totally separate system of lawyers, who would be paid salaries from public funds (as doctors are in the NHS), rather than being paid on a case by case basis. They chose to give legal aid work to lawyers in private practice, who would be paid per case. Kate Markus, writing in *The Critical Lawyer's Handbook* argues that this causes five main problems:

1 Rather than responding to need, legal aid practitioners in private practice are ruled by the requirements of running a business in a highly competitive marketplace. Private practitioners have to make a profit, even where they are paid by the Legal Aid Board, and therefore often feel that they must limit the time they spend on legal aid cases. This problem severely limits the services they can offer to the clients, and is also the reason why so many lawyers are refusing to do legal aid work, which given current funding problems, cannot compete with privately paid work.

2 The orientation of private practice towards money and property matters means that as far as general High Street solicitors are concerned, their expertise is often not developed in those areas affecting the poorer client.

3 Solicitors in private practice may be seen as intimidating by the majority of poorer clients, who are put off bringing their problems to them.

4 Private practice is geared largely to litigation, which is not always the best solution to the kind of problems facing the working class. Decisions made by some authorities may not be challengeable in the courts, and in some cases, combined action in the form of campaigns by groups of people affected by a particular problem can be more effective than court action. The working practices of private practitioners, and the case-by-case way in which legal aid is funded make it impossible for them to do much, if any, of this kind of work.

5 If justice is really to be accessible, widespread ignorance of legal

rights and how to assert them must be overcome. Private practice is in no way geared to this kind of educational work.

Tribunals

Legal aid has so far not been available for cases brought before most tribunals. This is a major anomaly, given that tribunals were created to give ordinary citizens a way of asserting their rights, and in many tribunals the 'ordinary citizen' faces an opponent with ready access to the best legal advice and representation – Government departments, for example, or large companies in the industrial tribunal. This can put the unrepresented litigant at a serious disadvantage (see p. 294). However, it is thought that legal aid may be extended to tribunals as part of Lord McKay's reform package.

Patchy coverage

The piecemeal development of the statutory schemes has brought about considerable overlap between schemes, while failing to fill important gaps.

▶ ## Criticisms: the individual schemes

The Green Form scheme

Failure to attract welfare problems
Part of the reason for creating the Green Form scheme was concerned with the issue of unmet legal need – the fact that some kinds of problems seem not to be dealt with adequately by the justice system (see p. 177). The Green Form scheme was intended to help bring in a new range of work, particularly welfare and similar problems, which individuals had traditionally been reluctant to bring to lawyers. It has largely failed to do this, probably because of the problems with the nature of private practice referred to by Kate Markus, above (p. 167). The percentage of welfare problems is now beginning to expand, but this may reflect the involvement of law centres, which specialize in this kind of work, rather than suggesting that private practice has begun to attract more welfare problems.

Bureaucracy
The initial limit for work to be done is thought to be too low, and where a barrister's advice (known as counsel's opinion) or expert reports are required, an extension will always be needed. Applying for an extension can waste time.

Lack of awareness
Public awareness of the scheme is generally low, which again hampers its ability to attract new areas of need.

Fraud

The scheme is said to be open to fraud, with claims that unscrupulous solicitors have paid people to fill in Green Forms, making up nonexistent claims, so that the solicitor can claim for work which has never been done. Around 100 firms have been investigated by the Legal Aid Board, some of which have been referred to the Serious Fraud Office.

Civil legal aid

The statutory charge

The statutory charge can claw back all a plaintiff's damages, which as far as the client is concerned, may make the whole action a waste of time. While the charge may be technically just – since privately-funded clients also face the risk of losing all their damages to costs – to the legally-aided client it does not look like a case of justice being seen to be done. To legally-aided clients who win their case and then come away empty-handed, it can look suspiciously as though the legal aid scheme is run purely for the benefit of lawyers.

Recovery of costs

Where a legally-aided client loses a case, it is difficult, sometimes impossible, for the opponent to get costs back, as would normally happen in a civil case. Clearly this can place the legally-aided client at an unfair advantage. There is some provision for payment from the Legal Aid Board, and though strictly applied at first, this has been more generous since Lord Denning recommended wider application in **Hanning** *v* **Maitland** (1970). Nevertheless, being sued by a legally-aided person is a risk for the average individual, which can work against justice since costs can be used as a weapon to force an early settlement.

Libel and slander

Civil legal aid is not available for cases of libel or slander, which means that only the wealthy and powerful can afford the luxury of defending their reputations. The knock-on effect of this is that unscrupulous newspapers know very well that they take little risk when they libel the ordinary person.

Criminal legal aid

Standards of work

Research by McConville (1993) has suggested that the standards of legally-aided criminal defence work is very low. Much of it is done by unqualified staff; there is little investigative work; and solicitors push clients towards pleading guilty, rather than taking time to prepare an effective defence. McConville claims that the heavy workloads and low pay of legal aid work force solicitors to see their clients as 'economic units', to be processed as quickly as possible; the result is a real danger of this leading to more miscarriages of justice.

Problems with the merits test

In concentrating on the seriousness of the charge and possible penalty, the merits test makes it more difficult for defendants to get legal aid for minor offences. These may be the least important ones, but the effects of a conviction on the individual may be profound – and if society does not want its members to see minor offences as trivial, the criminal justice system should not be seen to treat them as such.

A further problem is that it may be difficult to know whether the merits criteria apply until after a trial has started, and even if legal aid is then granted, the defendant may already have been disadvantaged.

Problems with the means test

Before 1984, the courts had only limited powers to order contributions in criminal cases, and few orders were made. Since the introduction in that year of new rules, many more contribution orders are made. It has been suggested that these moves were made with more concern for saving money than for pursuing justice. The Royal Commission on Criminal Justice 1993 acknowledged the need to keep public expenditure down, but stressed that it would be 'very seriously concerned' if it transpired that the changes meant a reduction in the number of defendants without legal representation, especially in the Crown Court.

However, it is also claimed that the system suffers from the opposite problem: failure to collect contributions from those who can afford them. In 1994, the National Audit Office reported that the information supplied on means test forms was rarely checked, so that it was easy to avoid contributions being ordered at all by lying about income. In addition, where contributions were ordered, experienced defendants avoided paying them before the trial began, knowing that once it started, the judge would not want to withdraw legal aid and end up with the delay and inconvenience of an unrepresented defendant, and once it was over, they were likely either to be in prison, with no income to pay the contributions, or acquitted, in which case the state would pay.

Inconsistency

In 1992, the Legal Aid Board produced a report showing that the chances of getting criminal legal aid varied widely from area to area. The percentage of cases in which it was granted could be as low as 35 per cent or as high as 100 per cent, depending on the court. The report found that whether an applicant received legal aid or not could depend as much on the personal views of the court clerks as it did on the seriousness of the charges or the possible implications for the defendant. The fact that application forms were often filled in by solicitors' junior staff also seemed to contribute to the problem.

Fixed fees

Originally, all legal aid was paid for on the basis of the amount of work done on each individual case, paid by the hour. In 1987, the Lord Chancellor announced that this arrangement would be changed, and fixed fees would by payable, assessed by the type of case and remaining the same regardless of the amount of work done on a particular case. As far as the Government was concerned, this was merely a 'swings and roundabouts' approach: lawyers would lose out on cases which took more work than usual, but gain on cases which were simpler and quicker than usual, and overall the fees would balance out. The Law Society saw it differently, pointing out that cases which could be processed without much work were in a definite minority. They claimed that standard fees would penalize solicitors who prepared their cases thoroughly, and reward those who cut corners. In addition, it was clear that fixed fees were to be used to keep costs down, and that meant the Lord Chancellor could choose to keep annual increases in the fees below the level of inflation, in effect forcing solicitors to take annual pay cuts.

The fixed fees were introduced in the Crown Court in 1986, but when the Lord Chancellor attempted to extend them to magistrates' courts in 1992, thus affecting higher numbers of solicitors, the solicitors dug their heels in, lobbying their MPs and even threatening industrial action by withdrawing from the duty solicitor schemes. When, in 1993, it was announced that the plans would still go ahead, the Law Society sought judicial review of the decision, though unsuccessfully.

Their opposition to the scheme was backed up by concerns expressed by the 1993 Royal Commission on Criminal Justice, which suggested that fixed fees in the magistrates' courts might discourage solicitors from doing all the work necessary for a case, or conversely, provide an incentive to take longer than necessary in order to qualify for a higher fee. The Royal Commission pointed out that such fees needed to be kept at an appropriate rate in order to attract sufficient numbers of able, qualified solicitors. The Commission noted that criminal legal aid appeared to be given a lower priority than civil legal aid by those who set the fees.

Payment for forensic work

The Royal Commission on Criminal Justice 1993 described the arrangements for legal aid to pay for scientific and forensic advice for the defence as 'far from satisfactory'. Scientific work commissioned for legally-aided defendants was often left unpaid for until at least a year after the end of the case, and this practice deterred good laboratories from taking on such work. Given the role which forensic evidence played in some of the well-known miscarriages of justice, this is a serious problem.

Duty solicitor schemes in police stations

Hours and pay

The pay for duty solicitors is higher than that for most legal aid work, but still low considering the irregular hours, with the result that few solicitors want to take part, and the burden on the rest can become intolerable. Some local schemes have collapsed as a result, and in 1992 the Law Society expressed its 'grave concern' at the drop in the number of solicitors involved.

The Royal Commission on Criminal Justice 1993 pointed out that unless fees paid for duty solicitor schemes were kept under regular review and maintained at an appropriate level, it would not be possible to attract sufficient numbers of properly trained solicitors and 'the suspect will not be properly protected'.

Rates of use

Although the number of people getting legal advice at police stations has increased, it is still quite low – less than 20 per cent according to Sanders' 1989 research – and varies widely between stations. This is partly due to unwillingness on the part of suspects, for any number of reasons: dislike of lawyers, desire to get things over with without delay, perception of the offence as trivial, confidence that their own innocence will save them, or conversely, belief that nothing can help them. However, Sanders's 1993 research revealed that police officers routinely circumvented the provisions of PACE by failing to inform suspects of their right to legal advice, or to inform them that it was free. They may also stress the delay caused by waiting for a solicitor, or suggest that it would be unlikely to help the suspect anyway. Research for the 1993 Royal Commission suggested that in about 25 per cent of cases, although information about the right to legal advice was supplied, it was given too quickly, incompletely, or incomprehensibly.

Delays

Sanders' research also suggested that there were problems with delays in provision of advice under the scheme. Responses were slow, especially at night, with less than 60 per cent reaching police stations within an hour – so helping the police to head off legal advisors by stressing delay. Nearly half of those respondents questioned for the 1993 Royal Commission who did not take up the offer of legal advice said they would have done so if a solicitor had been already available at the police station, rather than having to be called from elsewhere. However the Royal Commission saw little prospect of such a scheme being introduced.

Standards of work

Sanders' research found that advice was often given over the telephone rather than in person, or solicitors left the station after giving advice without attending the interrogation – a solicitor was present in only 14 per cent of interrogations. The Royal Commission 1993 found that where someone was sent to the police station, in many cases they lacked sufficient knowledge and experience. Its research showed that legal advisers sent under the scheme made few interventions during interrogation: in 66 per cent of cases they said nothing at all, and in only 9 per cent did they actively intervene on behalf of the subject and object to police questions. In some cases the legal adviser seemed to identify more with the police than with the suspect. They were also ineffective in discovering vital information about the case: in 45 per cent of cases, no attempt was made to seek information from the police, and the solicitor relied completely on information from the client. Advisers routinely failed to discover important information, or to adequately examine the legal position of the client.

In practice, firms often send an unqualified clerk rather than a solicitor; even where their legal knowledge is adequate, an effective duty solicitor also needs sufficient confidence to stand up to the police where necessary in the client's interests, and this is likely to pose problems for young, inexperienced personnel. Research by McConville found that almost half of firms studied sent employees who were former police officers.

OTHER PROVISION FOR LEGAL AID AND ADVICE

The statutory schemes are not the only sources of free or cheap legal advice and help. Two of the most important alternatives, Citizens Advice Bureaux and law centres, along with the conditional fee system, are discussed in detail below, but there are in fact several others. Some local authorities run money, welfare, consumer and housing advice centres to provide both advice and a mechanism for dealing with complaints, while charities such as Shelter, the Child Poverty Action Group and MIND often offer legal help in their specialist areas. Other organizations, such as trade unions, motoring organizations such as the AA and RAC, and the Consumers' Association give free or inexpensive legal help to their members. In 1994, the Law Society set up the Accident Line, a scheme under which accident victims can get a free initial interview with a solicitor specializing in personal injury.

It is also possible to insure against legal expenses, either as a stand-alone policy, or more usually, as part of household or motor insurance.

▶ Law centres

Law centres offer a free, non-means-tested service to people who live or work in their area. They aim to be accessible to anyone who needs legal help, and in order to achieve this usually operate from ground floor, high street premises, stay open beyond office hours, employ a high proportion of lay people as well as lawyers, and generally encourage a more relaxed atmosphere than that found in most private solicitors' offices. Most law centres are run by a management committee drawn from the local area, so that they have direct links with the community.

The first law centres were established in 1969, and by 1984 there were around 50 of them. The Law Society allowed them to advertise (before the restriction on advertising was lifted for solicitors in general) in exchange for the centres not undertaking certain areas of work which were the mainstay of the average high street solicitor – small personal injury cases, wills and conveyancing. Their main areas of work are housing, welfare, immigration and employment.

Law centres are largely funded by grants from central and local government, though a few have also managed to secure some financial support from large local private firms. This method of funding means that they do not have to work on a case-by-case basis but can allocate funding according to community priorities (though appropriate cases may be taken on under the statutory legal aid schemes, in which case the law centre gets paid as a private solicitor would).

Because they do not depend on case-by-case funding, law centres have developed innovative ways of solving legal problems. As well as dealing with individual cases, they run campaigns designed to make local people aware of their legal rights, act as a pressure group on local issues such as bad housing, and take action where appropriate on behalf of groups as well as individuals. The reasoning behind this approach is that resources and time are better used tackling problems as a whole, rather than aspects of those problems as they appear case by case. For example, if a council has failed to replace lead piping, or asbestos, in its council houses, it would seem more efficient to approach the council about all the properties rather than take out individual cases for each tenant as they become aware that they have a problem.

Law centres also provide valuable services in areas not covered by the statutory scheme, such as inquests, and several have set up duty solicitor schemes to deal with housing cases in the county court and help prevent evictions. They may offer a 24-hour general emergency service.

Most law centres face long-term problems with funding; several have closed, and others go through periodic struggles for survival.

▶ Citizens Advice Bureaux

There are around a thousand Citizens Advice Bureaux across the country, offering free advice and help with a whole range of problems, though the most common areas at the moment are social security and debt. They are largely staffed by trained volunteers, who can become expert in the areas they most frequently deal with. Where professional legal help is required, some Bureaux employ solicitors, some have regular help from solicitor volunteers, and others refer individuals to local solicitors who undertake legal aid work and/or fixed fee interviews. The Bureaux are overseen by the National Association of Citizens Advice Bureaux, and must conform to its standards and codes of practice.

One of their major advantages is a very high level of public awareness – because they are frequently mentioned in the press, and have easily recognizable high street offices, most people know where they are and what they do.

Like law centres, they have come under considerable financial pressure in recent years, with the result that many can only open for a very limited number of hours a week.

▶ Conditional fees

In other countries, notably the USA, lawyers have long been allowed to take on cases on a 'no win, no fee' basis (called a contingency fee); if they do win the case, they are paid an agreed percentage of the damages. The benefit of this system is that those who cannot afford litigation, but have good cases, can get a lawyer, while the lawyers have a direct incentive to do the best for their clients. However, critics in this country have always claimed that giving lawyers a financial interest in the outcome of the case would be an open invitation to unprofessional conduct, and lead to a tendency for lawyers to refuse to take on weaker cases, and to increased pressure to accept an early settlement (when actual costs will have been relatively low), rather than press on to trial and incur the costs this involves. In addition, while in the USA litigants under the contingency fee scheme risk nothing at all, the English rule that the losing side pays the other's costs means that here, some provision would have to be made for the other side's costs if the case lost.

Full contingency fees are still unenforceable in this country, but the Courts and Legal Services Act 1990 has taken a step towards them by introducing conditional fee agreements, a provision which took effect in 1995. Conditional fees will only apply to cases involving personal injury, insolvency or applications to the European Court of Human Rights; lawyers take on cases for nothing, but can charge up to double what their usual fee would be if they win. The problem of paying the other sides' costs if the case is lost has been addressed by the Law Society, which has launched an insurance scheme that accident victims can join after their accident, but before legal action begins.

The scheme will obviously help many of those in the middle income bracket – not poor enough for legal aid, not rich enough to pay standard fees – but it has its drawbacks. The first is the limited number of cases in which it will apply: only those in the categories listed above, and of those, only those where the solicitor is fairly certain the case can be won. Even if the Government eventually decides to extend the categories, conditional fees can only be of use in cases where compensation is sought – they would do nothing to meet the shortcomings in legal aid coverage of criminal or divorce cases, for example.

In addition, the fact that the increased fee is not related to the level of damages means that there is no incentive for the lawyer to get good compensation for the client, only to win the case; and in personal injury, the area where conditional fees are likely to be used most, there is a high rate of success anyway. Perhaps most importantly, it has been pointed out that doubling the lawyers' fees could wipe out any damages (especially given the lack of incentive to raise them), thus making the whole case pointless for the litigant. The scheme has been criticized, particularly on this last point, by a number of Law Lords, including the Lord Chief Justice, and it has been suggested that there should be a financial limit on the fees that can be earned this way, so insuring that some damages are left over for the client. The Law Society has drawn up a model conditional fee agreement, under which solicitors agree that their fee will be no higher than 25 per cent of the client's damages; its use will not be compulsory, but the Society believes many solicitors will use it.

ARE LAWYERS ALWAYS NECESSARY?

As we have seen, many of the non-statutory advice schemes use advisors who are not legally qualified. Some of these lay advisors appear as advocates in tribunals, and in some cases have been granted discretionary rights of audience before registrars in the county courts, as well as giving legal advice. In particular, advisors for charities such as MIND have shown themselves to be more than a match for most solicitors in their knowledge of the law in their fields. Many solicitor firms also employ non-qualified workers to do legal work.

The skills of a good advisor are not always the same as those of a good lawyer; what the client needs is someone who can interview sympathetically, ascertain the pertinent facts from what may be a long, rambling and in some cases emotional story, analyse the problem and suggest a course of action. The preliminary skills are just as likely to be possessed by a lay person as by a lawyer, even if a lawyer may be needed to advise on the course of action.

Nor are lawyers considered to be the best advocates in every situation. The National Consumer Council advised against allowing them to represent clients in the Small Claims Court, on the grounds that they could make the procedure unnecessarily long-winded and legalistic.

However, critics identify two possible problems in the growing use of lay advisors. First, although most organizations are scrupulous in training their advisors, some may be more casual, and there is no obligatory check on advisors before they are allowed to deal with cases. The general public may not always be in a position to assess the quality of the advice they are given. Secondly, the large number of overlapping agencies mean it can be difficult for consumers of legal advice to find the best source for them, and can be wasteful of scarce resources. However, the wide variation in sources of funding for these bodies, and in their areas of work mean co-ordination would probably be impossible.

Unmet need for legal services

The statutory legal aid and advice scheme attempts, however imperfectly, to address the problem of access to legal services for those who are not sufficiently well-off to pay their own costs. However, research has shown that although cost is very much a problem – a 1991 *Which?* report found one in ten people were put off seeking legal advice for that reason – there are also other reasons why people fail to secure help with their legal problems. A system designed to widen access to legal services must be judged on its contribution to meeting this gap by involving lawyers (or other advisors) in all the areas where help is needed.

Richard White's 1973 research suggested four situations in which need for legal services goes unmet;

- the person fails to recognize a problem as having legal implications, and so does not seek out legal advice;
- the problem is recognized as being a legal one, but the person involved does not know of the existence of a legal service that could help, or their own eligibility to use it;
- the person knows the problem is a legal one, and knows of the service that could help with it, but chooses not to make use of it because of some barrier, such as cost, ignorance of legal aid, or the unapproachable image of solicitors;
- the person knows there is a legal problem and wants legal help, but fails to get it because they cannot find a service to deal with it.

Clearly the problems involve more than just the cost of legal services – awareness of legal rights and the services available to help enforce them, the unapproachability of the legal profession and the matching of services to problems are all important.

This is backed up by the 1973 research of Abel-Smith *et al.*, which compared people's own perception of their need for legal help, and the action they took to get it. Almost all the respondents consulted a solicitor when they felt they needed advice on buying a house. For employment problems though, only 4 per cent consulted a solicitor; 34 per cent took advice from some other source, and 62 per cent took no advice at all. For social security problems, solicitors were consulted by even fewer people; just 3 per cent saw a solicitor, while 16 per cent took other advice, and 81 per cent took none at all. Yet in all these cases, the people surveyed realized that they did need some legal advice.

The Royal Commission on Legal Services concluded that the main reason for failure to get help on legal problems was poverty. Yet as we have seen, all sections of society took advice from a solicitor when buying a house, regardless of means (though of course this only includes those with sufficient means to buy their own home). Zander has pointed out that even the poorest members of society consult solicitors about divorce, while the middle classes seem no more likely than working class people to consult solicitors about employment or consumer problems.

American sociologists Mayhew and Reiss put forward a 'social organization' theory to explain why solicitors are consulted in some cases and not others. This theory suggests that certain types of work are related to social contact – most people know people who have used solicitors for conveyancing and divorce, and it becomes an obvious step to take. As Zander points out, lawyers adjust the services they offer to demand, and so it becomes a self-fulfilling prophecy. Another factor identified by the Royal Commission on Legal Services was the uneven distribution of solicitors throughout the country. A 1973 study showed that while there was one solicitor's office for every 4,700 people in England and Wales, their distribution varied enormously, from one office for every 2,000 people in prosperous owner-occupier areas such as Bournemouth and Guildford, to one for every 66,000 in working-class areas such as Huyton in Liverpool. The Commission concluded that the low rates for legal aid work had much to do with this; most private firms need to subsidize such work with privately-funded work, and the poorer areas may not provide enough of this to keep more than a few solicitors in each area in business. Other advice agencies, such as law centres and Citizens Advice Bureaux may also be thin on the ground in some, particularly rural, areas.

The image of lawyers as predominantly white, male and from privileged backgrounds may also contribute to the problem, making them unapproachable to many people. This is obviously more of a problem for solicitors, who deal direct with the public, and in recent years they have taken steps to address the issue, including the use of advertising and public relations campaigns. Many high street firms now advertise their services locally, while some of the firms currently involved in suing cigarette manufacturers for illnesses caused by smoking attracted potential clients by advertising specifically for people with smoking-related diseases. The Law Society too is playing its part – the new Accident Line scheme was widely publicised to the media, and in 1995, the Society ran its first National Law Week. Designed to 'increase public awareness of legal rights and give information about how solicitors can help people gain access to justice', it included regional activities and, perhaps a little optimistically, a 'my favourite solicitor' competition.

The profession is also looking at new ways to deliver legal services which could overcome public reluctance to consult solicitors. Much interest has been shown in QuickCourt, an electronic kiosk rather like a bank cashpoint machine, which is used in the USA to provide information about the legal system, accept fines for parking, and even allow litigants to file their own divorce proceedings; while such technology would not replace solicitors (at least not if solicitors have any say in the matter), it could be used for information services designed to bring clients into solicitors' firms. Another innovative idea is legal services by telephone. Inspired by direct telephone sales of insurance, a Hampshire solicitors' firm have set up a pilot scheme offering one particular service, an enduring power of attorney, through a simple telephone procedure. Power of attorney is used when a person, through age or illness, becomes unable to deal with their own legal and financial affairs; by signing a document known as an enduring power of attorney, they can authorize someone else (usually a relative or friend) to handle these matters for them. The firm's scheme allows clients, who will have seen the service advertised, to ring a recorded telephone message explaining the effect of enduring power of attorney. If they decide it is what they need, they call another number, give their details and pay the flat fee there and then by credit card, and the document can then be issued for them to sign. If the scheme is successful, it will be extended to other legal services, though obviously only the most straightforward types of work will be suitable.

▶ Proposals for reform of the statutory scheme

Lord McKay's reforms

When this book went to press, there was great controversy over plans drawn up by the Lord Chancellor to reform the legal aid scheme. Nevertheless, it seems likely that his reforms, or at least most of them, will take place. The most controversial of the proposals was that legal aid should be cash-limited, rather as NHS treatment has been for some years. Each region will have a budget, which it must spread out through the year; when the money is gone, legal aid cases will not be taken on, even though applicants pass the means and merits tests. The Law Society, the Bar, and the Labour Party are among those who have criticized this aspect of Lord McKay's reforms, arguing that they would make legal aid a lottery, in which the applicant's chances of getting help would depend not on their need or the strength of their case, but where they live and when they apply.

The Government however, argues that as well as cutting costs, cash limits will make providers of legal aid set priorities, so that help goes where it is needed most. It also proposes to set up a central 'emergency' fund to pay for exceptional cases.

Also controversial is a plan to franchise legal aid work, under which firms, or advice agencies such Citizens Advice Bureaux, would work under block contracts to provide legal aid in their area. In fact provision for these franchises was introduced in the Legal Aid Act 1988, and since then around 1,000 firms now have franchises. The advantage for the legal aid scheme is that such firms are vetted on the quality of their work before a franchise is awarded, and checked periodically afterwards; the firms gain both from payments on account, rather than claiming case by case, and from a reputation for legal aid work; both sides benefit from reduced bureaucracy. While there has been the odd teething problem with this arrangement – relating mainly to inefficiency on the part of the Legal Aid Board – the current criticisms relate not to the idea of franchising itself, but to Lord McKay's apparent plans to extend it, so that only those with a franchise will be allowed to do legal aid work, and to promote competitive tendering where there is competition for legal aid franchises. This development, it is argued, will reduce client choice, put many small firms out of business, and favour firms who offer low prices because they cut corners over those who take more care and so charge more. In the USA, competitive tendering is claimed to have led to an emphasis on cost over quality, and to experienced, efficient practitioners dropping out of the service, to be replaced by those with less experience or lower standards. In some areas firms simply colluded to put prices up, making the system pointless.

There are also fears that exclusive franchises could threaten the work of law centres; although they would be free to apply for franchises themselves, they will be unable to use the money granted under them for anything other than individual casework, so reducing the campaigning and educative work that has made them so successful. Those who have local authority funding might find this reduced to take account of franchise income.

The third main element of Lord McKay's plans was a change to the legal aid provisions for couples seeking a divorce. Such couples will be encouraged to try mediation before consulting lawyers; although this is not compulsory, those who could not afford to pay a lawyer themselves would have to show that one was necessary before they would be granted legal aid. Although mediation can often help divorcing couples split up with less bitterness, the Solicitor's Family Law Association warned that people should not be denied access to good legal advice in the cause of saving money.

Only one of Lord McKay's proposals seems to have won widespread support: the extension of legal aid to tribunal cases, initially on a pilot scheme basis. This could cover up to a million cases a year.

The Royal Commission on Legal Services 1979

The Commission on Legal Services made the following recommendations:

- the Green Form scheme should be merged into the main legal aid schemes, and eligibility levels should be standardized and raised;
- a free initial half-hour consultation should be offered to anyone who wants it, regardless of means;
- in criminal cases there should be a statutory right to legal aid for indictable and either way offences, and legal aid should be provided for summary offences unless the defendant was unlikely to receive a custodial sentence, or deportation order, or suffer major damage to livelihood or reputation, and where representation was not necessary to put the case properly;
- the Government should set up a Council on Legal Services to research into the provision of legal services, recommend and carry out any necessary changes, and generally keep the area under review.
- legal aid should be better remunerated;
- solicitors should be given interest-free loans to encourage them to set up business in less desirable areas.

None of these provisions were implemented.

The Legal Aid Efficiency Scrutiny

This was a Government team set up to investigate the workings of the statutory scheme in 1986. Its main recommendation was that the Green Form scheme should be abolished, and initial advice in civil cases be given by advice agencies such as the Citizens Advice Bureau. Cases should be referred to solicitors only when it became clear that litigation was needed, or in the case of family work, where detailed negotiations were required. The Government should spend £25m on the advice agencies to take account of the increased workload.

This proposal was met with disapproval by both the Law Society, which claimed that the cost of the plan, if done properly, would be more like £360m, and waste money on providing two parallel services; and the National Association of Citizens Advice Bureaux, which felt the change would threaten its independence and undermine its relationship with the legal profession. The plan was never implemented, but Lord McKay's current proposals envisage advice agencies playing a major role in providing franchised services.

Other reform proposals

A national legal service?

Perhaps the most radical reform would be to take the statutory scheme entirely out of the hands of private practice and establish a nationwide network of salaried lawyers on the law centre model. All funding could be given on a block rather than case by case basis, for centres to use in whatever ways best met the needs of their own locality, in consultation with management committees representing the community.

This would deal with some of the criticism of the current schemes made by Kate Markus and discussed above (p. 167). In particular the advantages of this idea include:

- state-funded work would no longer have to compete with private work for lawyers' time;
- state funding would no longer have to include an element of profit for the lawyer;
- resources could be more flexibly employed, on a combination of individual casework and litigation, education and campaigning, or any other approach that suited particular problems;
- this more flexible approach to dealing with problems would get away from the over-emphasis on litigation of solicitors in private practice;
- the ability to run educative campaigns would help deal with public ignorance of legal rights;
- law centres appear not to suffer from the unapproachable image of the legal profession in general;
- law centres have been successful in attracting problems not previously brought to lawyers, especially welfare and employment cases;
- a nationwide network of such centres would help overcome the uneven distribution of solicitors' firms.

The 1979 Royal Commission on Legal Services did suggest the establishment of a nationwide network of centrally-financed Citizens Law Centres, but felt that these should be restricted to individual casework only and not get involved in general work for the community. This idea would fail to take advantage of one of the real strengths of the law centre movement, and the fact that solicitors in private practice would still be allowed to undertake legal aid work would limit the improvements to be made in cost-efficiency. The Law Centres Federation rejected the idea.

Barrister Daniel Stilitz has argued for a similar scheme, though not necessarily based on law centres. Under his National Justice Service, anyone seeking to bring a legal action would need to show a reasonable cause (as legal aid applicants must now); if the case had a reasonable prospect of success, the NJS would decide what services were needed, fix a budget and allocate a lawyer on the basis of suitability and availability. Stilitz points out that for such a scheme to equalize access to justice, it would have to be compulsory – if one side was allowed to 'go private', the scales might be tipped unfairly in their favour. So, both sides would be obliged to use NJS lawyers. The service would be means-tested, with contributions of up to 100 per cent, ensuring that those who could afford to pay the whole cost did so, but could not use that wealth to secure an advantage in the justice system. Those who could not afford to pay would receive free or subsidized help. The result, says Stilitz, would be a level playing field, with cases decided on merits and wasteful tactics designed to drive up costs eliminated.

Stilitz acknowledges that the plan would remove client choice, but argues that improving access to justice is more important. He also points out that while many might object to the loss of independence involved in tying lawyers so closely to the state, this cannot have a worse effect on individual rights than the current system, under which financial pressures mean that for many citizens, their rights are useless because they cannot afford to enforce them.

Justice: a contingency fund
The law reform body, Justice, has suggested the establishment of a contingency Legal Aid fund, financed by the contributions from successful litigants. It would pay lawyers on the normal win or lose basis but would recoup costs in successful cases. However, as Zander has pointed out, the major problem with such a scheme is finding the initial funding, particularly if the fund were to be established on a voluntary basis.

The Law Society has proposed a fixed costs scheme, which people would join when they started a legal action. They would pay a fixed fee, win or lose, and the fees from successful cases would go to pay for unsuccessful ones.

Legal Action Group: A Strategy for Justice
The Legal Action Group, a campaigning organization, recommends ending the current piecemeal approach to legal advice and assistance, and creating an independent, publicly-funded Legal Services Commission. The Commission would be given an annual grant, and allowed to determine spending priorities – similar commissions are in place in Australia and other common law jurisdictions.

LAG also suggests that free advice should be given in areas of special need, including housing, custody, children, personal injury, employment protection, most criminal cases and immigration. Means testing would be retained, but there would be a free initial interview, regardless of means. But the plan goes further than merely dealing with the financial problems of access to justice; in order to address other problems of unmet need, it proposes that the Legal Services Commission should have responsibility for educating and informing people about their rights and duties, including alternative methods of dispute resolution, and for research into the provision of legal services.

The Marre Committee: action on unmet legal need

The Marre Committee on the legal profession tackled the problems of unmet need that were not cost-related. It suggested the following:

- Legal awareness to be taught in schools.
- Targeted information campaigns on legal rights and how to enforce them.
- Public relations activity on behalf of both the professions as a whole and individual firms.
- Shop floor premises for solicitors' firms.
- Changes in working practices to make them more 'client-friendly'.
- Improvements to be made in speed and responsiveness of service.
- Efforts to be made towards meeting the needs of ethnic communities.

Opening up the legal professions to a wider variety of people (see p. 117) would also go some way towards changing the unapproachable image of lawyers that puts some people off consulting them.

Public interest cases

It can be argued that cases raising important points of law (usually appeal cases) should be publicly-funded, regardless of means. In many such cases, losing litigants may have won every hearing up until the last, yet as the law stands, they still have to pay all the costs. This is unfair given that the outcome of the case may be impossible to predict; litigants should not be held financially responsible for lack of clarity in the law, and since such cases contribute to law reform, which is to society's benefit, it seems reasonable that society should pay for them.

No-fault compensation

A large amount of work could be taken out of the court system and therefore the legal aid scheme altogether if a system of no-fault compensation for personal injury cases was established, as it has been in New Zealand. Although this might not save money overall, at least all the money would be spent on helping the victim of injury, rather than paying lawyers; under the present system, public money is spent on paying lawyers even when the injured person loses the case and comes away empty-handed.

Lord Woolf's interim report

Lord Woolf's interim report is called *Access to Justice* and he makes various proposals related to the issue of the unmet need for legal services. He suggests that there should be permanent advice centres in courts, if these are found to be more effective than those located elsewhere. There should be a duty advice scheme funded by legal aid at all courts identified as handling substantial levels of debt and housing work. He says that legal aid funding for Citizens Advice Bureaux or similar facilities at court centres should be considered. In his opinion, alternative ways of providing court services in rural areas should be explored, including mobile courts providing small claims hearings as well as advice and information, while the possibility of holding evening or weekend courts should be re-examined. Finally he remarks that court buildings should be clearly signposted in appropriate minority languages as well as English.

ANSWERING QUESTIONS

1 **How far does the current provision of legal services for those who are unable to pay for them meet the needs of society?**
First of all, you need to define what you understand by the needs of society – you might mention equality of access to the law, and a system that allows all members of society to enforce their legal rights, but you also need to mention the need for such a scheme to be cost-effective, since society has to pay for it.

You can then go on to say why a scheme to provide legal services for those who are unable to pay for them is needed, mentioning the high cost of legal action. Then outline the provisions which are available, including the statutory scheme and the agencies outside it, such as law centres and Citizens Advice Bureaux. There is no need to go into too much detail here.

The main part of your essay should detail whether you think these provisions are adequate from the point of view of issues such as equal access to justice. You should of course discuss the financial problems of the various schemes, and the gaps in provision, but you also need to consider the other reasons for unmet legal need, and how far the provisions deal with these reasons.

You should then discuss the issue of cost effectiveness, perhaps bringing in the issues of reliance on private practice, of establishing no-fault compensation for personal injury, and Lord McKay's proposals.

Finally you could mention any reforms which you feel would improve the provision of legal services for those who cannot afford to pay for them.

2 **Brown has been involved in a road accident with Green, as a result of which the police have charged Brown with dangerous driving and Green has started civil proceedings against Brown, claiming damages in excess of £100,000.**
(a) Advise Brown as to how he may obtain legal aid and advice.
(b) Do you think that such provisions are adequate? *Oxford*
You need to keep the two parts separate and answer them in turn. In part (a) it is essential to make sure you are advising the right person. Accidentally advising Green instead would at best get you half marks, since you would not include criminal legal aid, and advising both would waste valuable time and gain no extra marks, so always check that aspect of a question carefully.

When advising Brown, you need to work through his two court cases in turn, starting with his possible prosecution. Using the material above, work through the types of legal aid that might be available under the statutory scheme, pointing out what help can be given, how Brown should go about getting it, and what criteria determine his eligibility for it. Then do the same with his civil case. After you have done this, go through the other sources of legal aid and advice to which he could turn – CABs, Law Centres, and of course motoring insurance and membership of motoring organisations if he has them.

(b) Here you need to highlight the problems with legal aid as it stands, with, if you have time, proposals for reform.

The criminal justice system

The criminal justice system is one of the most important tools available to society for the control of anti-social behaviour. It is also the area of the English legal system which has most potential for controversy, given that through the criminal justice system, the state has the means to interfere with individual freedom in the strongest way: by sending people to prison.

An effective criminal justice system needs to strike a balance between punishing the guilty and protecting the innocent; our systems of investigating crime need safeguards which prevent the innocent being found guilty, but those safeguards must not be so strong that it is impossible to convict those who are guilty. This balance has been the subject of much debate in recent years: a large number of miscarriages of justice, where innocent people were sent to prison, has suggested a system weighted too heavily towards proving guilt, yet shortly after these cases had been uncovered, there were claims, particularly from the police, that the balance had tipped too far in the other direction.

▶ The miscarriages of justice

Before looking in detail at the criminal justice system, it is useful to understand what happened to cause the miscarriages of justice which have hit the headlines over the past few years, causing a crisis of confidence in the system. The following are just some of those miscarriages (you may find it useful to read the section on criminal appeals, p. 299, before reading this).

The Guildford Four

In October 1974, the IRA bombed a pub in Guildford. A year later, Patrick Armstrong, Paul Hill, Carole Richardson, Gerard Conlon and two others were convicted of the five murders arising from the bombing. Mr Armstrong and Mr Hill were also convicted of two murders arising from an explosion in November 1974 at a pub in Woolwich. All were sentenced to life imprisonment.

The prosecution case was based almost entirely on confessions which were alleged to have been made while the four were in police custody. There was no other evidence that any of the four were members of the IRA, and they were certainly not the type of people that an effective terrorist organization would choose to carry out such an important part of its campaign – Patrick Armstrong and Carole Richardson, for example, took drugs, lived in a squat, and were involved in petty crime.

Like the other victims of miscarriages of justice, they tried to get their convictions referred to the Court of Appeal under s. 17 of the Criminal Appeal Act 1968, but were initially unsuccessful. In 1987, a Home Office memorandum recognized that the Four were unlikely terrorists, but the Home Office concluded that this could not be considered to be new evidence justifying referral to the Court of Appeal.

Then, in 1989, a police detective looking into the case found a set of typed notes of interviews with Patrick Armstrong, which contained deletions and additions, both typed and handwritten, as well as some rearrangements of material. Police evidence had consisted of a set of handwritten notes which they said were made at the time of the interview, and a typed version of these notes; both incorporated the corrections made on the newly discovered typewritten set, suggesting that this new set were made after the interviews had been conducted, and that the handwritten notes presented as being made at interview had actually been made much later. The implication was that the notes had been constructed so as to fit in with the case the police wished to present.

Patrick Armstrong's confession was central to the prosecution case. Anything which cast doubt on it would undermine all four convictions. The Director of Public Prosecutions, Alan Green, decided that he should not oppose a further appeal, and this took place in 1989. Giving judgment, the Lord Chief Justice said there were two possible explanations. The first was that the typescripts were a complete fabrication, amended to make them more effective and then written out by hand to appear as if they were contemporaneous. Alternatively, the police had started with a contemporaneous note, typed it up to improve legibility, amended it to make it read better, and then converted it back to a manuscript note. Either way, the police officers had not told the truth. The Lord Chief Justice concluded: 'If they were prepared to tell this sort of lie then the whole of their evidence became suspect.' As a result, the Guildford Four were released, after having spent fifteen years in prison for crimes which they did not commit.

The Maguires

In March 1976, the Maguire family, including Patrick Conlon, were convicted of unlawfully possessing the explosive nitroglycerine in December 1974. They were sentenced to between four and fourteen years.

The family came under investigation because Gerard Conlon, one of the Guildford Four, allegedly told the police, while being questioned about the Guildford bombings, that Mrs Maguire, his aunt, had shown him how to make bombs at her home in London. Two months after those bombings, the police raided Mrs Maguire's house and arrested the family. No explosives were ever found at the house, nor was there any evidence of what the family were supposed to have done with the explosives they were charged with possessing. The prosecution case was largely based on forensic tests which apparently showed minute traces of explosives on their hands (or, in Mrs Maguire's case, on her gloves). The Maguire family always maintained their innocence, but in the face of the test results, it was difficult to make a successful appeal.

An appeal was eventually allowed when new scientific evidence showed that the forensic tests were far from conclusive. A positive result in these tests could have been produced by the soap or detergent used to wash laboratory dishes, or in some cases, even from smoking cigarettes. Patrick Conlon died in custody. All the others served their sentences and were released.

The Birmingham Six

In November 1974, 21 people died and 162 were injured when IRA bombs exploded in two crowded pubs in the centre of Birmingham. The bombs caused outrage in Britain, and led to a wave of anti-Irish feeling.

The six Irishmen who became known as the Birmingham Six were arrested after police kept a watch on ports immediately after the bombings. Five of them were travelling to Northern Ireland, the sixth having gone to see them off, and the police asked them to undergo forensic tests in order to eliminate them from their inquiries. The men had told the police that they were travelling to Northern Ireland to see relatives; this was partly true, but their main reason for travelling was to attend the funeral of James McDade, an IRA man. Although some of the Six may well have had Republican sympathies, none were actually members of the IRA and none supported its campaign of violence. Nor had they suspected, until McDade was killed, that he was involved in terrorism. Nevertheless, they all knew his family, and intended to go to the funeral as a mark of respect for the family, a normal practice in Northern Ireland which would not necessarily suggest support for the dead person's political views.

Perhaps not surprisingly given the situation at the time, the men did not mention the funeral when the police asked why they were travelling, and equally unsurprisingly, when the police searched their luggage and found evidence of their real reason for travelling, they became extremely suspicious. When the forensic tests, conducted by a Dr Skuse, indicated that the men had been handling explosives, the police were convinced their suspicions were right.

At their trial, the case rested on two main pieces of evidence: the forensic tests, and confessions which the men had made to the police. A scientific expert for the defence argued that the forensic tests were unreliable, because contact with perfectly innocent substances such as paint could produce a positive result. In addition, the men had been playing cards while they waited for the boat; if one of the men's hands had been in contact with explosives, traces would have been transferred to the cards and from there to the hands of the others. Yet tests on the cards and the hands of two of the men proved negative.

The Six claimed that while at the police station, they had been beaten, kicked and threatened with death; they were also told that their families were in danger and would only be protected if the men confessed. As a result, they felt forced to confess to crimes they did not commit. There was clear evidence that the Six were beaten up; photos taken three days after their admission on remand to Winston Green prison show serious scars. However, the men were also beaten up by prison officers once they were remanded in custody, and the prosecution used this beating to explain the photographic evidence, stating that there had been no physical abuse by the police, and that therefore the confessions were valid. Yet a close examination of the confessions would have made it obvious that they were made by people who knew nothing about the bombings: they contradicted each other, none of them revealed anything about the way the bombings were done that the police did not know already, and some of the 'revelations' proved to be untrue – for example, three of the men said the bombs were left in carrier bags, when forensic evidence later showed them to have been in holdalls.

The men were never put on identity parades, even though at least one person who had been present in one of the bombed pubs felt he could have identified the bombers; nor were witnesses called from the bar where the men said they were at the time the bombs were placed. Nor was there any forensic evidence to suggest that the men had been in the bombed pubs, or to link their homes with bombmaking. Nevertheless, the Six were convicted and sentenced to life imprisonment, the judge commenting 'You have been convicted on the clearest and most overwhelming evidence I have ever heard in a case of murder.' On appeal, the judges reprimanded the trial judge for aspects of his summing up and a character attack on a defence witness; they acknowledged the weaknesses in forensic evidence, yet concluded that this evidence would have played a small part in the jury's decision; and as far as the confession evidence was concerned, one of them mentioned the black eye on one of the defendants, 'the origin of which I have forgotten', but said 'I do not think it matters much anyway'. The appeal was dismissed.

Fourteen prison officers were tried for assault of the Six; the Six were not allowed to appear as witnesses, and all fourteen were acquitted. Evidence given suggested that the men had already been injured when they arrived at the prison. The Six then brought a civil action for assault against the police force. This claim was struck out, apparently on the basis that since the jury had found the Six guilty at the original trial, they must have believed they had never been beaten by the police, and that therefore there was no reason to re-open that issue; the new evidence brought in the prison officers' trial could not be put forward because it could have been discovered in time for the original trial and should have been used then. Lord Denning's judgment summed up the legal system's attitude to the case, pointing out that if the Six won, and proved they had been assaulted in order to secure their confessions, this would mean that the police had lied, and used violence and threats, and that the convictions were false; the Home Secretary would have to recommend a pardon or send the case back to the Court of Appeal. This, said Lord Denning, was 'such an appalling vista that every sensible person would say "It cannot be right that these actions should go any further".'

In January 1987, the Home Secretary referred the case back to the Court of Appeal, on the basis of fresh scientific evidence casting doubt on the tests for nitroglycerine, witness evidence concerning the beatings in the police station, evidence rather like the various sets of notes in the Guildford Four case which suggested the confessions had been partially made up by the police, and a testimony from the Bishop of Derry concerning the strong Catholic tradition of attending funerals, regardless of approval for the deceased. The appeal took a year; the convictions were upheld. The Lord Chief Justice Lord Lane ended the court's judgment with remarks which were to become notorious: 'The longer this hearing has gone on, the more convinced this court has become that the verdict of the jury was correct. We have no doubt that these convictions were both safe and satisfactory.'

In the end, it took sixteen years for the Six to get their convictions quashed. In 1990, a new Home Secretary referred the case back to the Court of Appeal. A new technique had been developed, known as Electrostatic Document Analysis (ESDA) which could examine the indentations made on paper by writing on the sheets above. The test suggested that notes of a police interview with one of the Six had not been recorded contemporaneously, as West Midlands detectives had claimed in court. The scientific findings in the Maguire case also meant that the nitroglycerine tests could no longer be relied on. The prosecution decided not to seek to sustain the convictions and the Six were finally freed in 1991.

Judith Ward

Judith Ward was given a life sentence in 1974 for offences including the murder of twelve people, who died when a bomb exploded in a coach on the M62 motorway. During her trial she made admissions and confessions, some of which could be shown to be clearly untrue, and part of the scientific evidence against her was given by Dr Frank Skuse, the Home Office forensic scientist who also gave evidence against the Birmingham Six. In addition, the prosecution had in its possession over 5,000 items of evidence which would have pointed to her innocence, but failed to disclose them.

She was finally released and her conviction quashed after eighteen years in prison. The Court of Appeal said that a grave miscarriage of justice had occurred because: 'in failing to disclose evidence [to the defence] . . . one or more members of the West Yorkshire police, the scientists who gave evidence at the trial, and some of those members of the staff of the DPP and counsel who advised them . . . failed to carry out . . . their basic duty to seek to ensure a trial which is fair to both the prosecution . . . and the accused.'

The Tottenham Three

Engin Raghip, Winston Silcott and Mark Braithwaite were convicted of murdering PC Keith Blakelock in 1985 during rioting at the Broadwater Farm Estate in North London. As with the Irish miscarriages of justice, the crime was one which evoked strong feelings, among both police and ordinary people. Newspapers carried graphic details of the savage way in which PC Blakelock was killed, and exhorted the police to find the killer.

Again, confession evidence and statements given to the police proved unreliable. One apparent witness allegedly gave a 55-page statement, describing the murder in full detail, and incriminating himself and 27 others. The whole statement was later discovered to be complete fiction; the 'witness' had not even been at Broadwater Farm that night. The statement was obtained after the man had been held incommunicado for 55 hours in Barnet police station.

The Tottenham Three were convicted solely on alleged confessions to police; they were denied access to solicitors during the time these confessions were allegedly made. There were hundreds of police photos of the scene, yet the Three appeared in none of them, and nor was there any scientific evidence. Winston Silcott never signed his alleged confession, which was the only evidence against him. Mark Braithwaite was suffering from claustrophobia and was detained for long hours in a police cell when he gave his 'confession'.

Evidence was later produced that Mr Raghip was of low intelligence, and would be abnormally suggestible under the pressure of a police interview, and an appeal was sought on the basis of this new evidence. But leave to appeal was refused, a decision for which Lord Lane was later criticized by the Court of Appeal. Winston Silcott was also refused leave to appeal when he first applied in 1988.

Finally, the ESDA test, described above, satisfied the Court of Appeal that vital parts of the notes were inserted after other parts of Mr Silcott's interview were completed. As there was no other evidence against him, the conviction was quashed. The other two were cleared due to alleged misconduct by the police in the course of the original police investigation.

▶ The response to the miscarriages of justice

The miscarriages of justice described above, and others, showed that there was something seriously wrong with our criminal justice system. On 14 March 1991, when the Court of Appeal quashed the convictions of the Birmingham Six, the Home Secretary announced that a Royal Commission on Criminal Justice (RCCJ) would be set up to examine the criminal justice system from start to finish – from the time the police first investigate to the final appeal. The RCCJ (sometimes called the Runciman Commission, after its chairperson) considered these issues for two years, during which they received evidence from over 600 organizations and asked academics to carry out 22 research studies on how the system works in practice. In July 1993 they published their final report. In examining the workings of the criminal justice system, some of the research presented to the RCCJ, its recommendations and some changes that have subsequently been made will be considered.

▶ The adversarial process

The English system of criminal justice is what is known as adversarial. This means each side is responsible for putting their own case: collecting evidence, interviewing witnesses and retaining experts. In court they will present their own evidence and attack their opponent's evidence by cross-examining their adversary's witnesses. Both parties only call those witnesses likely to advance their cause and both parties are permitted to attack the credibility and reliability of the witnesses testifying for the other side. The role of the judge is limited to that of a referee ensuring fair play, ensuring that the rules on procedure and evidence are followed. It is often compared with a battle with each side fighting their own corner. The adversarial system is typical of common law countries.

The alternative is an inquisitorial system, which exists in most of the rest of Europe. Under that system, a judge plays the dominant role in collecting evidence before the trial. During the course of a lengthy investigation, the judge will interview witnesses and inspect documents, and the final trial is often just to rubber stamp the judge's findings. In France the judge in charge of the pre-trial investigation is called the 'juge d'instruction'.

In the light of the recent miscarriages of justice, some people have suggested that we should introduce the inquisitorial system into England. Arguments were put forward that in serious cases the inquisitorial system provides a properly organized and regulated pre-trial phase, with an independent figure supervising the whole investigation, so the Royal Commission ordered research into the French and German criminal justice system (Leigh and Zedner, 1992). The researchers rejected the idea of introducing the inquisitorial system into England. They did not think that the 'juge d'instruction' was a real protection against overbearing police practices, except in rare cases where physical brutality was involved. Furthermore, despite the fact that only 10 per cent of cases go before 'the juge d'instruction' in France, the system is overburdened and works slowly.

The French are themselves thinking of making changes. A French Commission has recommended that the pre-trial investigation should be transferred from the juge d'instruction to the public prosecutor, to avoid the potential conflict between the functions of investigator and judge. In Germany and Italy this has already been done.

▶ Police powers

Most people's first contact with the criminal justice system involves the police, and because they have responsibility for investigating crimes, gathering evidence, and deciding whether to charge a suspect, they play an important part in its overall operation. They also have wide powers over suspects, which may be used to help convict the guilty or, as the miscarriages of justice have shown, abused to convict the innocent.

The main piece of legislation regulating police powers is the Police and Criminal Evidence Act 1984 (PACE). The Act was the product of a Royal Commission set up following an earlier miscarriage of justice, concerning the murder in 1977 of a man called Maxwell Confait. Confait was found strangled with electric flex in a burning house, and three boys, aged fourteen, fifteen and eighteen, one of whom was educationally subnormal, were arrested, interrogated and, as a result of their confessions, charged with murder. Three years later, they were all released after an official report into the case (the Fisher Report) concluded that they had nothing to do with the killing.

In the light of concern over the police conduct of this case, and in particular the interrogation process, the then Labour Government set up the Royal Commission on Criminal Procedure (RCCP), sometimes known as the Philips Commission, to examine police procedures. It reported in 1981.

The Commission said that a balance needed to be reached between 'the interests of the community in bringing offenders to justice and the rights and liberties of persons suspected or accused of crime'. However, it, and the subsequent Act (PACE), were criticized by some as unjustifiably extending police powers, especially in the areas of stop and search, arrest and detention at the police station.

PACE was intended to replace a confusing mixture of common law, legislation and local bye-laws on pre-trial procedure with a single coherent statute. It provides a general, comprehensive and comprehensible code of police powers to stop people, search them, arrest them, hold them in police custody and interrogate them. It also lays down the suspects' rights. Although it did extend police powers, it also introduced a number of protections for the suspect. Since the implementation of PACE, the police have fought a campaign to reduce the effectiveness of these new protections, partly because of the bureaucracy they create, but also because they are said to tip the balance too far in favour of the suspect, making it too difficult for the police to convict the guilty.

The new Criminal Justice and Public Order Act 1994 (CJPOA) extends police powers significantly. It introduces some of the recommendations of the RCCJ, and other changes that the RCCJ was opposed to, for example, the abolition of the right to silence.

As well as the statutory rules on police powers, contained in PACE and the CJPOA, there are Codes of Practice, drawn up by the Home Office under s. 66 of PACE, which do not form part of the law, but which provide extra detail on the provisions of the Act. Breach of these Codes cannot be the ground for a legal action, but can give rise to disciplinary procedures, and if they are breached in very serious ways, evidence obtained as a result of such a breach may be excluded in a criminal trial. It has been argued that some of the Code provisions should be legally enforceable and form part of PACE itself.

The Codes have recently been revised, their third edition having come into force on 10 April 1995 in the light of changes in police powers made under the CJPOA and to take account of recommendations of the RCCJ and others.

Pre-arrest powers

Police officers are always free to ask members of the public questions in order to prevent and detect crime, but members of the public are not obliged to answer such questions, nor to go to a police station or be detained at a police station unless they are lawfully arrested. In **Rice** *v* **Connolly** (1966), the appellant was spotted by police officers in the early hours of the morning, behaving suspiciously in an area where burglaries had taken place that night. The officers asked where he was going and where he had come from; he refused to answer, or to give his full name and address, though he did give a name and the name of a road, which were not untrue. The officers asked him to go with them to a police box for identification purposes, but he refused, saying, 'If you want me, you will have to arrest me.' He was arrested and eventually convicted of wilfully obstructing the police contrary to s. 51(3) of the Police Act of 1964, but his conviction was quashed on appeal on the basis that nobody is obliged to answer police questions.

However, the line between maintaining the freedom not to answer questions and actually obstructing the police would appear to be a thin one. In **Ricketts** *v* **Cox** (1982), two police officers, who were looking for youths responsible for a serious assault, approached the defendant and another man in the early hours of the morning. The defendant was said to have been abusive, uncooperative and hostile to the officers, using obscene language which was designed to provoke and antagonize the officers and eventually trying to walk away from them. The magistrates found that the police officers acted in a proper manner and were entitled to put questions to the two men; the defendant's behaviour and attitude amounted to an obstruction of the police officers in the execution of their duty contrary to s. 51(3) of the Police Act 1964. An appeal was dismissed, and the implication appears to be that while merely refusing to answer questions is lawful, rudely refusing to do so may amount to obstruction of the police.

An even more problematic area is the question of how far the police are allowed to detain a person without arresting them. The courts appear to have concluded that under common law the police cannot actually prevent a person from moving away, though they can touch them to attract their attention (they also have some statutory powers in this area, discussed at p. 197).

In **Kenlin** *v* **Gardiner** (1967), two schoolboys were seen going from house to house. In fact they were reminding members of their rugby team about a game, but not realizing this, the two plain-clothes police officers who spotted them became suspicious and, producing a warrant card, asked what they were doing. The boys did not believe the men were police officers, and one of them appeared to try to run away. A police officer caught hold of his arm, and the boy responded by struggling violently, punching and kicking the officer, at which point the second boy got involved and struck the other officer. Both boys were convicted of assaulting a police constable in the execution of his duty in the magistrates' court, but an appeal was allowed, on the grounds that the police did not have the power to detain the boys prior to arrest, and so the boys were merely acting in self defence.

In **Donnelly** *v* **Jackman** (1970), the appellant was walking along a road one Saturday evening at about 11.15 pm, when a uniformed police officer came up to him, intending to make inquiries about an offence which the officer had reason to believe the appellant might have committed. The officer asked the appellant if he could have a word with him, but the appellant ignored him and walked on. The officer followed close behind him, repeating his request, and on being ignored, tapped the appellant on the shoulder. The appellant turned round and tapped the officer on the chest saying, 'Now we are even, copper'. When the officer tapped him on the shoulder a second time, the appellant turned round again, and this time hit the officer. He was convicted of assaulting an officer in the execution of his duty, and argued that in tapping him on the shoulder the officer had acted outside his duty. However, the court held that what the officer had done was not unlawful detention but merely 'a trivial interference with liberty', and the conviction was upheld.

Stop and search under PACE

PACE repealed a variety of often obscure and unsatisfactory statutory provisions on stop and search; the main powers in this area are now contained in s. 1 of PACE. Under s. 1 a constable may search a person or vehicle in public, for stolen or prohibited articles (defined as offensive weapons or articles used for the purpose of burglary or related crimes). A person or vehicle can be detained for this purpose. This power can only be used where the police have 'reasonable grounds for suspecting that they will find stolen or prohibited articles' (s. 1(3)).

The requirement of reasonable suspicion is intended to protect individuals from being subject to stop and search on a random basis, or on grounds that the law rightly finds unacceptable, such as age or racial group. Code of Practice A (concerning the exercise of statutory powers of stop and search) provides guidance on the meaning of 'reasonable grounds for suspecting'. Paragraph 1.7 of the Code provides:

> Reasonable suspicion can never be supported on the basis of personal factors alone. For example, a person's colour, age, hairstyle or manner of dress, or the fact that he is known to have a previous conviction for possession of an unlawful article, cannot be used alone or in combination with each other as the sole basis on which to search that person. Nor may it be found on the basis of stereotyped images of certain persons or groups as more likely to be committing offences.

A new paragraph 1.7A of the Code makes it clear that even if the police think that the particular individual is innocent of the relevant crime, they may still search if there are reasonable grounds for suspecting that person to be carrying the items concerned – so for example, they may search someone reasonably suspected of being in possession of stolen goods, even if they do not suspect that person of stealing them.

Research by Sanders ('Controlling the Discretion of the Individual Officer', 1993) has found that in practice, one of the main factors which prompts the police to search someone is knowledge that the person has previous convictions. Pre-PACE research by Smith and Gray found that in carrying out stop and search, the police often relied on instinct, which could lead to class and race bias in making stops, and in turn to those groups which were commonly stopped seeing the stops as harassment by police.

Before searching under these powers, police officers must, among other things, identify themselves and the station where they are based, and tell the person to be searched the grounds for the search. If not in uniform, police officers must provide documentary identification. Reasonable force may be used to conduct the stop and search (s. 117), but the suspect cannot be required to remove any clothing in public, except for an outer coat, jacket or gloves (s. 2(9)).

Any stolen or prohibited articles discovered by the police during the search may be seized (s. 1(6)). Details of the search must be recorded, and if requested a copy must be supplied to the person searched (s. 3). Searches must be recorded and the record be made available to a suspect on request, unless the suspect submitted to the search voluntarily.

Other powers to stop and search

Various other statutes give specific stop and search powers regarding particular offences. The Misuse of Drugs Act 1971, s. 23, allows the police to stop and search anyone who is suspected on reasonable grounds to be in unlawful possession of a controlled drug; the Sporting Events Act 1985 gives the power to stop and search people before entry into certain sporting events such as a football match; and there are also specific provisions concerning those who are suspected of unlawfully carrying firearms.

Stop and search powers have been further broadened by s. 60 of the CJPOA, which provides that where a senior police officer reasonably believes that serious violence may take place in an area, he or she may, in order to prevent its occurrence, give written authorization for officers to stop and search persons and vehicles in that area for up to 24 hours. This can be extended by a further six hours; after that a fresh 24 hour authorization must be made if necessary. When such authorization is in place, police officers can stop and search any pedestrian or vehicle for offensive weapons or dangerous instruments. Offensive weapon bears the same meaning as in s. 1 of PACE; dangerous instrument means an instrument which has a blade or is sharply pointed (s. 60(11)). Unlike s. 1 of PACE, these powers do not require reasonable grounds for suspicion – in fact their purpose is precisely to allow stop and search where it would not previously have been allowed because of that requirement.

In addition, under s. 65 of the Criminal Justice and Public Order Act, an officer can stop anyone on their way to a 'rave' and direct them not to proceed. Similar powers exist under s. 71, in relation to trespassory assemblies (defined on p. 36). These rather draconian powers can be exercised within five miles of the rave or assembly.

Section 81 creates a new power to stop and search persons and vehicles where it is expedient to do so to prevent certain acts of terrorism. This new provision was prompted by various IRA bombings, and is designed to safeguard the public against the dual threats of vehicle bombs and small explosive devices carried by individual terrorists and placed in sites such as litter bins.

There are clearly potential dangers in granting wide stop and search powers to the police if there is a possibility that the powers will be abused, with harassment of ethnic minority groups being a particular concern. A police operation against street robberies (muggings) in Lambeth in 1981, codenamed SWAMP 81, involved 943 stops, mostly of black youths, over a period of two weeks. Of these, only 118 led to arrests and 75 to charges, only one of which was for robbery. The operation, which had no noticeable effect on the crime figures, shattered relations between the police and the ethnic community, and was one of the triggers of the Brixton riots that occurred soon afterwards.

Nevertheless, in his report on the Brixton disorders, Lord Scarman thought such powers necessary to combat street crime, provided that the safeguard of 'reasonable suspicion' was properly and objectively applied.

Powers of arrest

Powers of arrest allow people to be detained against their will. However, in order to make such detention lawful, the arrest itself must be in accordance with the law. At one time, suspects were usually only arrested when the police had gathered enough evidence to make a case against them, and a charge usually followed very soon after arrest. Now arrest is usually undertaken earlier in the process, and is seen by the police as a prelude to gaining supplementary evidence, mainly through interrogation.

There are two basic types of arrest: arrest with a warrant; and arrest without a warrant, under PACE.

Arrest with a warrant

Under s. 1 of the Magistrates' Courts Act 1980, criminal proceedings may be initiated either by the issue of a summons, requiring the accused to attend court on a particular day, or in more serious cases by a warrant of arrest issued by the magistrates' court. The police obtain a warrant by applying in writing to a magistrate, and backing up the application with an oral statement made on oath. The warrant must specify the name of the person to be arrested and general particulars of the offence. In issuing a warrant for arrest, the magistrate may endorse it for bail. When an arrest warrant has been issued, a constable may enter and search premises to make the arrest, using such reasonable force as is necessary (PACE s. 117).

Arrest without a warrant

There are now three main categories of arrest without warrant, mentioned in ss. 24, 25 and 26 of PACE.

Reasonable suspicion concerning an arrestable offence. Under s. 24 of PACE, a police officer can arrest without a warrant a person whom they reasonably suspect has committed or is committing, or is about to commit an arrestable offence.

Arrestable offences comprise:

- all offences for which the sentence is fixed by law (for example, life imprisonment in the case of murder);
- all offences for which the maximum sentence for an adult is five years' imprisonment or longer.
- certain other specified offences (for example, offences contained in the Official Secrets Acts 1911–89, the Sexual Offences Act 1956, and the Theft Act 1968).

General arrest conditions. Section 25 of PACE gives the police a power to arrest anyone who they reasonably suspect has committed or attempted, or is committing or attempting, any offence, if serving a summons appears inappropriate or impracticable because of the existence of specified circumstances. Known as the 'general arrest conditions', these circumstances are:

- that the suspect will not give his or her name and address, or the police officer reasonably suspects that the name or address given is false, or the address is unsatisfactory for service of a summons; or
- that arrest is necessary to prevent physical harm and damage to property or obstruction of the highway or to protect a child or other vulnerable person from the suspect, or the suspect from harming themselves or suffering physical injury.

In **G** *v* **Director of Public Prosecutions** (1989), it was held that a belief by the police officer concerned that 'suspects generally give false names' was not sufficient to satisfy the general arrest conditions.

Arrest for breach of the peace. Section 26 of PACE preserves the old common law power of arrest for breach of the peace recognized in the important case of **R** *v* **Howell** (1982).

Other statutory powers of arrest

Certain other statutes provide powers of arrest. For example, s. 5 of the Public Order Act 1986 permits a police officer to arrest without a warrant anyone who commits the offence of disorderly conduct, provided the officer has warned the person in question to stop the disorderly conduct, and the person has continued; and the CJPOA gives a constable in uniform the power to arrest without a warrant a person reasonably suspected of committing attending or preparing for a rave or going to attend a rave.

Citizen's arrest
An ordinary citizen can arrest someone who is reasonably suspected to be committing an arrestable offence, and, where such an offence has been committed, anyone who is reasonably suspected of being guilty of it. If the offence has not actually been committed by anyone, the citizen may be liable for damages (**Walters** *v* **WH Smith** (1914)).

Manner of arrest
PACE requires that at the time of, or as soon as practicable after the arrest, the person arrested must be informed that he or she is under arrest, and given the grounds for that arrest, even if it is perfectly obvious that they are being arrested and why. This is in line with the previous case law, where in **Christie** *v* **Leachinsky** (1947) Viscount Simon said: 'No one, I think, would approve a situation in which when the person arrested asked for the reason, the policeman replied "that has nothing to do with you: come along with me" . . .'

There is no set form of words that must be used, and colloquial language such as 'You're nicked for doing a robbery' may be acceptable.

Police detention

Apart from powers given by anti-terrorist legislation, before 1984 the police in England and Wales had no express power to detain suspects for further investigations to be carried out, nor did they have a general power to detain individuals for questioning, whether as suspects or potential witnesses. In practice the police often acted as if they did have these powers.

The 1981 Royal Commission on Criminal Procedure recommended that the police should be given express powers to detain suspects for questioning, with safeguards to ensure that those powers were not abused. These express powers were granted by PACE. Before PACE, it was generally thought that the police were obliged to bring a suspect before a court within 24 hours, or release them; the Act allows suspects to be detained without charge for up to four days, although there are some safeguards designed to prevent abuse of this power.

PACE provides that an arrested person must be brought to a police station as soon as practicable after the arrest, though this may be delayed if their presence elsewhere is necessary for immediate investigation (s. 30). On arrival at the police station, they should usually be taken to the custody officer, who must decide whether sufficient evidence exists to charge the person. If not, then the person can be detained for the purpose of securing or obtaining evidence – often through interview (s. 37).

The custody officer is responsible for keeping the custody record, which records the various stages of detention, and checking that the provisions of PACE in relation to the detention are complied with by those involved in interrogating the suspect. These theoretical safeguards for the suspect have proved weak in practice. The 1981 Royal Commission on Criminal Procedure considered a properly-kept custody record to be essential, but research by Sanders and Bridge has suggested that over 10 per cent of custody records are falsified. PACE seems to see custody officers as quasi-judicial figures, who can distance themselves from the needs of the investigation and put the rights of the suspect first. In practice this has never been realistic; the custody officer is an ordinary member of the station staff, and likely to share their view of the investigation, and in addition, will often be of junior rank to the investigating officer. He or she is therefore highly unlikely to refuse to allow the detention of a suspect, or to prevent breaches of PACE and its codes during the detention.

If, on arrest, there is already sufficient evidence to charge the suspect, the suspect must be charged and then released on bail unless there are reasons why this is not appropriate. This includes the fact that the defendant's name and address are not known, or the address given is reasonably thought to be false, or too temporary for a summons to be served; or that the suspect may not answer to bail or may commit an offence while on bail (s. 38(1)).

Under s. 46 of PACE, a person who has been charged and is being held in custody must be brought before magistrates as soon as practicable, and in any event not later than the first sitting after being charged with the offence (s. 46(2)).

Section 40 of PACE provides that a review officer should assess whether there are grounds for continued detention, after the first six hours, and then at intervals of not more than nine hours. As a basic rule, the police can detain a person for up to 24 hours from the time of arrival at the police station, after which the suspect should generally be either released or charged (s. 41). However, there are major exceptions to this. Continued detention for a further twelve hours can be authorized by the police themselves, if the detention is necessary to secure or preserve evidence and the offence is a 'serious arrestable offence'. This category includes such offences as murder, manslaughter, rape, kidnap, drug-trafficking, hostage-taking and some sexual offences (PACE s. 117), plus any arrestable offence which has led or is intended to lead to serious harm to the security of the state or public order; serious interference with administration of justice or investigation of offences; death or injury; or substantial financial gain or loss to a person.

Further periods of continued detention, up to 96 hours, are possible with approval from the magistrates' court. After 96 hours the suspect must be charged or released. In fact prolonged detention is rare, with only 5 per cent of suspects detained for more than 18 hours, and 1 per cent for more than 24 hours.

Police interrogation

The usual reason for detaining a suspect is so that the police can question them, in the hope of securing a confession. This has come to be one of the most important investigative tools for the police, since it is cheap (compared, for example, to scientific evidence), and the end result, a confession, is seen as reliable and convincing evidence by judges and juries alike. Research by Mitchell (1983) suggests that in practice a high proportion of suspects do make either partial or complete confessions.

However, as the miscarriages of justice show, relying too much on confession evidence can have severe drawbacks. Instances of police completely falsifying confessions, or threatening or beating suspects so that they confess even when they are innocent may be rare, but the miscarriages show that police have been willing to use these techniques where they think they can get away with it. In addition, there are less dramatic, but probably more widespread problems. The 1993 Royal Commission raised questions about the poor standard of police interviewing; research by John Baldwin (*Video taping police interview with suspects: a national evaluation*) suggested that police officers went into the interview situation not with the aim of finding out whether the person was guilty, but on the assumption that they were and with the intention of securing a confession to that effect. Interviews were often rambling and repetitious; police officers dismissed the suspect's explanations and asked the same questions over and over again until they were given the answer they wanted. In some cases the researchers felt this treatment amounted to bullying or harassment, and in several cases the 'admissions' were one-word answers given in response to leading questions. Suspects were also offered inducements to confess, such as lighter sentences.

Obviously the implication here is that, under this kind of pressure, suspects might confess to crimes they did not commit – as many of the miscarriage of justice victims did. But such false confessions do not only occur where the suspects are physically threatened. A study by psychologist G.H. Gudjonsson (*The Psychology of Interrogations, Confessions and Testimony*) found that there were four situations in which people were likely to confess to crimes they did not commit. First, a minority may make confessions quite voluntarily, out of a disturbed desire for publicity, to relieve general feelings of guilt or because they cannot distinguish between reality and fantasy – it has been suggested that this was partly the case with Judith Ward. Secondly, they may want to protect someone else, perhaps a friend or relative, from interrogation and prosecution. Thirdly, they may be unable to see further than a desire to put the questioning to an end and get away from the police station, which can, after all, be a frightening place to those who are not accustomed to it. A psychologist giving evidence to the 1993 Royal Commission commented that 'Some children are brought up in such a way that confession always seems to produce forgiveness, in which case a false confession may be one way of bringing an unpleasant situation [interrogation] to an end.' (Report of the Royal Commission on Criminal Procedure 1979 p. 25). Among this group there may also be a feeling that once they get out of the police station, they will be able to make everyone see sense, and realize their innocence: Judith Ward has commented that she frequently felt that sooner or later someone would realize there had been a mistake.

Finally, the pressure of questioning, and the fact that the police seem convinced of their case, may temporarily persuade the suspect that he or she must have done the act in question. Obviously the young, as in the **Confait** case, the disturbed (such as Judith Ward), and the mentally sub-normal are likely to be particularly vulnerable to this last situation, but Gudjonsson's research found that its effects were not confined to those who might be considered abnormally suggestible. Their subjects included people of reasonable intelligence who scored highly in tests on suggest-ibility, showing that they were particularly prepared to go along with what someone in authority was saying. Under hostile interrogation in the psychologically intimidating environment of a police station, even non-vulnerable people are likely to make admissions which are not true, not realizing that once a statement has been made, it will be extremely difficult to retract it, or at least to make the police believe it was never true.

The RCCJ recommended that police training should be improved to recognize the dangers of bad interviewing, and the need to listen to what the suspect says and where practicable to follow up and check their story.

Certain safeguards do already exist to try to protect the suspect in the police station. Some of these – the custody officer, the custody record, and the time limits for detention – have already been mentioned, and we will now look at the rest. It was claimed that these safeguards would prevent miscarriages of justice in the future, yet the police station where Winston Silcott was questioned was meant to be following the PACE guidelines on a pilot basis (PACE was not officially introduced until the beginning of 1986). Mark Braithwaite was not arrested until February 1986, when the new law had been in force for more than a month, yet he was denied access to the legal advice guaranteed by the Act.

The caution

Under Code C, a person must normally be cautioned on arrest, and a person whom there are grounds to suspect of an offence must be cau-tioned before being asked any questions regarding involvement or sus-pected involvement in that offence. Until recently, the caution was: 'You do not have to say anything unless you wish to do so but what you say may be given in evidence.' Since the abolition of the right to silence (see p. 209), the correct wording is: 'You do not have to say anything. But it may harm your defence if you do not mention when questioned something which you later rely on in court. Anything you do say may be given in evidence.'

Tape-recording

Section 60 of PACE states that interviews must be tape-recorded. This measure was designed to ensure that oppressive treatment and threats could not be used, nor confessions made up by the police. However, it has proved a weaker safeguard than it might seem. In the first place, research presented to the RRCJ showed that police routinely got round the provision by beginning their questioning outside the interview room – in the car on the way to the police station, for example. In addition, they appeared quite willing to use oppressive questioning methods even once the tape recorder was running – the RCCJ listened to tapes of interviews with the Cardiff Three, victims of another miscarriage of justice, whose convictions were quashed in December 1992, and expressed concern at the continuous repetitive questioning that the tapes revealed.

The right to inform someone of the detention

Section 56 of PACE provides that on arrival at a police station, a suspect is entitled to have someone informed of their arrest. The person may be a friend or relative, or another person who is known to the suspect or who is likely to take an interest in their welfare. The person who the suspect chooses must be told of the arrest, and where the suspect is being held, without delay.

This right may be suspended for up to 36 hours if the detention is in connection with a serious arrestable offence, as defined at p. 200, and the authorizing officer reasonably believes that informing the person chosen by the suspect would lead to interference with or harm to evidence connected with a serious arrestable offence; the alerting of other, as yet unarrested, persons suspected of having committed such an offence; interference with or injury to others; hindrance in recovering any property gained as a result of a serious arrestable offence, or in drug-trafficking offences, hindrance in recovering the profits of that offence.

The right to consult a solicitor

Under s. 58 of PACE, a person held in custody is entitled to consult a solicitor privately and free of charge. This right may be suspended for up to 36 hours on the same grounds as the right to have another person informed. However, the courts take a strict view of these grounds in the case of refusal of legal advice, and wrongful refusal is one of the likely reasons for refusal to admit evidence gained in breach of PACE.

The leading case is **Samuel** (1988). The appellant was detained for six hours on suspicion of armed robbery and then refused lawyers because the police claimed there was a danger that other suspects might be warned. He was interviewed twice more, and denied the suspected offence but admitted two burglaries. After 48 hours, a lawyer sent by Samuel's mother arrived at the police station, but was refused access to Samuel for a further three hours, during which time Samuel confessed to the armed robbery. The Court of Appeal said that the denial of access to legal advice was unjustified, denying one of the citizen's most important rights, and the confession obtained as a result was inadmissible. They stated that a police officer who sought to justify refusal of legal advice had to do so by reference to the specific circumstances of the case. It was not enough to believe that giving access to a solicitor might generally lead to the alerting of accomplices; there had to be a belief that in the specific case it probably would, and such cases would be very rare – especially where the lawyer called was the duty solicitor.

However, in **R** *v* **Alladice** (1988), a suspect was refused access to a lawyer, but despite this clear breach of PACE, the courts held that the interview was in fact conducted with propriety, and that legal advice would have added nothing to the defendant's knowledge of his rights. In that case the suspect's confession was allowed in evidence.

Research by Sanders in 1989 showed that only about a quarter of all those arrested asked for a solicitor (*Advice and Assistance at Police Stations and the 24-hour Duty Solicitors Scheme*, Lord Chancellors Department). It appeared that part of the reason for this was a range of ploys used by the police to dissuade suspects from seeing a lawyer. The most common – and most successful – ploy was to suggest that asking for a solicitor would lead to delay, so that the suspect, who is generally keen to leave the police station as soon as possible, decides to go ahead without legal advice. In addition, defendants were not always given the leaflet advising them of their rights, were asked to sign at a particular point on their custody record without being told that in doing so they were waiving their right to see a solicitor, or were not told that the service was free.

This last ploy was addressed in April 1991, when a change in the relevant Code required the police to tell suspects that they were entitled to free legal advice, and research by Brown in 1993 found that after this the proportion of suspects requesting legal advice went up to 32 per cent. For cases ending up in the Crown Court, around half of defendants (53 per cent) have had a solicitor present during questioning.

The quality of legal advice

It has been assumed that access to legal advice before and during questioning is one of the strongest safeguards a suspect can have. While this may be true when the advice is skilled and the lawyer experienced in this kind of work, there is increasing evidence that this is all too rarely the case. Research by McConville and Hodgson (1993) found that only a quarter of those attending police stations were qualified solicitors; the rest were articled clerks, unqualified clerks or even former police officers. Firms tended to give this area of work very low priority, sending those employees who could most easily be spared from other work, rather than those who were most likely to have relevant skills and experience.

Nor, it seems, is the performance of solicitors in police stations of much use in protecting suspects. Research by Baldwin (1992) found that in 66 per cent of interviews, the legal representative said nothing at all, and in only 9 per cent of cases did they actively intervene on behalf of the suspect or object to police questions. Baldwin comments:

> The interview takes place on police territory and it is police officers who are in charge of it . . . Passivity and compliance on the part of lawyers are therefore the normal, the expected, almost the required responses at the police station. Solicitors are conditioned by their history, their experience, even their professional training and guidance, to be passive in the police interview room, and the existing rules reinforce this by giving police officers the upper hand. The junior staff who mainly turn up to police stations are more inclined to facilitate police questioning than they are to challenge it.

McConville and Hodgson (1993) found that legal advisers often lacked adequate legal knowledge or confidence, and sometimes appeared to identify more with the police than with the suspect. They were usually told very little about the case by the police, and had only minimal discussions with their client beforehand (around half spent less than ten minutes alone with the client). They were therefore rarely in a position to give useful advice.

Adding to these failings is the fact that the police may have questioned the suspect before the official interview, and may continue to do so after a lawyer has visited. In some situations, legal advisers have proved reluctant to visit the police station at all, preferring to speak to suspects on the telephone instead (Sanders *et al.*, 1989).

Taking into account these problems, the RCCJ recommended that the police should remind suspects of their rights to legal advice at the beginning of an interview, and to ask for reasons if the suspect chose to waive those rights; all this should be videoed (along with the interview itself). Police training should include formal instruction in the role that solicitors are properly expected to play in the criminal justice system. The Law Society should take appropriate action to ensure that the advice in its pamphlet for solicitors *Advising the Client at the Police Station* becomes more widely known, better understood, and more consistently acted upon. In the longer term, the RCCJ recommended that the training, education, supervision and monitoring of all legal advisers who operate at police stations should be thoroughly reviewed.

An 'appropriate adult'

PACE and Code C provide that young people and mentally disordered or mentally handicapped adults must have an 'appropriate adult' with them during a police interview, as well as having the usual right to legal advice. This may be a parent, but is often a social worker. Evans's 1993 research for the RCCJ found that parents were not necessarily a protection for the suspect, since they often took the side of the police and helped them to produce a confession.

With more and more patients of mental institutions being released into so-called 'community care', higher numbers of mentally vulnerable adults are finding themselves in police stations. However, unlike children, they may be difficult to identify, making it likely that the required safeguards will not be in place when they are interviewed. Research by the psychologist Gudjonsson (1992) calculated that between 15 and 20 per cent of suspects may need an appropriate adult present – considerably more than the 4 per cent whom the police currently identify. The RCCJ recommended that the police should be given clearer guidelines and special training in identifying vulnerable individuals, and that there should be a full review of who should be considered an 'appropriate adult', and what their role in the police station should be.

They also suggested that consideration should be given to establishing duty psychiatrist schemes at busy police stations in city centres, and that in any event, all police stations should have arrangements for calling in psychiatric help where necessary.

Treatment of suspects

PACE codes stipulate that interview rooms must be adequately lit, heated and ventilated, that suspects must be allowed to sit during questioning, and that adequate breaks for meals, refreshments and sleep must be given.

Record of the interview

After the interview is over, the police must make a record of it, which is kept on file. Baldwin's 1993 research checked a sample of such records against the taped recordings, and concluded that even those police forces considered to be most progressive forces were often failing to produce good quality records of interviews. Half the records were faulty or misleading, and the longer the interview, the more likely the record was to be inaccurate. These findings were backed up by a separate study carried out by Roger Evans (1993). He found that in some summaries, the police stated that suspects had confessed during the interview, but on listening to the tape recordings, the researchers could find no evidence of this, and felt that the suspects were in fact denying the offence.

Baldwin points out that the job of police officers is to catch criminals, and their temperament, aptitude and training are focused on this; the skills required for making careful summaries of complex material are not among those generally thought to be required in the job. However, he points out that while police officers will inevitably summarize interviews from the point of view of a prosecution, defence lawyers should be prepared to take this into account, and rather than taking the summaries on trust, to listen to the interview tapes themselves. In practice solicitors request interview tapes in only 10 per cent of cases.

Exclusion of evidence
One of the potentially most important safeguards in PACE is the possibility that the courts may refuse to admit evidence which has been improperly obtained. Given that the reason why police officers bend or break the rules is to secure a conviction, preventing them from using the evidence obtained in this way is clearly likely to be a deterrent.

PACE contains two provisions on the admissibility of evidence. Section 76(2) requires the prosecution to prove beyond reasonable doubt that a confession was not obtained by oppression (which is defined in s. 76(8) as torture, inhuman or degrading treatment or the use or threat of violence), or otherwise in circumstances likely to render the confession unreliable. Section 78 allows the court to refuse evidence (of any kind) if it appears to the court that the admission of such evidence would have such an adverse effect on the fairness of the proceedings that the court ought not to admit it.

These provisions have been used to render evidence inadmissible when the police have breached PACE or its Codes, although breaches of the Codes alone must be 'serious and substantial' in order to make evidence inadmissible. Such breaches were found in **R v Canale** (1990), where the court refused to accept evidence of interviews which was not contemporaneously written up, describing this breach of a Code as 'flagrant, deliberate and cynical'.

However, a serious drawback to the protection given by the s. 76(2) provisions are that even if confession evidence is excluded, this does not prevent the prosecution making use of facts obtained as a result of the confession, and they may also use part of the confession as evidence of the way suspects express themselves.

The right to silence
Until 1994, the law provided a further safeguard for those suspected of crime, in the form of the traditional 'right to silence'. This essentially meant that suspects were free to say nothing at all in response to police questioning, and the prosecution could not suggest in court that that silence implied guilt (with some very limited exceptions).

Once PACE was introduced, the police argued that its safeguards, especially the right of access to legal advice, had tipped the balance too far in favour of suspects, so that the right to silence was no longer needed. Despite the fact that the RCCJ opposed this view, the Government agreed with the police, and the right to silence was abolished by the CJPOA 1994. This does not mean that subjects can be forced to speak, but it provides four situations in which, if the suspect chooses not to speak, the court will be entitled to draw such inferences from that silence as appear proper. The four situations are where suspects, when questioned under caution or charge, fail to mention facts which they later rely on as part of their defence and which it is reasonable to expect them to have mentioned (s. 34); silence during the trial, including choosing not to give evidence or to answer any question without good cause (s. 35); failure to account for objects, substances or marks on clothing when requested to do so (s. 36); and failure to account for presence at a particular place when requested to do so (s. 37). Both of these latter sections require the accused to have been arrested and to be warned about the consequences of the failure to answer.

Interviews outside the station

PACE states that where practicable, interviews with arrested suspects should always take place at a police station. However, evidence obtained by questioning or voluntary statements outside the police station may still be admissible. Since such interviews are not subject to most of the safeguards explained above, the obvious danger is that police may evade PACE requirements by conducting 'unofficial' interviews – such as the practice known as taking the 'scenic route' to the station, in which suspects are questioned in the police car. The Royal Commission found that about 30 per cent of suspects report being questioned prior to arrest.

Even at the police station, research by McConville (*Videotaping interrogations: police behaviour on and off camera*) shows that illegal, informal and unrecorded visits were made to suspects in cells to prepare the ground for interview and to persuade them not to raise a defence. Sometimes suspects themselves ask to see police officers informally, in the hope of doing some kind of deal. In some cases the formal interview that followed was little more than a set piece, scripted by the police. Yet defence lawyers often accepted the police version of these events as the truth.

Despite the obvious dangers of these practices, the Royal Commission did not consider excluding evidence obtained in this way, but merely discussed the possibility of requiring tape-recording of all contact between suspect and police.

Search powers after arrest

Section 32 of PACE provides that the police may search an arrested person at a place other than a police station if there are reasonable grounds for believing they are in possession of evidence, or anything that might assist escape or present a danger. The police can also enter and search the premises where the suspect was at the time or immediately before the arrest.

Section 54 of PACE allows the police to search arrested persons on arrival at the police station, and to seize anything which they reasonably believe the suspect might use to injure anyone, or use to make an escape, or that is evidence of an offence or has been obtained as the result of an offence.

Finger printing and body samples

Section 55 of PACE gives police the power to conduct intimate searches of a suspect, which means searches of the body's orifices. Such a search must be authorized by a superintendent, who must have reasonable grounds for believing that a weapon or drug is concealed, and must be carried out by a qualified doctor or nurse.

The safeguards on the use of this power caused problems for the police when dealing with drug dealers. The dealers frequently stored drugs in their mouths, knowing that search of the mouth was regarded as an intimate search, and could not therefore be done without the special authorization, and the need for a nurse or doctor. To address this problem, s. 65 of PACE, as amended by the CJPOA now provides that a search of the mouth is not an intimate search.

Section 62 of PACE states that intimate samples, including blood, saliva or semen, can be taken from a suspect, but in some cases their written consent is required. Non-intimate samples, such as hair or nail clippings, can be taken from a suspect without their consent, under s. 63, although this procedure must be authorized by a superintendent in writing and recorded on the custody record. Section 61 of PACE permits the police to take fingerprints from suspects.

These powers have been extended by the CJPOA, which allows what the Act calls 'speculative searches', whereby fingerprints, samples or information drawn from them can be checked against other similar data available to the police. These changes broadly reflect the recommendations of the RCCJ, which proposed the creation of a national DNA database, and wider powers which would place body samples and fingerprints on an equal footing.

Powers to search premises

Part II of PACE (ss. 8–18) provides the police with statutory powers to enter and search premises for evidence. These powers can be executed either with or without a warrant.

Search with a warrant

A number of statutes allow the granting of search warrants, but the main provisions are to be found in PACE. The police apply for the warrant to a magistrate, who must be satisfied that the police reasonably believe that a serious arrestable offence has been committed, and that the premises concerned contain material likely to be of substantial use to the investigation or likely to be relevant evidence. In addition, it must be impractical to make the search without a warrant (which means with the consent of the person entitled to grant entry or access to evidence), because it is not practicable to communicate with that person, because entry would not be granted without a warrant, or because the purpose of the search would be frustrated or seriously prejudiced if immediate entry could not be obtained on arrival.

In practice, research by Lidstone (1984) indicates that magistrates rarely refuse to grant a warrant; if certain magistrates were known to refuse applications, the police would simply stop applying to them and go to another magistrate instead. About 12 per cent of searches are made with a warrant.

There are certain classes of material for which these basic powers cannot be used: privileged material, which covers communications between lawyers and their clients; excluded material, which includes medical records and journalistic material held in confidence; and special procedure material, which includes other journalistic material and material acquired through business and held in confidence.

Once the warrant is issued, entry and search must take place within one month, and must be undertaken at a reasonable hour, unless that would frustrate the search. Reasonable force may be used (PACE s. 117). The officers concerned should provide documentary evidence of their status, plus a copy of the warrant, unless it is impracticable to do so. The Codes also require that police hand out a notice giving information about the grounds for and powers of search, and the rights of the occupier, including rights to compensation for any damage done.

Search without a warrant

The police can always search premises if the occupier consents to this. In addition, PACE provides a range of powers of search which can be exercised without either a warrant or the occupier's consent. Section 17 allows the police to enter and search to execute a warrant of arrest; to make an arrest without warrant; to capture a person unlawfully at large; or to protect people from serious injury or prevent serious damage to property.

Under s. 18, after an arrest for an arrestable offence, the police can search premises occupied or controlled by the suspect if they reasonably suspect that there is evidence of the immediate offence or other offences on the premises.

Section 32 provides that, after an arrest for an arrestable offence, an officer can lawfully enter and search premises where the person was when arrested or immediately before they were arrested if the constable reasonably suspects that there is evidence relating to the offence in question on the premises.

There is also a common law power to enter and remain on premises 'to deal with or prevent a breach of the peace'. This is based on **Thomas v Sawkins** (1935), where it was held to be lawful for police to enter and insist on remaining in a hall where a political meeting was taking place, because their past experience of such meetings gave them reasonable grounds to apprehend a breach of the peace.

In **McLeod v Commissioner of Police of the Metropolis** (1994) Lord Neill said:

> I am satisfied that Parliament in s. 17(6) has now recognized that there is a power to enter premises to prevent a breach of the peace as a form of preventive justice. I can see no satisfactory basis for restricting that power to particular classes of premises such as those where public meetings are held. If the police reasonably believe that a breach of the peace is likely to take place on private premises, they have power to enter those premises to prevent it. The apprehension must, of course be genuine and it must relate to the near future.

It was also stressed that in exercising this power, the police should act with great care and discretion, especially where it involves entering private premises against the wishes of the owners or occupiers.

Searches of premises are governed by Code B, which states that searches should be made at a reasonable time, that only reasonable force should be used and that the police should show due consideration and courtesy towards the property and privacy of the occupier. How far this is observed in practice might be doubted by anyone who watched television news coverage of the anti-burglary campaign Operation Bumblebee, in which police broke down suspects' doors with sledgehammers at 6 am. The fact that in high profile cases, such searches are often accompanied by TV cameras suggests that the media may be tipped off by the police, which, whether such tip-offs are official or not, suggests little regard for the suspects' privacy.

Once the police are lawfully on premises, then under s. 19 of PACE they may seize and retain any item that is evidence of a crime.

▶ Prosecution

The initial decision on whether or not to prosecute is made by the police. If there is clearly insufficient evidence at this stage, the police should obviously not recommend prosecution, but even where there does appear to be sufficient evidence, the police may decide against prosecution for other reasons. In such cases, they may decide to take no further action or to issue a caution, a formal warning to offenders about what they have done, and their conduct in the future. Research suggests that no further action is taken in about 26 per cent of cases of arrested adults, and that a caution was issued in 14 per cent of such cases (McConville, Sanders and Leng, *The Case for the Prosecution*, 1993).

Home Office guidelines lay down the criteria on which the decision to caution should be made. A caution can only be given where the offender admits guilt, and there would be a realistic prospect of a successful prosecution. In the case of a juvenile, the parents or guardian must consent to a caution being given. If these criteria are met, other factors to be taken into account are the seriousness of the offence and the extent of the damage done; the interests and desires of the victim; the previous conduct of the offender; the family background of the offender; and the offender's conduct after the offence, such as a willingness to make reparation to the victim. The guidelines emphasize that, where the offender is a juvenile, prosecution should be a last resort.

Formal cautions are recorded and if the offender is convicted of another offence afterwards, can be cited as part of the offender's record. In 1993, 311,300 people were cautioned, almost double the number in 1983. The number of juveniles being cautioned has shown particular growth.

Cautioning appears to be effective in terms of preventing re-offending: 87 per cent of those cautioned in 1985 were not convicted of a standard list offence within two years of the caution. However, this may reflect the kind of individuals and offences who are seen as suitable for a caution: for example, 80 per cent of those cautioned had no previous cautions or convictions but for those who had been previously convicted, there was a much greater likelihood that they would re-offend. Prosecution is the most expensive method of dealing with offenders. The RCCJ recognized the value of diversionary schemes, stating that there could safely be more cautioning of petty offenders. However, they were concerned that rates of cautioning rather than prosecuting varied widely across the country, and recommended that cautioning should become subject to statutory guidelines. The initial decision on whether to caution should remain with the police, but the Crown Prosecution Service (CPS) should be able to require the police to caution instead of bringing a prosecution. Despite the RCCJ's recommendations for more cautioning the new national guidelines are more restrictive, removing any presumption that juveniles should be cautioned, and discouraging repeat cautions and cautions for serious offences.

The Crown Prosecution Service

Until 1986, criminal prosecutions were officially brought by private citizens rather than by the state; in practice most prosecutions were brought by the police but strictly speaking they were prosecuting as private citizens. Although the police obviously employed solicitors to help them in this task, their relationship with those solicitors was a normal client relationship, and so the police were not obliged to act on the solicitors' advice. Cases in the magistrates' court were sometimes actually presented by the police.

In 1970, a report by the law reform pressure group, Justice, criticized the role of the police in the prosecution process (*The Prosecution in England and Wales* 1970). It argued that it was not in the interests of justice for the same body to be responsible for the two very different functions of investigation and prosecution. This dual role prevented the prosecution from being independent and impartial: the police had become concerned with winning or losing, when the concern of the prosecution should be the discovery of the truth. As a result, there was a danger of the police withholding from the defence information that might make a conviction less likely. The report pointed out that public policy and the circumstances of the individual were relevant considerations in the decision to prosecute, and that the English system was unique in Europe in allowing the whole process from interrogation to prosecution to be effectively under the control of the police in the majority of cases. In addition, it noted, police officers were not trained as lawyers or advocates.

The prosecution process was reviewed by the Royal Commission on Criminal Procedure (RCCP) in 1981. Their report highlighted a range of problems. There was a lack of uniformity, with differing procedures and standards applied across the country on such matters as whether to prosecute or caution, and the system prevented a consistent national prosecution policy. The system was also said to be inefficient, with inadequate preparation of cases; research by McConville and Baldwin (1981) found many cases of defendants being acquitted due to judges stopping the trial at the end of the prosecution case, or directing the jury to acquit, because the prosecution evidence was insufficient. The failure of prosecution witnesses at trial accounted for many of these cases, but there were clearly some where it should have been foreseen that the evidence would be inadequate.

The RCCP agreed with Justice that, in principle, investigation and prosecution should be separate processes, conducted by different people. The goals of investigation and of prosecution were incompatible, although a total separation was thought to be impossible in practice. The RCCJ also accepted that there was no executive or democratic accountability or control over the existing system.

As a result of these findings, the RCCP recommended the establishment of a Crown Prosecution Service, divided into separate sections for each police force area, with a Chief Crown Prosecutor responsible locally to a supervisory body and nationally to the Director of Public Prosecutions.

The Government followed the recommendation, except that it preferred not to set up separate local services. The Crown Prosecution Service (CPS) was set up under the Prosecution of Offenders Act 1985, as a national prosecution service for England and Wales. It is divided into 31 areas, usually covering one or two police force areas each: the areas are each headed by a Chief Crown Prosecutor, and the service as a whole is headed by the Director of Public Prosecutions (DPP).

The areas are directly answerable to the DPP, who sets out national guidelines and procedures, appoints and supervises personnel and manages resources generally. He or she may also intervene in difficult or complex cases. The DPP reports on the running of the service to the Attorney-General, who is responsible in Parliament for general policy but not for individual cases. The only formal mechanism for accountability of the CPS is the requirement that an annual report must be presented to the Attorney-General, who is obliged to lay it before Parliament.

The establishment of the CPS means that the prosecution of offences is now separated from their detection and investigation, which is undertaken by the police. The CPS has no involvement in cases where the police decide not to prosecute, including those where the offender is given a caution. If the police decide the offender should be prosecuted, a file on the case will be sent to the CPS. They then review that decision, on the basis of criteria set out in the Code for Crown Prosecutors (CCP), issued by the DPP under s. 10 of the Prosecution of Offences Act 1985. The latest edition of this Code (published in June 1994) explains that the decision taken by the CPS has two stages. First, they must ask whether there is enough evidence to provide a 'realistic prospect of conviction' against each defendant on each charge. In assessing this evidential test, they will have to consider what the defence case may be, and how it is likely to affect the prosecution case. The 'realistic prospect of conviction' is an objective test, which requires that the evidence be such that a jury or bench of magistrates, properly directed in accordance with the law, would be more likely than not to convict the defendant of the charge alleged. If the case does not pass this evidential test, the prosecution must not go ahead, no matter how important or serious the case may be.

If the case does pass the evidential test, the CPS must then consider whether the public interest requires a prosecution. This is assessed by taking into account a number of factors, including the seriousness of the offence, the attitude of the victim, and various circumstances of the offender. The presence of some of these factors will point to a public interest in prosecuting, while others will suggest that a prosecution would not be in the public interest; in many cases, there will be factors pointing both ways, and the task of the CPS is to find the correct balance between them. For example, a prosecution is more likely to be in the public interest if a conviction is likely to result in a significant sentence, if the offence was committed against a person serving the public (such as a police officer) or if the offence, although not serious in itself, is widespread in the area where it was committed. On the other hand, a prosecution is less likely to be in the public interest where the court is likely to impose a very small or nominal sentence, or the defendant is elderly, or suffering from significant mental or physical ill-health, unless the offence is serious or there is a real possibility that it may be repeated. A long delay between the offence taking place and the date of the trial may be a public interest reason not to prosecute, except where the offence is serious, the delay is partly the defendant's fault, the offence has only recently been discovered, or its complexity has made a long investigation necessary.

At the end of this two-stage test, the CPS may decide to go ahead with prosecution, send the case back to the police for a caution instead of a prosecution, or take no further action. The decision is theirs, and the police need not be consulted.

How often does the CPS decide not to prosecute?

In the three years from October 1986, the CPS discontinued over 250,000 cases. The Service claims that this is evidence of its success, demonstrating that it 'has been effective in filtering a considerable number of unmeritorious cases out of the judicial system'. However, there are wide variations across the country, with some areas discontinuing 4 per cent of cases, while others discontinue 19 per cent. In 1990 the Home Affairs Committee expressed concern at the large proportion of discontinued cases which were not dropped until the court hearing, and was surprised that the CPS undertook no systematic analysis of the reasons for discontinuance.

In 1993 the RCCJ found that the CPS did exercise the power to discontinue appropriately, citing one study (Moxon and Crisp, 1994) which suggested that nearly a third of discontinuances were dropped on public interest grounds. Of these, nearly half were discontinued because the offence was trivial and/or the likely penalty was nominal. Other factors included the youth, age, previous good character or mental state of the accused, the attitude of the complainant or the offer of compensation. However, the study did reveal inefficiencies. Only 5 per cent of the cases were discontinued before any court appearance, and where cases were terminated at the court, the decision to discontinue was often taken before the hearing but not communicated to the defendant in time to save a court appearance – either because the decision had been taken too late in the day or because the CPS did not know where the defendant was.

In assessing the incidence of weak cases in the Crown Court (which may be cases that should have been discontinued), the numbers of ordered and directed acquittals are relevant. According to the 1991 Judicial Statistics, 43 per cent of acquittals were judge ordered, 16 per cent were judge directed, and 41 per cent were by the jury.

Private prosecutions

Private prosecutions can still be brought, and although statistically these are few, they can play an important role, particularly in highlighting or encouraging public concern over relevant issues.

In 1974, a PC Joy stopped a motorist and reported him for a motoring offence. The motorist was a Member of Parliament and PC Joy's superiors refused to pursue the case; PC Joy thought this unjust and successfully brought a private prosecution. Mary Whitehouse has also brought important private prosecutions in the past. More recently, the family of Stephen Lawrence, a teenager murdered in south London, have taken out a private prosecution against four men suspected of the killing, after the CPS dropped the case because it said there was insufficient evidence.

When a private prosecution is brought, the CPS may choose to take over the case, and although the service has so far shown itself reluctant to interfere in the individual's right to prosecute, it could probably take over such a case only to discontinue it, on either evidential or public interest grounds.

▶ Appearance in court

Persons charged with an offence can be called to court by means of a summons, or by a charge following arrest without a warrant. Arrest under a warrant signed by a magistrate under s. 1(1) of the Magistrates' Courts Act 1980 is not common today, and its main use is to arrest those who having been bailed do not turn up for trial.

In order to have a summons served, the prosecutor must give a short account of the alleged offence, usually in writing, to the magistrates or their clerk (a process called laying an information). The information may be substantiated by an oral statement from the police, given on oath before a magistrate; such a statement must be given if the information is to be used as the basis for a warrant for arrest. A summons setting out the offence is then issued and served, either in person or, for minor offences, through Recorded Delivery or Registered post.

▶ Bail

A person accused, convicted or under arrest for an offence may be granted bail, which means they are released under a duty to attend court or the police station at a given time. The criteria for granting or refusing bail are contained in the Bail Act 1976. There is a general presumption in favour of bail for unconvicted defendants, but there are some important exceptions. Bail need not be granted where there are substantial grounds for believing that, unless kept in custody, the accused would fail to surrender to bail, or would commit an offence, interfere with witnesses or otherwise obstruct the course of justice. In assessing these risks, the court may take account of the nature and seriousness of the offence and the probable sentence, along with the character, antecedents, associations and community ties of the defendant. The courts need not grant bail when the magistrates think the accused should be kept in custody for their own protection, where the accused is already serving a prison sentence or where there has been insufficient time to obtain information as to the criteria for bail; nor where the charge is murder, manslaughter, rape, attempted murder or attempted rape. If the court does choose to grant bail in such cases, its reasons for doing so must be included in the bail record. During 1994, concerns were raised about the so-called 'bail bandits': offenders, mainly young ones, who continue to commit crimes while on bail. The full extent of this problem is difficult to assess, but a recent Home Office study suggested that around 10 per cent of those on bail commit offences, and that as many as 16 per cent of burglaries are committed while offenders are on bail (Morgan, 1992). Whether or not fears of widespread offending on bail are justified, the CJPOA 1994 takes steps to address the apparent problem. It removes the presumption in favour of bail for anyone charged with a further indictable offence which appears to have been committed while on bail, and also aims to ensure automatic remand in custody with no opportunity for bail for those charged with murder, attempted murder, rape, attempted rape or manslaughter, where the person concerned has a previous conviction for any of those offences.

When bail is refused for any of the stated reasons, other than insufficient information, the accused will usually be allowed only one further bail application; the court does not have to hear further applications unless there has been a change in circumstances. Where the remand in custody is on the basis of insufficient information, this is not technically a refusal of bail, so the accused may still make two applications.

A defendant refused bail, or who objects to the conditions under which it is offered, must be told the reasons for the decision, and informed of the right to apply to the Crown Court or a High Court judge, who have power to grant bail or vary the conditions under which it has been offered (Criminal Justice Act 1967 s. 22). The 'bail bandit' concerns, particularly as regards dangerous offenders, have led to the CPS being given limited rights to appeal against a bail decision made in a magistrates' court. Appeal is to a judge of the Crown Court, and can only be made on the basis of new evidence, which was not previously available to the court or constable when the decision was taken.

In 1992 the average proportion of unconvicted and unsentenced prisoners was 22 per cent of the average prison population. Many of these remand prisoners, who have not been convicted of any offence, are kept in prison for between six months and a year before being tried, despite the fact that 60 per cent of them go on to be acquitted or given a non-custodial sentence.

▶ Classification of offences and mode of trial

There are three different categories of criminal offence.

Summary offences

These are the most minor crimes, and are only triable summarily in the magistrates' court. 'Summary' refers to the process of ordering the defendant to attend the court by summons, a written order usually delivered by post which is the most frequent procedure adopted in the magistrates' courts. There has been some criticism of the fact that more and more offences have been made summary only, reducing the right to trial by jury.

Indictable offences

These are the more serious offences, such as rape and murder. They can only be heard by the Crown Court. The indictment is a formal document containing the alleged offences against the accused, supported by brief facts.

Offences triable either way

These offences may be tried in either the magistrates' court or the Crown Court; the most common examples are theft and burglary, but the category also includes indecent assault, arson and criminal damage. The decision as to which court should try these offences depends on the seriousness of the case, and whether the magistrates' court is likely to have sufficient sentencing powers to deal with it. Even if it is felt that the case is suitable for summary trial, the defendant can insist on a Crown Court trial, as can the magistrates. In some cases the magistrates will hold a mode of trial hearing (Magistrates' Courts Act 1980) to decide whether the case is suitable to be heard summarily or not. In practice, unless the defendant demands jury trial, magistrates tend to follow the recommendations of the CPS.

Most offences tried in the Crown Court are 'either way' offences. Only 18 per cent are indictable only; the remainder are sent there because the magistrates so direct (52 per cent) or because the defendant so chooses (30 per cent). The reason for magistrates sending a case to the Crown Court is usually the assumption that their sentencing powers will be insufficient for it, or that it is too serious for them to try. In fact, the RCCJ found that in 62 per cent of the cases in which the magistrates declined

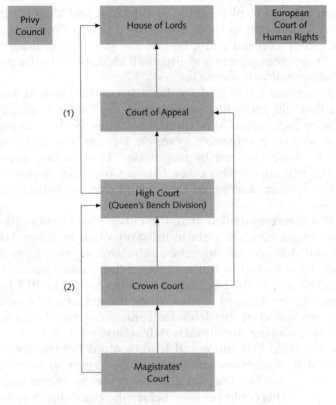

¹ Leap frog procedure
² Appeal by way of case stated.

The Criminal Court System

jurisdiction, the Crown Court imposed a sentence that would have been within the power of the magistrates to impose (Hedderman and Moxon, 1992).

There are three main reasons why defendants may choose to be dealt with by the Crown Court. First, it automatically puts off the day of trial. This has particular benefits to those who are remanded in custody and believe they will be found guilty and sent back to prison, because remand prisoners are entitled to privileges which are not available to sentenced prisoners (and time spent on remand is included in the time the prisoner eventually serves).

Secondly, many defendants believe they stand a better chance of acquittal in the Crown Court. A study by Vennard ('The Outcome of Contested Trials') suggests that they may be right: acquittal rates were significantly higher in the Crown Court (57 per cent) than in magistrates' courts (30 per cent). However, most of those who choose to be tried in the Crown

Court then proceed to plead guilty. Hedderman and Moxon's 1992 study found that 27 per cent of those who elected Crown Court trial intended from the outset to plead guilty, and on the day of trial, many more did so, with 70 per cent pleading guilty to all charges and a further 13 per cent pleading guilty to some charges.

Thirdly, around a half of defendants are under the mistaken impression that they will get lighter sentences in the Crown Court. The RCCJ noted that in fact, judges were three times more likely to impose prison sentences, and their sentences were, on average, two and a half times longer than those imposed by magistrates. Perhaps not surprisingly, a third of the defendants who chose Crown Court trial thought that they had made a mistake, and would have been better off being dealt with by magistrates.

The RCCJ recommended that for either way offences, defendants should no longer have the right to insist on a trial by a jury. Where prosecution and defence are in agreement about where a case should be tried, their views should be followed, but if they cannot agree, the matter should be referred to the magistrates for a decision. The RCCJ proposed that in making the decision in these cases, the magistrates should bear in mind the reputation of the defendant; this recommendation was widely criticized as favouring middle-class defendants.

In the Criminal Procedure and Investigations Bill the government is proposing that magistrates should have the power to invite a person charged with an offence that is triable either way, to give an indication of his or her plea. This could be done before the court decides whether the case is more suitable for summary trial or for trial on indictment. If the legislation is passed it is predicted that more defendants charged with such offences would be dealt with in the magistrates' courts.

▶ Disclosure

The issue of disclosure is concerned with the responsibility of the prosecution and defence to reveal information related to the case prior to the trial. At the time of writing the rules concerning disclosure were primarily covered by the common law. The prosecution had a duty to reveal 'material' evidence and the defence had only a very limited duty of disclosure, for example to inform the court in advance that they intended to call an alibi witness.

This area of law is likely to be reformed by the Criminal Procedure and Investigation Bill which will probably be passed by Parliament in 1996. Under the proposed legislation the prosecution would first disclose unused material which might undermine its case (known as 'primary prosecution disclosure') as well as a list of non-sensitive material held by the prosecution.

In response, the defence, in cases to be tried on indictment and after having received a limited amount of information about the prosecution case, would have to disclose information about its case to narrow the issues in dispute. This is a much broader duty of disclosure on the defence than currently exists. If the defence failed to do this or departed at trial from the defence previously disclosed the court would be free to draw inferences from this failure, such as that the defendant had something to hide, though such an inference could not provide the sole ground for a conviction.

After defence disclosure the prosecution would disclose any additional unused material which might assist the defence case (known as 'secondary prosecution disclosure'). The defence could apply for further disclosure where there was reason to believe it would assist the defence, and the prosecution would have a continuing duty to disclose information.

A new Code of Practice is to be written under the proposed legislation to support the new disclosure regime. It would lay down guidelines as to the recording and preservation by police of information obtained during an investigation and its disclosure to the prosecution. If the police could simply destroy evidence that favoured the defence the process of disclosure would clearly be undermined.

According to the Consultation Paper that preceded the Bill the proposed reforms are aimed to reduce the burdens on the investigating and prosecuting authorities, though it is questionable whether this will actually be achieved. They are also intended to prevent defendants 'ambushing' the trial by producing an unexpected defence at the last moment which the prosecution is unprepared for and therefore enabling the defendant to be wrongly acquitted. In fact research prepared for the RCCJ suggested that there was little evidence of this happening in practice.

▶ Transfer for trial

This area of criminal procedure is in transition. At the time of writing where cases are to be tried in the Crown Court, they begin with an initial hearing in the magistrates' court, called the committal proceedings. These proceedings were designed to allow the magistrates to check that there was in fact sufficient evidence to proceed to a full Crown Court trial, and to filter the weak cases. In practice, committal proceedings have proved to be highly ineffective as a filter, and the RCCJ recommended that they should be abolished, and replaced with a simple transfer to the Crown Court, with the option for preliminary argument before the judge that there is no case to answer. The CJPOA contains provision for the introduction of this reform but the relevant articles had not been brought into force at the time of writing. They are likely to come into force some time in 1996, when committal proceedings will be abolished and replaced by the new transfer for trial procedure.

In transfer proceedings, which will be largely conducted on paper rather than orally, the prosecutor serves notice on the magistrates and the accused that the case will be held in the Crown Court. The notice specifies the charge or charges, and includes documents containing the evidence (including oral evidence) on which the charge or charges are based. At this stage the defence can apply for the case to be dismissed on the grounds of insufficient evidence; if they do, there will be a hearing before magistrates. After considering the written evidence and any oral representations, they will have to dismiss a charge if it appears to them that there is not sufficient evidence against the accused to put him or her on trial by jury for the offence charged. If there is no successful application for dismissal, the magistrates will transfer the case to the Crown Court.

▶ Plea and direction hearings

The courts have the power to lay down their own rules as to how they should function. They sometimes do this by means of an official announcement known as a 'practice direction'. This procedure was used in 1995 to set up a new procedure known as a 'plea and direction hearing' (PDH). These were established for all cases in the Crown Court apart from serious fraud cases.

The PDH takes place after committal proceedings or when these are abolished after the transfer for trial proceedings. Their purpose is to ensure that all necessary steps are taken to prepare for the actual trial, and to provide sufficient information for a trial date to be arranged.

These hearings will normally be held in open court with the defendants present. The defendants will be required to plead guilty or not guilty to the charges against them. This process is known as the 'arraignment'. If the defendant pleads guilty, the judge will proceed immediately to sentence the defendant wherever possible.

Where they plead not guilty the prosecution and defence will have to identify the key issues, and to provide any additional information required to organise the actual trial, such as which witnesses will be required to attend, facts that are admitted by both sides and issues of law that are likely to arise.

Even prior to the PDH the defence must notify the probation service, the prosecution and the court as soon as it is known that the defendants intend to plead guilty to all or part of the charges against them.

▶ Preparatory hearings

If the Criminal Procedure and Investigations Bill is passed in its current form it would introduce preparatory hearings. Where the ultimate trial is likely to be long and complex a judge could choose to order such a hearing if it seems that there would be substantial benefits from doing so. Such a hearing would take place before the jury had been sworn in and therefore without the jury being present, though according to clause 23 of the bill this would be treated as the start of the trial. The aim of the procedure would be to identify the key issues of the case so that it will take less time in front of the jury, and to assist the judge generally in managing the trial.

If the defendant has not already been asked to do so then he or she will be arraigned, that is to say they will be asked whether they plead guilty or not guilty. At the hearing judges can rule on the admissibility of evidence and decide questions of law. They can require the prosecutor and then the accused to provide a statement giving information about their respective cases. Inferences can be drawn if the prosecutor or accused subsequently depart from the case disclosed at the preparatory hearing, or failed to comply with a requirement imposed at the hearing.

The exact relationship between PDHs and preparatory hearings is not made clear by the legislation. While the two proceedings have similarities, they do differ in nature in that PDHs seem to be prior to the trial while preparatory hearings are recognised to be part of the actual trial and the judge can determine issues of the admissibility of evidence and questions of law. But if the ultimate goal is efficiency then it would appear to be undesirable to have both a PDH and a preparatory hearing for the same case. It may be that in practice the two would be merged together and dealt with in one hearing in such a situation.

Plea bargaining

Plea bargaining is the name given to negotiations between the prosecution and defence lawyers over the outcome of a case; for example, where a defendant is choosing to plead not guilty, the prosecution may offer to reduce the charge to a similar offence with a smaller maximum sentence, in return for the defendant pleading guilty to that offence. Although plea bargaining is well-known in the US criminal justice system, for many years the official view was that it did not happen here, although those involved in the system knew quite well that in fact it happened all the time. Its existence in the English criminal justice system was confirmed in a 1977 study by Baldwin and McConville, and it is now recognized to be a widespread phenomenon.

Plea bargaining requires the active cooperation of the judge, but the Court of Appeal has consistently set itself against any such involvement. In **R** *v* **Turner** (1970), the defendant was indicted for theft and pleaded not guilty. He had been advised by his counsel to change his plea, on the grounds that a guilty plea normally reduces the sentence, so that if he pleaded guilty he was likely to receive a non-custodial sentence, whereas if he stuck with his plea of not guilty, he was likely to end up in prison.

This advice was repeated after the defence counsel had a meeting with the judge, and Turner then changed his plea. The Court of Appeal held that although there should be freedom of access between the judge and counsel and that counsel could advise a client in strong terms, any such discussion should involve both prosecution and defence, and should be restricted to matters that counsel could not mention in open court. The Court also stressed that judges should never indicate what sentence they had in mind in a particular case, except to say that, regardless of plea, the sentence would not take a particular form.

In practice there are serious concerns about judges breaching this guideline, and whether or not they should. The Court of Appeal has accepted that it is proper for a judge to ensure that the defendant was aware of the discount for pleading guilty, which usually means a sentence is reduced by 30 per cent (**Cain** (1976)), but it has also said that it would be improper to extend a sentence because the defendant has pleaded not guilty or has run a defence in a particular way (**Harper** (1967)). In theory the reason for reducing the sentence for a guilty plea is that this shows remorse; in practice, the saving of time and money this creates is probably more important.

Section 48 of the CJPOA allows the courts, when sentencing offenders, to take into account the stage at which they indicate an intention to plead guilty and the circumstances in which that indication was given. If the court imposes a less severe punishment as a result of this, it must state in open court that it has done so. In time this will lead to case law regarding the effect on discounts of the late or early guilty plea; since defence counsel and the court will need to make defendants aware of this, plea bargaining is likely to become more overt in the future.

Should plea bargaining be allowed?

It can be argued that plea bargaining offers benefits on all sides. For the defendant, there is obviously a shorter sentence. For the courts, the police, and ultimately the taxpayers, there are the financial savings made by drastically shortening trials; in fact without a high proportion of guilty pleas, the courts would be seriously overloaded, causing severe delays which in turn would raise costs still further, especially given the number of prisoners remanded in custody awaiting trial.

However, plea bargaining has been widely criticized as being against the interests of justice. Several studies have shown that plea bargaining may persuade innocent people to plead guilty; Zander and Henderson (1993) concluded that each year there were some 1,400 possibly innocent persons whose counsel felt that they had pleaded guilty in order to achieve a reduction in the charges faced or in the sentence. Critics also point out that the judge should be, and be seen to be, an impartial referee, acting in accordance with law rather than the dictates of cost-efficiency.

In addition, plea bargaining goes against the principle that offenders should be punished for what they have actually done. As well as leading to cases where people are punished more leniently than their conduct would seem to demand, it may lead to quite inappropriate punishments. For example, the high rate of acquittals in rape trials frequently leads to the prosecution reducing the charge to an ordinary offence against the person, in exchange for a guilty plea; this means that offenders who might usefully be given psychiatric help never receive it.

These criticisms are backed up by the fact that in practice, plea bargaining does not necessarily save time or money, because in many cases, it occurs at the last moment, so there is no time to arrange for another case to slot into the court timetable. Such cases are often known as 'cracked trials', and Zander and Henderson's study found that 43 per cent of those cases listed as not guilty pleas 'cracked', which represented 26 per cent of listed cases overall.

One of the reasons why so many defendants plead guilty at the last minute is that this change of plea tends to be made on the advice of their barrister, and often barristers only become involved in the case at this stage. The Royal Commission's Crown Court study found in over half of contested Crown Court trials, defendants did not see their barrister until the morning of the hearing; one-third complained that they had not had enough time with their barrister. A third of defence barristers only received the brief (the document which gives details of the case) the day before the trial. This means that vital decisions about plea are taken under time pressure, in the stressed atmosphere of the court, on the advice of a barrister who has never previously met the client and may have had a very short time to get acquainted with the case.

The RCCJ made two recommendations designed to address the problem of cracked trials. First, the discount for a guilty plea should be graduated, so that defendants who changed their minds at the last minute would receive only minimal advantage. Secondly, there should be what the RCCJ called a sentencing canvass – a preparatory hearing at which the judge would be able to indicate the maximum sentence that would be imposed on the basis of the facts available (a clear movement away from the principle established in **R** *v* **Turner**, above). At this point, the parties could discuss the possibility of the accused pleading guilty to a lesser charge so that there could be a 'full and realistic discussion about plea and especially sentence'.

▶ The trial

Apart from the role played by the jury in the Crown Court, the law and procedure in the Crown Court and magistrates' court are essentially the same. The burden of proof is on the prosecution, which means that they must prove, beyond reasonable doubt, that the accused is guilty; the defendant is not required to prove his or her innocence.

The trial will normally begin with the prosecution outlining the case against the accused, and then producing evidence to prove their case. They call their witnesses, who will give their evidence in response to questions from the prosecution (called examination-in-chief). These witnesses can then be questioned by the defence (called cross-examination), and then if required, re-examined by the prosecution to address any points brought up in cross-examination.

When the prosecution has presented all its evidence, the defence can submit that there is no case to answer, which means that on the prosecution evidence, no reasonable jury (or bench of magistrates) could convict. If the submission is successful, a verdict of not guilty will be given straight away. If no such submission is made or if the submission is unsuccessful, the defence then puts forward its case, using the same procedure for examining witnesses as the prosecution did. The accused is the only witness who cannot be forced to give evidence.

Once the defence has presented all its evidence, each side makes a closing speech, outlining their case and seeking to persuade the magistrates or jury of it. In the Crown Court, this is followed by the judge's summing up to the jury. The judge should review the evidence, draw the jury's attention to the important points of the case, and direct them on the law if necessary, but must not trespass on the jury's function of deciding what were the true facts of the case. At the end of the summing up the judge reminds the jury that the prosecution must prove their case beyond reasonable doubt, and tries to explain in simple terms what this means.

▶ Models of criminal justice systems

In order to judge the effectiveness of a criminal justice system (or anything else for that matter), you need first to know what that system sets out to do. The academic Herbert Packer has identified two quite different potential aims for criminal justice systems; the 'due process' model and the 'crime control' model. The former gives priority to fairness of procedure and to protecting the innocent from wrongful conviction, accepting that a high level of protection for suspects makes it more difficult to convict the guilty, and that some guilty people will therefore go free. The latter places most importance on convicting the guilty, taking the risk that occasionally some innocent people will be convicted. Obviously criminal justice systems tend not to fall completely within one model or the other: most seek to strike a balance between the two. This is not always easy: imagine for a moment that you are put in charge of our criminal justice system, and you have to decide the balance it should aim at. How many innocent people do you believe it is acceptable to convict? Bear in mind that if you answer 'none', the chances are that protections against this may have to be so strong that very few guilty people will be convicted either. Would it be acceptable for 10 per cent of innocent people to be convicted if that means 50 per cent of the guilty were also convicted? If that 10 per cent seems totally unacceptable, does it become more reasonable if it means that 90 per cent of the guilty are convicted? It is not an easy choice to make.

Looking at the balance which a criminal justice system seeks to strike, and how well that balance is in fact struck, is a useful way to assess the system's effectiveness. As mentioned at the beginning of this chapter, in recent years this balance has been the subject of much debate and disagreement as regards our criminal justice system, with the police, magistrates and the government claiming that the balance has been tipped too far in favour of suspects' rights, at the expense of convicting the guilty. On the other hand, civil liberties organizations, many academics, and the lawyers involved in the well-known miscarriages of justice feel that the system has not learned from those miscarriages, and the protections for suspects is still inadequate.

The latter group have particularly criticized the findings of the RCCJ. Sean Enright has written 'One would not guess from a reading of the Commission's proposals that this Royal Commission was set up in response to some astonishing miscarriages of justice. Rather the abiding impression is that this Commission was primarily concerned with a ruthlessly efficient and cost effective disposal of criminal business.' ('Notes from Cost Effective Criminal Justice'). Barrister Michael Mansfield, who represented Judith Ward, and some of the Birmingham Six and Tottenham Three, among others, agrees, pointing out that the RCCJ proposals and other Government plans for the criminal justice system are 'a complete denial of the basic principle of the presumption of innocence . . . the position has deteriorated to such an extent that further wrongful convictions are guaranteed.' (*Presumed Guilty*).

▶ Criticism and reform

Criticisms and suggestions for reform have been made throughout this chapter, but the following have been the subject of particular debate.

The right to silence

The abolition of the right of silence has been one of the most severely criticized changes to the criminal justice system in recent years. As the academic John Fitzpatrick has written (*Legal Action*, May 1994), the basis of the right to silence is the presumption of innocence, which places the burden of proof on the prosecutions: 'this burden begins to shift, and the presumption of innocence to dwindle, as soon as we are obliged to explain or justify our actions in any way.'

Those who objected to the right to silence claimed that only the guilty would have anything to hide, and that the innocent should therefore have no objection to answering questions. It was suggested that the calculated use of the right to silence by professional criminals in serious cases was leading to cases being dropped for lack of evidence, and that 'ambush' defences, in which defendants remain silent till the last moment and then produce an unexpected defence, were leading to acquittals because the prosecution had not had time to prepare for the defence.

These arguments were put to the RCCJ, by a Home Office Working Group among others, but after commissioning its own research into the subject, the RCCJ rejected the idea of abolishing the right to silence. The research, by Leng, McConville and Hodgson, showed that in fact only 5 per cent of suspects exercised their right to silence, and there was no evidence of an unacceptable acquittal rate for these defendants. Nor was there any serious problem with ambush defences.

As we have seen, the Government decided to ignore the RCCJ recommendations and abolish the right to silence – a somewhat strange decision considering that it was the same government which set up the Commission in the first place. The law reform body, Justice, has claimed that this decision will lead to increased pressure on suspects, and in turn, to more miscarriages of justice. Justice studied the effects of removing the right to silence in Northern Ireland (which took place five years before removal of the right in England and Wales). They found that suspects frequently failed to understand the new caution, and were put under unfair pressure to speak; lawyers found it difficult to advise suspects when they did not know the full case against them. Most importantly, Justice claims that while at first trial judges were cautious about drawing inferences of guilt from a suspect's silence, five years on, they were giving such silence considerable weight, and in some cases treating it almost as a presumption of guilt.

The role of the CPS

The CPS ran into problems from its very beginning. Because the Home Office had apparently under-estimated the cost of the new service, the salaries offered were low, making it impossible to find sufficient numbers of good lawyers. As a result, the CPS gained a reputation for incompetence and delay. In 1990 the House of Commons Public Accounts Committee noted that the CPS appeared to be costing almost twice as much as the previous prosecution arrangements, and the numbers of staff required was practically double that originally envisaged.

Relations between the police and the CPS did not begin well either: the police resented the new service, and its demands for a higher standard of case preparation from police. While the CPS see a high rate of discontinued cases as a success story (see above), the police see this as letting offenders off the hook.

While some of these teething problems have now been ironed out, there are still questionable aspects of the role of the CPS. In particular, it is debatable whether it can really be said to bring an independent judgment to the decision on whether to prosecute. First, the fact that the police still take the initial decision on whether to pass the file to the CPS means that such decisions are taken without any control by the CPS, which leads to wide variations in cautioning rates.

Secondly, where the police do refer a case for prosecution, the CPS makes its decision on the basis of information provided by the police – they cannot ask for further inquiries to be made. Given that the police, once satisfied that the suspect is guilty, will tend to look for evidence that supports this conclusion, and see any material that points in another direction as mistaken or irrelevant, this information may paint a very partial picture of the true situation.

This problem has led to some suggestions that the prosecutors should be given some powers of direction over investigations, and that the decision to prosecute should be removed altogether from the police. In their research for the RCCJ, Leigh and Zedner comment:

> It is remarkable that such procedures as application for search warrants need not be made by the CPS. It is surely remarkable, also, that applications to a magistrates' court for extended detention under PACE are made by the police, and not by the prosecutor. Prosecutorial involvement in such procedures would seem axiomatic in France and Germany. It enables the prosecutor both to review the file and to determine the necessity for a police procedure which affects the liberty of the subject. It can also serve to guard against error.

Leigh and Zedner suggest that in some types of case, police interrogations should be attended by a duty prosecutor. This would help overcome the problem of defence solicitors being reluctant to attend interviews, and would reinforce the status of the CPS.

Baldwin and Moloney's research ('Supervision of police investigations in serious criminal cases', 1993) found that the police were actually keen on the idea of early legal advice, and could see considerable benefits in involving the CPS early on in the investigative process. Baldwin and Moloney recommended that in complex cases the CPS should see all the evidence the police have collected and suggest any further enquiries that they feel should be made.

The general feeling of the researchers for the RCCJ seems to have been that the CPS should be given a greater role in the English criminal system, but that this should not go as far as giving them the functions of the French 'juge d'instruction'. However, the RCCJ failed to take this opportunity to clarify the future relationship between the CPS and the police; their Report merely suggests that the police should seek CPS advice in a greater number of cases in accordance with guidelines to be agreed between the two services. To that extent, the possibility of the CPS acting as a real check on police decisions seems to have been shelved for the immediate future.

A corroboration rule?

The major role played by confession evidence in the miscarriages of justice has led to suggestions that confession evidence alone should be regarded as insufficient to secure a conviction; in other words, the prosecution would be required to produce other evidence (such as witnesses, or forensic evidence) to back up confessions.

Research by McConville for the RCCJ suggests that in 95 per cent of cases where confession evidence played a part, supporting evidence was available, indicating that a requirement for such extra evidence would only lead to automatic acquittals in a handful of cases. He calculated that, even without changes in police investigative practices, only 8 per cent of prosecutions would be affected, and these would mostly be less serious cases. It can be argued that this is a reasonable price to pay for avoiding more miscarriages of justice.

Three members of the RCCJ agreed that there should be a requirement for corroborating evidence of confessions. However, the majority merely recommended that judges should warn juries that care was needed in convicting on the basis of the confession alone, and explain the reasons why people might confess to crimes that they did not commit.

Criminal appeals

A reluctance to refer cases back to appeal has been a major feature of most of the high-profile miscarriages of justice. This is discussed in chapter 14.

The role of the media and public opinion

It is noticeable that all the serious miscarriages of justice occurred in cases which had outraged public opinion, and led to enormous pressure on the police to find the culprits. In the case of the Birmingham Six, for example, feelings ran so high that Bridge J consented to the trial being heard away from Birmingham, on the grounds that a Birmingham jury might be 'unable to bring to the trial that degree of detachment that is necessary to reach a dispassionate and objective verdict'. Given the graphic media descriptions of the carnage the real bombers had left behind them, it was in fact debatable whether any jury, anywhere, would have found it easy to summon up such detachment. The chances of a fair trial must have decreased even further when, halfway through the trial, the *Daily Mirror* devoted an entire front page to photographs of the Six, boasting that they were the 'first pictures' (implying that they were the first pictures of the bombers).

Nor is it particularly uncommon for criminal cases to stir up strong public feelings; whenever a child is killed, for example, news that the police are questioning a suspect will draw hostile crowds to the police station, all but shouting for the suspect's blood. If the public can make up their minds at that stage that if the police suspect a person, that person must be guilty, is it any wonder that in such emotive cases, juries may be all too ready to convict, even when there are clear flaws in the evidence?

The role of the public does not end with the jury and the trial, however. As pointed out above, the miscarriages of justice were characterized by a reluctance to refer cases back to appeal. While campaigning by some newspapers and television programmes was eventually to help bring about the successful appeals, other sections of the media, and in particular the tabloid newspapers, were keen to dismiss the idea that miscarriages of justice might have occurred. Nor was there a great amount of public interest in the alleged plight of the Birmingham Six or the other victims – in stark contrast to the petitioning on behalf of Private Lee Clegg during 1995. There was a common feeling of satisfaction that someone had been punished for such terrible crimes, and the public did not want to hear that the system had punished the wrong people.

Even when the miscarriages of justice were finally uncovered, a lingering 'whispering campaign' suggested that the victims of those miscarriages had been let off on some kind of technicality – that there had been police misbehaviour, but that those accused of the bombings and so on were really guilty. Again, tabloid newspapers were only too pleased to contribute to this view. On the day that the report of the RCCJ was published, the *Daily Mail* published an article entitled 'The **true** victims of injustice'. In it, victims of the bombings expressed anger that the Guildford Four and the Birmingham Six had been released – as though justice for those wrongly convicted of a crime somehow meant less justice for the victims of that crime – and doubts as to their innocence. The newspaper commented that 'the decent majority' were more concerned to see measures designed to convict more criminals than to prevent further miscarriages of justice.

The implications of all this for the criminal justice system are important. Clearly such a system does not operate in a vacuum, and in jury trials in particular, public opinion can never really be kept out of the court room. That does not mean that juries should not be used in emotive cases, nor that the media should be gagged. What it does mean is that in those cases which arouse strong public opinion, the police, the prosecution, judges and defence lawyers must all be extra vigilant to ensure that the natural desire to find a culprit does not take the place of the need to find the truth – and to make clear to juries that they must do the same. In addition, measures must be taken to prevent 'trial by newspaper' – the Contempt of Court Act 1981 already provides powers in this respect, but in using these powers, the courts must be able to take into account the profits to be made from crime 'scoops' by newspapers, and punish breaches of the law accordingly. Rather than impose fines, which can be paid for from the increased profits, preventing newspapers from publishing for a day or more might be a more effective deterrent.

· ·

ANSWERING QUESTIONS

1 Discuss the rights of an arrested person, on arrest and during subsequent questioning by the police at a police station.
A good way to start this question would be to define an arrest explaining that it is the point at which an individual is deprived of liberty, and that this is the reason why the rights of an arrested person are so important. Point out the balance that needs to be struck between protecting the rights of the innocent in this situation, and allowing the guilty to be convicted.

Then go on to explain those rights, starting with rights on arrests, and going on to talk about rights in the police station. As well as stating what the arrested person's rights are, you should bring out any problems with or criticisms of those rights – issues you can discuss include police evasions of PACE, the quality of legal advice, and the demise of the right to silence. Your conclusion could sum up whether, in the light of the criticisms you have made, you feel that this area of the law strikes the right balance between protection of the innocent and detection of the guilty.

2 Outline the reasons for the creation of the Crown Prosecution Service. Describe its functions and assess its effectiveness. *WJEC*
You should briefly define what the CPS is, and then divide your answer into the two parts suggested by the question. First, discuss why the CPS was felt to be needed, including the points made by the Justice Report. Then go on to describe what the CPS does, and, in assessing its effectiveness, state how you think the creation of the CPS has improved the criminal justice system, if at all, and point out the problems with it.

10 Sentencing

This chapter is concerned with the punishment of those convicted of crimes, including the types of punishment available, and how the choice between them is made. But first, we need to ask why people are punished at all – what is it supposed to achieve? This will vary with the situation, but there are four main aims which may be present, alone or in combination: retribution; deterrence; rehabilitation or reform; and public protection.

AIMS OF PUNISHMENT

▶ Retribution

Retribution is concerned with recognizing that the criminal has done something wrong, and getting revenge for that wrong on behalf of both the victim and society as a whole. Making punishments achieve retribution has been given a high priority by the current Government. In the White Paper of 1990, *Crime, Justice and Protecting the Public*, references are made to the need for sentences to achieve 'just deserts', stating that punishments should match the harm done, and show society's disapproval of that harm. The problem with this is that other factors all too often intervene: for example, those whose crime is deemed to 'fit' a fine may end up in prison because they are too poor to pay it, while the choice of punishment is also affected by whether the offender is a 'good risk' – those from stable homes, with jobs, are more likely to get non-custodial sentences than those without, who may be sent to prison even though their crime more properly fits a non-custodial sentence.

▶ Deterrence

Deterrence is concerned with preventing the commission of future crimes; the idea is that the prospect of an unpleasant punishment will put people who might otherwise commit crime off the idea. Punishments may aim at

235

individual deterrence, dissuading the offender in question from committing crime again, or general deterrence, showing other people what is likely to happen to them if they commit crime.

One problem with the use of punishment as a deterrent is that its effectiveness depends on the chances of detection; a serious punishment for a particular crime will not deter people from committing that offence if there is very little chance of being caught and prosecuted for it. This was shown when Denmark was occupied during the Second World War. All the Danish police were interned, drastically cutting the risk of being arrested for ordinary criminals. Despite increases in punishment, the number of property offences soared.

Linked with this problem is the fact that a deterrent effect requires the offender to stop and think about the consequences of what they are about to do, and as the Government's 1990 White Paper points out, this is often unrealistic:

> Deterrence is a principle with much immediate appeal ... But much crime is committed on impulse, given the opportunity presented by an open window or unlocked door, and it is committed by offenders who live from moment to moment; their crimes are as impulsive as the rest of their feckless, sad or pathetic lives. It is unrealistic to construct sentencing arrangements on the assumption that most offenders will weigh up the possibilities in advance and base their conduct on rational calculation. Often they do not.

In addition, research by Walker in 1981 shows that the deterrent effect of punishment on individuals becomes weaker each time they are punished; the chances of those with five or more convictions re-offending are very high, no matter what sentence they are given. The more deeply a person becomes involved with a criminal way of life, the harder it is to reform, and at the same time, the fear of punishment becomes less because they have been through it all before.

It has been suggested that to treat this problem, offenders should be given a severe sentence – which politicians like to call a 'short, sharp, shock' – at an early stage, rather than having gradually increased sentences which are counterbalanced by the increased hardening of the offender to the effects of punishment. However, successive attempts at the 'short, sharp, shock' treatment have shown themselves to have no meaningful effect on reconviction rates. The latest move in this direction was the detention centre order, created by the Criminal Justice Act (CJA) 1982; it was abolished in the CJA 1988.

Where a specific crime is thought to be on the increase, the courts will sometimes try to increase the deterrent effects of punishment by passing what is called an exemplary sentence – a sentence higher than that which would normally be imposed in such cases, designed to show people that the problem is being treated seriously, and make potential offenders aware that they may be severely punished. There is some debate as to whether exemplary sentences actually work; their effectiveness depends on publicity, yet British newspapers tend to highlight only those sentences which seem too low for an offence which concerns society, or which seem too high for a trivial offence. In addition, even where there is publicity, the results may be negligible – Smith and Hogan point to an exemplary sentence passed for street robbery at a time when mugging was the subject of great social concern. The sentence was publicized by newspapers and television, yet there was no apparent effect on rates of street robbery even in the area where the case in question took place. We should also question whether exemplary sentences are in the interests of justice, which demands that like cases be treated alike; the person who mugs someone in the street when there has not been a public outcry about that offence is no better than one who mugs when there has.

An emphasis on deterrence is not favoured by the current Government, as the extract from the White Paper shows. The 1991 CJA, in ss. 1(2)(a) and 2(2)(a), suggests that courts must look to the seriousness of the offence, implicitly excluding any reference to the deterrent effect. In **Cunningham** (1993) the court said that '. . . what section 2(2)(a) does prohibit is adding any extra length to the sentence . . . simply to make a special example of the defendant'.

Rehabilitation

The idea here is to use sentencing to reform the offender, so that they are less likely to commit offences in the future – either because they now learn to see that it is wrong, or because through education, training and other help, they find other ways to make a living or spend their leisure time. During the 1960s, a great deal of emphasis was placed on the need for rehabilitation, but the results were seen as disappointing, and in government at least, there is now much less faith in this idea.

However, the CJA 1991 does suggest that the courts take rehabilitation into account when deciding which of various non-custodial community sentences is most suitable for the offender, even though the Act makes it clear that the primary aim must be to make the punishment fit the seriousness of the crime.

Although rehabilitation sounds like a sensible aim, Bottoms argues in *The Coming Penal Crisis* (1980) that it is more problematic than it seems. Firstly, it assumes that all crime is the result of some deficiency or fault in the individual offender; Bottoms, and many critical and Marxist lawyers, argue that crime is actually a result of the way society is organized. Secondly, it discriminates against the less advantaged in society, who are seen as in need of reform, whereas when an offender comes from a more privileged background, their offence tends to be seen as a one-off, temporary slip. This means that punishment is dictated not by the harm caused, but by the background of the offender. While this is unfair in itself, it causes few practical problems where the reformative aspect of the sentencing concerns training or education, which are after all an advantage. But these are not the only kinds of reformative practice; in some cases the pursuit of reform can encourage inexcusable interference with the dignity and privacy of offenders. In other countries this has included implanting electrodes in the brain, and even here, during the 1970s some units have tried experimental programmes involving hormone drug treatment for sex offenders.

▶ Public protection

The principle here is simply that by placing an offender in custody, you prevent them from committing further offences. While it has its merits where highly dangerous offenders are concerned, it is an extremely expensive way of dealing with crime prevention, and since prison is often the place where criminals pick up new ideas and techniques, may be ultimately counter-productive.

SENTENCING PRACTICE

Sentencing in England is the role of the judge. Once the defendant has been found guilty, the judge must decide first what category of sentence is appropriate, and then the amount, duration or form of that sentence, often described as the tariff.

The decision is guided by legislation on the types of sentence available, and the general circumstances in which each will be appropriate; these are currently contained in the Criminal Justice Act 1991, which is based on the policy of 'just deserts' outlined in the 1990 White Paper. It divides sentences into four categories: custodial sentences, community sentences, fines and certain miscellaneous sentences. Except where the sentence is fixed by law (such as life imprisonment for murder), the judge starts from the presumption that the sentence will be a fine. A custodial or community sentence can only be ordered where certain statutory conditions are satisfied.

▶ Custodial sentences

A custodial sentence means, in relation to a person aged 21 or over, a sentence of imprisonment or a suspended sentence; and, in relation to a younger person, a sentence of detention in a young offender's institution or detention under the Children and Young Persons Act 1933, s. 53(2). In defining when a custodial sentence is appropriate, the 1991 Act divides offences between offences which are neither violent nor sexual, and violent and/or sexual offences.

Non-violent and non-sexual offences

The majority of these are property offences, and in these cases, a court should not pass a custodial sentence unless it considers that the crime was so serious that only a custodial sentence is justified. If a non-custodial sentence can be justified then custody must not be imposed.

Traditionally, a major factor in the judge's decision on how severely to punish an offender would be that offender's previous record; those with a long string of similar offences would receive a heavier sentence than the first offender, or someone who had a very minor record. When the 1991 Act was passed, it ruled that judges could only take into account only one 'associated offence' when deciding whether the offence before them was so serious that a custodial offence was required. This followed strictly the principle of 'just deserts': the offender should primarily be sentenced on the basis of the seriousness of the particular offence for which he or she is before the court, and not on the basis of any past record, since punishment for those offences will already have taken place. However, this rule proved extremely unpopular with the judiciary and much of the public, and as a result, changes were quickly made. The 1993 Criminal Justice Act states that judges can look at all associated offences when deciding the seriousness of the offence before them; s. 29(1) (as substituted by the 1993 Act) allows them to take into account previous convictions, failure to respond to previous sentences and commission of an offence while on bail.

The legislation does not define seriousness, and so case law is likely to become important on this issue. In **Cox**, an eighteen-year-old defendant pleaded guilty to theft of some tools and reckless driving, and was sentenced to four months' detention. The Court of Appeal said that the phrase 'so serious that only a custodial sentence is justified' means:

> The kind of offence which when committed by a young person would make all right-thinking members of the public, knowing all the facts, feel that justice had not been done by the passing of any sentence other than a custodial one.

The focus on the seriousness could mean that the courts should not take into account rates of offending for that crime in society generally, which would prevent exemplary sentences; in fact s. 2(2)(a) prohibits making a sentence longer than it would otherwise be in order to make an example of the offender. However, in **Cunningham** (1993), a robbery case, Lord Chief Justice Taylor made it clear that seriousness could not be interpreted in isolation. The prevalence of the offence was a legitimate factor: whereas one violent sexual attack on a woman gravely harmed the victim, a series of attacks put women into fear and limited their freedom of movement, and accordingly such an attack might be viewed even more seriously.

One aggravating factor which the court must take into account is whether the offence was committed while the offender was on bail concerning another charge; this rule was introduced by s. 66(6) of the CJA 1993, substituting a new s. 29 in the CJA 1991. An offender who, while on bail for a particular offence, commits the same offence again, should forfeit the effect of any mitigating factors which might otherwise be available (see below).

Violent and sexual offences

Where an offence is violent and/or sexual, the Act moves away from focusing purely on 'just deserts', and requires the court to take into account the need to protect the public. A custodial sentence may be imposed where it is necessary to protect the public from 'serious harm', which the Act defines as 'death or serious injury, whether physical or psychological, occasioned by further offences'.

In such cases, the court can take into account not only the circumstances of the offence, but also 'any information about the offender which is before it'. Therefore even where the seriousness of the offence committed does not necessarily require custody, the court may decide custody is necessary because of what the defendant might do if left free. In exceptional circumstances, a court may impose a custodial sentence where it has proposed a community sentence which requires the defendant's consent, and the defendant refuses to give that consent.

Where a custodial sentence is imposed (whatever the offence, unless the sentence is fixed by law), a pre-sentence report must be prepared by the probation service, containing background information about the defendant, and the courts must give reasons for giving a custodial sentence.

▶ Community sentences

A community sentence means a sentence of one or more community orders. These include probation orders, community service orders, combination orders, curfew orders, supervision orders and attendance centre orders.

A community sentence can be ordered if the offence committed was sufficiently serious to justify such a sentence. Once this is established, the court must decide which order is the most suitable for the offender.

Section 6(2) requires that 'the restriction on liberty imposed by the order or orders shall be such as in the opinion of the court are commensurate with the seriousness of the offence, or the combination of the offence and other offences associated with it'.

In a few cases, particularly where young offenders are concerned, a pre-sentence report may be required before community sentence is imposed.

▶ The tariff system

The Criminal Justice Act 1991 regulates the type of sentence imposed, and in its focus on seriousness, clearly has implications for the length of a custodial or community sentence or the amount of a fine. In deciding the latter issues, judges also rely on what has been called the tariff principle, first recognized by Dr David Thomas in his book *Principles of Sentencing* (1970).

The tariff system is based on treating like cases alike; people with similar backgrounds who commit similar offences in similar circumstances should receive similar sentences. That does not mean that judges apply a rigid scale of penalties, but that for most types of criminal offence, it is possible to identify a range within which the sentences for different factual situations will fall. The system works in two stages: the initial tariff sentence, and the application of secondary tariff principles. To begin with, there will be a tariff sentence that is generally thought appropriate for the offence. This is the judges' starting point. It may then be lowered by what are called mitigating factors – reasons why the defendant should be punished less severely than the facts of the case might suggest. These include youth or old age; previous good character; the 'jump effect', a requirement that sentences for repeat offenders should increase steadily rather than by large jumps; provocation; domestic or financial problems; drink, drugs or ill-health; and any special hardship offenders may have to undergo in prison, such as the fact that sex offenders and police informers may have to be held in solitary confinement for their own protection. In some cases where an offender has already been held on remand, the courts may reduce the tariff sentence on the basis that the shock of being locked up at all has been a severe punishment. The offender's behaviour after committing the offence may also be a factor, including efforts to help the police and/or compensate the victim; a plea of guilty is usually taken as a sign of remorse and according to Thomas the initial tariff placement can be reduced by between one quarter and one third for this reason alone. As far as the offence itself is concerned, the fact that it was committed on impulse and not premeditated may be a mitigating factor, and the degree of harm done may be important too – a property crime where the value of the property is small, or a crime against the person where the injuries of the victim are minor may be treated less severely.

There may also be aggravating factors, as a result of which the court may want to pass an exemplary sentence. The Court of Appeal has stated that the correct way to deal with this is to ignore mitigating factors and not to increase the initial tariff placement.

▶ Individualized sentences

In some cases, the courts prefer not to use the tariff system, but to impose a sentence aimed at dealing with the individual needs of the offender. There are four main types of offender for whom individualized sentencing is used: young offenders; intermediate recidivists: inadequate recidivists; and offenders who need psychiatric treatment. Individualized sentences are often given to young offenders in the hope of steering them away from a life of crime. Intermediate recidivists are offenders in their late twenties or early thirties, with a criminal record dating back to their childhood. Rather than simply ordering steadily increased tariff sentences for them, the courts may give an individualized sentence if there is evidence that a new approach may work. Inadequate recidivists are middle-aged or elderly offenders who have a long history of relatively minor offences, which have resulted in imprisonment and most other types of sentence. Individualized sentences may be ordered for them on the simple basis that their record shows increasing tariff sentences to have been ineffective in stopping their offending. Finally, offenders who need psychiatric treatment are given individualized sentences within which such treatment can be undertaken.

TYPES OF SENTENCE

We stated above that there are four main categories of sentence: custodial sentences, community sentences, fines and other miscellaneous sentences. We will now look at the particular forms that these sentences can take.

▶ Fines

A fine may be imposed for almost any offence other than murder. Offences tried in the magistrates' court carry a set maximum, depending on the offence; the highest is £5,000. There is no maximum in the Crown Court. The CJA 1991 s. 18(2) requires magistrates to ensure that the amount of the fine reflects the seriousness of the offence, and also to take account of the offender's means, reducing or increasing it as a result. This consideration of financial circumstances is an important change to the pre-1991 law.

Advantages
Evidence suggests that re-offending following a fine is less than for other sentences, though this can be partly explained by the type of offenders that are given fines in the first place. Fines also bring income into the system, and they do not have the long-term disruptive effects of imprisonment.

Disadvantages
There are high rates of non-payment. This not only makes the sentence ineffective, but repeated non-payment of a fine can and often does lead to a custodial sentence, with the result that a high proportion of the inmates of English prisons are there for very minor offences, such as failure to pay for a television licence. At the moment magistrates' courts can arrange for the automatic deduction of a fine from the offender's earnings, known as an 'attachment of earnings order' once he or she has defaulted. If the Criminal Procedure and Investigations Bill is passed in its current form in 1996 then a magistrates' court would have the power to make an attachment of earnings order with the consent of an offender straight away when imposing the fine (or a compensation order) rather than only on default. It is thought this might reduce slightly the problem of unpaid fines.

Fines can also be criticized as being unfair, since the same fine may be a very severe punishment to a poor defendant, but make little impact on one who is well-off. In an attempt to address this problem, the 1991 Act originally laid down a system of unit fines for the magistrates' courts. A maximum number of units was allocated to each offence, up to a total of 50. Within that maximum, the court had to determine the number of units which was commensurate with the seriousness of the case. The value of the unit depended on the offender's disposable weekly income (their income after having deducted their regular household expenses), with the minimum value of a unit being £4, and the maximum £100. The unit fines system aimed to even out the effects of fines, so that although the fines were different, the impact on the offender would be similar. The pilot schemes for the unit fines suggested that fines were paid more quickly and there was a drop in debtors ending up in prison, because of the more realistic assessment of the fines.

Unfortunately, the idea aroused huge public opposition after press coverage of what seemed to be high fines for relatively minor offences and very low fines for the unemployed – despite the fact that even if some of these were unfair, they were less unfair than the previous system. As a result, unit fines were abolished, and the courts reverted to their previous practice, although as mentioned above, they are now required to take into account ability to pay when setting fines.

▶ Custodial sentences

For adult defendants, a custodial sentence means prison. Most of those given custodial sentences do not serve the full sentence. In the past, they could be released early on parole which essentially meant that they could be taken back into prison if they re-offended, or given remission, which shortened the length of the sentence to be served, provided the individual behaved well in prison. The 1991 Act abolishes remission and parole for most offenders, and puts in its place the single concept of early release. Offenders serving sentences of up to four years will automatically be released after half the sentence has been served. Where the sentence is more than twelve months, their release will be on licence, under the supervision of the probation service, for the next quarter of their sentence. Breach of licence has now become an offence punishable by a fine, or recall to prison.

Those serving more than four years may be released at a point somewhere between one half and two thirds of the sentence; the decision in each case will be made on the basis of a recommendation made by the Parole Board. Such offenders will be on licence until the three quarter point of the sentence. Breach of the licence can only be dealt with by recall to prison. An offender released early who commits a new offence during the duration of the original sentence may have to go back to prison and serve the complete sentence.

The system for those given mandatory life sentences was unchanged by the 1991 Act. The Parole Board can recommend release only if the Home Secretary has referred the case to the Board for its advice; if, on referral, the Board does advise release, the final decision is taken by the Home Secretary, after consultation with the Lord Chief Justice and, if possible, the trial judge. Prisoners released during a life sentence remain on licence.

The rules introduced by the 1991 Act mean that for many offenders the sentence actually served will increase. In particular, those sentenced to between one and four years would previously have served around a third of their sentence, and will now serve half. To try to avoid prison overcrowding a Practice Statement was issued, stating that whereas in the past, the courts were required to decide the appropriate sentence in each case without reference to questions of remission or parole, they were now to take into account the actual period likely to be served.

On the issue of early release Michael Howard announced at the end of 1995 his plans to reform the system that the government only introduced in 1991. He has proposed that automatic early release should be abolished. Instead there would be a maximum reduction in a person's sentence of only 15 per cent for good behaviour. No remission at all would be available if the sentence was for less than twelve months. The logic behind this proposal is that 'five years should mean five years', but the prison governors have expressed their concern that it might lead to greater difficulties in maintaining discipline in the prisons. The reform reflects the fact that the Government no longer seems to feel that sentences are too long.

Advantages
The Government has claimed that prison 'works', in the sense that offenders cannot commit crime while they are in prison, and so the public is protected.

Disadvantages
Around 65 per cent of offenders released from prison are reconvicted within two years. Recent research now suggests that these reconviction rates improve if prisoners undergo a period on licence between their custody and their return to the community (Ward, 1994). In her book, *Bricks of Shame*, Vivienne Stern highlights several reasons why imprisonment lacks any great reformative power, and may even make people more, rather than less, likely to re-offend. Prisoners spend time with other criminals, from whom they frequently acquire new ideas for criminal enterprises; budget cuts have meant there is now little effective training and education in prisons, and the stigma of having been in prison means their opportunities for employment are fewer when they get out; and families often break down, with the result that the ex-prisoner may become homeless. The result, says Stern, is that 'going straight can present the quite unattractive option of a boring, lonely existence in a hostel or rented room, eking out the Income Support'. All this can also mean that prison punishes the innocent as well as the guilty, with the prisoner's family suffering stigma, financial difficulties, the misery of being parted from the prisoner, and often family breakdown in the end.

Stern also rejects the idea that prison works because it protects the public. She points out that although it may prevent the individual offending for a while, the percentage of crime that is actually detected and prosecuted is so small that imprisonment has little effect on the crime rate.

Prison is also extremely expensive – according to Stern, three weeks in prison costs more than a whole community service order, or a year on probation. To this must be added the costs associated with the family breakdown and unemployment that imprisonment frequently causes.

Despite these criticisms, and the development of a range of alternative sentencing options over the past couple of decades, prisons have become more and more overcrowded – the UK has a higher proportion of its population in prison than any other country in the EU. The UK prison population currently stands at 52,000 people. While some people believe this is the result of growing lawlessness, others believe that in times of high unemployment and resulting social discontent, sentencers simply perceive a danger of increased lawlessness, and impose more prison sentences to counter it.

As well as those who find themselves in prison through non-payment of fines, many of those actually sentenced to prison have committed relatively minor offences and could be dealt with just as effectively and far more cheaply in the community. In 1978 the Advisory Council on the Penal System published a report pointing out that prison sentences could be reduced across the board without affecting the reconviction rates of those imprisoned. In 1979 the Committee of Inquiry into the Prison Service also stated that prison sentences were longer than they need to be.

The immediate impact of the CJA 1991 seems to have been a fall in the number of prison sentences, and a consequent increase in the use of other sentencing options. However, by the time the CJA 1993 was passed, it was clear that the mood among magistrates, judges and the Government had changed, possibly as a result of widespread press allegations that the system was becoming too soft on criminals. Along with the changes made to the 1991 provisions by the CJA 1993, this seems to have led to increasing use of custody, with a resulting rise in the prison population.

Suspended sentence

Where a court passes a sentence of up to two years' imprisonment, it may order that the sentence will not take effect unless the offender commits another imprisonable offence during a period fixed by the court, which must be between one and two years.

Suspended sentences were introduced in 1967, with the aim of reducing the number of people sent to prison. However, they turned out to have the opposite effect. This might not have been the case if courts had confined suspended sentences to those cases where they would otherwise have sent the offenders to prison, but the courts failed to do this. Suspended sentences were frequently used as an alternative to a community sentence, as a kind of warning. If the offender committed another offence, the suspended sentence was often activated, so that the offender ended up in prison, even though the original offence had not demanded a prison sentence.

The CJA 1991 s. 5 addressed this problem by requiring the court to satisfy itself that the exceptional circumstances of the case justify use of the power to suspend. An offender should not receive a suspended sentence of imprisonment unless imprisonment would have been appropriate if the power to suspend had not existed. The case of **Okinikan** (1993) indicates that circumstances must be out of the ordinary; in that case, good character, youth and an early plea were held not to be sufficiently exceptional, either by themselves or together. Where courts seek to impose a suspended sentence, they are still required by the 1991 Act to state in open court why the defendant requires a custodial sentence within the terms of the Act.

The impact of s. 5 has to be considered in the context of the 1991 Act's restrictions on the use of custody generally, but use of suspended sentences has certainly lessened. In 1991 10 per cent of adult offenders sentenced for indictable offences received a suspended sentence; for the first three-quarters of 1992 the figure was 9 per cent, but by the final quarter of that year, it had gone down to 3 per cent.

For a time, the courts had the power to order that part of a prison sentence should be served immediately, and the rest suspended; this has been abolished by the Criminal Justice Act 1991.

▶ Community sentences

In order to encourage the use of community sentences, rather than custody, these sentences have been restructured by the 1991 Act, and the Government has emphasized that they do present substantial restrictions on the offender's freedom, and should not be seen as 'soft options'.

There are a range of different community sentences available to the courts.

Probation orders

A probation order places the offender under the supervision of a probation officer for a fixed period of between six months and three years. After consulting with a probation officer, the court may impose conditions on the probation order. These commonly require the offender to attend a specified place and engage in specified activities for a maximum of 60 days (or longer if the convict is a sex offender), or not to undertake specified activities for either the whole or part of the period on probation. Other possible conditions include requiring the offender to live in a specified place, such as a probation hostel, or undergo psychiatric treatment; the CJA 1991 adds a power to require offenders who have drug or alcohol problems to undergo medical treatment.

A probation order can be made for any offender aged sixteen or over. The court must be satisfied that supervision is desirable in the interests of rehabilitating the offender, or preventing them from committing further offences or harming the public. As such an order cannot succeed without the offender's cooperation, it may only be made if the offender consents to it. A court cannot impose a fine and a probation order for the same offence.

Where conditions are imposed, and the offender breaks one of them, the probation officer may decide that the offender should be brought before the court again. In that case the court can fine the offender up to £400, make an attendance centre order (see p. 264), or pass a new sentence for the original offence. An offender who commits another offence while on probation may be dealt with for both the subsequent offence and the original offence.

Advantages

Probation orders have fewer disruptive effects than prison, and sensibly-applied conditions may help keep the offender away from criminal influences.

Disadvantages

Reconviction rates are disappointing. Recent research shows that with the exceptions of juveniles and adult males with between one and four previous convictions, offenders are more likely to re-offend after being placed on probation than if they had been given any other non-custodial sentence.

Community service orders

Community service orders were introduced in 1972, and designed to be an alternative way of dealing with offenders who would otherwise have been sentenced to a short term of imprisonment. The order requires the offender to perform, over a period of twelve months, a specified number of hours of unpaid work for the benefit of the community; the number of hours must be between 40 and 240. The kind of work done includes tasks on conservation projects, archaeological sites and canal clearance. An additional requirement imposed by the 1991 Act is that the offender must keep in touch with the probation officer, and notify them of any change of address.

The general conditions for making such an order are much the same as for a probation order and it is in fact supervised by a probation officer. The offender must be sixteen or over and have been convicted of an imprisonable offence.

If the offender fails to comply with a condition of the order, and the probation officer decides to bring the matter before the court, the court may impose a fine of up to £400 and allow the order to continue, or revoke the order and pass another sentence for the original offence.

Advantages

Community service orders are less disruptive than prison; allow useful community work to be done; and may give the offender a sense of achievement which helps them stay out of trouble afterwards.

Disadvantages

Community service orders were designed to be an alternative to imprisonment, but there is evidence that they have frequently been made for offenders who would otherwise have been given another non-custodial sentence. Re-conviction rates are unimpressive: in one Home Office study, they were even higher for young adult men than for those released from detention centres. Community service orders have also suffered from being seen as a 'soft option', giving them little deterrent value.

Combination orders

The Criminal Justice Act 1991 allows a probation order of between one and three years to be combined with between 40 and 100 hours community service.

Curfew orders

The Criminal Justice Act 1991 gave courts the power to impose a curfew order for offenders aged sixteen or over. Under this power, the court may order that, within a six month period, an offender should remain in a specified place or specified places for periods of not less than two hours or more than twelve hours in any one day. A curfew order can only be imposed with the offender's consent, and the meaning of the order and the consequences of failing to comply with it must be explained to the offender. The court should avoid imposing conditions which would interfere with the offender's work or education, or cause conflict with the offender's religious beliefs or the requirements of any other community order. A specified person must be made responsible for monitoring the offender's whereabouts.

Advantages
Curfew orders have the potential to keep offenders out of trouble, and protect the public, without the disruptive effects, or the costs, of imprisonment. In the American city of Atlanta, a night curfew has been imposed on anyone under sixteen, which was introduced to protect children, but has also had the effect of considerably reducing juvenile crime. While such use of curfew orders on those who have not been convicted of crimes offends against the right to freedom of movement, the effects show that as a sentence, it could prove very useful.

Disadvantages
The police have said they are concerned about the enforceability of curfew orders, and perhaps as a result, they are not greatly used. The 1991 Act allows courts to require that offenders wear electronic tags, which allow their whereabouts to be monitored, but technical problems delayed the introduction of these tags.

Tagging is also said to be degrading to the person concerned, but supporters of tagging – including one or two well known former prisoners – point out that it is far less degrading than imprisonment. This argument applies only where tagging is used as an alternative to imprisonment: its opponents, however, claim that it is likely to be used in practice to replace other non-custodial measures. Home Office experiments which allowed tagging as a condition of bail have not been particularly successful: in Nottingham, for example, nine out of seventeen defendants breached their bail conditions.

▶ Other miscellaneous sentences

Death

Although it is widely believed that the death sentence has been abolished in this country, it is still available for a small number of uncommon offences, including high treason and piracy with violence, provided the person committing the offence is over eighteen.

Compensation orders

Where an offence causes personal injury, loss or damage (unless it arises from a road accident), the courts may order the offender to pay compensation. This may be up to £1,000 in a magistrates' court, and is unlimited in the Crown Court. Courts can also order that stolen property is given back to its owner, or where stolen property has been disposed of, it may order that compensation be made to the victim from any money taken from the offender when arrested. Offenders who have used their own property for criminal purposes (such as a car used in connection with a robbery) may be ordered to give up that property.

Mental health orders

Under the Mental Health Act 1983, the Crown Court can order the detention of an offender in a hospital on conviction for an imprisonable offence if he or she is suffering from a mental disorder, the nature or degree of which makes detention in hospital for medical treatment appropriate; and, if psychiatric disorder or mental impairment is present, the court is satisfied that the treatment is likely to help the condition or stop it getting worse. The order can only be made if the court considers that such an order is the most suitable way of dealing with the case. Alternatively, the court may place the offender under the guardianship of a local authority.

Where detention in hospital is ordered by the Crown Court, and it believes that the public needs to be protected from the offender, it can make an order restricting the discharge of the offender either for a specified period or without limit.

A magistrates' court can make an order for detention in a hospital when an offender has been convicted of an imprisonable offence, or even if the offender has not been convicted, if the court is satisfied as to guilt.

Binding over to be of good behaviour

This order dates back to the thirteenth century. It can be made against any person who is before the court – not just the defendant, but also any witness. People who are bound over have to put up a sum of money, or find someone else to do so (sometimes both), which will be forfeited if the undertaking is broken. A person who refuses to be bound over can be imprisoned, despite the fact that they may not have been convicted of any offence. The order usually lasts for a year.

Absolute and conditional discharges

If the court finds an offender guilty of any offence (except one for which the penalty is fixed by law), but believes that in the circumstances it is unnecessary to punish the offender and probation is inappropriate, it may discharge the defendant either absolutely or conditionally.

An absolute discharge effectively means that no action is taken at all, and is generally made where the defendant's conduct is wrong in law, but no reasonable person would blame them for doing what they did. A conditional discharge means that no further action will be taken unless the offender commits another offence within a specified period of up to three years. This order is commonly made where the court accepts that the defendant has acted wrongly as well as illegally, but the mitigating circumstances are very strong. If an offender who has received a conditional discharge is convicted of another offence during the specified period, the offender may, in addition to any other punishment imposed, be sentenced for the original offence. A discharge does not count as a conviction unless it is conditional and the offender re-offends within the specified period.

Deferred sentences

The Powers of the Criminal Courts Act 1973 allows the courts to defer passing sentence for a period of up to six months after conviction. The Act contains few guidelines on the use of the power, but does state that it can be exercised only with the consent of the offender, and where deferring sentence is in the interests of justice. Deferred sentences are intended for situations where the sentencer has reason to believe that within the deferral period, the offender's circumstances will materially change, with the result that no punishment is necessary, or that the punishment imposed should be less than it would have been if imposed at the time of conviction. For example, offenders may make reparation to the victim, settle down to employment, or otherwise demonstrate that they have changed for the better.

Disqualification

This is most common as a punishment for motoring offences, and for certain driving offences (most notably drink driving) disqualification for twelve months is mandatory unless there are special reasons against disqualification. A conviction for offences concerning cruelty to animals may also lead to disqualification from keeping pets or livestock.

▶ Appeals against sentence

The defence may appeal against a sentence considered too harsh, while the prosecution can appeal if they feel the sentence was too lenient. In addition, ss. 35 and 36 of the Criminal Justice Act 1988 give the Attorney General the power to refer a case to the Court of Appeal where the sentence is believed to have been too lenient.

▶ Problems with sentencing

The role of the judge

We have seen that the sentence in England is essentially a decision for the judge, and this has been held to give rise to inconsistencies, especially among magistrates' courts. This situation clearly offends against the principle of justice that requires like cases to be treated alike.

The Government has tried to restrict judicial discretion through legislative guidelines, such as those in the 1991 Act, and has also set up a Judicial Studies Board for Crown Court judges. Overseen by the Lord Chancellor's Department, its functions include running seminars on sentencing, which seek to reduce inconsistencies, courses for newly-appointed judges and refresher courses for more experienced judges. The Board also publishes a regular bulletin summarizing recent legislation, sentencing decisions, research findings and developments in other countries. The Magistrates' Association also issues a *Sentencing Guide for Criminal Offences* to its members.

Other jurisdictions generally allow judges less discretion in sentencing. In the USA, for example, many states use 'indeterminate' sentencing by which a conviction automatically means a sentence of, say, one to five years' imprisonment, and the exact length of the sentence is decided by the prison authorities. However, in this country, control of sentencing is seen as an important aspect of judicial independence, and proposals for more legislative control have been criticized as interfering with the judiciary's constitutional position. The same reaction faced proposals for the creation of a sentencing council. Such a council could comprise senior judges, circuit judges and lay and stipendiary magistrates, representatives of the prison and probation services, academic lawyers and criminologists, and would formulate and review guidance for the courts on sentencing matters, but at the moment it seems unlikely to be created. (See the section on reform at the end of this chapter for the most recent controversy to arise from proposals to reduce judicial sentencing discretion.)

Community sentences

Over the past couple of decades, a range of community sentences have been introduced, with the aim of reducing the prison population, and improving reconviction rates. None of them have been particularly successful.

In 1995, the Government issued a consultation paper arguing that community sentences would benefit from restructuring:

> It is the view of the Government that the role of community sentences is poorly understood and – perhaps as a result – that they have failed to command the confidence of the public despite the greater prominence and extra resources given to the probation service in recent years. Probation supervision is widely regarded as a soft option. Although in many cases this perception is misconceived, it must be addressed. Both courts and the public have found difficulty in squaring their concept of the probation order (with its additionally high social work content) with the notion of punishment involving significant restriction of liberty.

The paper proposes 'a single integrated sentence integrating and extending the present range of community orders'. The current range of different community orders – probation, community service, attendance centre, curfew, and so on – would be replaced by a single order known as 'the community sentence'. This could include measures to restrict liberty, make reparation to the victim or society, and prevent re-offending; in each case the court would specify precisely what mix of these functions was required.

There is an obvious drawback to this plan, which the consultation paper recognizes: 'wider choice and potentially more complex orders, while offering the opportunity for more closely targeted sentences, also have the potential for confusion and the overloading of sentences with unnecessary elements'. And of course, budget constraints are not forgotten, with the Government apparently requiring these changes to be made at no extra cost: the paper points out that the new plans 'will have to be delivered within planned resources. Any increased demand can only lead to a reduction in the level of service. Greater choice should not necessarily entail greater consumption'.

Racism

Critics of sentencing practice in England have frequently alleged that members of ethnic minorities are treated more harshly than white defendants. For example, black men form 1.9 per cent of the population of England and Wales, yet according to Home Office figures for June 1993, they comprise 10.8 per cent of the male prison population. The percentage of black women in prison is even more out of proportion to their presence in the population as a whole, though this difference becomes much less if only UK nationals are considered, because a high proportion of black females in prison are foreign nationals imprisoned for illegally importing drugs. Whether these figures actually point to racial discrimination in sentencing is difficult to say with certainty, but research has strongly suggested that there are differences in the way black and white people are treated by sentencers.

In 1985, David Martin of the South East London Probation Service conducted a survey of 117 young men in youth custody or released on licence. At that time, 29 per cent of the service's youth custody cases concerned black people, compared with 4.7 per cent of the total population. Of the young men studied, those who were black were less likely than white men to be offered supervision or probation orders before being sentenced to youth custody, and were sentenced to youth custody with fewer previous convictions than white men, even though they generally came from more stable backgrounds than the white subjects, which would normally make them a 'better risk' for non-custodial sentences.

In 1986, a study by the West Midlands Probation Service looked into the role of Social Inquiry Reports (information on the defendant, with a recommendation for sentencing, usually prepared by the Probation Service) in sentencing differences between whites and blacks. The study showed that where the defendant was black, sentencers were less likely to follow the sentencing recommendations than they were if the defendant was white, and the result of not following recommendations was more likely to be a custodial sentence where defendants were black, than if they were white. In cases where the Social Inquiry Report made no sentencing recommendation, all the black defendants were given custody, compared to only 57 per cent of the white defendants.

The study then looked at the offences committed, to see if this could explain the sentencing differences. It found that on balance, the white defendants had committed a higher proportion of the more serious offences than the black defendants, and that where the offence was the same, black people were more likely to receive custodial sentences; for example, 79 per cent of black defendants for burglary received custody, compared with 25 per cent of white defendants. Nor were the differences explained by previous records of sentencing: of those receiving a custodial sentence, 58 per cent of the white defendants had previously been in custody, compared with 37 per cent of the black defendants.

In addition to any racism in the system, the legal and procedural factors which affect sentencing may account for some of the differences. More black offenders elect for Crown Court trial and plead not guilty, which means that if convicted, they would probably receive harsher sentences, because the sentences in the Crown Court are higher than those in the magistrates' court, and they would not benefit from a discount for a guilty plea.

The proposal for a sentencing council, discussed above, might be one way to bring greater coherence, rationality and consistency to sentencing.

Sexism

There is enormous controversy over the treatment of women by sentencers. On one hand, many claim that women are treated more leniently than men. A recent Home Office study (Hedderman and Hough, 1994) reported that, regardless of their previous records, women were far less likely than men to receive a custodial sentence for virtually all indictable offences except those concerning drugs, and that when they do receive prison sentences these tend to be shorter than those imposed on men. This has been variously attributed to the fact that women are less likely to be dealt with at the Crown Court; to chivalry on the part of sentencers; to assumptions that women are not really bad, but offend only as a result of mental illness or medical problems; and to reluctance to harm children by sending their mothers to prison.

On the other hand, other surveys have suggested that women are actually treated less leniently than men. A 1990 study by the National Association for the Care and Resettlement of Offenders found that one-third of sentenced female prisoners had no previous convictions, compared with 11 per cent of men, and most of them were in prison for minor, non-violent offences. A 1994 report from the County Durham Probation Service said that the numbers of women jailed had risen by one-third in less than a year, with no equivalent rise in the numbers of men being imprisoned; again, most of the women were imprisoned for small thefts or deception offences. Because they are usually on lower incomes than men, women are thought more likely to end up in prison for non-payment of fines.

Several critics have suggested that women who step outside traditional female roles are treated more harshly than both men and other women – almost as if they have committed two crimes. Sociologist Pat Carlen studied the sentencing of a large group of women, and found that judges were more likely to imprison those who were seen as failing in their female role as wife and mother – those who were single or divorced, or had children in care. This was reflected in the comments made by sentencers, including 'It may not be necessary to send her to prison if she has a husband. He may tell her to stop it' and 'If she's a good mother we don't want to take her away. If she's not, it doesn't really matter.'

▶ Reform

At the end of 1995, Michael Howard, the Home Secretary, announced further controversial plans for reforming the sentencing system. He has proposed that mandatory life sentences should be imposed on repeat rapists, attempted murderers and other serious violent offenders. Habitual burglars and hard drug dealers would face an automatic minimum prison sentence for a third conviction if they were over 18.

The proposed reforms were heavily criticised by Lord Taylor, a senior member of the judiciary. He was particularly concerned by the introduction of minimum sentences as this took away sentencing discretion from the judges. Michael Howard has tried to appease the judges on this point by saying after his initial announcement that judges would still be able to exercise their discretion in exceptional cases. Lord Taylor has stated publicly that money would be better channelled into policing than sentencing. He stated:

> I make no criticism of the police, who do their best within the
> limited resources they are given. But does anyone believe that a
> professional burglar who knows he has at most only three chances
> in 20 of being caught will be deterred by the possible addition of 6
> months or even 2 years to his sentence?

The philosophy behind these proposals can be traced back to the USA and in particular California where in their attempt to 'get tough on crime' they have introduced a system known as 'three strikes and you're out'. Under this system a person is convicted of committing a third offence classified as a 'felony' will get an automatic life sentence. The result of this has been a rapid increase in the prison population. Eleven new prisons have had to be built in California in the last decade to cope with the increase. Prison officials are now seeking $2 billion to build a further 15–20 prisons – in the USA as a whole they are now spending more on their prison system than they are on schools. The scheme is also over-burdening the court system. Defendants are becoming reluctant to agree to a plea bargain and are demanding a jury trial more often. As a result in Los Angeles alone there is a backlog of 1,500 cases. Some juries are refusing to convict people of offences even though there is strong evidence against the person because of a reluctance to be responsible for sending them to a life in prison. There are suggestions that suspects are more likely to resist arrest with sometimes dangerous gunfights ensuing. The possible injustice that can arise was illustrated by the case of Jerry Williams, who was a 27-year-old man who was sentenced to life, on conviction of his third offence which was the stealing of a piece of pizza from a group of children when he was drunk.

On the other hand in the first six months of the introduction of the scheme robberies dropped by 12.7 per cent, rape by 10.8 per cent, murders by 10.6 per cent and burglaries by 6.3 per cent. But these statistics must be handled with care as there is apparently a general fall in the crime rate across the USA which some have linked with the drop in the number of young people in the country, since young people are among those who are most likely to be convicted of crimes.

ANSWERING QUESTIONS

1 Margaret, aged 26, is charged with manslaughter and has appeared before Hattown magistrates.
(i) What are the powers of Hattown magistrates to deal with Margaret?
(ii) How may Margaret obtain legal aid and advice?
(iii) If Margaret is convicted what sentences might be passed upon her?
Part (i): the information needed for this part is covered fully in chapter 9 but essentially the powers of the magistrates concern bail and transfer of the case to the Crown Court, since manslaughter is a crime triable only on indictment.

Part (ii): these issues are covered in chapter 8 – the relevant areas are the duty solicitor's scheme in court and criminal legal aid.

Part (iii): as we are given no details about the form of manslaughter or the circumstances, and as Margaret is an adult offender, in theory any of the sentencing options described above could be relevant. You need to outline what these options are and the criteria that would be used to decide which of these is imposed on Margaret.

2 How do judges arrive at decisions as to what sentences should be imposed on persons convicted of offences? *London*
You could start your answer to this question by pointing out the important role that judges play in sentencing in our system, highlighting the fact that although there are some mandatory sentences and now greater statutory guidance to judges, they still maintain a wide discretion in sentencing. You could then point out that there are a number of principles which are officially accepted as guiding such judicial decisions but that it is alleged that these decisions may also be affected by certain unadmitted factors, such as racism and sexism.

You can then go on to look at the official factors first, discussing the four key principles that can underlie the sentence (retribution, deterrence, rehabilitation and public protection) and the process of sentencing (the statutory guidance in the Criminal Justice Act 1991 and 1993, the tariff system and individualized sentences). After this you could examine some of the allegations that racism and sexism also influence judges in arriving at sentencing decisions, mentioning the research studies detailed in the relevant sections above.

11

Young offenders

Offenders who are under eighteen years old are dealt with differently by the criminal justice system to the way in which adults are treated. There are a number of reasons for this, including a belief that children are less responsible for their actions than adults, a wish to steer children away from any further involvement in crime, and the feeling that sentencing can be used to reform as well as, or instead of, punishing them.

▶ Young people and the police

Most of the police powers concerning adults also apply to young suspects, but because they are thought to be more vulnerable, some extra rules apply. For example, Code C of the Police and Criminal Evidence Act 1984 (PACE) states that young suspects should not be arrested or interviewed at school, and when brought to a police station they should not be held in a cell. The police must find out who is responsible for the young person's welfare as quickly as possible, and then inform that person of the arrest, stating where and why the suspect is being held. If the person responsible for his or her welfare chooses not to come to the police station, the police must find another 'appropriate adult', who should be present during the various stages of cautioning, identification processes, intimate searches and questioning. Where the suspect's parent is not present, the appropriate adult will often be a social worker, though it may be anyone defined as a responsible adult, except someone involved in the offence, a person of low intelligence, hostile to the young person, or a solicitor acting in a professional capacity.

The adult's role is to ensure that the young person is aware of his or her rights, particularly to legal advice. The adult should be told that his or her role is not just that of observer, but also of adviser to the young person, ensuring that the interview is conducted properly, and facilitating communication between suspect and interviewer. However, research by Brown (1992) suggests that some adults are so overawed by the whole process that they are of little use as advisers; they may even side with the interviewer.

▶ Remand and bail

A young person charged with an offence has the right to bail under the Bail Act 1976 (see chapter 9). Where the police refuse bail, children under seventeen are usually remanded to local authority accommodation, which can range from remand fostering schemes to accommodation with high levels of supervision. Children under seventeen should not be held in police custody before being brought to court, unless the custody officer certifies that it is impracticable to transfer them to local authority accommodation, or, so long as they are over twelve, that no local authority secure accommodation is available and that other accommodation would be inadequate to protect the public from serious harm.

For many years, there has been criticism of the fact that many young offenders are held on remand in adult prisons, because of the lack of other secure accommodation; a number of young men held in this way have committed suicide. Under new provisions, local authorities will be expected to provide secure accommodation for young persons, and adult prisons and remand centres should no longer be used for those under seventeen.

Defendants aged seventeen and over are subject to the same rules as adults with regard to conditions in police custody, bail and remand.

▶ Cautions

In an effort to divert young offenders from what often becomes a cycle of court appearances, punishments and further offending, often aggravated by contact with other offenders during the process, the police will often caution them rather than prosecute. A caution is an official warning about what the person has done, designed to make them see that they have done wrong and deter them from further offending (it is quite separate from the caution administered before questioning, concerning the right to silence).

A problem with the use of cautioning is that the extent to which the police choose to caution rather than prosecute varies widely between different police forces, so that like cases appear not to be treated alike. In some areas the decision has been taken over by multi-agency panels, and these can be very successful where they form part of a planned approach to youth offenders, involving cooperation between social services, education and youth services and the police.

Some areas also run schemes which aim to divert offenders from prosecution, yet still make them very aware of the damage done by their offence; vandals, for example, might be required to apologize to those whose property has been damaged, and make good the damage done.

The Children Act 1989 gives local authorities the responsibility to take reasonable steps to discourage young people in their area from committing crime, and this may in time lead to more diversionary schemes.

▶ Trial

Young offenders are usually tried in youth courts (formerly called juvenile courts), which are a branch of the magistrates' court. Youth courts must sit in a separate court room, where no ordinary court proceedings have been held for at least an hour. Other than those involved in the proceedings, the parents and the press, nobody may be present unless authorized by the court. Parents or guardians of children under sixteen must attend court at all stages of the proceedings, and the court has the power to order parents of older children to attend.

Young persons can only be tried in a Crown Court if the offence charged is murder, manslaughter or causing death by dangerous driving, or if they are at least fourteen and are likely, if convicted, to be detained under s. 53 of the Children and Young Persons Act 1933 (in practice this means that they are charged with a very serious offence, usually involving violence). They may also sometimes be tried in an adult magistrates' court or the Crown Court if there is a co-defendant who is an adult.

▶ Sentencing

Sentencing for young offenders has always posed a dilemma: should such offenders be seen as a product of their upbringing and have their problems treated, or were they to be regarded as bad, and their actions punished? Over the past couple of decades, sentencing approaches have swung between the two. In 1969, the Labour Government took the approach that delinquency was a result of deprivation, which could be 'treated', and one of the aims of the Children and Young Persons Act of that year was to decriminalize the offending of young people. Instead of going through criminal proceedings, they would be handed over to the social services, under either a supervision order or a care order, the latter giving the social services the power to take the young person into some form of custody. The magistracy constantly fought against this approach, and when a Conservative Government was elected in 1970, they declined to bring much of the Act into force, and the care order has now been repealed.

The opposite approach introduced by the Conservatives led to the UK having a higher number of young people locked up than any other Western European country, but reconviction rates of 75–80 per cent suggested that this was benefitting neither the young offenders themselves, nor the country as a whole.

The 1982 Criminal Justice Act took the approach that sentencing for young people should be based on the offence committed, and not on the offender's personal or social circumstances, and the consequent chances of reform. This succeeded in lowering the level of detention for young offenders, and the 1991 CJA continued this approach for young persons, and extended it to adults.

Custodial sentences

Currently, the courts may not pass a sentence of imprisonment on an offender under the age of 21. Such offenders may be detained in other places, such as a young offenders' institute, local authority accommodation or a secure training centre, but in order to pass a sentence of this kind, the court must satisfy the same conditions under the 1991 Act as for adults, (discussed in chapter 10), and in some cases additional criteria as well.

Detention in a young offenders' institute
The minimum age for a young offenders' institute order is 15, and the maximum is 21. For those aged between 15 and 17, the maximum term is 24 months, and the minimum 2 months.

Detention 'during her Majesty's pleasure'
Under s. 53(1) of the Children and Young Persons Act (CYPA) 1933, an offender convicted of murder who was under eighteen when the offence was committed must be sentenced to be detained indefinitely, known as 'during her Majesty's pleasure'. In 1993, 24 such orders were made.

Detention under s. 53(2) CYPA 1933
The CYPA 1933 s. 53(2) provides that where a person aged ten or over has been convicted in the Crown Court of an offence with a maximum sentence of fourteen years' imprisonment or more, the court may pass a sentence not exceeding that maximum.

Secure training orders
Under the CYPA 1969, a care order gave the local authority the power to remove a young person from his or her home. The 1989 Children Act abolished the care order, leaving the courts with no powers to impose a sentence of detention on children under the age of fifteen. This situation was changed by s. 1 of the Criminal Justice and Public Order Act 1994, which provides for the introduction of a secure training order for twelve- to fourteen-year-old offenders.

Secure training orders allow such offenders to be detained in a secure training centre for half their sentence, and placed under supervision for the second half. The minimum total sentence is six months, and the maximum two years. These orders can only be used for offenders who have been convicted of three or more imprisonable offences, and who have re-offended or been in breach of a supervision order.

It is debatable whether this new power is either necessary or useful. The vast majority of crime committed by this age group is minor property offences, and for more serious cases, s. 53 still applies. Given the problems associated with custodial sentences, putting young persons at risk of custody for more minor offences does not seem a sensible option – yet this may be exactly what these new powers do, given that three imprisonable offences could mean a couple of shoplifting episodes and some criminal damage.

The tariff
Because the maximum custodial sentences for young offenders are usually quite short, the tariff approach described in the chapter on sentencing is of limited application to the sentencing of young offenders, except in the sense that young offenders can usually rely on their youth as strong mitigation.

Community sentences

As far as sixteen- and seventeen-year-olds are concerned, the youth courts have much the same powers for community sentences as the adult courts, though an order of compensation must not exceed £2,000 per offence. Attendance centre orders and supervision orders are specific to young people.

Supervision orders
These are applied to offenders aged between ten and sixteen, and require a probation officer or social services department to supervise the offender for up to three years. The order is basically a junior version of probation, except that a stronger emphasis is placed on assisting the personal development of the young person; it was introduced by the CYPA 1969 to replace probation for young offenders. The consent of a young person to a basic supervision order is not required.

As with probation, the supervisor must assist, advise and befriend the offender. The 1969 Act also gives the power to order the offender to undertake intermediate treatment, by living in specified accommodation, attending a specified place, or taking part in specified activities, or any combination of the three, for up to 90 days. The purpose of this is to remove the young person from their home environment, and make them take part in challenging activities – these might include rock climbing, pot-holing or even simply attending a local youth club. Youth court magistrates, after consultation with the supervisors, can also specify activities which the offender should not participate in; in such cases consent must be obtained from the young person and a parent or guardian. The CJA 1991 allows a young offender of compulsory school age to be ordered to comply with arrangements for their education.

If an offender breaches a requirement in a supervision order and the supervisor brings this to the court's attention, the court may change the order, fine the offender up to £100, or make an attendance centre order. If the offender has reached the age of seventeen, the court may discharge the order and pass a new sentence for the original offence. However, unlike probation, an offender who re-offends while under supervision cannot be sentenced for the original offence.

Young offenders over sixteen may be made subject to a probation order.

Attendance centre orders

Under the Criminal Justice Act 1982, an offender under 21 convicted of an imprisonable offence may be ordered to go to an attendance centre for a specified number of hours spread over a specified period. The number of hours of attendance that may be ordered is not less than twelve (unless the offender is under fourteen and twelve hours seems excessive), and not more than 24 in the case of those under sixteen, and 36 for those aged sixteen to twenty. Breach of an attendance centre order may result in the offender being dealt with for the original offence. The centres are normally run by the police, and tend to involve attendance on Saturday afternoons for physical education classes or practical courses.

Unless there are special circumstances, such an order should not be made if the offender has previously been sentenced to detention in a young offenders' institute.

▶ Parents of young offenders

The Criminal Justice Act 1991 states that where a young offender is under sixteen, a parent or guardian must be required to attend the court hearing, unless the court considers that this would be unreasonable. Where such an offender is convicted, the court is required to bind over the parents to take proper care and exercise proper control over their child; the courts also have discretion to do this in the case of sixteen- or seventeen-year-olds. Although the consent of the parents is required, an unreasonable refusal can attract a fine of up to £1,000. Following an amendment in the 1994 Act, parents or guardians can also be bound over to ensure that the young offender complies with a community sentence. A parent whose conduct has been found to have contributed to the offence may be ordered to pay compensation.

Where an offender under sixteen is sentenced to a fine or compensation order, the parents are required to pay it. The court may also order parents to pay in the case of sixteen- and seventeen-year-olds fined or given compensation orders. In both cases, the fine or compensation order will be assessed taking into account the financial situation of the parent, rather than the young offender. Where a local authority has parental responsibility for a young person who is in their care or has provided accommodation for them, the local authority is to be treated as the young person's parent for these purposes.

▶ 'Boot camps'

In 1995 the Government was said to be considering the introduction of American-style 'boot camps' for young offenders. These are a form of custodial sentence, featuring short-term detention in a military-style regime. This appears to be yet another attempt at the 'short, sharp shock' approach to young offenders, and is quite similar to the detention centres set up under the 1982 Criminal Justice Act, despite the fact that these centres led to a sharp rise in the use of youth custody and a poor rate of re-offending – just like the other 'short, sharp shock' regimes before them. While this approach may be a good way temporarily to appease the 'law and order' lobby, it seems to offer little hope of reducing youth crime.

ANSWERING QUESTIONS

1 Deborah, aged 15, has been seen by a police officer attacking an old man. He arrests her and takes her to the police station.
(i) Explain the rules concerning the police powers to question Deborah about the offence;
(ii) If Deborah is charged and prosecuted, which courts are likely to deal with her case (excluding possible appeals)?;
(iii) What sentencing powers do the courts have in respect of her offence?
(i) Note that because of Deborah's age, you are talking about a young offender and not an adult. The general rules concerning a suspect in the police station are explained in chapter 9 (p. 201), but you also need to include the particular rules that apply to Deborah because of her age which are detailed at p. 259.
(ii) Special rules apply to the trial of young offenders, which are discussed in this chapter.
(iii) The material in chapter 10 covering the statutory guidance contained in the Criminal Justice Acts 1991 and 1993 is relevant here. As to the specific sentences that can be passed, starting with the most serious, custodial

sentences, note that Deborah cannot be sent to prison; she can only be sentenced to a young offenders' institute. As regards a community sentence, supervision orders and attendance centre orders are specific to young offenders, but the other forms of community sentences discussed in chapter 10 are also relevant here. Note that the maximum length of sentences is often shorter for young offenders. Fines are also a possibility, and if imposed, will have to be paid by Deborah's parents. You might also want to mention the possibility that her parents may themselves be subject to sanctions, such as being bound over.

12

The civil justice system

The civil justice system is designed to sort out disputes between individuals, rather than between citizens and the state, as the criminal system does – though in legal terms an 'individual' may be a company or other organization, as well as one person (see p. 441). One party, known as the plaintiff, sues the other, called the defendant, usually for money they claim is owed, or because they claim the other party has done some harm to their interests (a civil wrong like this is called a tort). Typical examples might be the victim of a car accident suing the driver of the car for compensation, or one business suing another for payment for goods supplied.

Major changes have been made to the civil justice system in recent years, as a result of recommendations made by the Civil Justice Review and implemented in the Courts and Legal Services Act 1990.

HISTORY

The civil justice system developed in a rather piecemeal fashion, responding to different needs at different times, with the result that at the end of the eighteenth century, civil matters were being dealt with by several different series of courts. Three common law courts, supplemented by the Court of Chancery, did most of the work, but there was also a Court of Admiralty and the ecclesiastical (church) courts. They had different but often overlapping jurisdictions, and between them administered three different 'systems' of law: civilian law (based on Roman law), common law and equity. The courts were also largely centralized in London, making access difficult for those in the provinces.

With no coordination of the increasingly complex court system, inefficiency, incompetence and delays were common, and the courts acquired a reputation for binding themselves up in cumbersome procedural rules. Until well into the nineteenth century, litigation in the higher courts was an extravagance which could be afforded only by the very rich, and in many respects the system benefited the judges and the legal profession far more than litigants.

267

Reform began in 1846, with the creation of a nationwide system of county courts, designed to provide cheaper, quicker justice at local levels for local businessmen, and was followed in the early 1870s, by the creation of one Supreme Court, consisting of the High Court, the Court of Appeal and the Crown Court, although the High Court was still divided into five divisions. In 1881, these were reduced to three: Queen's Bench; Chancery; and what is now known as the Family Division.

▶ The civil courts today

Today there are around 300 county courts, concerned exclusively with civil work. About 170 of them are designated as divorce county courts and thereby have jurisdiction to hear undefended divorces and cases concerning adoption and guardianship.

In the High Court, the three divisions mentioned above remain today – they act as separate courts, with judges usually working within one division only. Lord Woolf has recently recommended that these divisions should remain. The Family Division hears cases concerning marriage, children and the family, such as divorce, adoption and wills. The Chancery Division deals with matters of finance and property, such as tax and bankruptcy. The Queen's Bench Division is the biggest of the three, with the most varied jurisdiction. The major part of its work is handling those contract and tort cases which are unsuitable for the county courts (see below). Sitting as the Divisional Court of the Queen's Bench, its judges also hear certain criminal appeals originating in the magistrates' courts, and applications for judicial review (for details see chapter 14). High Court judges usually sit alone, but the Divisional Court is so important that two or three judges sit together.

High Court trials happen either in London or in one of the 26 provincial trial centres. In theory, they are all presided over by High Court judges, but in fact there are not enough High Court judges to cope with the case load. Some cases therefore have to be dealt with by circuit judges, others by barristers sitting as part-time, temporary, deputy judges. In 1987, only half of all High Court sitting days were taken by High Court judges.

Although most civil cases are dealt with by either the county courts or the High Court, magistrates' courts have a limited civil jurisdiction, and some types of case are tried by tribunals.

▶ Jurisdiction of the High Court and county courts

The Civil Justice Review in 1985, was set up by the Lord Chancellor in response to public criticism of the delay, cost and complexity of the civil

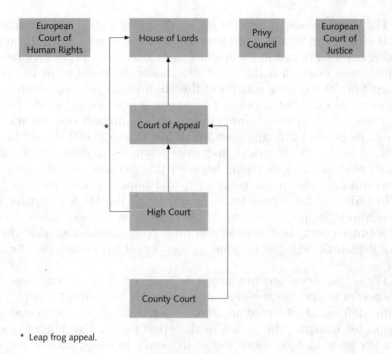

* Leap frog appeal.

The Civil Court System

court system. Unusually, it was chaired by a non-lawyer, Maurice Hodgson, the Chairman of Bhs, and only a minority of its members were lawyers. They therefore tended to be less pro-lawyer than previous committees that had been dominated by judges and barristers, which may explain why many of the Review's more innovative suggestions were ignored or only partially implemented. Important changes were made to the division of work between the county courts and High Court by the Courts and Legal Services Act 1990, in response to some of the proposals of the 1985 Review. The Review's report described its purpose as being to 'improve the machinery of civil justice in England and Wales by means of reforms in jurisdiction, procedure and court administration and in particular to reduce delay, cost and complexity.'

One of its main findings was that too many cases were being heard in the High Court rather than the cheaper and quicker county courts, often for relatively small amounts of money: in 1987, half of all money claims started in the Queen's Bench Division were for less than £3,000. Consequently it aimed to increase the number of cases heard in the county courts, thereby freeing High Court time for public law cases, specialist cases and cases considered to be of importance, complexity and substance.

The position now is that claims worth under £3,000 are automatically dealt with by the Small Claims procedure of the county court, the amount having been increased at the beginning of 1996 from £1,000. All personal injury cases worth less than £50,000 should be brought in the county court. Both the county court and the High Court have jurisdiction over any other tort or contract case. There is no longer a fixed maximum limit for cases heard in the county court, nor a minimum one for the High Court. In general though, cases worth less than £25,000 should be commenced in the county court, and cases worth more than £50,000 in the High Court; for actions falling between £25,000 and £50,000, the proper court will depend on the complexity and importance of the case.

In order to discourage unnecessary use of the High Court for small or relatively simple cases, the High Court can transfer cases down to the county court, and may also impose cost sanctions so that the successful plaintiff will not be able to recover all his costs from the other side.

These sanctions are not applied, however, if there was reasonable ground for supposing the amount recoverable to be more than £50,000, if the defendant objected to transfer, or if there was sufficient other reason for bringing the action in the High Court. The High Court has recently been making more use of its power to order such transfers.

The High Court can also transfer cases worth over £50,000 down to the county court if the parties agree, and the High Court considers that the proceedings are not likely to raise any important question of law or fact and are suitable for determination by a county court. In such cases the county court may award any relief, including any amount of damages, which could have been awarded by the High Court.

Equally, the county court can transfer cases worth less than £25,000 up to the High Court, if the High Court thinks this is appropriate, due to the complexity of the case, or the fact that it has some importance for people other than the parties in the case. When deciding whether to transfer a case in either direction, the courts must consider both the financial value and whether the case is otherwise important, in the sense of affecting other parties outside the case, raising an important point of law or some other question of public interest.

To back up these changes, provision was made for improved trial facilities at county courts, and a new tier of circuit judges to take additional civil jurisdiction burdens; and the number of people eligible for appointment as district judges was increased. However, the changes have not been without new problems of their own – see criticisms, p. 280.

The number of civil court cases dropped dramatically in 1994, apart from cases relating to children. The 25 per cent reduction in High Court writs and 11 per cent in county court summonses was largely in recession-related work, such as insolvency and mortgage repossessions. The drop in High Court writs was largely expected due to the jurisdiction changes.

CIVIL PROCEDURE

▶ Which court?

In many cases the choice of court will be straightforward, given the jurisdiction rules discussed above and the fact that the courts are increasingly
willing to transfer cases if the 'wrong' court is chosen. Still there are clearly
cases where a plaintiff will potentially have a choice between High Court
and county court, and even though the core procedural rules are being
harmonized, there are still differences between them.

The county court procedure tends to be simpler, especially for the
unrepresented litigant; if representation is felt to be needed, it can be
performed by the solicitor alone, rather than the more expensive solicitor and barrister combination still considered prudent for High Court
work; the courts are local, so probably more convenient; and the case is
likely to be dealt with more quickly. The danger of cost sanctions must
also be taken into account.

On the other hand, there is still a feeling that a High Court writ will
have a greater threatening effect than a county court summons, which is
especially important given the high number of civil cases settled out of
court. Although the 1990 reforms have made the same remedies available in both courts, the idea that damages awarded in the High Court are
likely to be higher may linger, and judgment enforcement procedures
are thought to be more effective.

As far as lawyers are concerned, a further important difference between
the courts is that the county courts do much of the pre-trial work for the
parties, issuing the various documents needed during the course of the
action, whereas when an action is brought in the High Court, solicitors
take responsibility for preparing and serving most of the court documents. Such a degree of direct control gives a great strategic advantage
to the plaintiff, enabling them to co-ordinate the timing of different stages
of an action with the arduous, time-consuming task of gathering witness
statements and medical evidence.

▶ Pre-trial procedure

This is perhaps the most important area of civil process, since few civil
cases actually come to trial. Usually an out-of-court settlement is negotiated before they ever reach the trial stage. For every 9,000 personal injury
cases commenced only 300 are submitted for judgment. Outside personal
injuries, for every 100,000 writs fewer than 300 actually come for trial.

Civil procedure is governed by the Rules of the Supreme Court, found in documents called the 'White Book' (for the High Court) and the 'Green Book' (for the county courts). The purpose of these rules is supposed to be to ensure that the case comes to court with the issue or issues clearly defined, and with what is agreed or disagreed clearly spelt out so that the trial can be conducted as quickly and efficiently as possible.

High Court actions start with a writ, county court ones by a summons. These are documents served informing the defendants that a case is being brought against them; they must acknowledge service. The plaintiff serves a statement of claim if bringing an action in the High Court, or the particulars of a claim in the county court. Both are formal documents outlining the facts and legal basis of the claim, and the remedy sought. The defendant responds with a defence. Either party may request more details from the other, in a document known as 'a request for further and better particulars'. These will then be supplied. Each party then provides the other with a list of the documents which they have in relation to the action. The parties can then ask to see some or all of these documents. This process is known as discovery.

▶ Out of court settlements

The case may be settled out of court at any of these points – around a third of such settlements happen almost literally at the door of the court. The obvious advantage of this is a quicker end to the dispute, and a reduction in costs, although these start to build up from the time each side consults a lawyer, the trial itself is by far the most expensive part.

For the plaintiff, a settlement means they are sure of getting something, and do not have to risk losing the case altogether and probably having to pay the other side's costs as well as their own, but they must weigh this up against the chances of being awarded a better settlement if the case goes to trial and they win. The defendant risks the possibility that they might have won and therefore had to pay nothing, or that they may be paying more than the judge would have awarded if the plaintiff had won the case, against the chance that the plaintiff wins and is awarded more than the settlement would have cost.

A further complication is that the defendant may, at any time during the process, make a payment into court, which the plaintiff may accept as settlement of the claim. If not, the process continues as before, but if the case continues to trial and the plaintiff wins but is awarded less than the sum paid in, they must pay the defendant's costs from the time of the payment in – which can result in the winner of the case being worse off than the loser. Although the judge knows that a payment into court has been made, the amount is not revealed, so that there is no way of ensuring that the award matches the payment in.

▶ The trial

Civil trials are usually presided over by a single judge, with juries used in only a handful of cases (see chapter 5). The burden of proof is usually on the plaintiff, who must prove their case on a balance of probabilities – that it is more likely than not. Obviously this is a lower standard of proof than the 'beyond reasonable doubt' of the criminal courts, and for this reason it is possible to be acquitted of a criminal charge yet still found negligent with regard to the same action – for example, one might be found not guilty of dangerous driving, yet still successfully sued for negligence by the person knocked down.

The trial is conducted along adversarial lines, with each side calling its own witnesses and cross-examining those of the other. As in a criminal trial, judges rely on the parties to present the evidence, rather than making their own investigations. However, unlike the judges in a criminal trial, since they do not usually need to ensure that everything has been explained so that a jury can understand it, they can read the papers beforehand, and direct the parties or their representatives that they need only cover unclear or disputed points in court.

In 1995 the Lord Chief Justice issued guidelines to the High Court in his Practice Direction ('Civil Litigation: Case Management'). The Practice Direction was aimed to streamline civil litigation and reduce costs in the High Court. It stated that judges should assume tighter control over the preparation and conduct of hearings and should penalize lawyers who failed to conduct cases economically. Judges were to exercise their discretion to limit discovery and the time spent giving oral evidence and reading aloud from documents in open court. Where possible witness statements could stand as the evidence-in-chief of the witness.

▶ Costs

The cost of bringing or defending a civil action can be very high. Legal aid may be available (see chapter 8); in many cases, especially those involving personal injury, the defendant's, and sometimes the plaintiff's, costs will be paid by their insurance companies – when car accidents are involved, for example, one or both parties are likely to have been insured, and professionals such as doctors are insured against claims of negligence against them. As Hazel Genn's 1987 study showed, where only one party is insured, this can place great pressure on the other, unless they have been granted legal aid. The insured side may try to drag out the proceedings for as long as possible, in the hope of exhausting the other party's financial reserves and forcing a low settlement.

If the case comes to trial, the winner is usually awarded costs; the loser must pay the legal costs of both parties, as well as any damages ordered.

If at any time in the trial any representative of a party incurs costs as a result of any improper, unreasonable or negligent conduct they will not receive payment for those wasted costs: s. 51 of the Supreme Court Act 1981 as substituted by the Courts and Legal Services Act 1990. In **Ridehalgh** *v* **Horsefield** (1994) the Court of Appeal held that an advocate would not be liable to a wasted costs order simply because he or she acted for a party who pursued a claim or defence which was doomed to fail, provided the proceedings did not constitute an abuse of the court.

▶ The small claims court

This is not actually a separate court, but a procedure used by county courts to deal with claims worth under £3,000. It was introduced in response to a report from the Consumers Association in 1967, claiming that county courts were being used primarily as a debt collection agency for businesses: 89.2 per cent of the summonses were taken out by firms and only 9 per cent by individuals, who were put off by costs and complexity.

The special procedure known as the Small Claims Court was introduced in 1973, with the aim of providing a cheap, simple mechanism for resolving small-scale consumer disputes. It is now mandatory for claims of under £3,000. Actions for possession and actions for damages for personal injuries in which the amount claimed exceeds £1,000 are exempted from automatic reference. The court also has a discretion to allow a case that would ordinarily be heard by the small claims procedure to be heard by the main county court where a complex factual issue is involved. In **Afzal** *v* **Ford Motor Co Ltd** (1994) the Court of Appeal commented that it would be an abuse of court procedure to overstate the amounts involved in a claim simply to avoid the small claims procedure.

Claimants start proceedings in the normal way by taking out a summons – county court officials can help with form filling – and have to pay a small sum, based on the amount claimed. Once the summons is served, the defendant has fourteen days to send back a defence; if none is returned, the court may simply rule in the claimant's favour.

These days the courts aim to sort out small claims in a single hearing, but the procedure does also allow for a pre-trial hearing, at which the judge – usually the district judge of the court – attempts to conciliate the parties, and if this is not possible, to at least isolate the issues in the case, and give directions on how to prepare and conduct the case.

If the case comes to court, the hearing is usually held in private rather than in open court, and the procedure is simple and informal, with few rules about the admissibility or presentation of evidence. The arbitrator plays a more interventionist role than most judges, asking questions and examining evidence as necessary, and must give both parties a fair and equal opportunity to present their case. It is usually a fairly quick process, with 60 per cent of cases taking less than 30 minutes.

The procedure is designed to make it easy for parties to represent themselves, without the aid of a lawyer, and legal aid for representation is not available. Litigants who do choose to be professionally represented have to pay the costs themselves, win or lose, as the judge may only award minor costs against a losing party. Under the Lay Representatives (Rights of Audience) Order 1992 made under s. 11 of the Courts and Legal Services Act 1990, a party can choose to be represented by a lay person, who will have a right of audience in the Small Claims Court, though the party must also attend.

There is little right of appeal from the Small Claims Court: the judge's decision can be set aside but only on the ground that he or she acted contrary to the rules of natural justice in not granting the parties a fair hearing, or that the record of the proceedings showed that an error of law was made. As the court records of arbitrations are concise and do not usually state the reason for the award, the proceedings rarely give rise to an appeal.

Advantages of the small claims procedure

The procedure is quicker, simpler and cheaper than full county court procedure, which is useful to both litigants and the overworked court system. It gives individuals and small businesses a useful lever against creditors or for consumer complaints. Without it, threats to sue over small amounts would be ignored on the basis that going to court would cost more than the value of the debt or compensation claimed. Public confidence is also increased by proving that the legal system is not only accessible to the rich and powerful.

Disadvantages

Small claims are not necessarily simple claims; they may involve complex and unusual points of law. Is the small claimant entitled to be judged by the law of the land or by speedier, more rough-and-ready concepts of fairness?

The procedure is not simple enough. The Consumers Association magazine *Which* reported in 1986 that the process was still 'quite an ordeal', and the level of formality varied widely. The submissions of both the National Consumer Council and the National Association of Citizens Advice Bureaux to the Civil Justice Review echoed this feeling. The Civil Justice Review recommended that court forms and leaflets should be simplified. The procedure is still largely used by small businesses chasing debtors, rather than for the individual consumer cases for which it was set up. A consultation paper was issued in 1995 suggesting that in limited cases the arbitrator might be given the power to award an additional sum of up to £135 to cover the cost of legal advice and assistance in the preparation of the case. If this reform is introduced it might assist individual consumers to bring their cases.

There are also problems with enforcement. A survey by the Lord Chancellor's Department in 1986 found that 25 per cent of parties were failing to get the payment owed to them.

The financial limit needs regular updating – the Consumers Association has suggested replacing it with a list of the type of goods and services covered by the procedure, and establishing an annual review of average expenditure on these in order to ensure the Small Claims limit keeps pace with inflation.

▶ Aims of a civil justice system

The civil justice system is currently being reviewed by Lord Woolf due to concerns with the system in practice. In his interim report he stated that a civil justice system should:

- be just in the results it delivers;
- be fair in the way it treats litigants;
- offer appropriate procedures at a reasonable cost;
- deal with cases with reasonable speed;
- be understandable to those who use it;
- be responsive to the needs of those who use it;
- provide as much certainty as the nature of particular cases allows;
- be effective, adequately resourced and organized.

He has concluded that the current system fails to achieve all those goals. It is possible that this failure is inevitable as some of the aims conflict with others. A system based on cost-efficiency alone would make it difficult to justify claims for comparatively small sums, yet these cases are very important to the parties involved, and wide access to justice is an important aim. Promoting efficiency in terms of speed can also conflict with the need for fairness. Making the courts more accessible could lead to a flood of cases which would make it impossible to provide speedy resolution and keep costs down. One practical example of the conflict between different aims is that the availability of legal aid to one party, part of the aim of widening access to justice, can put pressure on the other side if they are funding themselves, and so clash with the need for fairness.

In addition, changes made to the system may have effects outside it – making it easier to bring personal injury actions, for example, could push up the costs of insurance, and it has been suggested that in the USA, this has led to unwillingness on the part of doctors to perform any risky medical treatment. It is widely thought that the changes made to the civil legal system by the Courts and Legal Services Act 1990 will affect the structure of the legal professions, with possible implications for the kind of services on offer to consumers.

It is never likely to be possible to completely resolve these conflicts, and a successful legal system must simply aim for the best possible balance. Lord Scarman has said of civil procedure:

> To be acceptable to ordinary people, I believe legal process in litigation must be designed to encourage, first, settlement by agreement; secondly, open and speedy trial if agreement is not forthcoming. In other words, justice, not truth is its purpose. It is against the criteria of justice and fairness that the system must be assessed.

In the final analysis, it is up to the Government to decide the balance they wish to strike, and how much they are prepared to spend on it.

▶ Criticisms of civil procedure

We shall now consider the problems that Lord Woolf and others before him have highlighted in the criminal justice system.

Too expensive

The Civil Justice Review found that total costs in personal injury cases in the High Court amounted to 99 per cent of the amount recovered in damages; in the county court they were around 25 per cent. A survey carried out for Lord Woolf's inquiry found numerous cases where costs had outstripped the value of the financial sums in dispute. The bill for one claim of just £2,000 came to £69,295; that for another of £1,000 was £26,398. The survey concluded that the simplest cases often incurred the highest costs in proportion to the value of the claim.

Because of the complexity of the process, lawyers are usually needed, and High Court litigation especially is not a game for the inexperienced, so barristers draft the pleadings and advise on the evidence, which is expensive. The sheer length of civil proceedings also affects costs. Though both county court and High Court costs are high, moving more cases to the county courts under the provisions of the Courts and Legal Services Act should go some way to reducing costs overall.

Lord Woolf has said that, fifteen years ago, his report would not have been necessary, because most lawyers made their money from other work such as conveyancing, seeing litigation as a loss maker that they would only undertake reluctantly for their client. But with the huge increase in the number of lawyers, combined with the recession in the propety market, lawyers have suddenly found that litigation can generate a steady income.

He has said that costs were now so high that even big companies were wary, some even preferring to fight cases in New York.

Delays

The Civil Justice Review found that the system was overstretched, and the time between the incident giving rise to the claim and the trial could be up to three years for the county courts, and five for the High Court. The current average waiting time for a county court claim is 79 weeks. The Review found that long delays placed intolerable psychological and financial burdens on accident victims, and undermined the justice of the trial, by making it more difficult to gather evidence, and making that evidence less reliable, since witnesses may have to remember the events of several years before. The overall result was to lower public estimation of the legal system as a whole.

So far the reforms made by the Courts and Legal Services Act seem to have done little to ease delays. Originally, the main complaint was that county courts had not been given enough administrators to cope with their new workload, so High Court delays had simply been transferred to the county courts; the county courts were said to be too understaffed and underfunded to cope easily with the increase in business. The work of the county courts was increasing rapidly even before the reforms, largely as a result in the increase in debt over the last few years – in 1990 a massive 3.5 million cases were started in the county courts. Most do not involve a court hearing, but the workload in terms of pre-trial procedure was still heavy. However, it was noted above that the statistics for 1994 show that there was actually a drop in the case load of the county court as well as the High court.

In any case, not all the reasons for the delay are the fault of the system – in some cases, for example, it may be necessary to wait for an accident victim's medical condition to stabilize enough for any long-term or permanent results to be assessed. Accident victims in particular often do not seek legal advice until some time after the accident has occurred. However, much of the responsibility does lie with the legal system – there are time limits laid down for every stage of an action, but both lawyers and the courts disregard them. Sometimes time limits are waived by the lawyers to create time to negotiate, which is reasonable, but the problem is that there is no effective control of when and why it is done. The High Court's long vacation (the two months during the summer when the judges do not sit) also contributes to delay.

Injustice

The high number of out of court settlements can create injustice, because the parties usually hold very unequal bargaining positions. In the first place, one party may well be in a better financial position than the other, and therefore under less pressure to keep costs down by settling quickly.

Secondly, as Galanter's 1974 study revealed, litigants can often be divided into 'one-shotters' and 'repeat players'. One-shotters are individuals involved in litigation for probably the only time in their life, for whom the procedure is unfamiliar and traumatic; the case is very important to them and often occupies most of their thoughts while it continues. Repeat players, on the other hand, include companies and businesses (particularly insurance companies), for whom litigation is routine. They are used to using the law and lawyers, and while they obviously want to win the case for financial reasons, they do not have the same emotional investment in it as the individual one-shotter. Clearly where a repeat player and a one-shotter are on opposing sides – as is often the case in personal injury litigation, where an individual is fighting an insurance company – the repeat player is likely to have the upper hand in out-of-court bargaining.

A third factor was highlighted by Hazel Genn's 1987 study of negotiated settlements of accident claims. She found that having a non-specialist lawyer could seriously prejudice a client's interests when an out-of-court settlement is made. A non-specialist may be unfamiliar with court procedure, and reluctant to fight the case in court, and therefore not encourage his or her client to hold out against an unsatisfactory settlement; specialist lawyers on the other side may take advantage of this inexperience, pressuring for acceptance of a low settlement. Repeat players are clearly more likely to have access to their own specialist lawyers, whereas for the one-shotter, finding a specialist lawyer can be something of a lottery, since they have little information on which to base their choice.

Clearly these factors do affect the fairness of out-of-court settlements. In court, the judge will treat the parties as equals, but in out-of-court negotiations one party often has a very obvious advantage.

The rule on payment into court can increase the unfairness of pre-trial procedure. As Zander points out, the rule is 'highly favourable' to the defendant, putting extra pressure on the plaintiff to accept an offer.

Pressures of time may be causing injustice. Special continuous trial centres have been set up, in which most of the business is heard very quickly, thus allowing the court to hear a number of cases each day. This can lead to an emphasis on processing people through the system at speed, rather than examining the evidence and making a judicial decision. One research report put the average court time spent on local authority repossession cases at 90 seconds, and a judge has described the judicial role in such cases as 'purely administrative, somebody independent of the local authority to rubber-stamp the document'.

Too complex

This is largely a result of the adversarial process: it would be far simpler and cheaper for each side to state precisely what it alleges in the pleadings, disclose all the documents it holds, and give the other copies of its witness statements – in other words, for the two sides to cooperate. The adversarial system encourages tactical manoeuvring rather than cooperation, giving away as little as possible of your side's strengths and weaknesses.

However, attitudes appear to be slowly changing, with a growing appreciation that the public interest demands that justice be provided as quickly and economically as possible. Some of the procedural rules, for example on expert witnesses, have changed recently and there is less scope for tactical manoeuvring.

Emphasis on oral evidence

Too much emphasis is placed on oral evidence at trial. This may have been appropriate when juries were commonly used in civil proceedings, but it is now less necessary – much of the information the judge needs can be provided on paper and read before the trial. Oral evidence slows down proceedings, adding to cost and delays.

There are also doubts about the usefulness of oral evidence. In particular, there is a danger that the ordinary witness, often giving evidence years after the events occurred, will be so intimidated by the nature of the questioning and the formality of the proceedings that their evidence will appear far less credible than should be the case, while the evidence of an expert witness familiar with court room antics may well have an aura of authority which it does not deserve.

There has been a limited move away from oral evidence – in 1986 it was decided that the written statements of witnesses could be accepted as evidence.

Enforcement

It can be difficult to enforce judgments against debtors; responsibility for it is largely left to the parties.

Changes in jurisdiction

Though designed to ease the problems of the civil system, the reforms implemented by the 1990 Courts and Legal Services Act to the jurisdiction rules of the High Court and county court have caused some new ones of their own. The changes have caused delay in the county courts (see p. 278). There is also a suggestion that the High Court has been preserved as a small, elite court hearing only a few public and commercial cases, while smaller cases, such as accidents at work or on the roads, wrongful arrests, contracts of employment or tenancies and housing conditions – in other words, the problems of the average citizen – are getting second-class justice in the county court.

Lawyers specializing in personal injury litigation (most of whom would previously have been dealing with the High Court) say problems in county courts are considerable: papers lost, letters and phone calls unanswered, inadequate pre-trial procedures, too few administrators and a shortage of experienced, informed judges. The rule changes have coincided with a huge rise in housing repossessions, arrears and debt cases, mostly brought by volume creditors who have established a close relationship with their local courts. Some personal injury solicitors claim that, as a result, their cases are getting short shrift in terms of both court time and attention from court staff.

Specialist personal injury firms also regret the loss of direct control over the running of cases they enjoyed in the High Court. While solicitors may, with the court's permission, prepare and serve their own documents in county court actions, it is not always possible to do so, and there are long waits in some cities as summonses are sent to typing centres. Even if solicitors take on the work themselves, they must keep in touch with the court; telephones are often busy and correspondence goes unanswered. Many solicitors report that contact by letter or phone is so difficult that they send employees to the county court in person several times a week to check on progress with cases.

Not all county courts have the same procedural rules, and differing procedures are creating confusion for firms dealing with a number of differing county courts (the Civil Justice Review called for an integrated set of procedural rules, but this has only been partially introduced). Some solicitors are avoiding problematic county courts, and as the news spreads about courts to avoid, delays could build up in the more popular courts.

There is also concern that the quality of judges will be lower, and that damages will be smaller than in the High Court.

REFORM

There are three main types of approach which might be adopted in seeking a solution to some of the problems above. The first simply aims to improve the current system; the second would involve a more radical alteration, rejecting the adversarial system altogether and moving towards an inquisitorial model; and the third would change the substantive law to do away with the need for personal injury claims, the main area of civil litigation.

▶ The Civil Justice Review

The main proposals for reform made by the Review that have been implemented have been discussed above; those which were amended or not implemented at all included a suggestion that the upper financial limit to the county court jurisdiction should be abolished altogether. Instead there would be a one court entry system, with all civil cases starting in the same way, with a writ, and being allocated to the county courts or the High Court on the basis of their complexity. The ability to transfer cases, and the cost sanctions of unnecessary use of the High Court have gone some way towards achieving this, but do not amount to the streamlined approach envisaged by the Review. The two courts would have had a unified cost system and a common core of procedural rules. A new case flow management system giving a timetable of the progress of cases was recommended, which would have entailed considerable administrative effort and expense. They suggested that there should be incentives and penalties for speedy resolution or delay.

Within the High Court it was suggested that the divisional structure should be relaxed, with judges being easily transferable from one division to another and the heads of the divisions meeting under the presidency of the Lord Chancellor to coordinate their work. They thought that the London bias of the High Court should go, with some judges being required to reside in the regions rather than visiting them on circuit tour from London. The judges were not at all keen on this idea.

Judicial productivity would have been increased by restricting the High Court's long vacation to one month, and adding an extra hour's sitting per day. Recommendations were made for better judicial training, including seminars directed at High Court judges and registrars with the aim of creating closer working relationships and shortening trials. Some limited improvements have been made in this area.

▶ Lord Woolf's interim report

Lord Woolf's review was set up within ten years of the Civil Justice Review, so clearly one can only conclude that the reforms introduced in the light of the previous review were not sufficient. The leading academic Zander has pointed out that in fact Lord Woolf's review is the 63rd such review in a hundred years. At the time of going to press Lord Woolf had only produced his first interim report for consultation so his final conclusions are not yet available. Some of his current proposals bear similarities with those already recommended but not implemented by the Civil Justice Review, but some of them are quite new. He certainly seems to have the same aims in mind of reducing the cost and delay of the current system. The general approach of Lord Woolf is reflected in his statement: 'If "time and money are no object" was the right approach in the past, then it certainly is not today. Both lawyers and judges, in making decisions as to the conduct of litigation, must take into account more than they do at present, questions of cost and time and the means of the parties.' Lord Woolf has provisionally recommended that the division between the High Court and the county courts should remain, though they would generally have the same jurisdiction, and outside London they would share the same administration.

Three track system

One of his more radical suggestions is that there should be a three-tier system with cases being allocated to the appropriate system or 'track' for case management and trial depending on their importance. On receipt of a defence all cases would be considered by a procedural judge who would allocate them to their appropriate track. Minor cases would be dealt with by the small claims procedures which would be extended to claims of up to £3,000 (except personal injury claims) – a proposal that has since been introduced. The increase would be monitored with a view to a possible further extension to £5,000. Small claims would normally be dealt with in one hearing or through a paper disposal.

There would be a new 'fast track' for straightforward claims of up to £10,000, with restricted discovery, a trial confined to a maximum of three hours (with no oral expert evidence), fixed timetables (20 to 30 weeks to trial) and fixed costs. This would be the appropriate track for most cases now currently heard by the county court and High Court. All small claim and fast track cases would be dealt with at local county courts.

Finally there would be a new 'multi-track' for cases above £10,000 providing individual hands-on management by judicial teams for the heaviest cases, and standard or tailor-made directions where appropriate. For heavier cases on the multi-track there would be a case management conference shortly after the defence is filed, and a pre-trial review a few weeks before the trial. Even on this track timetables would be set and there would be limits on costs and controls on the use of expert witnesses.

Case management

Lord Woolf recommends that the courts should go much further down the road of case management, meaning that judges should have more responsibility for managing cases, taking this responsibility out of the hands of the litigants and into the hands of the judges under all three procedures. The courts would decide on the appropriate procedure for each case; set timetables, and make sure that these were followed. The main aim of case management is to encourage settlement and, if this fails, to ensure that cases progress to trial as quickly and economically as possible. This is similar to the Civil Justice Review's proposal for case flow management.

Costs

On the issue of legal costs, Lord Woolf recommends that there should be a professional obligation on lawyers, before they are retained in connection with litigation, to inform the client what their costs are likely to be, and let them know if their estimate is likely to be exceeded and why. At the moment clients commit themselves to open ended payment by the hour, which he has described as being equivalent to handing out a blank cheque. The other side should also be informed of costs incurred and likely to be incurred in the future. He is reported to have said that this is the only way that market forces can operate properly: 'If you and I are having our house repaired, we don't do it on a time and materials basis, because we know it will be a disaster. There is no incentive for the builder to do it in the least time and do it with the most economical materials.'

Settlements

He argues that settlements outside court should be further encouraged. To this end alternative dispute resolution should be suggested where it is likely to be beneficial (discussed at p. 329), including the use of ombudsmen (see p. 324) and parties should be encouraged to be more cooperative. The present practice of making payments into court would be replaced by a system which permits the parties to make an 'offer of settlement', which could be made by either side and could relate to individual issues; they could be made before proceedings had even commenced and no actual payment into court would be required. Litigants who are considered to have behaved unreasonably would be penalized by costs orders.

Judicial teams

Lord Woolf recognizes that problems arise when different judges deal with a case at different stages causing lack of continuity, consistency and incentive to get to grips with a case at an early stage. To deal with some of these problems he proposes that judges should work in teams. But it has been argued that this is only a partial solution and that it would be more desirable for a single judge to be allocated to a case throughout its duration, sometimes known as the 'single docket system'. This is already usually the case in large commercial cases. It means that a judge increases his knowledge and understanding of a case with each successive hearing.

Streamlining of civil procedure

Civil procedure could be streamlined with a 'trimming of procedural frills', in order to make litigation quicker, cheaper and less complicated.

There would be a single simplified and combined set of rules for both the High Court and the county court. All claims would be started in the same way, with litigants able to start in any court and the court would take the responsibility of allocating the case to the appropriate court and track. Discovery would generally be limited to documents which are readily available and of direct relevance to the case, 'standard discovery', though this could be extended for multi-track cases.

Statements of case would replace statements of claim which would give more information about the facts relied upon and would be sworn on oath. After a case management session this could be replaced by a statement of issues which would specify exactly what was in issue. Leave would be required both to raise points not made in a witness statement (witness summaries for the fast track) or to cross-examine. The use of expert witnesses would be further restricted.

Information technology

Lord Woolf suggests that greater use should be made of developments in information technology such as computers and telecommunications. Attendance would not always be required by the court if the matter could be dealt with over the telephone. Computers would be used to provide information and assistance to the public, including 'information technology kiosks' in courts.

Civil Justice Council

To sustain the pace of change in the longer term he has suggested that a Civil Justice Council should be created, which would also prepare the new rules of procedure.

Criticism of Lord Woolf's interim proposals

Lord Woolf has suggested that if his proposals are implemented legal bills would drop by as much as 75 per cent, though it might also mean that some lawyers would lose their livelihoods. Whether this is true remains to be seen. Zander is reported to have said that his proposals amount to taking a sledgehammer to crack a nut and questioned the need for such major reforms, arguing that they would actually increase the cost of litigation.

Zander has remarked that judges do not have the time, skills or inclination to undertake the task of case management. To fulfil this role, more judges would probably be required but Lord Woolf has said that his approach '... involves reforms which can be achieved by redeployment of existing judges ... without a substantial injection of new resources ...'

On the payment into court procedures Zander had earlier suggested that the procedure for payment into court should be reformed to allow a reasonable margin of error, so that the rule only applies when the award is a great deal less than the payment into court, or allowing either side to make a proposal for settlement, with implications for costs. This system has been adopted in Canada.

▶ Other possible reforms

Class actions

Disasters such as the sinking of the ferry *Herald of Free Enterprise*, or the Opren and Thalidomide drug tragedies create a vast number of victims, who are all potential co-plaintiffs, seeking to prove negligence against the same defendant. In the USA, 'class actions' enable one or more plaintiffs to bring an action on behalf of all the members of that class, reducing costs and time. The Legal Aid Board is examining how to fund multi-party actions through the legal aid scheme, by directing legal aid cases to a single firm or small group of firms of solicitors.

More efficient enforcement of judgments

In 1969 the Payne Committee recommended the establishment of an Enforcements Office which would select the most appropriate method of enforcing a judgment. The proposal has not been implemented, mainly because of cost – the Civil Justice Review considered the idea to be expensive and inefficient.

Integration

A proposal to integrate the High Court and the county court to produce a simpler system was considered by the Gorell Committee on county court procedure, but rejected, mainly on the grounds that hearing big cases in the county courts would prejudice the handling of smaller ones.

The proposal was also considered by the Civil Justice Review, which pointed out that the two-court system was inflexible, making it difficult to make rational allocations of judges' time and administrators between the different courts. Consequently some courts have much longer delays than others. In a unified court, all cases would start in the same way, and be allocated to different sorts of judges on the basis of their complexity. The Lord Chancellor's Department could send judges where they were needed most, and some higher level judges could be based outside London.

The proposal was supported by solicitors, advice centres and consumer organizations but strongly opposed by barristers and judges, for rather unattractive reasons. Barristers feared that solicitors would have greater rights of audience in the unified court, and that the London Bar would lose business to provincial solicitors; High Court judges thought that the proposals would reduce their standing and destroy their special way of life, especially if they were expected to be based for long periods of time in the provinces.

In the end the Review rejected the idea of a unified court, on the grounds that there was no general support for it, the financial implications were uncertain, a unified court would require major legislation and a lengthy implementation period, and it might have adverse effects on the standing of the High Court judiciary. It did, however, recommend some streamlining (see p. 270).

Inquisitorial system

In theory, the civil justice system could move to an inquisitorial system, in which the judge would take a more investigative role, and the two parties would be required to cooperate by revealing all their evidence to each other. Tactics would become less important, and since delay is often a part of these tactics, the whole process could be speeded up. Some would suggest that this system might also be fairer, since being able to afford the best lawyer would be less important.

In fact, a full change away from the adversarial system seems extremely unlikely, but there have been proposals for such movement in certain areas: the Civil Justice Review suggested that a paper adjudication scheme might be considered for handling certain claims, which would move to an oral hearing only if the adjudicator felt there were difficulties which made one necessary. The procedure would be compulsory for road accidents and claims under £5,000 and could also be used in other cases where the parties agreed. However, this idea has been opposed by both the National Consumer Council and the National Association of Citizens Advice Bureaux, on the grounds that those who could afford a skilled lawyer to draft their papers would have too much of an advantage. Some of the Woolf proposals also favour a move towards an inquisitorial approach and a less aggressive form of litigation.

The move towards full pre-trial disclosure of evidence, and the facts that Small Claims Court arbitrators now take a more interventionist approach can be seen as moves towards a more inquisitorial system.

Reform of compensation for personal injury

Tort law dictates that the victims of an accident (other than industrial accidents, which are covered by a compensation scheme) can get compensation only if they can prove that the harm caused to them was somebody else's fault. The result of this is that individuals with identical injuries may receive hundreds of thousands of pounds in compensation, or nothing more than state benefits, depending not on their needs but on whether they can prove fault – often very difficult to do conclusively. In many cases, the state has to spend money, in the form of legal aid, but if the case is lost, the only person to benefit from that expenditure is the lawyer.

Because of this, it is often suggested that the tort action for personal injury should be abolished, and the financial savings should be used to provide improved welfare benefits for all those injured by accidents. New Zealand has adopted such an approach and established a no fault system of compensation.

ANSWERING QUESTIONS

1 **Assess the changes made to the civil justice system by the Courts and Legal Services Act 1990 (ignoring changes to the legal profession).**
You will need to outline the reforms made by the CLSA, the most important here being the changes in distribution of cases between the High Court and county courts. As usual, don't spend too much time describing these.

In order to assess these changes, you need to point out what problems they were designed to solve – they stem from recommendations of the Civil Justice Review, so you could talk about its aims, and say a little about the problems that existed before – delay, complexity and cost are described in the section on criticisms of the civil procedure on p. 277 *et seq*.

Then go on to evaluate how far these problems have been solved by the CLSA changes – you can point out that it is still too early to be sure of exactly how they will work out in the long term. You should point out that the reforms have caused problems of their own.

If you have time, you could discuss some of the reforms suggested by the Civil Justice Review which were not implemented, or any other suggested reforms, and say whether you think these could have contributed to dealing with the problems you have described. In particular you could look at the current review of the civil justice system by Lord Woolf.

Alternatively (or as well if you have time), you might mention one or two of the problems not addressed by the Courts and Legal Services Act, such as the unfairness of out of court settlements and the difficulties with enforcement – you could say whether you think these should have been considered, and whether you feel that the fact that they were not weakens the value of the CLSA to the civil justice system.

Your conclusion might state how effective you find the CLSA reforms to be in improving the civil justice system.

2 **How satisfactory are the current arrangements for the resolution of the civil law disputes through the courts? Suggest what improvements may be necessary.** *AEB*

You could begin this essay by discussing some of the theoretical aims of a civil justice system described above, and pointing out that as they may conflict, it is not always possible to fulfil them all – so a balance needs to be struck. You might give some examples of such aims in conflict. You could introduce a discussion on justice (see p. 429) but as applied to the context of the civil justice system.

You could then look at how the different aims are approached in practice, by looking at the proposals of the Civil Justice Review and Lord Woolf's interim report. You could mention that in real life, less noble principles may play a part – as the vested interests of lawyers and judges did in the provisions of the Civil Justice Review.

You might then go on to talk about the fact that the CLSA adopts the priorities set by the Review, and analyse how this is working in practice – think about, for example, whether the CLSA's championing of speed and cost-efficiency has any implications for the aims of getting a fair result, finding out the truth, and making the system accessible. How have reforms aimed at making the system quicker, cheaper and simpler affected the overall balance? Note that soon after the CLSA the Woolf committee has been established.

You can then discuss reforms which you feel would improve the civil justice system. For example, the suggestions made by Lord Woolf on p. 282 or the other possible reforms on p. 286.

13 Tribunals

Many claims and disputes are settled not by the courts, but by tribunals, each specializing in a particular area. The Industrial Tribunal is probably the best-known example, but there are around 60 in all, dealing with subjects ranging from social security and tax to forestry and patents. Not all are actually called tribunals – the category includes, for example, the Education Appeal Committee, which hears appeals concerning the allocation of school places, and the Criminal Injuries Compensation Board, which assesses applications for compensation for victims of violent crime. The majority deal with disputes between the citizen and the State, though the Industrial Tribunal is an obvious exception.

Tribunals are generally distinguished from the other courts by less formal procedures, and by the fact that they specialize. However they are all expected to conduct themselves according to the same principles of natural justice used by the courts: a fair hearing for both sides and open and impartial decision-making.

Individual tribunals may differ quite markedly from each other in terms of procedure, workload and membership. For example, Industrial Tribunals operate on an adversarial model, whereas procedure in the social security tribunals is much more inquisitorial.

▶ History

Tribunals were in existence as long ago as 1799, but the present system has really grown up since the Second World War. The main reason for this was the growth of legislation in areas which were previously considered private, and therefore rarely interfered with by the state, such as social security benefits, housing, town and country planning, education and employment.

This legislation gave people rights – to a school place, to unemployment benefit, or not to be unfairly sacked, for example – but its rules also placed limits on these rights. Naturally, this leads to disputes: employer and employee disagree on whether the latter's dismissal was unfair under the terms of the legislation; a social security claimant believes she has been wrongly denied benefit; a landowner disputes the right of the Local Authority to compulsorily purchase her field.

Given the potentially vast number of disputes likely to arise, and the detailed nature of the legislation concerning them, it was felt that the ordinary court system would neither have been able to cope with the workload, nor be the best forum for sorting out such problems, hence the growth of tribunals.

As well as the administrative tribunals dealing with this kind of dispute, there are domestic tribunals, which deal with disputes and matters of discipline within particular professions – trade unions and the medical and legal professions all have tribunals like this, the Solicitors Complaints Tribunal being an example. The decisions of these tribunals are based on the particular rules of the organization concerned, but they are still required to subscribe to the same standards of justice as the ordinary courts and in the case of those set up by statute, their decisions can be appealed to the ordinary courts – as can those of most administrative tribunals.

▶ The Franks report

In 1957, the Franks Committee investigated the workings of tribunals. It reported that the tribunal system was likely to become an increasingly important part of the legal system, and recommended that tribunal procedures should be marked by 'openness, fairness and impartiality'. Openness required, where possible, hearings in public and explanations of the reasoning behind decisions. Fairness entailed the adoption of clear procedures, which allowed parties to know their rights, present their case fully, and be aware of the case against them. Impartiality meant that tribunals should be free of undue influence from any Government departments concerned with their subject area. The Committee was particularly concerned that tribunals were often on ministry premises, with ministry staff.

The Committee also recommended the establishment of two permanent Councils on Tribunals, one for England and Wales and one for Scotland, to supervise procedures. Although a Council was set up (with a Scottish committee), its functions are only advisory – it has little real power, and cannot reverse or even direct further consideration of individual tribunal decisions. In 1980, it put forward a report asking for further powers, but these were not granted.

▶ Tribunals today

Composition

Most tribunals consist of a legally trained chairperson, and two lay people who have some particular expertise in the relevant subject area – doctors in the Medical Appeal Tribunal for example, and representatives of both employees' and employers' organizations in the Industrial Tribunal. The lay members take an active part in decision-making.

Tribunals composed entirely of lay people are considered to have been less effective than those with a legally qualified chairperson.

Status

Tribunals are regarded as inferior to the ordinary courts, even though they are largely independent from them in their own jurisdictions.

Workload

The 1979 Royal Commission on Legal Services found that in 1978, tribunals heard six times as many contested cases as the High Court and county courts. Although they have often been seen as an unimportant part of the legal system, this caseload clearly shows that they are now playing a major role.

▶ Appeals from tribunals

There is no uniform appeals procedure from tribunals, though most do allow some right of appeal. The 1992 Tribunals and Inquiries Act provides for appeals to the High Court on points of law from some of the most important tribunals. These appeals are heard by the Queen's Bench Division.

In addition to appeal rights, decisions of tribunals are always subject to judicial review by the High Court on the grounds that they have not been made in accordance with the rules of natural justice, or were not within the powers of the tribunal to make (see p. 314).

▶ Controls over tribunals

Aside from the judicial review procedure, which supervises the actual decisions of tribunals, the workings of tribunals are overseen by the Council on Tribunals. This consists of ten to fifteen members appointed by the Lord Chancellor and the Secretary of State for Scotland. It reviews and reports on the constitution and workings of certain specified tribunals, and is consulted before any changes to their procedural rules are made; it also considers and reports on matters referred to it concerning any tribunal. However, it has no firm say in any of these matters, and cannot overrule any decisions.

▶ **Advantages of tribunals**

Speed
Tribunal cases come to court fairly quickly, and many are dealt with within a day. Many tribunals are able to specify the exact date and time at which a case will be heard, so minimizing time-wasting for the parties.

Cost
Tribunals usually do not charge fees, and each party usually pays their own costs, rather than the loser having to pay all. The simpler procedures of tribunals should mean that legal representation is unnecessary, so reducing cost, but that is not always the case (see below).

Informality
This varies between different tribunals, but as a general rule, wigs are not worn, the strict rules of evidence do not apply, and attempts are made to create an unintimidating atmosphere. This is obviously a help where individuals are representing themselves.

Flexibility
Although they obviously aim to apply fairly consistent principles, tribunals do not operate strict rules of precedent, so are able to respond more flexibly than courts.

Specialization
Tribunal members already have expertise in the relevant subject area, and through sitting on tribunals are able to build up a depth of knowledge of that area that judges in ordinary courts could not hope to match.

Relief of congestion in the ordinary courts
If the volume of cases heard by tribunals was transferred to the ordinary courts, the system would be completely overloaded.

Awareness of policy
The expertise of tribunal members means they are likely to understand the policy behind legislation in their area, and they often have wide discretionary powers which allow them to put this into practice.

Privacy
Tribunals may, in some circumstances, meet in private, so that the individual is not obliged to have their circumstances broadcast to the general public (but see the first disadvantage below).

▶ **Disadvantages of tribunals**

Lack of openness
The fact that some tribunals are held in private can lead to suspicion about the fairness of their decisions.

Unavailability of legal aid
Full civil legal aid is available for only a couple of tribunals. The Legal Aid Act 1988 allows the Lord Chancellor to make assistance by way of representation available to tribunals, but so far it has been extended only to the mental health review tribunals and some prison disciplinary proceedings. Assistance with preparing a case is available under the Green Form scheme, but this cannot pay for representation.

Tribunals are of course designed to do away with the need for representation, but the fact is that in many of them, the ordinary individual will be facing an opponent with access to the very best representation – an employer, for example, or a Government department – and this clearly places them at a serious disadvantage. Even though the procedures are generally informal compared to those in ordinary courts, the average person is likely to be very much out of their depth, and research by Genn and Genn in 1989 found that much of the law with which tribunals was concerned was complex, their adjudicative process sometimes highly technical; individuals who were represented had a better chance of winning their case.

There is however some dispute as to the desirability of such representation necessarily involving lawyers; although in some cases this will be the more appropriate form of representation, there are fears that introducing lawyers could detract from the aims of speed and informality. If money for tribunal representation were available, it may be better spent on developing lay representation, such as that offered by specialist agencies such as the United Kingdom Immigration Advisory Service, or the Child Poverty Action Group, who can develop real expertise in specific areas, as well as general agencies such as the Citizens Advice Bureaux. However this aspect of the question is largely academic since there is no sign of money being made available.

Involvement of interested parties
The requirement of independence defined by the Franks Committee is compromised by the fact that members of some tribunals are appointed by the Minister on whose decisions they are to adjudicate. Although there is no evidence that this results in bias, clearly it makes it difficult for tribunals to achieve the appearance of impartiality.

Reasons for decisions not always given
Although the majority of tribunals are obliged to explain their reasoning if requested, a few are not.

Too complex
The 1979 Royal Commission on Legal Services recommended a review of tribunal procedures, with a view to simplifying matters so that applicants could as far as possible represent themselves, yet if anything, tribunal procedures have become more legalistic. Genn and Genn's study points out that the complexity of the legal provisions many tribunals deal with may make self-representation impossible, in which case better representation will become even more necessary.

Lack of accessibility
The Franks Committee recommendation that tribunals should be 'open' requires more than just a rule that hearings should usually be held in public; it also demands that citizens should be aware of tribunals and their right to use them. In cases where the dispute is between a citizen and the Government, the citizen will usually be notified of procedures to deal with disputes, but in other cases more thought needs to be given to publicizing citizens' rights.

Problems with controls over tribunals
- Although considered together, tribunals vary widely, and make thousands of decisions each year in very different types of case. It is not easy to supervise this diversity.
- The Council on Tribunals is a watchdog with no teeth. It has no real power, and can only advise the Government of problems.
- There is no absolute right to appeal from a tribunal; such rights exist only when laid down by statute with regard to a particular tribunal. Consequently there is no uniform appeals system, and some tribunals offer no appeal rights at all. An example is the Vaccine Damage Tribunals, set up under the Vaccine Damage Payments Act 1971 to assess claimants' rights to damages for disabilities caused by vaccination. Some tribunal appeals can only be made to the relevant minister, who can hardly be seen as a disinterested party. Others have appeal rights to the High Court, which is expensive, complex and time-consuming, and therefore inconsistent with the basic aims of tribunals.
- The use of judicial review is as always limited by the fact that it cannot consider the merits of decisions, and that where wide discretionary powers are given to a minister, Government department or local authority, the court will find it difficult to prove that almost any decision was outside those powers (see p. 314).

ANSWERING QUESTIONS

1 **Consider the role of tribunals in the administration of justice.** *London*
You can begin by considering what the role of tribunals is. You should
point out that they do vary widely, but broadly their job in the legal system
can be said to include providing justice in a quick, inexpensive and accessible
way, making independent decisions in disputes between the citizen and the
state, putting into effect the policy behind legislation, and taking pressure off
the courts. You then need to assess how well tribunals do these jobs.

The following are points you might mention:

- Speed – they are quicker than courts, but since the Franks Committee have
  adopted more court-like procedures, which may slow things down;
- Inexpensive – some charge no fees, and costs are not usually awarded
  against a losing party as they would be in a court. However, the need for
  representation, and the fact that legal aid is not available may eradicate
  these advantages for some;
- Accessibility – procedures are usually simpler than in courts, but again, the
  fact that representation is allowed means that powerful litigants will have
  it, so less powerful ones are disadvantaged by representing themselves;
- Independence – though this has improved, there are still criticisms (see
  above);
- Helping the citizen to assert rights against the state – this may be
  compromised by lack of independence, and also the problems with legal
  aid, putting the individual at a disadvantage.
- Effecting policy – tribunals do often have wider discretionary powers than
  courts;
- Taking pressure off the courts – you could point out the vast numbers of
  cases which arise in the kinds of matters dealt with by tribunals.

2 **Analyse the role played by tribunals in the English legal system. How far
are the methods of supervising and reviewing their judgments adequate?**
The role of tribunals is described above – if you have time, it is worth
mentioning some of the assessment points, since you are being asked what
role is actually played, rather than just what role tribunals aim to play.

For the second part of the question, you need to outline what methods of
supervising tribunals and reviewing their decisions are available. The problems
with these methods are outlined above, and you should also refer to the
section on judicial review in general (p. 314), and to any relevant points made
by chapter 14.

14

APPEALS

The appeals system provides a way of overseeing the lower courts, and has two basic functions:

- Putting right any unjust or incorrect decisions, whether caused by errors of fact, law or procedure. An error of fact might be that a victim was stabbed with a knife rather than a broken bottle; an error of law might be that the judge has wrongly defined an offence when explaining to the jury what needs to be proved; and an error of procedure means that the trial has not been conducted as it should have been.
- Promoting a consistent development of the law.

In some circumstances appeal lies 'as of right', and appellants need no permission to take their case to a higher court. In other circumstances they will have to get leave, meaning permission, either from the higher court or from the court which has considered their case, and without leave, they have no right to appeal or further appeal.

Judicial review is not technically an appeal, though it is a way of reviewing the decisions of courts and tribunals. It will be considered after the appeals system.

▶ Appeals in civil law cases

Civil appeals may be made by either party to a dispute.

From the county court

Appeals based on alleged errors of law or fact are made to the civil division of the Court of Appeal. Leave to appeal is usually as of right under s. 7 of the Courts and Legal Services Act 1990. Appeals from a district judge's decision have to go first to a circuit judge.

The Court of Appeal does not hear all the evidence again, calling witnesses and so forth, but considers it on the basis of the notes made by the trial judge, and/or other documentary evidence of the proceedings. It may affirm, vary (for example by altering the amount of damages) or reverse the judgment of the county court. It is generally reluctant to overturn the trial judge's finding of fact because it does not hold a complete rehearing: since the trial judge has the advantage of observing the demeanour of witnesses giving their evidence, the Court of Appeal will hardly ever question his or her findings about their veracity and reliability as witnesses.

From the Court of Appeal, there may be a further appeal to the House of Lords, for which leave must be granted.

Judicial review by the High Court is also possible.

From the High Court

Cases started in the High Court may be appealed to the Civil Division of the Court of Appeal. Leave is not usually necessary, but the process is expensive. The case is examined through transcripts rather than being reheard, as above. From there, a further appeal on questions of law or fact may be made, with leave, to the House of Lords.

The exception to this process is the 'leap frog' procedure, provided for in the Administration of Justice Act 1969. Under this procedure an appeal can go directly from the High Court to the House of Lords missing out the Court of Appeal. The rationale behind this is that the Court of Appeal may be bound by a decision of the House of Lords so that money and time is wasted by going to the Court of Appeal when the only court that could look at the issue afresh is the House of Lords. In order to use this procedure, all the parties must consent to it and the High Court judge who heard the original trial must certify that the appeal is on a point of law that either:

(a) relates wholly or mainly to the construction of an enactment or of a statutory instrument, and has been fully argued in the proceedings and fully considered in the judgement of the judge in the proceedings, or
(b) is one in respect of which the judge is bound by a decision of the Court of Appeal or of the House of Lords in previous proceedings, and was fully considered in the judgments given by the Court of Appeal or the House of Lords (as the case may be) in those previous proceedings (s. 12(3)).

The trial judge has a discretion whether or not to grant this certificate, and there is no appeal against his or her decision. Even if this certificate is granted leave will still need to be obtained from the House of Lords.

From the civil jurisdiction of the magistrates' court

Appeals concerning family proceedings go to the Family Division of the High Court. From there, appeal with leave then lies to the Court of Appeal and the House of Lords. Appeals on licensing matters go to the Crown Court.

It is also possible for the magistrates to state a case (see point 3 on p. 300) and for judicial review to be applied.

From tribunals

These may have their own appeal system – the Employment Appeal Tribunal, for example, hears cases from industrial tribunals. Otherwise appeals from tribunals tend to be limited to points of law, which are usually referred to the High Court. They are also subject to judicial review by the High Court (see chapter 13).

▶ Appeals in criminal law cases

The criminal appeal process is in a period of transition having come under heavy criticism following high profile miscarriages of justice. The appeal process is supposed to spot cases where there have been wrongful convictions at an early stage so that the injustice can be promptly remedied. A wrongful conviction could arise because of police or prosecution malpractice, a misdirection by a judge, judicial bias, or because expert evidence, such as forensic evidence, was misleading. However, the Court of Appeal in particular failed in the past to detect such problems and this has led to demands for reform. The Criminal Appeal Act 1995 has therefore been passed to make major amendments to the current criminal appeal procedure. This Act was given the royal assent in July 1995 but has not come into force at the time of writing. According to the Home Office its provisions concerning the establishment of the new Criminal Cases Review Commission (CCRC) are likely to come into force around mid-1996 and the other provisions at the beginning of 1996. We will need to look at the criminal appeal process prior to and after the Act coming into force.

From the magistrates' court (criminal jurisdiction)

There are four routes of appeal:

1 The magistrates can themselves rectify an error they have made. In the past this could only be done if the defendant pleaded not guilty at the original trial, but the Criminal Appeal Act 1995 extends the power to where the defendant pleaded guilty as well.

2 A defendant who has pleaded not guilty may appeal as of right
   to the Crown Court on the grounds of being wrongly convicted or
   too harshly sentenced. Defendants pleading guilty may only appeal
   against sentence. The appeal has to be made within 28 days of the
   conviction. These appeals are normally heard by a circuit judge
   sitting with between two and four magistrates (not those who heard
   the original trial). Each person has an equal vote, but if the court
   is equally divided the circuit judge has the casting vote.

   The court will rehear the facts of the case and either confirm
   the verdict and/or sentence of the original magistrates, or
   substitute its own decision for that of the magistrates' court. It can
   impose any sentence that the magistrates might have imposed –
   which can occasionally result in the accused's sentence being
   increased. In 1993 there were 23,722 such appeals, which is less
   than 0.01 per cent of all cases heard by magistrates. Of those
   appeals, 7,998 (33.7 per cent) were successful.

3 Alternatively, either the prosecution or the accused may appeal on
   the grounds that the magistrates have made an error of law, or
   acted outside their jurisdiction, by asking the magistrates (or the
   Crown Court when hearing an appeal from the magistrates) to
   'state the case' on the question to the High Court for a decision.
   This is known as an appeal by way of case stated. These appeals are
   heard by two or three judges of the Queen's Bench Division and
   the sitting is known as a Divisional Court. The court can confirm,
   reverse or vary the decision; give the magistrates their opinion on
   the relevant point of law; or make such other order as it sees fit,
   which may include ordering a rehearing before a different bench.

4 The new Criminal Cases Review Commission will be able to refer
   appeals from the magistrates' court to the Crown Court. This body
   is discussed in more detail from p. 303 onwards.

If an appeal has been made to the Crown Court, either side may then
appeal against the Crown Court's decision by way of case stated; however
a party appealing by way of case stated first may not afterwards appeal to
the Crown Court. In 1993 there were 199 appeals from magistrates' courts
and 37 appeals from Crown Court under this procedure, of which 39 per
cent were allowed.

From the Divisional Court there may be a further appeal, by either
party, to the House of Lords, but only if the Divisional Court certifies that
the question of law is one of public importance and the House of Lords
or the Divisional Court gives permission for the appeal to be heard.

Criminal cases heard by magistrates are also subject to judicial review.

In practice, appeals from the decision of magistrates are taken in less
than 0.5 per cent of cases. This may be because most accused plead guilty,
and since the offences are relatively minor and the punishment usually a

fine, many of those who pleaded not guilty may prefer just to pay up and put the case behind them, avoiding the expense, publicity and embarrassment involved in an appeal.

From the Crown Court

There are two types of appeal for cases tried in the Crown Court.

1 Where a prospective appeal concerns the sentence, or is to be made on grounds that involve the facts, the accused must get leave from the Court of Appeal. The Court of Appeal cannot impose a sentence that is more severe than that imposed by the Crown Court. An appeal against sentence will only be successful where the sentence is wrong in principle or manifestly severe; the court will not interfere merely because it might have passed a different sentence.

   The accused could appeal as of right to the Court of Appeal on a question of law under the Criminal Appeal Act 1968 s. 1(2). However s. 1 of the Criminal Appeal Act 1995 will remove this automatic right. In order to bring any appeal on a question of law to the Court of Appeal the trial judge must either certify that the case was fit for appeal, or leave to appeal must be given by the Court of Appeal.

   While only the accused can appeal to the Court of Appeal, from there either the accused or the prosecution may appeal on a point of law to the House of Lords, provided that either the Court of Appeal or the House of Lords grant leave for the appeal and that the Court of Appeal certifies that the case involves a matter of law of general public importance. The Royal Commission on Criminal Justice 1993 (set up after the release of the Birmingham Six) has recommended that this latter requirement should be abolished.

2 **The section 17 procedure**. In the past the Home Secretary had an important additional role in allowing appeals from the Crown Court. A person convicted in the Crown Court could apply to the Home Secretary to have their case referred to the Court of Appeal under s. 17 of the Criminal Appeals Act 1968, and the Home Secretary could also refer a case under this section of his own accord, without having received such an application. Section 17 appeals could take place regardless of the fact that the normal time limit for appeals had expired, that there had already been an unsuccessful appeal, or even that the defendant had since died.

   Only the Home Secretary could make such a referral, and he or she had considerable discretion in deciding whether or not to do so: the statute simply required a reference to be made 'if he thinks fit'. Much of the groundwork was done for the Home Secretary by a small department in the Home Office. In fact, the Home Secretary only usually referred cases where new evidence had come to light suggesting that there may have been a miscarriage of justice, and only after appeal rights had been exhausted; usually cases referred were those which continued to cause media comment and public concern long after the trial had taken place. The Court of Appeal reviewed the whole case once it had been referred. It treated the case as an appeal by the convicted person and had all the powers that it had in dealing with criminal appeals.

However there were serious difficulties with the s. 17 procedure as seen in cases such as the Birmingham Six and the Tottenham Three, where references were only made after years of persuasion and publicity. The original appeal of the Birmingham Six was rejected in 1976. It was not until 1987 that the Home Secretary referred their case back to the Court of Appeal though that appeal was rejected. Three years later, he referred the case to the Court of Appeal again, and this time the Director of Public Prosecutions did not resist the application so that the Court of Appeal had little choice but to allow the appeal and quash the convictions in 1991.

Successive Home Secretaries had been reluctant to refer cases, and whether they eventually did so depended too much on pressure from people of influence – usually cases were only referred back to appeal after pressure from MPs, the media, and sometimes high-ranking members of the clergy. Refusals to refer could be challenged on an application for judicial review, but no such applications were successful. Each year there were about 730 applications to the Home Office and its equivalent in Northern Ireland, but only ten to twelve of those cases were actually referred to the Court of Appeal.

The Court of Appeal showed a general reluctance to allow s. 17 appeals in cases where it had already dismissed an appeal, and in fact appeared to dislike s. 17 referrals generally: in the first (unsuccessful) s. 17 appeal from the Birmingham Six, the court stated that: 'As has happened before in references by the Home Secretary to this court, the longer the hearing has gone on the more convinced this court has become that the verdict of the jury was correct.' As MP Chris Mullins' book on the Birmingham Six points out, this seemed to be a thinly-veiled message to the Home Secretary that referring such cases was a waste of time.

A further problem was that once the reference was made, the appeal was governed by the Criminal Appeal Act 1968, and the expense and responsibility of preparing the appeal lay with the defendant, who would probably be in prison, and have been there for quite some time. Legal aid might be available but investigation in these circumstances would be difficult.

Criminal Cases Review Commission

When the relevant provisions come into force (predicted to be mid-1996) the Criminal Appeal Act 1995 will abolish the s. 17 procedure and replace it with a Criminal Cases Review Commission, following a proposal made by the Runciman Commission. This Commission will consist of no fewer than 11 members, at least a third of whom will be lawyers and two thirds of its members must have had knowledge or experience in the criminal justice system. At least one will have knowledge of the criminal justice system in Northern Ireland. They will be appointed by the Queen on the advice of the Prime Minister. The Commission will not be a court deciding appeals, rather it will be responsible for bringing cases where there may have been a miscarriage of justice to the attention of the Court of Appeal if the case was originally heard by the Crown Court (or the Crown Court if the case was originally heard by a magistrates' court). Either a person can apply to the Commission to consider their case or the Commission can consider it on their own initiative if an ordinary appeal is time barred. The Commission can carry out an investigation into the case, which may involve asking the police to re-investigate a matter. Before making a reference the Commission will be able to seek the Court of Appeal's opinion on any matter.

The Commission can make such a reference in relation to a conviction where it appears to them that any argument or evidence, which was not raised in any relevant court proceedings, gives rise to a real possibility that the conviction would not be upheld were the reference to be made. A reference in relation to a sentence will be possible if 'any argument on a point of law, or any information' was not so raised and again there is a real possibility that the conviction might not be upheld. Where the Commission refer a conviction or sentence to the Court of Appeal it will be treated as a fresh appeal by the person concerned.

Whichever appeal route is taken to reach the Court of Appeal, once the case is in the Court of Appeal it is dealt with under the same procedure which will now be considered.

Admission of fresh evidence

Unlike an appeal from the magistrates' court to the Crown court, the Court of Appeal in criminal cases does not rehear the whole case with all its evidence. Instead it aims merely to review the lower court's decision. This is at least partly because the Court of Appeal is reluctant to overturn the verdict of a jury, apparently fearing that to do so might undermine the public's respect for juries in general.

Under the old law, the Court of Appeal **could** admit fresh evidence or examine or re-examine a witness 'if they think it necessary or expedient in the interests of justice' (Criminal Appeal Act 1968, s. 23(1)).

They **had** to receive fresh evidence if:

- it appeared to them it was likely to be credible; and
- it would have been admissible in the original proceedings; and
- they were satisfied that there was a reasonable explanation why it was not adduced at the trial (s. 23(2)).

The reluctance of the Court of Appeal even to admit fresh evidence was repeatedly criticized. Although the legislation gave it a wide discretion to admit new evidence, in practice the Court of Appeal required a particular type of explanation why evidence was not called at the time of trial, such as that it was not available. If it was available but for some reason not called, the Court of Appeal was unlikely to accept it. One of the reasons for the court's approach was that they were reluctant to turn what should be a process of review into a full re-hearing. But, in effect, defendants could be punished, and denied the right to a fair hearing, for omissions caused by their lawyers' incompetence, the underfunding of the legal aid system, or the prosecution's obstructiveness. Malleson in his research for the Runciman Commission, 'A Review of the Appeal Process' (1993), found that 80 per cent of successful appeals were based on a wrong decision regarding the admissibility of evidence or a misdirection by the judge.

The Runciman Commission concluded that the court's current powers to admit fresh evidence were sufficient, but the problem was that in practice the court was interpreting these powers too narrowly. Thus they encouraged the court to take a more flexible approach. In the light of past experience, it seems unlikely that the court will take this approach of its own initiative and this may be why the Criminal Appeal Act 1995 will actually change the current law to encourage the admission of more evidence. The Act will amend s. 23(2) of the Criminal Appeal Act 1968. It will lower the threshold for admitting fresh evidence, so that such evidence should be admitted if it is 'capable of belief', instead of the current test that it is 'likely to be credible'.

In addition, under the 1995 Act, the Court of Appeal can direct the proposed new Criminal Cases Review Commission to investigate, and report on, any matter relevant to the determination of a case being considered by the Court. Thus the Court of Appeal would have a radical new power to seek out new evidence themselves, something that no other criminal court in England currently has due to our traditional adversarial procedures.

At one time the Court of Appeal considered new evidence in the light of the effect it might have had on the decision of the jury, but in **Stafford** *v* **DPP** (1974), Viscount Dilhourne said that if the court was satisfied that there was no reasonable doubt about the guilt of the accused, the conviction should not be quashed even though the jury might have come to a different view. The court was not bound to ask whether the evidence might have led to the jury returning a verdict of not guilty. The judges are therefore replacing the jury's opinion with their own, and this is viewed by some as weakening the right to trial by jury.

At present the Court of Appeal may order a re-trial where it feels this is required by the interests of justice. It will only do so if it accepts that the additional evidence is true but is not convinced that it is conclusive – in other words that it would have led to a different verdict.

Section 2 and the outcome of the appeal

Another area that is to be reformed by the 1995 Act concerns the powers of the Court of Appeal to deal with the appeal. Under s. 2 of the Criminal Appeal Act 1968 the Court of Appeal can allow the appeal, dismiss it or order a new trial. They should allow an appeal against conviction if they think:

- that the jury's verdict is unsafe and unsatisfactory; or
- that there was an error of law; or
- that there was a material irregularity in the course of the trial.

The drafting of section 2 of the Criminal Appeal Act 1968 was criticized by the Runciman Commission. They concluded that the paragraphs were unnecessarily complex and overlapped. Their recommendation was that the sole test should be whether the court thinks that the conviction 'is or may be unsafe'. In which case the conviction should be quashed, and where it appeared to the court that the conviction 'is' unsafe the appeal should be allowed and where it appeared that it 'may' be unsafe, a retrial should be ordered.

Zander (one of the Commissioners and a leading academic on the English legal system) along with one other Commissioner took the view that where there had been serious police malpractice then the conviction should always be quashed to discourage such conduct, and to prevent the police believing that they could benefit in terms of getting convictions by such behaviour. However, this approach was not accepted by the majority.

The Criminal Appeal Act 1995 essentially follows the majority's recommendation, though the ground for allowing the appeal is significantly narrowed as it only covers where the conviction 'is' unsafe and not where it 'may' be so.

The proviso

Under the 1968 Act there is a proviso to section 2, which states that if any of the section 2 criteria apply, but the court feels that nevertheless no miscarriage of justice has occurred, they may dismiss the appeal – if, for example, it is clear that something was wrong with the trial, yet the court believes the defendant was nevertheless genuinely guilty, and that no reasonable jury would have found the accused not guilty even if the trial had been carried out properly. Dismissing an appeal for any of these reasons is called applying the proviso.

Particular concern has been expressed in the past that the Court of Appeal applied the proviso too often, to avoid overturning a verdict, even when there have been serious irregularities in the trial. Malleson looked at 118 appeals that were dismissed in 1990 and found that the proviso was applied in 113 of them.

The Criminal Appeal Act 1995 will abolish the proviso.

▶ Appeals by the prosecution against acquittal

In general this is not allowed, on the basis of double jeopardy, and because it would be a means by which the state could abuse its power over the prosecution process (though it does exist in other countries, such as Canada). There are, however, some exceptions:

- The prosecution can state a case for consideration of the High Court, following the acquittal of a defendant at the magistrates' court. This is restricted to a point of law or jurisdiction.
- The prosecution can also, with leave, appeal to the House of Lords against a decision of the Court of Appeal (see above).
- The Criminal Justice Act 1972 gives the Attorney-General powers to refer any point of law which has arisen in a case, for the opinion of the Court of Appeal, even where the defendant was acquitted. Defendants are not identified (though they may be represented) and their acquittal remains unaffected even if the point of law goes against them – so this procedure is not, strictly speaking, an appeal. The purpose of this power is to enable the Court of Appeal to review a potentially incorrect ruling before it gains too wide a circulation in the trial courts.

  The procedure is not much used, perhaps because it is felt to be appropriate only for exceptionally difficult points of law – though the statute contains no such limitation and Lord Widgery has made the point that the Court of Appeal hoped to see it used extensively for 'short but important points' as well as more complex problems – **Attorney-General's Reference (No. 1 of 1975)**.

- The Criminal Justice Act 1988 enables the Attorney-General to refer to the Court of Appeal cases of apparently too lenient sentencing, including cases where it appears the judge has erred in law as to his or her powers of sentencing. Leave from the Court of Appeal is required.

  The Court of Appeal may quash the sentence and pass a more appropriate one. This is the first time that the prosecution is involved in the sentencing process. The provision was enacted in response to the Government's view that public confidence in the criminal justice system was being undermined by unduly lenient sentences, which had been given great publicity by the tabloid press.

▶ Criticism and reform of the appeals system

Delays

Lord Donaldson MR has suggested that too many appeals are being made, and are clogging up the system. He argues that leave should be required in more categories of cases; at present there are still many circumstances in which a party who has dismally failed to succeed before the judge or tribunal at first instance can try again in the Court of Appeal, however limited the prospects of success. This uses up scarce judicial resources, and delays other appeals, as well as benefiting litigants who know they have no chance of success, but appeal because the delay confers some commercial or other advantage.

While this approach may be appropriate for civil cases, restricting rights of criminal appeal may seem highly undesirable, in view of the fact that refusal of leave to appeal has been one of the factors keeping many of the well-known miscarriages of justice unresolved for so long. Nevertheless, steps have been taken to deter criminal appeals with no merit, in the form of practice notes issued in 1970 and 1980 by the then Lord Chief Justice, pointing out that the Criminal Appeal Act provision that time spent in custody pending appeal should be counted as part of the eventual sentence ('subject to any direction which the Court of Appeal may give to the contrary'), would not be applied if unsuccessful appeals were considered unmerited – on both occasions the number of appeals dropped afterwards.

The Criminal Division of the Court of Appeal

The Criminal Cases Review Commission

One problem with the CCRC is that, while it is predicted that more cases will reach the Court of Appeal than they did under the s. 17 procedure, one of the weaknesses with that procedure was that even when the case was referred to the Court of Appeal the convictions were often upheld even though later it was acknowledged that there had been a miscarriage of justice. Thus cases such as the Birmingham Six had to be repeatedly referred back to the Court of Appeal before they would eventually allow the appeals. In that case the appeal was allowed on the basis that there was 'fresh' evidence as to the police interrogation techniques and the forensic evidence. In reality this evidence had in essence been before the Court of Appeal in 1987; the difference was that the Court was forced to accept that the evidence raised a lurking doubt in 1991. Only if the other provisions are adequate to improve the Court of Appeal process will the same problems be avoided. An alternative solution would have been to give the Commission the power to decide appeals themselves.

The Director of the pressure group Justice, Anne Owens (1995), has criticized the fact that the CCRC has no power to assign in-house staff as investigating officers. She argues that without this power the Commission could not guarantee the independence of an inquiry.

Reluctance to overturn jury verdicts

The Court of Appeal seems to feel that overturning jury verdicts weakens public confidence in the jury system, and it is therefore very reluctant to do it. This view was spelt out during the final, successful appeal of the Birmingham Six, in 1991, in which the Court of Appeal stated:

> Nothing in s. 2 of the Act, or anywhere else obliges or entitles us to say whether we think that the appellant is innocent. This is a point of great constitutional importance. The task of deciding whether a man is innocent or guilty falls on the jury. We are concerned solely with the question whether the verdict of the jury can stand.
>
> Rightly or wrongly (we think rightly) trial by jury is the foundation of our criminal justice system . . . The primacy of the jury in the criminal justice system is well illustrated by the difference between the Criminal and Civil Divisions of the Court of Appeal . . . A civil appeal is by way of rehearing of the whole of the case. So the court is concerned with fact as well as law . . . It follows that in a civil case the Court of Appeal may take a different view of the facts from the court below. In a criminal case this is not possible. . . . the Criminal Division is perhaps more accurately described as a court of review.

The case of Winston Silcott (discussed on p. 192) illustrates the dangers. He had been convicted in 1985 of murdering PC Blakelock during the Tottenham riots. The offence had been committed by a group of 30 people. Six had gone on trial and only three were convicted including Silcott. The only evidence against Silcott was a statement he was alleged to have made: ('You won't pin this on me . . . nobody will talk'), which he had not signed. Despite these obvious weaknesses in the case, conviction was initially upheld by the Court of Appeal and was only overturned in 1991.

The major problem with the Court of Appeal's approach is that in many cases, the fault lies not with the decision-making powers of the jury, but in the evidence presented to them. Where a jury has not seen all the evidence, or where the evidence it has seen has been falsified by the police (as was alleged in some of the well-known miscarriages of justice), or where the jury has in any other way failed to have the case properly presented to it, overturning the verdict should not automatically be seen as a criticism of its ability to make correct decisions. A better way to demonstrate confidence in the jury system might be to order a retrial with a new jury.

The Runciman Commission concluded that the Court of Appeal should show greater willingness to substitute its judgment for that of the jury. They pointed out that in gauging the evidence juries could make errors particularly where it was a high profile case in which emotions run high. The case of Winston Silcott is a classic case in point. We will have to wait and see whether the Criminal Appeal Act 1995 might instigate a change of philosophy in this regard particularly in the light of the changes to the rules on the admissibility of fresh evidence.

Criticism of the case of *Stafford v DPP*

Lord Devlin, in his book *The Judge*, criticised the Court of Appeal's decision in **Stafford** *v* **DPP** to follow their own view of whether new evidence makes a conviction unsafe (or unsatisfactory), rather than assessing the effect such evidence might have had on the trial jury. He felt that this involves the judges in findings of fact, a function that properly belongs to the jury. The jury ends up playing a subordinate part in the verdict, since it has not heard all the evidence. He believes the change from assessing the possible effect of new evidence on the trial jury has not been sanctioned by Parliament and is an attack on the jury system.

Unwillingness to order retrials

Many have argued that the Court of Appeal should use its power to order re-trials more often. The number of such retrials has been growing from (three in 1990 to 23 in 1992) though the numbers are still small.

Lord Devlin has argued, as stated above, that a retrial should be ordered wherever fresh evidence could have made a difference to the verdict – the original verdict being clearly unsatisfactory since it was given without the jury hearing all the evidence.

Opponents argue that it may be unfair to the accused to reopen a decided case, and that a second trial cannot be a fair one, especially if some time has passed and/or the case has received a lot of publicity. But as Lord Devlin argues, this does not stop retrials being ordered where the jury has failed to agree a verdict, nor are prosecutions necessarily stifled because witnesses have to speak of events many years before. In fact, at the same time as the Birmingham Six were told that a retrial thirteen years after the original one was inappropriate, the Government was debating the prosecution of war criminals, some 44 years after the end of the Second World War. Shortly after the Six's unsuccessful appeal, an IRA man was brought to trial on charges dating back thirteen years.

As far as publicity is concerned, the second jury may well know of the defendant's record and have noted other adverse publicity, as well as knowing that the defendant has been convicted. On the other hand, it could be argued that in all the high-profile miscarriages of justice, no further publicity could have affected the attitudes of potential jurors more than that surrounding the original offences and trials – in fact prejudicial media reporting was one reason given for finding the convictions of the Taylor sisters unsafe and unsatisfactory in 1995.

Many wrongful convictions result from mistaken identity, and it is difficult for the Court of Appeal, which does not usually re-examine witnesses, to assess the strength of such evidence. Retrials might be the best way of dealing with this problem. A general power to order retrial could also be a way of convicting offenders who escape on a technicality first time round, and might be a more obviously just solution than applying the proviso, or letting such defendants go free, which has a negative effect on the public, the jury and the victim. However, it could also subject genuinely innocent defendants to a second ordeal.

It has been suggested that wider use of retrials would 'open the floodgates' to a deluge of appeals, yet this does not appear to be a problem in other countries with wider powers of retrial, including Scotland. In any case, it can be argued that, as Lord Atkin has put it, 'Finality is a good thing but justice is better'. The Runciman Commission considered the issue and concluded that the Court of Appeal should use the power to order a retrial more extensively.

The single test for quashing convictions

Anne Owens and the leading criminal law academic, JC Smith, have both criticized the new single test for quashing convictions. They have suggested that there is a danger that this will be interpreted more narrowly than the previous tests and the Scottish experience would appear to support this fear.

Legal advice

Legal advice should be available immediately after the conviction, including advice on the possibility of an appeal. Research carried out for the Runciman Commission by Plotnikoff and Wilson – 'Information and Advice for Prisoners about Grounds for Appeal and the Appeal Process' (1993) – found serious defects in the provision of such legal advice. Nine per cent of those convicted were not visited afterwards in the cells in order to be given legal advice, 23 per cent not advised about appeal and nearly 90 per cent received nothing in writing about an appeal. Malleson, in his research for the Runciman Commission – 'A Review of the Appeal Process' (1993) – found that lawyers themselves were often ill-informed about the powers of the Court of Appeal, some believing that they had the power to increase sentences on appeal by defendants. Not surprisingly those applicants who sought to appeal without legal advice were less successful. In the light of this evidence the Runciman Commission argued that appellants needed to receive more legal advice.

General unwillingness to address faults in the system

The problems outlined above can be seen as symptomatic of a more general reluctance to uncover the extent of miscarriages of justice in our system. This attitude was typified by Lord Denning's speech in **Chief Constable of the West Midlands** *v* **McIlkenny** (1980), the case in which the police successfully appealed against a civil action brought against them by the Birmingham Six in respect of injuries sustained after their arrest. Lord Denning said:

> If the six men win, it will mean that the police were guilty of perjury, that they were guilty of violence and threats. . . . and that the convictions were erroneous . . . the Home Secretary would have either to recommend that they be pardoned or he would have to remit the case to the Court of Appeal . . . This is such an appalling vista that every sensible person in the land would say 'It cannot be right that these actions should go any further'.

The implication was that even if the men were innocent, the damage such a revelation could do to confidence in the justice system meant it was better not known.

It has been argued that the review of a case in which a miscarriage of justice is alleged to have occurred where there has already been an unsuccessful appeal should not be an appellate process; what is alleged is a serious wrong committed by the state to the individual, which it should be the state's duty to investigate and the burden should not be left on the individual. The Criminal Cases Review Commission may go part of the way to acknowledging this.

The acquitted

There are two situations where the victim of an injustice has little or no possibility of appeal or redress:

- Acquittals – 55 per cent of defendants who pleaded not guilty to all charges in the Crown Court in 1989 were acquitted. Many of these people will have spent time on remand. Clearly not all of these are victims of injustice but those that are have no legal remedy except a civil action against the police for malicious prosecution, which is notoriously difficult to prove.

- Where a person has been kept in custody and released without charge – again there is no remedy except a civil action for false imprisonment.

It appears that in recent years there has been an increase in out-of-court settlements agreed by police authorities in actions for false imprisonment and/or malicious prosecution.

▶ The role of the House of Lords

From time to time the question is asked whether we need two courts with purely appellate jurisdiction. For those who consider that we do not, the answer is usually to abolish the House of Lords (as a court) – the Court of Appeal could not be abolished because its much larger caseload could not be absorbed by the House of Lords. Efforts to abolish the appellate jurisdiction of the House of Lords date back over a hundred years – in fact the Judicature Act of 1873 contained a section which did just that, but was never enacted. The following are some of the arguments on both sides.

For abolition

- The Court of Appeal should be sufficient; a third tier is unnecessary and illogical. A.P. Herbert points out that giving appellants the chance to get their case decided by two appellate courts is like having your appendix taken out by a distinguished surgeon, and then being referred to another who might confirm the first surgeon's decision, but might just as easily recommend the appendix be replaced! Reversing legal decisions might not pose the same practical problems as medical ones, but nevertheless, it may seem odd that the decisions of the eminent judges in the Court of Appeal can be completely overturned by the House of Lords.
- It allows a litigant with the support of a minority of judges to win. Take the example of a litigant losing a civil case, appealing to the Court of Appeal and losing, but finally winning in the House of Lords. Counting all the judges involved together, they may have had six against them (the original trial judge, the three judges hearing the case in the Court of Appeal, and two out of five in the House of Lords). Yet if three judges in the House of Lords are in their favour, they win the case overall, even though twice as many judges supported their opponent.
- It adds cost and delay to achieving a decision. Usually QCs are instructed in appeals to the House of Lords, substantially increasing

costs, and extra time is taken up. This can add to emotional stress and financial hardship for one or both litigants.

- It has failed to make any adequate contribution to development of the criminal law – this point is made by the eminent criminal law specialists JC Smith and Glanville Williams. Unlike the Court of Appeal, the House of Lords has no specialist divisions, and criticisms of the quality of their decisions in criminal appeals may stem from this. Glanville Williams points out that 'It is particularly inapt that a Chancery judge should have the casting vote in the House of Lords in a criminal case, as Lord Cross did in **Hyam**'. He also suggests that the age of judges in the House of Lords is a problem, since old men are 'often fixed in their opinions' and 'tend to ignore the opinions of others'; this may be true, but the judges of the Court of Appeal are hardly in the first flush of youth either.

  Part of the problem may be due to the strict conditions for appealing to the House of Lords, which mean that few criminal cases get there, and the Law Lords actually have very little chance to make notable contributions to this area of law.

- It tends to side with the establishment, and usually the Government. This is the argument advanced by Griffiths (see p. 94), but there is little evidence to suggest that the Court of Appeal would be very different in this respect if it became the highest court.

- The House of Lords offers nothing beyond finality, and that could be more efficiently achieved without it. Jackson, an academic in the field, examined the fifteen appeals made to the House of Lords in 1972, and found that eight involved Government departments or national authorities, and five were disputes between commercial concerns. He deduced that in the case of both Government departments and commercial concerns, the reason for taking the case to the House of Lords was nothing more than the fact that it is the final court.

  In the case of Government departments, where judicial decisions appear to obstruct them, their object is to remove that obstruction; appeal to the House of Lords may achieve this, but if not, the matter can be put right by legislation. However, they must have the final decision of the judiciary before this can happen, and must therefore go to the House of Lords – not because of any innate quality of its decision-making, but simply because it is the final court. Jackson felt that the commercial cases were also likely to be based on the pursuit of finality. If this is correct, abolishing the House of Lords would enable finality to be achieved more quickly and cheaply.

Against abolition

- Its small membership allows the House of Lords to give a consistent leadership that the Court of Appeal, with its much greater number of judges, could not, and therefore to guide the harmonious development of the law. Louis Blom-Cooper QC has argued that, especially since the Practice Direction of 1966, allowing the House of Lords to overrule its own decisions, the House of Lords is in a unique position to be able to reform the law from the top. The much larger size of the Court of Appeal, and its division into different courts means there would always be a danger of different courts within it applying different views of the law.
- The combination of the two appellate courts allows the majority of appeals to be dealt with more quickly than the House of Lords could hope to deal with them, while still retaining the smaller court for those matters which require further consideration, and for promoting consistent development of the law.
- The House of Lords plays a valuable role in correcting decisions by the Court of Appeal – in 1988 it reversed nearly 40 per cent of civil and 33 per cent of criminal appeals that were referred to it.
- It has made some important contributions to the development of our law, including making marital rape a crime, in **R *v* R** (1991), and confirming the restricted scope of parental rights in a modern society in **Gillick** (1985).

JUDICIAL REVIEW

The system of judicial review by the High Court oversees the decisions of public bodies and officials, such as inferior courts (magistrates' and county) and tribunals, local councils, and members of the executive such as police officers and Government ministers. Cases are heard by the Queen's Bench Division.

Judicial review does not examine the merits of the decision, as an appeal does. It can only quash a decision if the public body had no power to make it, known as *ultra vires* (*ultra* is latin for 'beyond' and *vires* is latin for 'powers'). There are two forms of *ultra vires*: procedural *ultra vires* and substantive *ultra vires*.

Procedural *ultra vires*

Where there has been procedural *ultra vires* it is often said that there has been a breach of natural justice. This means either that the body reaching the particular decision complained of was biased, or that the applicant was not given a fair opportunity to be heard.

In **Dimes** *v* **Grand Junction Canal Proprietors** (1852), a dispute about land, Lord Chancellor Cottenham found in favour of the canal company. It was then discovered that he owned several thousands of pounds worth of shares in Grand Junction Canal Proprietors, and the decision was set aside. Note that there is no need to prove that the decision was in fact biased, only that there is a financial interest or some other reason why bias is likely – this is on the grounds that justice must be seen to be done as well as actually be done.

▶ Substantive *ultra vires*

This occurs where the content of the decision was outside the power of the public body that made it. Sometimes legislation may make it clear what the limits on the public body's powers are. Thus the limits on the magistrates' jurisdiction are clearly laid down in legislation. If a magistrates' court decides to hear a case which is indictable only and should therefore have been heard in the Crown Court the magistrates' decision can be ruled *ultra vires* and quashed.

Often, however, the legislation does not lay down clear limits on the public body's powers. For example, the legislation might simply say that the minister can appoint 'who he thinks fit'. If the minister then appoints someone who is totally unqualified for the job, it is very difficult for the court to prove that the minister did not think he was fit for the job. To get round some of the problems caused by broadly drafted powers such as these, the courts are prepared to imply certain limitations on the official's power even where they are not laid down by the relevant legislation.

Wednesbury unreasonable

A decision will be held to be outside the public body's power if it was so unreasonable that no reasonable public body could have reached the decision. This is known as the Wednesbury principle and was laid down in **Associated Picture Houses Ltd** *v* **Wednesbury Corporation** (1948). It will only be used for quashing a decision if that decision was one which no reasonable authority could have made; Lord Diplock described such a decision in **Council of Civil Service Unions** *v* **Minister for the Civil Service** (1984) as 'a decision which is so outrageous in its defiance of logic or of accepted moral standards that no sensible person . . . could have arrived at it'.

A decision cannot be struck out simply because the courts think it was the wrong decision; it can be struck out only if it was so perverse that no reasonable official could have made it.

Irrelevant considerations

If the court concludes that a public body took into account irrelevant considerations then its decision may be quashed. **Secretary of State for Education *v* Tameside Council** (1977) was a House of Lords decision. Under the Education Act 1944 s. 68 it was provided that 'if the Secretary of State is satisfied' that an education authority was proposing to act unreasonably he or she could issue directions to that authority to make them act reasonably. A newly elected Conservative education authority proposed to cancel the previous Labour education authority's plans to abolish the grammar school system and replace it with a comprehensive school system. To do this an 11 plus examination had to be arranged at very late notice to select pupils for the grammar schools. The Secretary of State issued directions that they should not do so. On appeal the House of Lords concluded that he had behaved *ultra vires* because, according to the House, he could only have concluded that the education authority were behaving unreasonably by taking into account irrelevant considerations.

Improper purpose

The idea of a body acting outside its powers has been extended to include abusing those powers by using them for an improper purpose. In **R *v* Derbyshire County Council ex parte The Times Supplements** (1990), *The Times* challenged Derbyshire County Council's decision to withdraw its advertising for educational appointments from *Times* publications, after the *Sunday Times* had printed two articles accusing the council of improper and legally doubtful behaviour. The Divisional Court held that the Council's decision bad been motivated by bad faith and vindictiveness, and was therefore an abuse of power.

Fettered discretion

Where the public body does have a discretion, that is to say a choice, they must exercise that choice. In **British Oxygen Co *v* Board of Trade** (1971) a scheme had been set up where grants towards capital expenditure (the purchase of large pieces of machinery, etc.) could be awarded from the Ministry of Trade at the Ministry's discretion to industry. The Ministry developed a rule that grants would not be given for machinery costing less than £25. The British Oxygen Company had spent over £4 million on gas cylinders which cost £20 each. They applied for a grant to assist with this expenditure and applying this blanket rule the Ministry rejected their application. On appeal the House of Lords concluded that a public body was only allowed to develop such general policies where legislation had given them a general discretion, if they were prepared to listen to arguments for the exercise of individual discretion in particular cases.

Error on the face of the record

Where the decision-making body's own record of the proceedings reveals that it has made a mistake concerning the law, the decision may be quashed.

▶ Remedies

In addition to any of the ordinary civil law remedies of damages, injunction, or declaration, the High Court may order a public law remedy only available through the judicial review proceedings. These remedies are often called prerogative orders, and three such remedies exist.

Certiorari

This order quashes (nullifies) an *ultra vires* decision. For example, it might be used to quash the refusal of a mandatory student grant. It is not available against the Crown, but usually a declaration in that situation will be sufficient.

Mandamus

This is an order to do something, and might be used, for example, to force a local authority to produce its accounts for inspection by a local resident, or to compel a housing tribunal to hear a previously refused appeal. *Mandamus* is not available against the Crown or a Crown servant. Often an applicant will seek both an order of *certiorari* and a *mandamus* order. *Certiorari* could quash an *ultra vires* decision and *mandamus* could compel the public body to decide the case according to their legal powers.

Prohibition

This can order a body not to act unlawfully in the future. Thus while *certiorari* quashes decisions already made, a prohibition prevents a decision being made which, if made, would be subject to a *certiorari* order. For example, it can prohibit an inferior court or tribunal from starting or continuing proceedings which are, or threaten to be, outside their jurisdiction, or in breach of natural justice.

The former Labour leader Michael Foot made an unsuccessful application for a prohibition order in **R *v* Boundary Commission for England ex parte Foot** (1983). He had challenged the recommendations of the Boundary Commission on amendments to the boundaries of electoral constituencies, as he thought they were unjust. His application was rejected.

Discretion

All the prerogative remedies are discretionary, so even if an applicant proves that the public body behaved illegally, the court can still refuse a remedy. This discretion is reflected in s. 31(6) of the 1981 Act. This provides that in deciding whether to grant a remedy the court should take into account whether it would be detrimental to good administration. If an alternative remedy is available such as through the appeals process or a specialized tribunal, the court is unlikely to grant a prerogative order. Examples of other factors that might influence their use of their discretion are consistency with other cases, the nature of the remedy sought, delay, and the motive of the applicant.

▶ Procedure

When the current procedure for judicial review was laid down in 1978, safeguards were included to protect public authorities from unreasonable or frivolous complaints, and prevent abuse of the legal process. The procedure for applications for judicial review are now laid down in s. 31 of the Supreme Court Act 1981 and Order 53 of the Supreme Court Rules.

Time limit

An application should normally be made within three months of the date when the grounds for the application arose. Even where the application is made within three months, if the court concludes that it was not made promptly it may still not be allowed. On the other hand, the court has a discretion to allow applications made outside the three month time limit if there was good reason for the delay.

Leave

Before the case can be heard, leave must be obtained from a single judge in the High Court. To obtain leave the applicants must prove that they have an arguable case. This is quite a low threshold, but the aim is to sift out very weak cases at this early stage to avoid too much unnecessary inconvenience to the administration.

Locus standi

Section 31(3) of the Supreme Court Act 1981 provides that the applicant must have 'a sufficient interest in the matter to which the application relates.' They must therefore have a close connection with the subject of the action. This is known as *locus standi* or standing. Again this rule aims to prevent time being wasted by vexatious litigants or unworthy cases. The issue can be considered both when leave is sought and at the main hearing.

The leading case in the field is **R *v* Inland Revenue Commissioners ex parte National Federation of Self-Employed and Small Businesses** (1982), often called the Fleet Street Casuals case. An application for judicial review had been made by a tax payers' association. They wanted to challenge an agreement that had been made by the Inland Revenue to waive the income tax arrears for 6,000 freelance workers in the newspaper printing industry based at the time in Fleet Street, if they declared their earnings fully in the future. The House of Lords held that they lacked *locus standi*. In deciding whether there was *locus standi* the merits of the case could be taken into account and the case had no merit as the Inland Revenue had no duty to collect every penny of tax due. The tax payers' association did not have a sufficient interest in other tax payers' affairs.

Since that case the concept of *locus standi* has been broadened to include some interest and pressure groups. The Attorney-General always has *locus standi*. If a party has failed to prove *locus standi* the Attorney-General can choose to permit the action through a proceeding known as a 'relator action'. Under this mechanism the action officially proceeds under the Attorney-General's name.

There is only limited discovery of documents and cross-examination is only allowed in certain circumstances.

Where an application for judicial review is refused by the Divisional Court, application may be made to the Court of Appeal, which, if it accepts that the case should be heard, may refer it back to the Divisional Court, or conduct the hearing itself. Decisions made in judicial review may be appealed to the Court of Appeal, and from there to the House of Lords.

Criticisms of judicial review

Problems with control of wide discretionary powers

While the courts have been prepared to imply certain limits to apparently broad discretionary powers of public bodies, it is still very difficult for such powers to be controlled. The Housing Act 1980, for example, empowers the Secretary of State for the Environment to 'do all such things as appear to him necessary or expedient' to enable council tenants to buy their council houses. In 1982 the then Secretary of State decided that this allowed him to take the sale of council houses out of the hands of local authorities who were not proceeding with such sales as quickly as he wished, and in **R *v* Secretary of State for the Environment**

ex parte Norwich City Council (1982), the courts had to agree. The powers granted were so wide that very little could be considered *ultra vires*.

Strictness of 'Wednesbury principles'

As Geoffrey Robertson points out in his book *Freedom, the Individual and the Law*, the very narrow test of unreasonableness severely limits the court's power to supervise the executive. An example of this was the Campaign for Nuclear Disarmament's failure to get a blanket ban on marches in the central London area revoked. The decision was taken by the Home Secretary, who has power to ban such marches, on the advice of the Metropolitan Police Commissioner. The courts agreed that the reasons for the ban (which was not aimed at CND) were meagre, and accepted that CND demonstrations were commonly and peacefully held, and that the right to demonstrate on matters of public concern was a fundamental civil right. However it declined to quash the ban; as Robertson points out, to do so under the Wednesbury principles would effectively mean that the court would have to find that the Home Secretary had taken leave of his senses in making the decision.

From time to time the courts have toyed with the idea of adopting the principle of proportionality as a ground for judicial review. This principle, which is recognized by the administrative law of many European countries, would allow a decision to be struck down on the grounds that although not irrational on *Wednesbury* terms, it is out of proportion to the benefit it seeks to obtain, or the harm it wishes to avoid – in other words, where a sledgehammer is being use to crack a nut. Clearly this would be a wider test than *Wednesbury* principles, and could lead to more decisions being struck down.

The idea of proportionality as a criteria for judicial review has been mentioned in **Council of Civil Service Unions** *v* **Minister for the Civil Service** (1984), and **Brind** *v* **Secretary of State for the Home Department** (1991), where journalists unsuccessfully sought to challenge the Home Secretary's ban on broadcasting direct interviews with members of the IRA and other Northern Ireland groups. In both cases the courts felt it was not open to them to accept it as a criteria at the time, but indicated that case-by-case development might eventually bring it into consideration.

Political nature of decisions

The nature of cases brought under judicial review means they inevitably become political at times. Critics, notably Griffiths, have noted that the judiciary seem more reluctant to interfere in decisions made by the executive where the executive concerned is a Conservative one. Cases such as **Secretary of State for Education** *v* **Tameside Council** and **R** *v* **Boundary Commission for England ex parte Foot** mentioned at p. 316 and p. 317 respectively, would support this argument.

Restrictions on applications

The procedural limitations on applications for judicial review can be seen as necessary to safeguard good administration from unnecessary distractions, vexatious litigants, and busybodies. One of the advantages of the judicial review procedure is that it is relatively quick and if the volume of cases were increased this would cease to be true. On the other hand, they can also be seen as ways to discourage ordinary people from seeking to challenge Government or other authorities. There is no leave requirement for ordinary civil proceedings. It could be argued that the current time limits are too short and the courts' discretion is too vague so that sometimes justice is not done.

The concept of national security

Some have criticized the use of the concept of national security to inhibit judicial review of Government decisions. In **Council of Civil Service Unions** *v* **Minister for the Civil Service**, the Civil Service union challenged the Government's decision to ban employees of Government Communications Headquarters (GCHQ, the Government intelligence centre, which monitors communications from abroad and ensures security for UK military and official communications) from membership of trade unions. The Divisional Court upheld the complaint on the grounds that the decision had been made unfairly, since the unions had not even been consulted. On appeal, the Government argued that its decision had been motivated by considerations of national security, because the centre had been disrupted by industrial action some years earlier. Despite the fact that this argument had not been advanced in the initial proceedings, and that a no-strike agreement was offered by the union, the House of Lords overturned the original decision and upheld the ban. The Government was not required to prove that the ban was necessary, or even justifiable, in the interests of security, only that the decision had been motivated by national security concerns.

Similarly, in **R** *v* **Secretary of State for Home Affairs ex parte Hosenball** (1977), Mark Hosenball, an American journalist, was made the subject of a deportation order on the grounds that his presence in the UK was not conductive to the public good. He challenged the order on the grounds that he had been given no details of the case against him, and therefore the rules of natural justice had not been followed. The Court of Appeal held that although the proceedings had been unjust, the rules of natural justice were not to be applied to deportation decisions made on grounds of national security.

As Geoffrey Robertson points out, where national security is invoked, the courts are reluctant to assess the strength of evidence presented, even to assert whether decisions made on such grounds were made rationally. He alleges that so long as there appears to be some evidence of national security concerns, however slight or dubious, or contradictory, the courts will take a 'hands-off' approach. Obviously this problem occurs in only a minority of cases, but as the above examples show, they may be those which affect fundamental civil liberties.

ANSWERING QUESTIONS

1 Assess the likely impact of the Criminal Cases Review Commission.
This is a very topical area, and therefore one which you would be wise to study carefully. You could start your essay by stating what the Commission is, and looking at the reasons for its creation – what were the problems with criminal appeals? You could mention the role that these problems played in the well-known miscarriages of justice – these are highlighted in the section on criticisms in this chapter, while the stories of some of the miscarriages of justice are told in more detail in chapter 9.

Then move on to look in detail at the Commission itself; its membership, function and powers. One of the points you might want to make is that it is not an appeal court as such, but can merely refer cases for appeal, and that it replaces the old s. 17 procedure under which the Home Secretary referred cases back to appeal. You are asked to assess its likely impact; this essentially means considering how far it will solve the problems it was set up to address. In answering this, you should highlight ways in which it is an improvement on the previous situation – the problems with the s. 17 procedure are relevant here for example – and also any criticisms which can be made of it.

2 Harriet has been injured in a road traffic accident caused by Angela's negligence and wishes to claim damages for pain and suffering.
(a) Advise Harriet as to where and how she should start civil proceedings against Angela;
(b) If she is dissatisfied with the result of her case what appeals are open to her?
(c) To what extent have the changes in jurisdiction under the Courts and Legal Services Act 1990 improved the Court as a forum for personal injury disputes?
Part (a) is dealt with in detail in the chapter on the civil justice system, but in brief, the relevant court for Harriet to start her action will primarily depend on the value of her claim and the complexity of the case. As we are not given

details you can only conclude that it might either be the county court or the High Court, and say how the decision would be made.

As regards part (b), appeals from both the county court and the High Court are taken to the Court of Appeal. You could mention that the Court of Appeal does not hear all the evidence again, so is generally reluctant to overturn a trial judge's finding of fact; therefore Harriet is more likely to be successful if her appeal is based on an issue of law rather than fact. Further appeals can be made to the House of Lords, though leave is required. You should also discuss the special 'leap frog' procedure and the requirements that have to be satisfied in order to use that procedure.

The details required to answer part (c) are contained in the chapter on the civil justice system.

15

Ombudsmen

The rights and duties of the state, and the limits of its powers over individuals form what is called administrative law. In some countries, such as France, this forms a comprehensive branch of law, with its own courts and case law. In this country however, such issues are dealt with by various unrelated systems, the most important being administrative tribunals and judicial review (discussed on pp. 290 and 314), and the two ombudsmen empowered to investigate complaints against central and local government respectively.

The Parliamentary Commissioner for Administration and Health Service Commissioner

The Parliamentary Commissioner Act 1967 established the office of Parliamentary Commissioner for Administration, popularly called the Ombudsman. He or she is appointed by the Crown (on the advice of the Prime Minister), and remains in office until reaching the age of 65. No qualifications for the position are specified, and the office has been held by lawyers and civil servants. His or her role is to investigate complaints by individuals who claim to have suffered injustice as a result of maladministration by Government departments. Following the Courts and Legal Services Act 1990 jurisdiction has been extended to be able to look at complaints of maladministration by administrative staff of courts and tribunals, but does not include the judiciary or tribunal members.

Examples of the kind of complaints dealt with include general inattention or delay; rudeness, bias, discrimination or inconsistency; misleading or inaccurate advice; or failure to follow, or properly follow, administrative rules or procedures. Around 1,000 complaints are dealt with every year, with around 90 per cent proving wholly or partly justified.

The Ombudsman will not consider complaints if alternative remedies exist through courts or administrative tribunals, unless it is unreasonable to expect the complainant to use these, and may not deal with complaints concerning any of the following matters:

- nationalized industries;
- relations with other Governments or international organizations;
- actions taken by Crown officials outside the UK;
- the administration of governments of the dependencies;
- extradition proceedings;
- investigation of crime;
- security of the state;
- contractual or commercial transactions by Government departments (other than those relating to compulsory purchase of land);
- conduct of legal proceedings, whether civil or criminal;
- conditions of service in the Civil Service or Armed Forces;
- granting of awards, honours and royal charters.

The Ombudsman cannot act on his or her own initiative, not even on a complaint direct from a citizen. Complaints must initially be made, in writing, to an MP, who can refer them to the Ombudsman. On receiving a complaint the Ombudsman assesses whether it is within his jurisdiction, and if so, conducts a private investigation, giving the head of the relevant department the opportunity to comment on the allegations. He has full powers to examine departmental documents (though not Cabinet papers) and take written or oral evidence, and wilful obstruction of an investigation is punishable as if it were contempt of court. Under the Act of 1967 the Parliamentary Commissioner has a discretion whether to investigate a complaint or not. It was held in **R** *v* **Parliamentary Commissioner ex parte Dyer** (1994) that the exercise of this discretion could be controlled by judicial review.

The results of an investigation are reported to the MP who referred the complaint, and to the heads of the departments concerned, and the Ombudsman may request that the causes of any injustice be put right, but has no power to alter administrative decisions. The Ombudsman reports annually to Parliament, and may in this report draw attention to any problems that have been revealed and not remedied by the department concerned. These are then considered by a House of Commons Committee.

The **Sachsenhausen** case was the first occasion on which the Commissioner found a department to be seriously at fault. Under the Anglo-German Agreement of 1964 the German Government provided £1 million to compensate UK citizens who suffered from Nazi persecution during the Second World War. Its distribution was at the discretion of the British Government. The UK Foreign Secretary approved rules for its distribution, and under these rules twelve people who had been detained in the Sachsenhausen concentration camp were refused compensation. The Commissioner investigated their case and found that there were serious defects in the Foreign Office's procedures. By this time all of the £1 million had been distributed. The Foreign Secretary maintained that the decisions were correct but nonetheless made an additional £25,000 available in order that the claimants might receive the same rate of compensation as successful claimants on the fund.

The most elaborate investigation ever undertaken by the Ombudsman concerned the Barlow Clowes affair, which 159 MPs had referred to him. The Barlow Clowes investment business had collapsed in 1988, leaving millions of pounds owing to investors, many of whom were elderly persons of modest means. The Department of Trade and Industry had licensed the business under the Prevention of Fraud (Investments) Act 1958 (since repealed), despite indications that the business was not properly conducted. The Parliamentary Commissioner found that there had been maladministration on the part of civil servants. The Government rejected the findings of maladministration, but nonetheless undertook *ex gratia* to provide £150 million to compensate investors for up to 90 per cent of their loss. An action in negligence against the DTI would almost certainly have failed (because the investors would have been owed no duty of care).

▶ Commissioners for Local Administration

This office was established under the 1974 Local Government Act, and deals with the same sort of complaints as the Parliamentary Commissioner, but with regard to local authorities, including planning boards and police authorities. Local commissioners will not deal with complaints on the following:

- anything that affects all or most of the local inhabitants (such as the size of its Council Tax);
- conduct of court proceedings;
- investigation or prevention of crime;
- conduct of police officers;
- personnel matters;
- internal affairs of schools and colleges;
- contractual and commercial transactions (unless relating to land);
- public transport;
- docks and harbours;
- industrial establishments and markets.

The relevant authority must have been given a chance to solve the problem before a complaint is accepted, and complaints must usually be referred by a local councillor. The Commissioners consider whether it is within their jurisdiction, then investigate, and finally send a report to the authority, which must be available to the public for at least three weeks. Like the Parliamentary Commissioner, Local Commissioners cannot interfere with a decision, only make a report – which the local authority is under no obligation to heed. If they do not, the Commissioners may make further reports, which, especially if given press coverage, may well be persuasive. There are however no provisions for enforcing recommendations if a council is really obstinate.

Miscellaneous ombudsmen

In recent times more specialist ombudsmen have been created. In 1994 a Prison Ombudsman was created. The Courts and Legal Services Act 1990 created the office of Legal Ombudsman whose function is to help people who have a genuine cause for complaint against members of the legal profession but have not been able to find an alternative remedy. He or she can investigate the handling of complaints by the Law Society, the Bar and the Council for Licensed Conveyancers, reinvestigate complaints and recommend remedies including the payment of compensation, and reports annually to the Lord Chancellor and Parliament. The 1990 Act also created a Conveyancing Ombudsman. The Pension Schemes Act 1993 provides for a Pensions Ombudsman to adjudicate disputes concerning pension schemes. There is now a European Ombudsman under a new Article 138e of the EEC Treaty, appointed by the European Parliament to investigate maladministration by Community institutions including the non-judicial functions of the EC courts. He or she can be approached directly or through an MEP, or may carry out an investigation on his or her own initiative. The European Ombudsman holds office for the duration of the Parliament and can only be dismissed by the European Court at the request of Parliament.

Strengths of Parliamentary and Local Commissioners

- The Parliamentary Commissioner in particular can help the ordinary citizen penetrate the maze of secrecy in which Government departments habitually conduct their business.
- Both Commissioners can draw attention to problems. This can be very persuasive, especially in investigations conducted by local commissioners where the local press take up the story.
- They both provide some means of redress when other avenues fail. The Parliamentary Commissioner has been known to persuade the Inland Revenue to modify or waive tax demands which, while legal, are likely to cause major hardship, and in the **Sachsenhausen** case, uncovered maladministration in the Foreign Office's dealings with compensation claims by former prisoners of war.
- Their services are free.

▌Weaknesses of Parliamentary and Local Commissioners

- Neither has the power to change decisions and practices, or to compel redress of grievances. Local councils have fairly frequently ignored the recommendations of Local Commissioners.
- They can only deal with maladministration, which means they have no way of questioning a decision taken in accordance with proper procedures, even if the decision itself seems unfair or wrong.
- Both have a long list of areas with which they will not deal, which include some areas of potential concern for citizens.
- Neither will handle complaints submitted directly from citizens, and complainants must therefore find a sympathetic MP or counsellor, who must then find time to look at the complaint, before the process can even start. This seems an unneccessary waste of everybody's time, and may prevent problems from being dealt with. The current Parliamentary Commissioner, William Reid, has said that he would prefer to be able to receive complaints directly, after pointing out that 150 MPs, almost a quarter of the House, have not referred a single complaint from their constituents; either their constituents are unusually content, or the complaints are not getting through.
- Complaints can take a long time to deal with – around a year is usual for complaints to the Parliamentary Commissioner.
- The services of the ombudsmen are not well publicized – even the literature of Community Health Councils gives the addresses of Local Commissioners for complaints about the NHS, which should go to the Parliamentary Commissioner.

▌Reform

Lord Woolf in his interim report on the civil justice system has recommended that the retail sector should be encouraged to develop private ombudsman schemes to cover consumer complaints similar to those which now exist in relation to service industries. He has also suggested that the relationship between ombudsmen and the courts should be broadened, enabling issues to be referred by the ombudsman to the courts and the courts to the ombudsmen with the consent of those involved.

ANSWERING QUESTIONS

Ombudsmen rarely merit an examination question in their own right, but they are often relevant to answering general questions about the remedies available if, for example, a person's civil liberties have been breached.

16
Alternative methods of dispute resolution

Court hearings are not always the best methods of resolving a dispute, and their disadvantages mean that for some types of problem, alternative mechanisms may be more suitable. The main uses of these at present are in family, consumer, commercial and employment cases, but proposals put forward by Lord Woolf, in his review of the civil justice system, suggest that these alternative mechanisms should play a more important role in solving civil disputes.

▶ Problems with court hearings

The adversarial process

A trial necessarily involves a winner and a loser, and the adversarial procedure combined with the often aggressive atmosphere of court proceedings divides the parties, making them end up enemies even where they did not start out that way. This can be a disadvantage where there is some reason for the parties to sustain a relationship after the problem under discussion is sorted out – child custody cases are the obvious example, but in business too, there may be advantages in resolving a dispute in a way which does not make enemies of the parties. The court system is often said to be best suited to areas where the parties are strangers and happy to remain so – it is interesting to note that in small-scale societies with close kinship links, court-type procedures are rarely used, and disputes are usually settled by negotiation processes that aim to satisfy both parties, and thus maintain the harmony of the group.

Technical cases

Some types of dispute rest on detailed technical points, such as the way in which a machine should be made, or the details of a medical problem, rather than on points of law. The significance of such technical details may not be readily understandable by an ordinary judge. Expert witnesses or advisors may be brought in to advise on these points, but this

329

takes time, and so raises costs. Where detailed technical evidence is at issue, alternative methods of dispute resolution can employ experts in a particular field to take the place of a judge.

Inflexibility

In a court hearing, the rules of procedure lay down a fixed framework for the way in which problems are addressed. This may be inappropriate in areas which are of largely private concern to the parties involved. Alternative methods can allow the parties themselves to take more control of the process.

Imposed solutions

Court hearings impose a solution on the parties, which since it does not involve their consent, may need to be enforced. If the parties are able to negotiate a settlement between them, to which they both agree, this should be less of a problem.

Publicity

The majority of court hearings are public. This may be undesirable in some business disputes, where one or both of the parties may prefer not to make public the details of their financial situation or business practices because of competition.

ALTERNATIVE DISPUTE RESOLUTION MECHANISMS

Where, for one or more of the reasons explained above, court action is not the best way of solving a dispute, a range of alternative methods of dispute resolution may be used. One of the simplest is of course informal negotiation between the parties themselves, with or without the help of lawyers – the high number of civil cases settled out of court are examples of this. Formal schemes include the Advisory, Conciliation and Arbitration Service (ACAS) which mediates in many industrial disputes and unfair dismissal cases; the role of ombudsmen in dealing with disputes in the fields of insurance and banking, and in complaints against central and local government and public services; the pre-hearing arbitration sometimes used in the Small Claims Court; the work done by trade organizations such as the Association of British Travel Agents (ABTA) in settling consumer complaints; inquiries into such areas as objections concerning compulsory purchase or town and country planning; the conciliation schemes offered by courts and voluntary organizations to divorcing couples; and the arbitration schemes run by the Institute of Arbitrators for business disputes. We will look at some of these in more detail below. Though procedural details vary widely, what they all have in common is that they are attempting to provide a method of settling disagreements that avoids some or all of the disadvantages listed above.

▶ Conciliation in unfair dismissal cases

A statutory conciliation scheme administered by ACAS operates before cases of unfair dismissal can be taken to an Industrial Tribunal. ACAS conciliation officers talk to both sides with the aim of settling the dispute without a tribunal hearing; they are supposed to procure reinstatement of the employee where possible, but in practice most settlements are only for damages.

A conciliation officer contacts each party or their representatives to discuss the case and advise each side on the strength or weakness of their case. They may tell each side what the other has said, but if the case does eventually go to a tribunal, none of this information is admissible without the consent of the party who gave it.

Evaluation
The success of the scheme is sometimes measured by the fact that two-thirds of cases are either withdrawn or settled by the conciliation process. However, this ignores the imbalance in power between the employer and the employee, especially where the employee has no legal representation – the fact that there has been a settlement does not necessarily mean it is a fair one, when one party is under far more pressure to agree than the other. Dickens's 1985 study of unfair dismissal cases found that awards after a hearing were generally higher than those achieved by conciliation, implying that employees may feel under pressure to agree to any settlement. The study suggested that the scheme would be more effective in promoting fair settlements – rather than settlement at any price – if conciliation officers had a less neutral stance and instead tried to help enforce the worker's rights.

▶ Mediation in divorce cases

In many ways, the court system is an undesirable forum for divorce and its attendant disputes over property and custody, since the adversarial nature of the system can aggravate the differences between the parties. This makes the whole process more traumatic for both parties, and clearly is especially harmful if there are children involved, since the couple will usually have to maintain some kind of contact after divorce. Consequently conciliation has for some time been made available to divorcing couples, not necessarily to get them back together (though this can happen), but to try to ensure that any arrangements between them can be made as amicably as possible, reducing the strain on the parties themselves as well as their children.

In 1995, the Lord Chancellor announced changes to the divorce laws which place more emphasis on mediation. There will be a compulsory year-long 'pause for reflection' before a divorce can be obtained, and couples will be required to attend an information session, explaining the implications of divorce. Further voluntary mediation to resolve property and child access arrangements will be available, and it is intended that couples should iron out these issues before coming to court. Legal aid will be unavailable for divorcing couples, unless they can show some clear reason why they need to consult a lawyer rather than a mediation service.

Evaluation

It is too early to assess the impact of the new reforms, but in divorce cases generally, success depends on the parties themselves and their willingness to cooperate. The parties may find that meeting in a neutral environment, with the help of an experienced, impartial professional helps them communicate calmly, and can make the process of divorce less painful for the couple and their children, by avoiding the need for a court battle in which each feels obliged to accuse the other of being unfit to look after their children – a battle which can be as expensive as it is unpleasant, at a time when one or both parties may be under considerable financial strain.

A three year study undertaken as a pilot scheme for the new reforms found that eight out of ten couples reached agreement on some issues through mediation, and four in ten reached a complete settlement. However, the Solicitors' Family Law Association point out that because men are usually the main earners in a family, and women's earning abilities may be limited by the demands of childcare, women may need lawyers to get a fair deal financially; in fact the SFLA says the reforms may well turn out to be 'A rogue's charter for unscrupulous husbands'.

▶ Trade association arbitration schemes

The Fair Trading Act 1973 provides that the Director-General of Fair Trading has a duty to promote codes of practice for trade associations, which include arrangements for handling complaints. So far, more than twenty codes have received approval from the Office of Fair Trading (OFT), and there are many other voluntary schemes not yet approved. Many include provisions for an initial conciliation procedure between consumers and retailers or suppliers in case of complaints, often followed by independent arbitration if conciliation fails.

One of the best-known examples is that set up by the Association of British Travel Agents (ABTA), which in the case of disputes between tour operators and consumers, offers impartial conciliation. If this fails, disputes may be referred to a special arbitration scheme – about half of all claims referred to it succeed, though not always winning the amount originally claimed.

A less well-known scheme is that run by the footwear industry, which offers an independent testing scheme for complaints involving faulty footwear. Where a retailer disputes that the product is faulty – blaming damage on inappropriate use by the consumer for example – an expert opinion can be obtained from the independent Footwear Testing Centre in Kettering. A small test fee is shared by retailer and consumer, with the consumer's share (as well as the cost of the shoes) refunded if testing proves the complaint.

Evaluation

The best of the schemes offer quick, simple dispute resolution procedures, but standards do vary – the National Consumer Council has reported that some are very slow, and there is some concern about the impartiality of arbitrators. These problems could be addressed relatively easily, but the main drawback is the diversity of the codes, and widespread ignorance of their existence, not only among consumers but even among some of the retailers covered by them! Tighter controls by the OFT and better publicity could make them much more useful mechanisms.

▶ Commercial arbitration

Many commercial contracts contain an arbitration agreement, requiring any dispute to be referred to arbitration before any court proceedings are undertaken – the aim being to do away with the need for going to court. Where such an agreement exists, if one party starts court proceedings without having tried arbitration, the other may apply to the court to stop the action.

Arbitrators usually have some expertise in the relevant field, and lists of suitable individuals are kept by the Institute of Arbitration. The parties themselves choose their arbitrator, ensuring that the person has the necessary expertise in their area and is not connected to either of them. Once appointed, the arbitrator is required to act in an impartial, judicial manner just as a judge would, but the difference is that they will not usually need to have technical points explained to them, so there is less need for expert witnesses.

Disputes may involve disagreement over the quality of goods supplied, interpretation of a trade clause or point of law, or a mixture of the two. Where points of law are involved the arbitrator may be a lawyer.

Under the Arbitration Act 1950, hearings must be conducted in a judicial manner, in accordance with the rules of natural justice, but proceedings are informal and held in private, with the time and place decided by the parties. The arbitrator's decision, known as the award, is often delivered immediately, and is as binding on the parties as a High Court judgment would be, and if necessary can be enforced as one.

The award is usually to be considered as final, but appeal may be made to the High Court on a question of law, with the consent of all the parties, or leave from the Court. Leave will only be given if determination of the question could substantially affect the rights of one of the parties, and provided (with some exceptions) that they had not initially agreed to restrict rights of appeal. The High Court may confirm, vary or reverse the award, or send it back to the arbitrator for reconsideration.

Evaluation

Arbitration fees can be high, but for companies this may be outweighed by the money they save through being able to get the problem solved as soon as it arises, rather than having to wait months for a court hearing. The arbitration hearing itself tends to be quicker than a court case, because of the expertise of the arbitrator – in a court hearing time and therefore money can be wasted in explanation of technical points to the judge.

The ability of the parties to choose their arbitrator promotes mutual trust in and respect for the decision, and arbitration is conducted with a view to compromise rather than combat, which avoids destroying the business relationship between the parties. Privacy ensures that business secrets are not made known to competitors. Around 10,000 commercial cases a year go to arbitration, which tends to suggest that business people are happy with the system.

▶ Advantages of alternative methods of dispute resolution

Cost

Many procedures try to work without any need for legal representation, and even those that do involve lawyers may be quicker and therefore cheaper than going to court. However, concerns have been expressed that a bigger role for alternative dispute mechanisms, as suggested by Lord Woolf, could simply be a way of solving disputes cheaply, offering a form of second-class justice.

Accessibility

Alternative methods tend to be more informal than court procedures, without complicated rules of evidence.

Speed

The delays in the civil court system are well known, and waiting for a case to come to court may, especially in commercial cases, add considerably to the overall cost, and adversely affect business.

Expertise

Those who run alternative dispute resolution schemes often have specialist knowledge of the relevant areas, which can promote a fairer as well as a quicker settlement.

Conciliation of the parties

Most alternative methods of dispute resolution aim to avoid irrevocably dividing the parties, so enabling business or family relationships to be maintained.

▶ Disadvantages of alternative methods of dispute resolution

Imbalances of power

As the unfair dismissal conciliation scheme shows, the benefits of voluntarily negotiating agreement may be undermined where there is a serious imbalance of power between the parties – in effect, one party is acting less voluntarily than the other.

Lack of legal expertise

Where a dispute hinges on difficult points of law, an arbitrator may not have the required legal expertise to judge.

No system of precedent

There is no doctrine of precedent, and each case is judged on its merits, providing no real guidelines for future cases.

No legal aid

Legal aid is not available for any of the alternative methods of dispute resolution.

Enforceability

Decisions not made by courts may be difficult to enforce.

▶ Lord Woolf's proposals

Lord Woolf, in his review of the civil justice system, has given his support to alternative dispute resolution. He thinks that developments abroad, particularly those in the USA, Australia and Canada in relation to ADR should be monitored. He suggests that consideration should be given to making legal aid available to fund voluntary organizations providing mediation services. Where there is a satisfactory alternative to the court system then the courts should encourage parties to use that alternative. To this end court staff and the judiciary should make themselves more aware of the ADR facilities that exist. Parties would be required to state at preliminary court hearings whether the question of ADR had been discussed and, if not, why not. Finally, a court would be able to penalize a party for unreasonably refusing to attempt ADR.

· ·
ANSWERING QUESTIONS

1 Do the courts provide the best means of solving disputes?
Your introduction might mention the fact that although courts are accepted as a means of resolving disputes, there are some types of dispute where they are not helpful, and so other methods of dispute resolution have developed. You can then examine the disadvantages of courts as means of dispute resolution, and then relate these disadvantages to the types of dispute where courts have not been found to offer the best solution.

You could then go through the four types of alternative dispute resolution we have examined, pointing out why they have advantages over the court system for those types of dispute. In this essay you could also look at tribunals (see chapter 13), and examine how and why they provide a useful alternative to courts.

You might then discuss some of the disadvantages of alternative methods of dispute resolution, pointing out the kinds of case for which these disadvantages might make them unsuitable. Your conclusion might simply point out that courts may provide the best way of solving some disputes, but be unhelpful in others.

2 'Courts and tribunals do not provide the only means of resolving disputes'. What other existing methods provide alternatives? How satisfactory are they? *London*
This question uses much the same material as the previous one, but you are required to evaluate the alternative methods of dispute resolution. Also note that you could not bring tribunals into this answer.

17 The administration of justice

Our legal system is currently administered by a range of Government departments, with the Lord Chancellor's Department (LCD) and the Home Office taking the most important roles. The LCD has responsibility for the appointment of judges, judicial salaries and the disciplining of the lower judiciary. It also administers the courts and oversees legal aid and advice, and has some responsibility for law reform. The Home Office is responsible for the police, national security, reform of the criminal law, prisons, immigration, elections and civil rights.

There is also a small Law Officers' Department. The Law Officers are the Attorney-General and the Solicitor-General, who are both ministers, though not members of the Cabinet. The Attorney-General is the Government's main legal adviser, and is responsible for major domestic and international litigation involving the Government. Other functions of the post include giving consent to certain categories of prosecution, granting immunities from prosecution, and terminating prosecutions where appropriate, through a process known as *nolle prosequi*. The Director of Public Prosecutions answers to the Attorney-General in relation to the running of the Crown Prosecution Service. The Solicitor-General carries out such functions as the Attorney-General delegates to that office.

In addition, ministers from other departments play a role in legal matters through their responsibility for law reform in their particular area. There is therefore no single minister with responsibility for legal affairs, but a range of ministers who might be involved at any one time.

This situation has been subject to a number of criticisms. First, the division of most of the important legal work between the Home Office and the LCD seems illogical. Why should two different departments each play a leading role in the same area?

Secondly, the role of the Home Office gives rise to a potential conflict of interests, given that it is responsible both for protecting civil liberties, and for maintaining public order. Since public order requirements frequently clash with those of civil liberties, it is a tall order to ask one department to balance the two, and chances are that one or other will suffer – especially if, as over the past decade or so, the Government has been elected with 'law and order' highlighted in its manifesto. In such situations there is little political advantage for the Home Secretary who argues for the enlargement of civil rights, and since such enlargement is often inconvenient for governments, the temptation is to give much less attention to this aspect of the department's job.

A further problem is that legal matters may be easily ignored when the Government is unenthusiastic about them, since there is no single minister who can be pressurized in Parliament. An example is the issue of funding for law centres. While the Department of the Environment has given grants to set up centres, their continued funding appears not to be the responsibility of any department, and so they have been forced to rely on local authorities – themselves under severe financial restraints – and any other sources of funding they can drum up themselves. The Lord Chancellor's Advisory Committee on Legal Aid has described the lack of clear ministerial responsibility for legal services in general as a chronic problem, and has criticized the Government's failure to decide on future funding for law centres.

The position of the Lord Chancellor has caused particular concern. Despite being the minister at the head of the LCD, the Lord Chancellor does not sit in the House of Commons, but is the Speaker of the House of Lords. This means that MPs are not able to ask direct questions in the House of Commons about the work of the LCD, and limits the department's democratic accountability. In addition, neither the LCD nor the Law Officers' Department are subject to the select committee system, which is another way in which MPs can question the running of departments. Instead, the Attorney-General takes parliamentary questions every four weeks or so, including questions about the LCD. However, in most cases such questions are merely referred back to the Lord Chancellor, rather than being answered by the Attorney-General, and replies are not always forthcoming after such referrals.

It is sometimes claimed that the Lord Chancellor is accountable through the House of Lords, but while such accountability may be possible in theory, in practice it is fake. For example, during Lord Hailsham's Chancellorship there were incidents such as the removal of a circuit judge in 1983, and refusals to renew temporary judicial posts, which would certainly have provoked challenges to a minister sitting in the House of Commons. Yet, despite many opportunities for peers to inquire into these matters, and other issues relating to the judiciary, there were no questions or debate in the Lords about any of these issues.

This overall lack of accountability is important not only because of the importance of the issues with which the LCD deals, but also because it is responsible for spending a great deal of public money.

▶ A Ministry of Justice?

The situation described above is unusual in countries with a developed legal system, most of which have a Ministry of Justice to take responsibility for the legal matters which in Britain are spread over many different departments. Given the criticisms detailed above, and the problems listed in the chapter on law reform (which also suffers from the lack of a specific department), it has frequently been suggested that England should introduce such a ministry.

If this were to take place – and at the last General Election the main opposition parties appeared to be in favour of some kind of reform in this direction – there is some debate as to what form the new ministry should take.

The simplest option would be to merge the Home Office and the LCD. However, this would produce a huge department which might be too large to work efficiently, and it would not avoid the problem of concentrating the functions of public order and protection of civil liberties in the same department.

A leading public law expert, Rodney Brazier, has argued that we should keep two separate ministries, by retaining the Home Office and substituting a new Law Department (simply another name for a Ministry of Justice) for the LCD, but dividing functions between them logically, with the Law Department responsible for all issues of law reform, administration of the courts and protection of civil liberties.

Opponents of a Ministry of Justice argue that the political pressure a minister in the House of Commons would be under would endanger the independence of the judiciary, which should be completely free of political involvement. This fear seems to be somewhat overcautious, given that the vast majority of the work done by a Ministry of Justice (like that done by the LCD now) has nothing to do with matters of judicial service – and as Brazier points out, the current system does not avoid the danger of political decisions being made in relation to judges, since the Lord Chancellor is both head of the judiciary and a member of the Government. If there is a choice to be made between political decisions based on pressure from Government, or political decisions based on pressure from Parliament, the second would seem to be the more attractive option. In any case, the problem could be avoided – and the present system improved on – if, as Brazier suggests, the creation of a Ministry of Justice was accompanied by a new Judicial Service Commission, responsible for judicial appointments, promotions and the disciplining of judges. It would not be a ministry and would therefore avoid problems of political patronage.

Another possibility would be to have one large Ministry of Justice, with a minister in the House of Commons, and in addition, keep the Lord Chancellor's responsibility for the judiciary and his function as Speaker of the House of Lords. In such a situation the Lord Chancellor could cease to be a party politician and a member of the Cabinet, and so remove the problem of political pressure altogether.

A small scale reform was proposed by the Royal Commission on Legal Services in 1979, which noted the heavy workload of the Lord Chancellor and suggested that the Prime Minister appoint a junior minister in the

House of Commons to help with the administrative and parliamentary work. This suggestion has not been taken up.

. . . .

ANSWERING QUESTIONS

1 Would the English legal system be improved by the creation of a Ministry of Justice?

Your answer could start by briefly describing what a Ministry of Justice is, and pointing out that most other countries have one. You could then explain how the normal functions of such a Ministry are distributed in this country, and detail the criticisms of this system. You can go on to describe the possible forms a Ministry of Justice might take in this country, and point out the objections to it. Your conclusion should state, drawing on the points you have made, whether you think such a reform would be justified.

18 Introduction to civil liberties

In democratic societies, it is usually felt that there are certain basic rights – often called civil liberties, civil rights or human rights – which should be available to everyone. Exactly what these rights are vary in different legal systems, but they generally include such freedoms as the right to say, think and believe what you like (freedom of expression, thought and conscience), to form groups with others, such as trade unions and pressure groups (freedom of assembly), to protest peacefully, and to be imprisoned or otherwise punished only for breaking the law, and after a fair trial. Part of the reason why these freedoms are considered important is the nature of democracy; citizens can only make the kind of free choice of government required by a democratic system if they can discuss and debate freely.

Most democratic countries have a written Bill of Rights, which lays down the rights which, by law, can be enjoyed by citizens of that country. These rights have to be respected by the courts, Parliament, the police and private citizens, unless the Bill of Rights allows otherwise (for example, some rights may be suspended in times of war or national emergency, or where it is necessary in the interests of national security). Such a Bill may form part of a written constitution or sit alongside such a constitution; either way, like a constitution it will usually have a status which is superior to that of ordinary law, in that it can only be changed by a special procedure. This will vary from country to country, but might involve holding a referendum, or securing a larger than usual majority in Parliament. Legislation which is protected in this way is said to be entrenched.

Britain is unusual among democratic countries in having neither a Bill of Rights nor a written constitution. In this country, our rights and freedoms are traditionally considered to be protected by a presumption that we are free to do whatever is not specifically forbidden by either legislation or the common law. Anyone prevented by the state from doing something which they are legally free to do should have a remedy against the state – an example is that anyone wrongly kept in custody by the police can sue for false imprisonment. Citizens' rights in the UK may be said to be residual, in that they consist of what is left after taking into account the lawful limitations.

One result of this approach is that the law on civil rights is complex and disorderly. In most similar countries, a lawyer wanting to know about, for example, freedom of expression would simply look at the relevant clause in the Bill of Rights, and perhaps a few cases interpreting that clause. In this country, the task would be much more difficult; there is no clear definition of any right to freedom of expression, only a collection of statutes and cases which state when and how such a freedom can be restricted. Nor are these found in a body of constitutional law; restrictions concerning freedom of expression, for example, can be found in such diverse areas as the Official Secrets Act, the Public Order Act and the laws on libel and slander, among others.

▶ The European Convention on Human Rights

The European Convention on Human Rights (ECHR) is one of the best known Bills of Rights. It was drawn up by the Council of Europe, which was set up after the Second World War when countries tried to unite to prevent such horrors ever happening again. The Council now has 25 members, including the fifteen members of the European Union.

The Convention was signed in Rome in 1950, ratified by the UK in 1951, and became binding on those states which had ratified it in 1953 (it is only binding on those countries who have chosen to ratify it). A special court, known as the European Court of Human Rights, was set up to deal with claims concerning breaches of the Convention. The Court sits in Strasbourg, and deals with claims made by one state against another, and by individuals against a state. However, it will only hear individual claims where the relevant state has accepted the right of individuals to bring such cases; not all states accept this right of individual petition, and the UK Government has only done so since 1966.

The Convention in domestic law

The fact that a state has ratifed the Convention does not mean that it has to incorporate Convention provisions into its domestic law; each state can choose whether or not to do this, and about half have done so. In these cases, citizens can claim their rights under the Convention through domestic courts, and the parliaments of these countries cannot usually legislate in conflict with the Convention.

The UK has not incorporated the Convention, and so it is not recognized by the courts as part of English law. UK citizens who believe that their rights under the Convention have been breached cannot bring their claim through the normal domestic courts, but must take their case to the European Court of Human Rights; if they succeed there, the UK Government is expected to change whatever aspect of domestic law caused the problem.

As with any other international treaty, domestic courts may take the Convention into account when interpreting UK legislation, and presume that Parliament did not intend to legislate inconsistently with it. Where a statute is ambiguous, they may use the Convention as a guide to the correct interpretation; an example of this is the case of **Waddington** *v* **Miah** (1974), where the House of Lords referred to art. 7 of the Convention to support its view that s. 34 of the Immigration Act 1971 could not be interpreted as having retrospective effect. However, where the words of a statute are clear, domestic courts must apply them, even if they obviously conflict with the Convention.

The scope of the Convention

The rights protected by the Convention include the right to life (art. 2); freedom from torture or inhuman or degrading treatment or punishment (art. 3); freedom from slavery or forced labour (art. 4); the right to liberty and security of the person (art. 5), including the right of arrested persons to be informed promptly of the reasons for arrest and of any charge against them; the right to a fair trial by an impartial tribunal (art. 6), including the right to be presumed innocent of a criminal charge until proved guilty and the right to be defended by a lawyer and to have free legal assistance 'when the interests of justice so require'; the prohibition of retrospective criminal laws (art. 7); the right to respect for a person's private and family life, home and correspondence (art. 8); freedom of thought, conscience and religion (art. 9); freedom of expression (art. 10); freedom of peaceful assembly and association, including the right to join a trade union (art. 11), and the right to marry and found a family (art. 12). The Convention states that citizens should be able to enjoy these rights without discrimination on any ground such as sex, race, colour, language, religion, political or other opinion, national or social origin, association with a national minority, property, birth or other status (art. 14). Some additions, known as Protocols, have been made to the Convention since it was first drawn up. The First Protocol was written in 1952, and provides three new rights: the right to to peaceful enjoyment of one's possessions (art. 1); the right to education, which includes the provision that states should respect parents' rights to the education of their children in conformity with their religious and philosophical beliefs (art. 2); and the right to take part in free elections by secret ballot (art. 3). The other important Protocol is the fourth, concluded in 1963, which guarantees freedom of movement within a state and freedom to leave any country; it also precludes a state from expelling or refusing to admit its own nationals. This protocol has not been ratified by the United

Kingdom, which has chosen not to ratify this protocol, and in the past some citizens from Northern Ireland have been excluded.

Many of the rights provided under the Convention are limited in some circumstances. For example, the Convention states that such restrictions on freedom of expression may be imposed 'as are necessary in a democratic society, in the interests of national security, territorial integrity or public safety, for the prevention of disorder or crime, for the protection of health or morals, for the protection of the reputation or rights of others, for preventing the disclosure of information received in confidence, or for maintaining the authority and impartiality of the judiciary' (art. 10).

Member states may decline to carry out most of their obligations under the Convention in time of war or some other national emergency. The United Kingdom has done so in respect of Northern Ireland. In such cases a state must inform the Secretary-General of the Council of Europe of the Government's actions and the reasons (art. 15). There are some rights, most importantly freedom from torture or inhuman or degrading punishment or treatment, from which states are not permitted to derogate under any circumstances.

The Convention does not cover the whole field of human rights. It omits general economic and social rights, such as a right to housing, or to a minimum income, or free health care, which some would argue should be guaranteed in a civilized society. This is because there is less agreement between different countries on this type of rights than there is on the kind of freedoms which the Convention does protect.

The administration

In addition to the Court, the main institutions concerned with the Convention are the Committee of Ministers of the Council of Europe, which is made up of one political representative from each member state, and the European Commission of Human Rights, which also comprises one member from each member state, but requires them to act independently for the Commission, rather than as representatives of their own country.

Most cases brought under the Convention are individual petitions; between 1955 and 1991, there were only eleven inter-state cases, and over 17,000 individual petitions. Individual petitions are first examined by the Commission for admissibility: they are admissible only after the applicant has exhausted all available domestic remedies and brings the petition no more than six months after the final national decision (art. 26). The Commission must also reject as inadmissible any petition which it considers to be outside the scope of the Convention or manifestly ill-founded (art. 27). In fact only 1,038 of the petitions considered between 1955 and 1991 were declared admissible.

The next step (and the first for inter-state claims) is for the Commission to investigate the facts fully and try to help the parties achieve a friendly settlement of the dispute if possible (art. 28). If this cannot be done, the Commission sends a secret report on the dispute to the state or states concerned, and to the Committee of Ministers (art. 31). If two-thirds of the Committee vote that there has been a breach and, if so, may refer the case within three months to the European Court of Human Rights.

▶ The European Court of Human Rights

The Court of Justice at Strasbourg is comprised of 21 judges, each from different member states; usually cases are heard by seven judges sitting together. As well as deciding whether a state is in breach of the Convention, the Court can award compensation or other 'just satisfaction' of the complaint (art. 50). Its decision is final (there is no appeal). Although the Court has no way of forcing states to abide by its rulings, every state which is a party to its proceedings undertakes to do so, and the force of international law and inter-state relations means that in practice member states do tend to follow the findings of the Court. Changes introduced in the United Kingdom as a result of decisions of the Court include the Contempt of Court Act 1981, the Homosexual Offences (Northern Ireland) Order 1982 and the Interception of Communications Act 1985.

Cases brought against the United Kingdom

Since 1966, over 60 individual petitions have been brought against the UK Government, and there have also been inter-state references to the Commission by the Republic of Ireland. Of the 49 individual cases decided by September 1994, the UK lost 31 and won 18. This figure is often quoted as suggesting that the UK has one of the worst records of breaching the Convention (only Italy has a worse record of losing cases). However, while it is certainly true that our record is open to criticism, the figures must be read in the light of the fact that many states have not recognized the right of individual petition for so long as the UK, and therefore have had less time to build up a record of individual petitions. In addition, those countries which have incorporated the Convention into domestic law will obviously have a lower rate of petitions, successful or otherwise, because most cases will be dealt with in their domestic courts.

The first individual petition from a UK citizen to be considered by the Court was **Golder** *v* **United Kingdom** (1975), which alleged breaches of the right to privacy for private correspondence (art. 8) and to a fair hearing (art. 6). Golder was a prisoner who had been refused access to a solicitor under the Prison Rules, and denied the opportunity to bring an action against a prison officer. The Court held that the Prison Rules were inconsistent with the ECHR. This resulted in a change in the Prison Rules. It was held that the refusal of legal advice to a prisoner who was contemplating a defamation action against a prison officer infringed the right of respect for private life and correspondence (art. 8), and the guarantee of a fair hearing (art. 6).

In **Campbell and Cosans** *v* **United Kingdom** (1982), the complainants alleged that the use of corporal punishment in schools amounted to inhuman and degrading treatment, in breach of art. 3. The Court disagreed with this allegation, but stated that while art. 3 had not been breached, there was a breach of art. 2 of the First Protocol, which requires the State to 'respect the rights of parents to ensure such education and teaching in conformity with their own religious and philosophical convictions'. Since 1986, corporal punishment has been prohibited in state schools in England, Wales and Scotland, though it may still be used on fee-paying pupils at independent schools.

The practice of telephone tapping came under scrutiny in **Malone** *v* **United Kingdom** (1984), and was held to infringe the right to privacy under art. 8. At the time, telephone tapping was regulated only by guidelines, and as a result of the decision, the Government introduced the Interception of Communications Act 1985, regulating the circumstances in which telephone tapping may take place, and giving individuals a right of redress against improper use.

The case of **Dudgeon** *v* **United Kingdom** (1981) challenged laws making homosexual practices between consenting males illegal in Northern Ireland. The laws were held to infringe the individual's right to respect for private life (art. 8), and as a result the Homosexual Offences (Northern Ireland) Order 1982, changing the law on homosexual conduct in Northern Ireland, was passed.

The law on contempt of court, and its relationship with the right to free expression was considered in **Sunday Times** *v* **United Kingdom** (1991). One of the purposes of contempt of court legislation is to prevent the publication of any information which is likely to prejudice the result of a court case. This case arose out of the thalidomide scandal, when thousands of expectant mothers were prescribed a drug, thalidomide (see p. 441). During the parents' long drawn-out struggle for compensation, the *Sunday Times* published an article on the subject which, among other things, urged the drug manufacturers, Distillers, to pay generous compensation. The common law of contempt was used to obtain an injunction against the paper, preventing any further publication of such articles, and the paper challenged this order in the European Court of Human Rights, alleging breach of art. 10, the right to freedom of information. The Court ruled by a majority of eleven votes to nine that the injunction was inconsistent with the ECHR. The Contempt of Court Act 1981 changed the law on contempt to avoid the conflict highlighted by the case.

While there are many instances of UK Governments changing the law as a result of losing cases in the European Court of Human Rights, it is not always keen to do so. In **Brogan** *v* **United Kingdom** (1988), the provisions of the Prevention of Terrorism (Temporary Provisions) Act 1984 allowing detention of suspects for up to seven days without judicial authority were found to violate art. 5, which protects freedom of the person and requires that the accused should be charged 'promptly'. The Government responded by declaring that the power was necessary on security grounds and by depositing at Strasbourg a limited derogation under art. 15 from the Convention to the extent that the legislation violated art. 5.

In another case, **Abdulaziz** *v* **United Kingdom** (1985), the Government technically complied with the Court of Human Rights decision, but in such a way as to decrease rather than increase rights. The case alleged that British immigration rules discriminated against women, because men permanently settled in the United Kingdom were allowed to bring their wives and fiancées to live with them here, but women in the same position could not bring their husbands and fiancés into the country. The European Court of Human Rights agreed, but the Government was determined not to increase immigration rights. Instead of allowing husbands and fiancés to settle here, they removed the right of wives and fiancées to do so, so ending the sexual discrimination but making the immigration laws even more restrictive. Since then the Commission has dealt with a number of individual petitions alleging that United Kingdom immigration law was in breach of the Convention.

As mentioned before, the UK has also been the subject of interstate actions brought by the Republic of Ireland. In 1971, Ireland lodged complaints with the Commission alleging that the security forces had failed to protect life, as required under art. 2, that detained suspects were subject to treatment which amounted to torture, inhuman and degrading treatment contrary to art. 3, and that internment without trial violated arts. 5 and 6 and in its operation it violated art. 14. Finally the allegation was made that the United Kingdom Government had failed to honour the rights and freedoms contained in art. 1 of the ECHR. The Court upheld complaints relating to interrogation methods as a breach of art. 3, but rejected the claim that focusing internment on Republican terrorists was discrimination contrary to arts. 4 and 5, accepting that this focus was justifiable because of the level of violence from that element in the community. As a result of the Court's decision, the United Kingdom Government sought to incorporate the substance of art. 3 into the domestic law in Northern Ireland, and enacted art. 5 of the Northern Ireland (Emergency Provisions) Act 1987 which allows the courts in Northern Ireland to exclude evidence where there is *prima facie* evidence that the accused was subject to 'torture, to inhuman or degrading treatment, or to any violence or threat of violence'.

Many petitions against the United Kingdom have been withdrawn when the British Government has agreed to take action in particular cases, or to change the general law.

The European Court of Human Rights and the European Court of Justice

The European Court of Human Rights is often confused with the European Court of Justice, but these are quite separate institutions, as are the Commission of Human Rights and the EU Commission. The phrase 'taking your case to Europe' tends to be used interchangeably, but the process and grounds for taking a case to the ECJ is quite distinct from that for the European Court of Human Rights.

However, there are growing links between the ECHR and EU law. Article 164 of Treaty of Rome provides that one of the functions of the ECJ is to ensure observance of the general principles of law contained in that Treaty. In recent cases – such as **Johnston** *v* **Chief Constable of RUC** (1986), **EC Commission** *v* **Germany** (1987) and **Orkem** *v* **EC Commission** (1989) – the ECJ has suggested that respect for human rights is one of these principles, and that for guidance in this principle, they can look to the Convention. In addition, the preamble to the Single European Act pledges members to 'work together to promote democracy on the basis of the fundamental rights recognized in the Convention'. It has been suggested that as a result, the Convention may become incorporated into UK law through the back door of law made by the ECJ.

▶ Do we need a Bill of Rights?

As we have seen, the UK is unusual in having no Bill of Rights, and although the ECHR has clearly provided important protections for civil rights in this country, the inconvenience of having to take cases to Strasbourg – and the embarrassment of losing so many of them – have led to widespread support for a Bill of Rights to be incorporated into UK law. This movement gained considerable support during the later years of the Thatcher regime, when the Government showed itself willing to compromise many important civil rights, in incidents such as the banning of trade unions at Government Communications Headquarters (GCHQ), the attempts to ban the publication of *Spycatcher*, the memoirs of a retired security service agent, and the use of the Official Secrets Act 1911 to prosecute civil servants Sarah Tisdall and Clive Ponting who leaked official information which the government had wished to keep secret.

The system of residual freedoms which traditionalists claim protects civil rights in the UK has shown itself to be seriously flawed over the past couple of decades. The idea that a person is free to do anything not specifically prohibited by law also applies to the state, so that the Government may violate individual freedom even though it is not formally empowered to do so, on the ground that it is doing nothing which is prohibited. An example of this is **Malone** *v* **Metropolitan Police Commissioner** (1979). Mr Malone's telephone had been tapped, and he was able to prove that this was done without any lawful authority – that is, there was no law which allowed the Government or its agencies to tap his phone. But equally, there was no law which forbade them to do so; English law gives no general right to privacy. As a result, Mr Malone's action failed.

The fact that, given a decent majority in Parliament, governments can make whatever law they like, means that they can simply legislate freedoms away, secure in the knowledge that the courts cannot refuse to apply their legislation, as they can in countries which have a Bill of Rights or written constitution. The 1994 Criminal Justice and Public Order Act, for example, severely restricts rights of peaceful protest, of assembly and of movement, and aspects of it are likely to be challenged in the Court of Human Rights, but the English courts must apply it nevertheless.

Even where the constitution does allow for judicial protection of civil rights, the British judiciary have frequently proved themselves unequal to the task. As Griffith has famously pointed out, they show a tendency to view the public interest as the maintenance of established authority and traditional values. Though exceptions can always be found, the overall result has been that the maintenance of 'order' and the suppression of challenges to established authority – whether of trade unions or terrorists – have taken precedence over the kind of liberties a Bill of Rights might seek to protect. To give just a few of many examples, the degree of respect the British judiciary accord to freedom of expression can be seen in **R** *v* **Secretary of State for the Home Department ex parte Brind** (1989), where they upheld a broadcasting ban on members of a legitimate political party in Northern Ireland; to rights of association in **Council of Civil Service Unions** *v* **Minister for the Civil Service** (1984), where they upheld the ban on trade unions at GCHQ; and to rights of peaceful assembly in **Kent** *v* **Metropolitan Police Commissioner** (1981), where they upheld a blanket ban on protest marches through an area of London.

As a result of all this, many people believe that civil liberties in Britain are very poorly protected. The numerous miscarriages of justice suggest there is little protection of the right to a fair trial, nor, given the treatment of some of those involved while in police custody, to freedom from torture and inhuman treatment. The wide powers of surveillance allowed under statute to the police and security services, prove the right to privacy a fallacy, while the wide discretion allowed to police under both the

Public Order Act 1986 and the Criminal Justice Act 1988 mean that the rights to peaceful assembly and protest are very limited indeed.

Although the current Government maintains, as Mrs Thatcher did, that civil rights are adequately protected in the UK and a Bill of Rights is unnecessary, there is a growing body of opposition to that view. In 1977 the Standing Advisory Commission on Human Rights in Northern Ireland recommended that a Bill of Rights for the whole United Kingdom would be the best way to protect individual rights in the province; Lord Scarman has suggested that, had such a Bill existed before, the eruption of violence in Northern Ireland might have been prevented. Both the Labour Party and the Liberal Democrats are in favour of a Bill of Rights, and the need for a Bill is the centrepiece of a package of constitutional reform advocated by Charter 88, a large and fairly influential pressure group.

In 1995 the Institute for Public Policy Research published its own detailed proposals for a new written constitution, including proposals for a Bill of Rights based to a large extent on the European Convention.

Arguments for a Bill of Rights

Curbs on the executive

Perhaps the main argument for a Bill of Rights is the need for better checks on the enormous powers of the executive (the government of the day, and its agencies, such as the police, the army and government departments). Constitutional writers of the nineteenth century, such as Dicey, made much of the role of Parliament as a watchdog over the executive, ensuring that oppressive legislation could not be passed. However, since Dicey's time, the growth of a strong party system has fundamentally altered the nature of Parliament; in the vast majority of cases, a government can expect its own members to obey party discipline, so that Government proposals will almost invariably be passed (during the 1980s, for example, only one Government Bill was defeated). Not only do those in opposition lack the numbers to prevent this, but the pressures of parliamentary time may even prevent a detailed scrutiny of exactly what is being passed. As we have seen, this can result in governments being able to legislate against individual rights and freedoms almost at will.

Supporters of a Bill of Rights claim it would curb executive powers, since the courts could simply refuse to apply legislation which conflicted with it. This in turn would be a powerful incentive for government to avoid introducing such legislation in the first place.

Ratification of the ECHR

Many supporters of a Bill of Rights argue that it makes no sense for us to ratify the ECHR, and yet not make it part of English law. If the British Government agrees with the aims of the Convention, which ratification of it clearly suggests, why should citizens have to make the long trek to Strasbourg in order to assert their rights under it? If the Government supports those rights, why should their enforcement rely on individual citizens having the knowledge, determination and financial resources to take a case all the way to Strasbourg? As Lord Taylor, the Lord Chief Justice, pointed out in the 1992 Dimbleby lecture, 'It is as if we said, in 1950, the well-known prayer: God make us good – but not yet.' Taking a case to Strasbourg can take up to six years, and this delay can mean that remedies come too late to be effective. In the meantime, other domestic cases on similar issues are likely to be decided, and if the Strasbourg case goes against the UK Government, these decisions may turn out to be wrong. In addition, it hardly does the country's image abroad much good to be frequently found in error by a 'foreign' court, as it has been many times.

Clarity and accessibility

A Bill of Rights would provide a comprehensive and easily accessible statement of rights and freedoms enforceable in the United Kingdom, as opposed to the scattered and complex legislation concerning civil rights at the moment.

Education

A Bill of Rights would set out for citizens, government and the judiciary the basic rights and freedoms we would all be entitled to expect. Supporters say this would lead to better awareness by citizens of their legal rights, and to legislation and judicial decisions which take those rights as their starting point, rather than just one of many things to be considered.

Other countries

Among developed Western countries, Israel and the UK are the only ones without a Bill of Rights. Supporters of a Bill argue that this gives us a lower standard of protection than comparable jurisdictions.

Arguments against a Bill of Rights

Unneccessary

As we have seen, the present Government are among those who assert that civil liberties are already adequately protected in this country. The points made above would seem to argue against this conclusion.

Increased power for the judiciary

Among those who oppose a Bill of Rights, mistrust of the judiciary, and constitutional objections to taking power from Parliament and giving it to judges, are perhaps the most frequently expressed. There is no doubt that a Bill of Rights would considerably increase judicial power. Unlike English statutes, the language of a Bill of Rights is typically open and imprecise, setting out broad principles rather than detailed provisions. This gives judges a wide discretion in interpretation – so wide that in the USA, for example, the provisions against racial discrimination in their Bill of Rights were once held to allow a form of apartheid, yet since 1954, such a system has been held to violate the Bill of Rights. Even within the last decade, the US Bill of Rights has been interpreted to allow discrimination against minorities, in, for example, the Supreme Court's decision in **Bowers** *v* **Hardwick** (1986), that the constitutional right of privacy should be effectively denied to homosexuals.

A Bill of Rights also calls upon judges to decide the relative importance of protected rights, where two of them clash. Should, for example, the right to free expression of members of the British National Party override or give way to that of ethnic minorities to be free of racial harassment? Does a foetus have a right to life which overrides its mother's right to liberty and security of the person? There are no obvious right or wrong answers to questions like these, and nor are there always obvious legal answers, even where there is a Bill of Rights. In many such cases the real problem is not what the law **is**, but what the law **should be**. Many people believe that is not a question which should be answered by a group which is not elected, but appointed by the Government through a secretive procedure undisturbed by any parliamentary scrutiny, and which is, currently at least, drawn from a narrow social group, unrepresentative of society as a whole. As Griffith has pointed out, these questions are political, and political questions should, as far as possible, be answered by politicians, elected to do so.

Supporters of a Bill of Rights might argue that the problems associated with greater judicial power could be dealt with by reforming judicial selection, and drawing judges from a wider spread of the population. While this is clearly desirable in itself, it would not remove the fundamental objection that judges are not elected, and nor, whatever the reforms, is it likely to avoid the fact that by virtue of their education and their lifestyle, judges would be unrepresentative of the mass of the population. Those, like Griffiths, who oppose a Bill of Rights, argue that what is needed is not so much reform of the judiciary, but political reforms that would allow a democratically elected legislature genuinely to supervise the acts of the executive, and to fetter the exercise of executive discretion. The protection of fundamental freedoms and rights should not be for the individual to establish in court, but for the legislature to safeguard as part of their job.

Inflexibility

Supporters of our current constitutional arrangements argue that without a written constitution, our system can adapt over time, meeting new needs as they arise. They contend that a Bill of Rights would lack this flexibility. Two answers to this point are that, first, the open and imprecise language of a Bill of Rights allows flexibility, and secondly, the Bills of Rights can be changed when necessary; the arrangements for entrenchment will usually set down a special procedure that can be used to make amendments. The fact that these procedures may be long and difficult simply protects those rights originally set down from rash or unpopular change; it does not set them in stone.

Too much flexibility

Ironically, it is also argued that the imprecise language typical of a Bill of Rights would lead to uncertainty about the law, leading to increased litigation, with no clear objectives as to how general principles might emerge and policies be interpreted. This is clearly linked to the problem of mistrust of the judiciary.

Rights are not powers

A more fundamental problem with the claims made for a Bill of Rights is the idea that merely granting rights is enough to secure individual freedom and empowerment. It is all very well to grant rights, but unless they are underpinned by economic and social provision, they may prove to be useless. Freedom of labour is effectively useless in times of high unemployment, when it becomes nothing more than the freedom to live in poverty. Freedom of movement fails to help disabled people who cannot use public transport or afford their own. Freedom of association offers little advantage if employers refuse to recognize trade unions, and liberty of the person means little to the battered wife or abused child who has neither the personal nor the practical resources to escape.

Similarly, where there are huge imbalances in power in society, giving equal rights to all may be of limited use, because those who have the most power can use it to find a way round the rights of those who are less powerful. For example, recent compensation payments made to women sacked for being pregnant have led to speculation that as a result, employers may simply become even less keen than before to employ women; cases on racial discrimination may have had similar effects on the employment prospects of members of ethnic minorities. While it should not be denied that this kind of provision helps people, it can be argued that in focusing on individual rights, rather than social duties, a Bill of Rights might detract attention from any real commitment to a just society. The point is not that a Bill of Rights is undesirable, but that on its own, it could not make the kind of changes supporters claim for it.

The UK constitution and a Bill of Rights

Even if agreement is ever reached on the introduction of a Bill of Rights, there is further debate as to the constitutional form it could or should take. There are three main options.

An entrenched bill of rights

The most powerful type of Bill of Rights is an entrenched provision, which is superior to all other law. Any other law which does not comply with it can be struck down by the courts, and the Bill of Rights itself can be changed only by special procedures such as a referendum or an increased parliamentary majority; in some cases, it cannot be altered at all.

Whether or not such a Bill would be desirable in the UK, many experts believe its introduction would be constitutionally impossible. This is because the doctrine of parliamentary sovereignty provides that no sitting Parliament can bind a future one; in other words, every Parliament is free to unmake laws made by their predecessors. Not only does this mean that a future Parliament could simply abolish a Bill of Rights, but more importantly (given that political pressure would probably prevent that), it gives rise to a doctrine known as implied repeal. This means that where two pieces of legislation conflict, the courts must apply the one most recently passed; therefore they would have to apply legislation passed since the Bill of Rights even if it took away rights protected by the Bill. Any arrangements for entrenchment could simply be legislated away.

Not everybody agrees that such entrenchment would be impossible (one result of an unwritten constitution is that experts frequently disagree on its details and effect). It may be that the political implications of entrenchment, particularly when associated with referenda, would limit the actions of Government; when citizens have directly voted for a set of provisions, it would be an unwise government which would legislate to remove them, even if legally able to do so. Many commonwealth countries which have inherited our ideas of sovereignty from the United Kingdom have enacted entrenched Bills of Rights without these constitutional problems.

A written entrenched constitution

If the UK were to adopt a written constitution, this could include entrenched clauses devoted to fundamental rights. The problems of entrenchment, discussed above, also apply here.

Ordinary legislation

The Bill of Rights passed as an ordinary statute would, by the doctrine of implied repeal, automatically prevail over all existing legislation, so that any previous law which conflicted with it would no longer apply. This would leave the problem of conflicts between the Bill and later legislation. If the doctrine of implied repeal applied as usual, there would be little point in having the Bill, since all its protections could be easily legislated away. There are two possible approaches to this problem. First, the courts could assume that statutes were to be interpreted in line with the Bill of Rights, unless they clearly stated that provisions were to apply even if in conflict with the Bill of Rights. Although this would mean that freedoms could still be legislated away, the need to make such a clear statement would ensure that at the very least, there would be proper discussion of proposals to do so, and there would obviously be political pressure not to do this often. This approach was taken to the Canadian Bill of Rights between 1960 and 1982; Canada followed a doctrine of parliamentary sovereignty exported by the British.

Alternatively, a Bill of Rights enacted as an ordinary statute could serve as an interpretation Act, so that the provisions of every other Act, whether passed before or after it, would be interpreted by reference to it. This approach is favoured by the House of Lords Select Committee on the Bill of Rights.

Content of a Bill of Rights

The possible content of a Bill of Rights provokes as much debate as its constitutional form. An obvious suggestion is simply to incorporate the ECHR into domestic law as our Bill of Rights; this has the advantage of widespread acceptance and familiarity, and was recommended by the House of Lords Select Committee on a Bill of Rights in 1978 (the committee was actually divided on the issue of whether we should have a Bill of Rights, but unanimously agreed that if we ever do, it should take the form of incorporation of the ECHR).

However, there are objections: the ECHR is now over 30 years old, and since its creation, new rights have become important – for example, the Convention makes limited provision for preventing racial discrimination, and none at all for preventing discrimination on the basis of disability or sexual orientation. Some people feel that a UK Bill of Rights should cover a wider range of rights, including environmental, economic and social rights.

A further problem is that the ECHR follows the more general, looser European style of legislative drafting, in contrast to the more tightly worded legislation our courts are used to applying – though as EU law becomes more important, our courts are developing more expertise in this area. There is also the question of whether the same Bill of Rights would be appropriate for all parts of the United Kingdom. It has been suggested that Northern Ireland may require special treatment given the intensity of religious and political animosity.

An alternative to incorporating the ECHR would be to draw up a completely new Bill of Rights, but given the level of dispute over whether we need one at all and what constitutional form it should take, the difficulties in determing potential content would be enormous. Some argue that it should bring together every kind of right which should be protected in a civilized society; some favour an approach similar to that of the ECHR, but updated; others feel that a Bill of Rights should simply cover those areas not currently protected by the common law, such as the right to privacy or the freedom from improper discrimination. While the ECHR itself has its defects, one advantage is that it at least gives a basic standard which is already accepted and used.

Complementary reforms

Supporters of a Bill of Rights, such as the Charter 88 group, advocate a package of complementary reforms to maximize the effect of such a Bill. These include more open and egalitarian systems for the appointment and removal of the judiciary; improved training and education in human rights law for citizens; freedom of information legislation; and electoral reforms designed to restore the power of Parliament over the executive.

. . . .

ANSWERING QUESTIONS

1 **Assess the impact of the European Convention on Human Rights on UK law.** *WJEC*

You should begin your essay by stating what the Convention is, **briefly** outlining its origins and stating some of the rights and freedoms which it protects – remember to point out that states can depart from these principles under certain circumstances.

Then discuss the relationship of the Convention to UK law, pointing out first of all that it does not give directly enforceable rights here, as it does in those countries which have incorporated it into domestic law. Explain how UK citizens who believe that their rights under the Convention have been breached have to bring a claim in the European Court of Human Rights, and the expectation that the UK Government will change the law if they are found in breach. You could then talk about some of the cases in which this has happened, emphasizing the important changes in the law that have been made as a result of them. You could mention at this point that such cases do not always lead to better protection for the rights of UK citizens and cite the cases of **Brogan v United Kingdom** and **Abdulaziz v United Kingdom**.

You should also discuss the influence of the Convention on the interpretation of UK statutes, mentioning **Waddington v Miah**, but remember to point out that this influence is limited by the principle of parliamentary sovereignty, in that where the words of a statute are clear, domestic courts must apply them, even if they obviously conflict with the Convention. You should also discuss the relationship of the Convention and EU law, and the view that EU law is becoming a way in which the Convention is incorporated 'by the back door'. Make it very clear to the examiners at this point that you know the two systems are separate – many students confuse the two.

Finally, you could discuss the question of whether the impact of the Convention should be increased, by incorporating it into UK law.

2 (a) Explain and illustrate the approach of English law to the protection of fundamental rights and freedoms *(15 marks)*;
(b) Discuss what changes to that approach might be desirable *(10 marks)* AEB

Part (a): you should first define what fundamental rights and freedoms are, giving examples of the kinds of rights and freedoms generally considered fundamental in modern, democratic societies. Then explain the English approach to these rights – the idea of residual freedoms, giving examples of this approach from case law, such as **Malone**. In order to explain the approach fully, you might want to briefly contrast it with the Bill of Rights approach. You could also point out the problems which spring from this approach to fundamental rights: the complexity, and the way in which freedoms can be legislated away, for example.

Part (b): the main change which could be made to this approach would be some form of a Bill of Rights. Explain how this would work, and in what way it would improve the situation; you could also highlight any drawbacks to it.

19

Forms of civil liberties

FREEDOM OF ASSEMBLY AND PUBLIC ORDER

Freedom of assembly means the right to meet together with other people. The aspect of freedom of assembly which has most relevance to civil rights law is the right to meet for the purposes of public protest, whether in a static assembly, or a march. The danger of such meetings leading to public disorder – especially where rival groups hold meetings or marches in the same area – has led to a number of provisions restricting rights of assembly. For the sake of convenience, this chapter also includes other important public order offences, which are more loosely concerned with freedom of assembly but are often combined with restrictions on freedom of assembly in exam questions.

▶ The Legislation

The Public Order Act 1986 was passed after over a decade of periodic public order problems. During the 1970s, there were a series of public order problems arising from confrontations between rival processions organized by the National Front and anti-fascist groups. These came to a head on a Saturday afternoon in June 1974, when a march to Red Lion Square by the National Front antagonized many people. A counter march was organized and despite police efforts public order broke down. In clashes that ensued one student was killed and many other people were injured.

The Home Secretary appointed Lord Scarman to conduct an inquiry into the incident. In his report on the disorders Lord Scarman considered the relationship between public protest and public order and said that the law needed to reach a balance between these often conflicting interests. The early 1980s saw even more public order problems, beginning with inner city riots, apparently sparked off by heavy-handed policing among the ethnic minorities, followed by violent scenes on picket lines during the Wapping newspaper dispute and later the miners' strike, when around 140 charges of riot and over 500 of unlawful assembly were brought. Finally, there was an increase in violence at football matches, culminating in the Heysel stadium tragedy. All these incidents were the subject of a massive media outcry, and right-wing papers in particular suggested that public order was breaking down. The Government responded by passing the Public Order Act 1986, which, building on the provisions of the 1936 Act, establishes potentially severe limits on freedom of assembly.

These limits have been taken further in the 1994 Criminal Justice and Public Order Act, a highly controversial piece of legislation which was opposed by a wide variety of groups. The civil rights pressure group, Liberty, has stated that many of its provisions may be against the European Convention on Human Rights in respect of the restrictions they make on freedom of assembly and movement.

There are also common law offences concerning freedom of assembly, and torts which may be committed when attending an assembly. We will now look at some of these, along with the statutory restrictions.

▶ Powers to control assemblies

The common law

Under common law, public authorities traditionally had very little power to prevent the holding of assemblies. This can be seen in the case of **Beatty** *v* **Gillbanks** (1882), which concerned regular Sunday marches held by the Salvation Army in Weston-super-Mare. These marches antagonized some inhabitants of the town, who set up a rival group, which they called the Skeleton Army, and attempted to disrupt Salvation Army marches. In order to try to prevent these breaches of the peace, the Salvation Army were banned from holding their marches. When they ignored this ban, this was held to be an offence and they were bound over to keep the peace. However, the order binding them over was set aside on appeal. The court held that they could not be prohibited from assembling merely because their lawful conduct might induce others to act unlawfully.

More recently, the common law has increased the powers of the police to deal with assemblies. In **Moss** *v* **McLachlan** (1985), which took place during the miners' strike, the four defendants were stopped at a motorway exit by police officers, who suspected that they were travelling to attend a picket line, and told them to turn back. The men refused, and the police arrested them on the basis that they had reasonable grounds to suspect a breach of the peace would occur if the men were allowed to travel on. Despite the fact that the men were some miles away from the nearest picket line, the arrests were found to be justified. The court held that if the police reasonably apprehend that the holding of a gathering in a public place will give rise to a breach of the peace, they are under a common law duty to take reasonable steps to prevent that gathering from taking place or to break it up. The court clearly felt that questions of public order outweighed strong restrictions on both freedom of assembly and freedom of movement.

Statutory controls

These are contained in the Public Order Act 1986 and the Criminal Justice and Public Order Act 1994. Different provisions apply to static assemblies (such as public meetings or rallies) and moving ones (marches and processions).

Static assemblies

The Public Order Act 1986 defines a public assembly as a gathering of twenty or more people, in a public place which is wholly or partly open to the air. It does not therefore include assemblies in buildings, including public buildings (s. 16).

The Act gives no power to ban static assemblies, but it does allow conditions to be imposed on them by the police, either before an assembly takes place, or during it. This power allows the police to limit the number of people attending, or the duration of the assembly, or to direct the organizers to hold it somewhere other than the intended place. The police can issue such conditions where they reasonably believe that the assembly may result in serious public disorder, serious damage to property, or serious disruption to the life of the community, or that the purpose of organizing the assembly is to intimidate others.

These powers are potentially very strong. Take the example of a meeting held outside a town hall to demonstrate opposition to council policies, or outside a foreign embassy to highlight the relevant country's bad record on human rights. The whole point of such a demonstration is to draw attention to a cause. By moving the demonstration to a local park or a side street, where nobody will notice it, or limiting it to a handful of people, or a very short duration, police have the power to make the demonstration all but useless. In addition, the conditions under which those powers can be exercised show how far the Act tips the balance in favour of public order and against freedom of assembly; in the White Paper which preceded the 1986 statute an example given of disruption to the life of the community was that of marches held on Saturdays in shopping centres. As far as the Act is concerned, it appears that getting your shopping done is more important than being able to exercise a fundamental civil right.

Further controls over static assemblies were introduced in the Criminal Justice and Public Order Act 1994, which inserts a new s. 14A, covering trespassory assemblies, into the Public Order Act 1986. Where an assembly is intended to be held on land to which the public has no or only limited access, the relevant chief constable may apply to the local council for a banning order, provided that (a) the assembly is likely to be held without the owner's permission or to exceed that permission or the public's right to be on the land, and there is a risk of serious disruption to the life of the community, or (b) the land is of historical, architectural, archaeological or scientific interest, and serious damage may result. Such banning orders must be approved by the Home Secretary, and may ban all assemblies within a five-mile radius for up to four days. Once the order is in place, people may be turned back from attempting to attend the proposed assembly; and it is an arrestable offence to organize, participate in, or incite others to participate in the assembly, knowing that the banning order has been made.

The exact scope of this provision is not yet clear, and there are a number of grey areas. There seems to be no requirement to publicise a banning order, which makes it difficult to know how intending participants, particularly in large assemblies, can be expected to know about it; while participating without knowledge of a ban is not an offence, there are clearly going to be problems of proof, and in any case, it is surely better to give people the means of avoiding an offence if possible. Nor is it clear whether chief constables would be under a duty to ascertain from the occupier (if he or she is known and can be found) whether or not there is permission.

More importantly, it is unclear exactly what type of location the section may cover. It clearly makes some types of protest impossible: many of the demonstrations that occurred during the miners' strike, which took place wholly or partly on National Coal Board land, would be covered, as would be sit-ins, worker occupations and so on; there is no problem with proving that these disrupt the life of the community, since that is precisely their purpose. But the dividing line between private and public property is nowhere near as clear cut as is presumed by the legislation. What about, for example, protests in a shopping-mall, or at an airport? Even in a public park, access is limited by virtue of bye-laws. The potential coverage of this section is vast; its extent in practice will only be known once it begins to be interpreted by the courts, but previous case law gives little hope of the courts upholding freedom of assembly by interpreting the provision narrowly. Contrast, for example, the following two cases, the first from Canada and the second from England. In both cases, airport authorities tried to prevent a group of individuals from carrying placards and distributing pamphlets within the airport area. In **Committee for the Commonwealth of Canada** *v* **The Queen in Right of Canada** (1986) the court held that the airport's action was in breach of the Canadian Charter; according to the court, the Government owns its property 'not for its own benefit but for that of the citizen', and, therefore has an obligation to 'devote certain property for certain purposes and to manage "its" property for the public good'. But in **British Airports Authority** *v* **Ashton** (1983) the courts, when weighing individual freedom against property rights, came down firmly in favour of the latter; as owner of the land, the airport authority was entitled to prevent the behaviour they objected to. If the courts take the same approach to trespassory assemblies, rights of assembly in this country may become very limited indeed. Liberty have already asserted that this provision is contrary to art. 11 of the ECHR.

Public processions

Statutory controls of public processions were first introduced by the Public order Act 1936, and the relevant provisions are now contained in the Public Order Act 1986. The 1986 Act introduced a requirement that the organizers of a public procession should give advance notice to the police (s. 11). The requirement covers public processions designed to demonstrate support for, or opposition to, the views or actions of any person or body, to publicize a cause or campaign, or mark or commemorate any event. Unless it is not reasonably practical to do so (if a march is organized at very short notice, for example), or the procession is commonly or customarily held in that area, the organizers must notify the police at least six days in advance (or as soon as reasonably practical) of the date, route and time of the proposed march, and the name and address of the organizer (or organizers). If notice is not given, or the procession deviates in time, date or route from the notice given, organizers will be guilty of an offence, unless they can prove they neither knew of, suspected nor had reason to suspect the failure to give notice of the deviations, or that the deviation arose from circumstances beyond their control, or was done with the agreement or direction of the police.

The 1936 Act allowed for conditions to be imposed on processions, and the 1986 Act extends the grounds on which this can take place. The grounds on which conditions can be imposed are the same as those for static assemblies; provided these are satisfied, the police may impose any conditions or limitations which seem to them necessary.

If a chief constable reasonably believes that his or her powers to impose conditions on the procession would not be enough to prevent serious public disorder, he or she may apply to the district council for a ban of up to three months on all public processions or a specified class. Banning orders must be approved by the Home Secretary. It is an offence knowingly to organize or participate in a procession which violates a banning order, or to incite another to participate.

Other powers

Bye-laws regulating the use of public areas for meetings, and requiring advance notice of processions are in effect in many local authority areas in England and Wales. Public rallies in Trafalgar Square in London, for example, must be authorized by the Secretary of State for the Environment at his discretion (Trafalgar Square Regulations 1952, reg. 3).

In many other countries, there is a right to hold meetings in public areas and publicly-owned buildings, but this is not the case here. There are however some positive rights. Meetings organized as part of a candidate's election campaign are entitled to be held in a state school or in other publicly owned rooms (Representation of the People Act 1983), and universities, polytechnics and colleges have a general duty to make their halls available to all groups, whether popular or unpopular, without discriminating between them on political or other grounds, under the Education (No. 2) Act 1986. By s. 43, the governing bodies of such establishments must 'take such steps as are reasonably practicable to ensure that freedom of speech within the law is secured for members, students and employees of the establishment and for visiting speakers'. This includes an obligation 'to ensure, so far as it is reasonably practical, that the use of any premises of the establishment is not denied to any individual or body of persons on any ground connected with (a) the beliefs or views of that individual or of any member of that body, or (b) the policy or objectives of that body'. To this end, governing bodies must issue and keep up to date a suitable code of practice.

In **R v University of Liverpool ex parte Caesar-Gordon** (1990), the university authorities refused permission for a meeting at the university to be addressed by two first secretaries from the South African Embassy. The authorities feared that the meeting might spark off public violence in Toxteth, the residential area adjacent to the university. In an application for judicial review by the chairman of the student Conservative Association, the Divisional Court held that, on a true construction of s. 43(1), the duty imposed on the university is local to the members of the university and its premises. Its duty was to ensure, so far as is reasonably practical, that those over whom it had control – its members, students and employees – do not obstruct the exercise of freedom of speech within the law by other members, students and employees, and by visiting speakers in its premises. But under s. 43(1) the university was not entitled to take into account threats of 'public disorder' outside the confines of the university by people over whom they had no control, and a declaration was granted that the university acted *ultra vires* in denying permission to hold the meeting. The court suggested, however, that had the university authorities confined their reasons for refusing permission to the risk of disorder on university premises and among university members, then their decision would have been perfectly lawful.

Offences committed during assemblies and marches

As well as the offences detailed above, there are a number of other criminal offences which are specific to public order situations, some of the most important of which are detailed in Part I of the Public Order Act 1986. The section modernizes the old common law, replacing the common law offences of riot, rout, unlawful assembly and affray, which the Law Commission had concluded were unsatisfactory. The section creates new statutory crimes of riot, violent disorder, affray, threatening behaviour and disorderly conduct.

Riot

The offence of riot is committed when twelve or more people, who are present together, use or threaten unlawful violence for a common purpose, and their conduct (taken together) is such as would cause a person of reasonable firmness present at the scene to fear for their personal safety (s. 1). A common purpose may be inferred from their conduct, and a riot may take place in private or in a public place; no person of reasonable firmness need actually be present at the scene. The offence carries a maximum penalty of ten years imprisonment and a fine. It is clearly the most serious public order offence, and the consent of the Director of Public Prosecutions is necessary for any prosecution of it. Although charges of riot are unusual today, they were brought during the miners' strike of 1984/85, but most, if not all, of the prosecutions collapsed.

Violent disorder

Section 2 of the Public Order Act 1986 created the new offence of violent disorder. Violent disorder is committed when three or more persons who are present together use or threaten unlawful violence and their conduct (taken together) is such as would cause a person of reasonable firmness present at the scene to fear for their personal safety. Again, the offence can take place in a public or private place, and no person of reasonable firmness need actually be present. The defendant must intend to use or threaten violence, or be aware that their conduct may be violent or threaten violence. The maximum sentence on indictment is a five-year prison sentence and a fine, or on summary conviction six months imprisonment or a fine of up to £5,000.

Affray

Affray is committed by using or threatening unlawful violence towards another, such as to cause a person of reasonable firmness present at the scene to fear for their personal safety (s. 3). The threat must come from more than just words, and again, the offence can be committed in a public or private place, and no person of reasonable firmness need actually be present. On indictment the maximum sentence is three years imprisonment and a fine; summarily it is three months imprisonment and a fine up to £5,000.

Threatening behaviour

By s. 4 of the Public Order Act 1986:

A person is guilty of an offence if he –
  (a) uses towards another person threatening, abusive or insulting words or behaviour, or
  (b) distributes or displays to another person any writing, sign or other visible representation which is threatening, abusive or insulting, with intent to cause that person to believe that immediate unlawful violence will be used against him or another by any person, or to provoke the immediate use of unlawful violence by that person or another, or whereby that person is likely to believe that such violence will be used or it is likely that such violence will be provoked.

The offence can be committed in a public or private place, but not where both the person committing the offence, and the person in whose sight or hearing it is committed are inside a dwelling. It is a broadly defined offence with a maximum sentence of six months imprisonment and a fine of £5,000.

Case law on this offence has examined the question of how soon after insulting conduct the violence must be likely to take place. The case of **R *v* Horseferry Road Magistrate ex parte Siadatan** (1991) concerned the publication of the book *The Satanic Verses*, by Salman Rushdie, which many devout Muslims found offensive. The applicant alleged that publication and distribution of the book was an offence under s. 4(1), on the ground that the book contained abusive and insulting writing which was likely to provoke unlawful violence. On a strict construction of the Act, the Divisional Court held that the magistrate was correct in refusing to issue a summons. In the view of the court, the requirement in the Act that the insulted person should be 'likely to believe that such violence will be used' should be restricted to where the victim is likely to believe that the violence will be used immediately.

Disorderly conduct

This offence, defined in s. 5, is committed where one or more persons use threatening, abusive or insulting words or behaviour, or disorderly behaviour, or display threatening, abusive or insulting writing, signs or other visible representation, within hearing or sight of anyone likely to be caused harassment, alarm or distress by any of these. The offence can be committed in public or private places, but not where the offender and the person likely to be caused harassment, alarm or distress are both inside a dwelling.

There are three defences; the first applies where the defendant had no reason to believe that any person likely to be caused harassment, alarm or distress was within sight or hearing; the second where the defendant was inside a dwelling and had no reason to believe that words, behaviour, signs and so on would be heard or seen by anyone outside the dwelling; the third where the defendant's conduct was reasonable. The latter was examined in **Morrow** *v* **Director of Public Prosecutions** (1994), where demonstrators outside an abortion clinic claimed that the abortions prevented by their demonstration must have included unlawful ones, and their action was therefore reasonable for the purposes of preventing crime. The court agreed that the defence would be more easily established where the disorderly behaviour was part of a campaign which had a strong moral basis, but in this case it did not justify the defendants' conduct.

A person committing this offence can be arrested only if they are first warned to stop it, but continue regardless. The conduct which takes place after the warning need not be the same as that before, so long as both fall within the scope of the offence. The maximum penalty is a £1,000 fine.

Incitement to racial hatred

This offence is defined in the Public Order Act 1986, ss. 17–23. 'Racial hatred' means 'hatred against a group of persons in Great Britain defined by reference to colour, race, nationality (including citizenship) or ethnic or national origins' (s. 17).

Section 18 of the Act makes it an offence to use threatening, abusive or insulting words or behaviour, or to display any material which is threatening, abusive or insulting, if done with intent to stir up racial hatred, or if in circumstances where racial hatred is likely to be stirred up. The Act applies to theatrical performances (s. 20), the distribution, showing or playing of a recording of visual images or sounds (s. 21), and television and radio broadcasts (s. 22). Under s. 23 of the Act it is an offence to possess material which if published or displayed would amount to an offence under s. 18. It is not an offence to publish a fair and accurate report of proceedings in Parliament or of proceedings publicly heard before a tribunal or court where the report is published contemporaneously with the proceedings (s. 26). No prosecution may occur in England and Wales without the consent of the Attorney-General (s. 27).

Obstruction of the police

Obstructing the police in the execution of their duty is a statutory offence under the Police Act 1964, s. 51(3). Its scope is very wide, and it is heavily used in public order situations. It covers most cases where the police lawfully request someone to do something, and the person refuses, as was the case in **Moss** *v* **McLachlan** (see p. 359).

The courts have shown themselves very willing to uphold a wide use of this offence, even where its use severely restricts freedom of assembly. In **Duncan** *v* **Jones** (1936), a speaker addressing a crowd from a box on the highway was told to stop, because the police feared a breach of peace. Despite the fact that the only ground for this fear was the fact that a disturbance had occurred in the same place a year earlier, the courts upheld the arrest of the speaker for obstruction, after she refused to stop speaking.

Obstruction of the highway

This is another offence with very wide application. Under the Highway Act 1980, s. 137, it is an offence 'if a person without lawful authority or excuse in any way wilfully obstructs the free passage along a highway'. For the purposes of this offence, the highway includes the pavement as well as the road. There is no need for any kind of violent or disorderly behaviour, nor does the defendant have to be completely blocking the highway – in **Nagy** *v* **Weston** (1965), it was held that it is no defence that a way round is left, nor that nobody is in fact obstructed by the defendant. The case is among several in which, as with obstruction of the police, the courts have supported very wide definitions of the offence. In **Hubbard** *v* **Pitt** (1976), demonstrators picketed an estate agent, protesting about the way he conducted his business. Despite the fact that no physical obstruction was caused, and the police had no objection to the protest, a majority of the Court of Appeal granted the estate agent an interlocutory injunction to stop the demonstrators. In **Arrowsmith** *v* **Jenkins** (1963), an obstruction caused by a speaker was considered unlawful even though the police had been notified of the gathering, and the area was frequently used for meetings.

The offence thus gives wide powers to the police, which may be used to disperse perfectly peaceful assemblies. If a police officer orders a speaker, distributor, vendor or audience to 'move along', and they refuse to do so, they are likely to be arrested for obstruction of the highway or obstruction of a constable in the execution of his duty.

Public nuisance

A procession or public meeting may amount to a public nuisance if it entails an unreasonable use of the highway, causing obstruction or excessive noise. There may be a difference in the degrees of obstruction needed to obtain convictions for a public nuisance and for wilful obstruction under the Highways Act 1980.

▶ Torts

Assemblies held without permission on land which is in private owner-ship constitute trespass. If they are held on a highway, they often consti-tute a trespass at common law against the person or body in whom the highway is vested, unless the owner has given his or her consent. This is because the primary purpose of a highway is for passage and repassage. This means that public processions are *prima facie* lawful, since they sim-ply involve collective exercise of the right to passage along the highway. However, their use of the highway must still be reasonable; a procession becomes a nuisance if the right is exercised unreasonably or with reckless disregard of the rights of others'. This might cover, for example, demon-strators linking arms so as to block the highway as they walked.

FREEDOM OF ASSOCIATION

Freedom of association is concerned with the right to meet with other people, and to form organizations, such as trade unions and pressure groups. This right is an essential part of a democratic system, allowing the formation of political groups, and of groups which oppose government policies.

In general, English law imposes no restrictions upon the freedom of individuals to associate together for political purposes; in less democratic countries, political parties, action groups, campaign committees and so on have to be officially registered, and in some cases may be forbidden altogether. However, freedom of association in this country is not entirely unrestricted. The following are some of the important restrictions.

▶ Terrorist organizations

The situation in Northern Ireland has led to special restrictions on membership of organizations viewed as terrorist. The Prevention of Ter-rorism (Temporary Provisions) Act 1989 covers association with the Irish Republican Army (IRA) and the Irish National Liberation Army (INLA). The Act makes it an offence to be a member of either organization; soli-cit or invite financial or other support; solicit or invite membership or carry out tasks on behalf of either organization; arrange a meeting of three or more people, knowing that the meeting is to support or further the activities of one of the banned organizations, or will be addressed by a person who belongs to or professes to belong to such an organization; or to dress or display an article in a public place in such a way as to arouse the reasonable apprehension that the person is a member of a proscribed organization.

The Public Order Act

The 1936 Public Order Act was passed largely in response to problems caused by a Fascist organization known as the 'Blackshirts'. Against the background of growing Nazi influence in Germany, this organization held provocative marches through the East End of London, an area which then, as now, had a high ethnic minority population.

The Public Order Act 1936 s. 1 made it an offence to wear a political uniform in a public place or at a public meeting (except with the permission of the Home Secretary). Although designed to cope with the Blackshirts, the offence has been used more recently against IRA members, in the case of **O'Moran** *v* **Director of Public Prosecutions** (1975). Here individuals who attended the funeral of an IRA member in London, wearing the recognized IRA uniform of black berets and dark glasses were prosecuted for the s. 1 offence.

Section 2 of the Public Order Act 1936 makes it an offence to organize or train a body to usurp the functions of the police or the armed forces, or to train such a body to use or display force in promoting any political object. In 1963, the leaders of a neo-Nazi movement known as Spearhead, whose members wore uniforms and exchanged Nazi salutes, were convicted under this section, even though there was no evidence of specific training for attacks on opponents. During the same decade, the offence was also successfully used against leaders of the Free Wales Army.

Measures against subversion

Subversion is defined as measures which are intended to undermine or overthrow parliamentary democracy in the UK and Northern Ireland by political, industrial or violent means. While membership of organizations defined as subversive is not banned in this country, members of such organizations are prohibited from holding certain kinds of civil service jobs. These restrictions are implemented by means of what is called the purge procedure, which aims to remove existing civil servants found to be members of subversive groups, and positive vetting, which seeks to exclude the members or supporters of disapproved organizations from being appointed to posts which are considered to be vital to the security of the state, by examining their political and other connections during the recruitment process.

A further restriction on the freedom of association for those in government service was the controversial banning of trade union membership at Government Communications Headquarters (GCHQ). This was not imposed because of the risk of infiltration by extremist organizations, but because the Government argued that the possibility of industrial action by union members threatened national security, even though the relevant union had offered a no-strike deal.

▶ Trade union membership

With the exception of certain government posts, workers in the UK are free to join trade unions if they wish. However, the benefit of this free-dom is compromised by the strict anti-union laws introduced since 1979, which make it very difficult to take industrial action which is both effect-ive and within the law. Collecting union subscriptions has also been made more difficult, and secondary action, in which union members not dir-ectly affected by a particular situation take action in support of fellow union members who are affected, has been made illegal. There is no requirement for UK employers to negotiate with unions, even where a high proportion of their employees are union members. This situation shows how the presence of formal rights can conceal the fact that such rights may have little effect in practice.

FREEDOM FROM DISCRIMINATION

At common law, English law provided no protection from discrimination, but over the past couple of decades, legislation has introduced protection from both sexual and racial discrimination, and to a more limited extent, discrimination on the basis of disability. Campaigners are currently trying to extend this to cover discrimination on the basis of age.

The need for protection from discrimination actually stems from the basic freedom of British law, that a person may do anything not prohib-ited by the law. In the past, this meant that, for example, landlords were free not to accept black tenants, and employers not to employ female workers. The law itself did not discriminate – it did not state postively that women or black people should have fewer rights than others – but by not specifically preventing discrimination on these grounds, it allowed those with power in society to discriminate against those without.

▶ Racial discrimination

The issue of racial discrimination was first addressed in the Race Rela-tions Act 1965, though it is now covered by the Race Relations Act 1976. The 1976 Act was introduced to remedy some of the defects in the earlier legislation, and also to bring racial discrimination provisions into line with those covering sex discrimination, which were enacted in 1976 (see below).

Under English law, racial discrimination is defined as treating someone less favourably than you would treat other people, on racial grounds; the question to be asked is not whether the person's treatment was good or bad, fair or unfair, but simply whether it would have been different but for his or her racial background. The Act makes it an offence to discriminate on racial grounds, or to incite, instruct or induce someone else to do so.

Discrimination may be either direct or indirect; the Act prohibits both. Direct discrimination occurs where a person treats another less favourably on directly racial grounds – examples would include excluding black people from membership of a club, or refusing to employ Irish people. Indirect discrimination can be less easy to spot. It occurs where conditions imposed – on employees, applicants for membership of a club, or potential tenants, for example – are such that the proportion of persons of a particular racial group who can comply with it is considerably smaller than the proportion of other persons who can comply, and such conditions are not justifiable for any reason which does not concern racial considerations, and have a detrimental effect on those who are unable to comply. This kind of discrimination was examined in **Mandla** *v* **Dowell Lee** (1983). The case concerned the application of a Sikh schoolboy to a school which forbade the wearing of any kind of headgear. The Sikh religion requires that men wear turbans, and so the boy's father alleged that the school rule indirectly discriminated against Sikhs. The school did not say it would not accept Sikh pupils (which would have been direct discrimination) but by enforcing a rule with which Sikhs could not comply and other people could, it treated Sikhs differently on the basis of their race alone. The House of Lords upheld this argument. They stated that the term 'can comply' in the Act was not to be interpreted as meaning 'can physically comply', which the Sikhs clearly could do, but 'can in practice comply' or 'can consistently with the customs and cultural conditions of the racial group comply'. The House also pointed out that the result might have been different had the same rule been in place for a different reason, such as in a factory, where headgear might be banned for health and safety reasons.

It is illegal to discriminate when offering employment, except where the work is in a private household, or where membership of a particular racial group is a genuine qualification for a stated job (for example a role in the theatre). It is unlawful to dismiss an employee for refusal to carry out racially discriminatory instructions, or to advertise in terms which suggest an intention to discriminate – though it is now legal to state that a job requires a member of a particular racial group (for example, a Chinese waiter for a Chinese restaurant) (s. 29). It is illegal

to discriminate on racial grounds in the choice of partners for partnerships of six or more persons, admission to trade unions and professional
organizations, granting of licences and qualifications for trades or voca-
tions, vocational training and employment agency services (ss. 10–14).
Discrimination is also unlawful in education and in the provision of goods,
services and facilities to the public or a section of the public. There are
exceptions for residential accommodation in small premises and for the
fostering or care of children in a person's home (s. 23(2)). Clubs which
have more than 25 members may not discriminate in admission to membership or the treatment of associate members (s. 25) but a club whose
main aim is to provide benefits to persons of particular racial group may
discriminate on grounds of race, nationality or ethnic origin but not as
regards colour (s. 26).

Allegations of discrimination in relation to employment are brought
before an industrial tribunal, which can declare the rights of the parties
in regard to the alleged discrimination, order compensation to be paid,
or recommend other steps to be taken by way of a remedy (ss. 53–55).
Other types of discrimination may be brought before designated county
courts, which can award damages, including compensation for injury
to feelings. Where indirect discrimination is alleged, it is a defence to an
action for damages for the alleged discriminator to prove that there
was no intention to discriminate against the claimant on racial grounds
(s. 57(3)). In some cases the Commission for Racial Equality will help
complainants bring cases, and fund the necessary legal advice.

The Commission consists of a chairman and not more than fourteen
members. The members are appointed by the Home Secretary, though
the Commission is formally independent of Government, and the various
ethnic minorities are substantially represented in its membership. One of
its main functions is to conduct investigations into alleged discriminatory
practices. This can only be done where there is a reasonable suspicion
that acts of discrimination have occurred, but if so, it may order the
organization or person concerned to supply information and produce
documents, and hold a hearing. If the investigation does find discrimination, the Commission may issue a non-discrimination notice requiring it
to stop; there is a right of appeal to the county court, or to an industrial
tribunal in the case of employment discrimination. The Commission can
follow up a notice within five years of issue, to ensure that it has been
complied with, and if not, it may apply to the county court for an injunction. The Commission also makes an annual report to the Home Secretary which is laid before Parliament.

The Act has been criticized for laying the burden of preventing discrimination on the individuals affected. Many people may be reluctant to
report discrimination, especially in employment, for fear that their chances
of work may be further threatened, and it is arguable that such a practice
as anti-social as discrimination should be viewed rather as crimes are, as

something which makes society less pleasant for all of us, and which should therefore be the responsibility of society, in the form of the state, rather than the individual. Some more severe racist behaviour is made a criminal offence under Part three of the Public Order Act 1986 (see p. 366).

A further problem with our race discrimination legislation is the difficulty of proof. Given the large numbers of people looking for jobs, for example, it can be difficult to prove that a person has been refused a job on the basis of race, when he or she may have been one of many applicants with similar qualifications. Coupled with the problems mentioned above on reporting and challenging discrimination, it can be argued that our approach to discrimination law can never really lead to the eradication of racial discrimination in practice. Given this point of view, some experts argue that what is needed is positive discrimination or reverse discrimination; measures which aim to compensate for the disadvantages caused by racial discrimination, by making rules which discriminate in favour of ethnic minorities. One way of doing this is to put in place quota systems, whereby the intake of a university, or the staff of a firm, for example, would be required to reflect the percentage of ethnic minorities in society as a whole. In a culture where we are used to the idea that treating everybody the same is fair, this can seem unjust, but the alternative view is that if people start off with unequal chances – because of the effects of racial discrimination, for example – treating them as though they were equal will simply maintain their inequality. Positive discrimination aims to promote a 'level playing field', redressing the balance between those who have most opportunity to succeed and those who have least. However, with certain exceptions, it is illegal under our legislation.

▶ Sex discrimination

Although the cause of equality for women had been a major issue since the beginning of the century, Britain did not create laws against sex discrimination until 1976. The field is now covered by two inter-related Acts, the Equal Pay Act 1970 and the Sex Discrimination Act 1975.

The Equal Pay Act 1970

The Equal Pay Act states that women are to have equal pay with men where they are doing the same work. This does not mean that their jobs must be identical; different jobs done by men and women will be considered as 'like work' where the differences in job content are not significant or though significant do not occur frequently. The same applies where an official job evaluation study has been made, and rates the work

374 Forms of civil liberties

done by women as equivalent to men's work. In **Hayward** *v* **Camell Laird Shipbuilders Ltd** (1988), it was held that a female cook was entitled to the same wage as a carpenter, or a joiner, or a thermal insulation engineer, employed by the same company, because her work and theirs were of equal value to the company.

Where a collective bargaining agreement between employer and trade union provides different rates for men and women, it can be referred to the Industrial Arbitration Board so that any offending clauses may be removed.

A woman who believes that she is not getting equal pay has to make her claim before an industrial tribunal (a man who believes he is paid less than a woman doing like work has the same rights, but in practice the victim of lower pay is usually a woman). So long as she can satisfy the tribunal that her work is the same as or similar to a man's, the onus is on her employer to prove that there are material differences between the man's situation and the woman's, other than sex, and that these differences constitute a genuine reason for the difference in the treatment awarded them – an example might be where women and men did the same work, but the man worked night shifts and the woman days. As well as gaining equal pay, an employee who succeeds in her claim may win compensation.

As well as pay, the Act covers other terms and conditions of employment, including sickness pay and holiday bonuses.

The Sex Discrimination Act 1975

The Sex Discrimination Act 1975 has a broader application than the Equal Pay Act, and is similar in scope to the Race Relations Act 1976. Four types of discrimination are covered: treating a woman less favourably than a man on account of sex; treating a man less favourably than a woman (maternity provisions excepted); treating a married person less favourably, on grounds of their marital status, than a single person; and victimization because someone has invoked either the 1970 or 1975 Act. Like the Race Relations Act 1976, it prohibits both direct and indirect discrimination; an example of indirect sex discrimination might be a requirement that all plumbers employed by a company should be at least 5ft 10in tall, a requirement that is clearly likely to be satisfied by more men than women.

Part II of the 1975 Act prohibits discrimination in employment, covering terms and conditions of employment, access to training, promotion and benefits and dismissal. It includes job advertisements, and makes it illegal deliberately to refuse employment on grounds of sex. There is an exemption for employment which involves working in a private house, with a degree of contact which might reasonably lead to objections to a worker of a particular sex, and for cases where the job can genuinely only be performed by one sex or the other.

The Act established the Equal Opportunities Commission, which has similar powers to the Commission for Racial Equality. Complaints about discrimination in employment and training are made to an industrial tribunal which may award compensation; the EOC can help with this action, as well as with complaints not related to employment.

▶ Discrimination against disabled people

Legislation is likely to be passed in the near future to give disabled people rights against discrimination. The Government-backed Disability Discrimination Bill is currently being considered by Parliament. The Bill aims to outlaw discrimination of disabled people in the field of employment and in the provision of services, goods and facilities. But it has already been criticized for containing too many exceptions and being too narrowly drafted. It has been suggested that the two Private Member's Bills which were opposed by the Government (primarily on the basis of the cost of compliance for businesses) would have given disabled people more rights.

Looking at the proposed legislation in more detail, clause 1 defines disability for the purposes of the Bill as 'An impairment (either physical or clinically well-recognised mental illness) which has a substantial and long term effect on his ability to carry out day to day activities.' Schedule 1 of the Bill states that a 'long term effect' is one which has lasted or is likely to last 12 months or more. The Law Society has criticized this definition as excluding people who have recovered from a mental illness, such as a nervous breakdown, but are perceived as not having recovered by, for example, a potential employer.

Clause 3 provides that it is unlawful to treat disabled people less favourably than others because of their disability, in relation to offering employment and the terms of that employment: promotion, transfer, training and other benefits and the decision to dismiss or impose some other disadvantage.

Less favourable treatment is allowed under clause 5 if the employer reasonably believes that the nature of the disability substantially affects the disabled person's ability to perform a requisite task. So, problems of access to the office are no longer a sufficient excuse, but inability to perform even a very minor task is. The employment provisions of the Bill only apply where twenty or more people are employed.

The Bill would also make it illegal to refuse to provide disabled people with goods, facilities or services, or to fail to amend a practice or procedure which makes it impossible or unreasonably difficult for a disabled person to use them. Thus, automatic ticket machines at a car park will have to be at a height accessible to disabled people.

Clause 14 states that less favourable treatment will be justified, however, if the service provider reasonably believes that it is necessary so as not to endanger the health or safety of any person; or the disabled person (with sufficient mental capacity) has given their agreement to less favourable treatment; or it is necessary if the service is to be provided to other members of the public. A disabled person can be required to pay more for a service if this reflects the greater cost to the provider. The Bill excludes protection against discrimination in the fields of education or transport.

An action under the Bill in employment matters would be heard by an industrial tribunal and in other matters would go to the county court. Unlike the legislation against race and sex discrimination, no commission is established.

• •

FREEDOM OF THE PERSON

Freedom of the person (sometimes called personal liberty) refers to a person's right to go about their lawful business without interference from the state, and in particular, their freedom to go where they want to, and not to be imprisoned in any way. Although this is a right which we often take for granted, it is subject to some restrictions.

Freedom of movement also offers one of the few examples of a positive right in English law, as oppposed to a residual right, though this springs originally from Britain's membership of the European Union rather than from Parliament or the common law. The Treaty on European Union spells out the rights to be enjoyed by every citizen of the European Union, and the first of these is the right to move and reside freely throughout the territory of the member states.

▶ Deportation, extradition and unlawful immigration

In theory, freedom of the person includes the right to travel and live anywhere, but this aspect of personal liberty is severely restricted in Britain. While all British citizens have the right to enter the country and live here, anyone who is not a British citizen can be deported, under the Immigration Act 1971 as amended by the British Nationality Act 1981, and the Immigration Act 1988 and the Immigration Rules 1990 (which deal with asylum seekers). Anyone who is not a British Citizen, with certain specified exceptions, is subject to deportation. Deportation can be ordered on four basic grounds:

- If the Home Secretary deems it 'conducive to the public good';
- If the person is over seventeen and has been convicted of an offence which is punishable by imprisonment, and the court recommends deportation;

- Where a person breaks any entry conditions or overstays the period of entry permitted by the immigration officer;
- Where the person is the infant child or wife of someone against whom a deportation order is made.

The first ground offers a wide discretion to the Home Secretary, and is often used against convicted offenders, even where the court does not recommend deportation.

There are no rights of appeal against decisions relating to work permits, to the issue of a special voucher status available to British Overseas Citizens, or against refusal to issue a passport or the decision to withdraw a passport. Rights of appeal are also limited where individuals are to be deported at the Home Secretary's discretion, because of an apparent threat to national security. In such cases, persons affected can appear before a panel known as the 'Three Wise Men' to try to oppose deportation, but in doing so, they are not entitled to know the reasons for the deportation order, making it very difficult to make a case against it. This was highlighted in the case of **R** *v* **Secretary of State for the Home Department ex parte Cheblak** (1991), which arose during the Gulf War. Cheblak was one of over 160 Iraqis and Palestinians who the Home Office decided to deport in the interests of national security, and who were detained pending their deportation. The individuals were chosen on the advice of the police, MI5, Special Branch and the Home Office, but the accuracy of the information was open to question and the procedures for vetting the information appeared inadequate. The detainees appeared before the 'Three Wise Men', and as a result, a handful of them were released, but the reasons why some were allowed to go and not others were never made public. In an application for *habeas corpus*, Cheblak challenged the fact that no reasons were given for his detention, but the courts held that where national security was an issue, such reasons did not have to be produced.

Restrictions on travel

It is commonly believed that British citizens can go in and out of the country without problems, but there are two restrictions on this aspect of personal freedom. First, the government can refuse to issue a passport, or insist that one is handed back, in four classes of case:

- Where it is suspected that the applicant or passport holder intends to take children out of the jurisdiction illegally;
- Where tourists stranded abroad have been brought back home at the UK Government's expense, and have not repaid the cost;
- Where the applicant or passport holder is suspected of intent to leave the country in order to avoid arrest;

- Where the activities of the applicant or passport holder are 'so notoriously undesirable or dangerous that Parliament would be expected to support the action of the Foreign Secretary in refusing them a passport'. This category has been used to deny a passport to those travelling abroad for purposes which the UK Government finds politically unacceptable, such as scientists attempting to attend conferences in Eastern Europe during the Cold War.

It has been established that the decision to withdraw or refuse to issue a passport can be reviewed by the courts.

A second restriction on travel by UK subjects is that of exclusion orders. These are used to prevent those suspected of terrorism from travelling to the mainland from Northern Ireland, or sometimes vice versa. Involvement in terrorism does not have to be proved, and the only possible appeal consists of making written representations to the Home Secretary, or putting the case in an interview with a Home Offive adjudicator, neither of which is likely to be successful.

Mental illness

The personal liberty of those suffering from mental illness can be restrained by orders requiring their detention in hospital or a psychiatric institution. This kind of detention can be used as a sentence against those convicted of criminal offences.

Police powers

For majority people in England, the most important legal restrictions on personal liberty can be found in the powers of the police to stop, search and arrest those suspected of crime. These are discussed on p. 194 *et seq.*

FREEDOM OF EXPRESSION

The right to freedom of expression in most democratic countries includes freedom to hold opinions, 'and to receive and impart information and ideas without interference by public authority and regardless of frontiers. This is one of the most fundamental rights in democratic society; democracy is based on the consent of the people to their government, and this consent is meaningless if people cannot debate and discuss ideas without government permission. Without free speech, opposition to government cannot be expressed, and new ideas cannot be introduced.

Moreover, freedom of expression is an integral part of the artistic, cultural and intellectual freedom of a free society.

In the USA, freedom of speech is guaranteed by the First Amendment to the Constitution, and carries great weight even when in conflict with other rights; here, like other 'rights', our freedom of speech is what is left when you take into account the restrictions on it, and these are many. Where freedom of speech has conflicted with other interests, it often comes a very poor second.

Restrictions on freedom of expression take two main forms: censorship of material by state authorities before it is published or displayed; and the imposition of penalties, or the granting of redress in the case of someone specifically harmed by the material, after the event. Prior censorship is particularly controversial, and tends to be associated in the public's minds with totalitarian regimes, but it is actually alive and well in Britain today.

We will look first at restrictions which are aimed at specific sections of the media, and then at those which apply across the board.

▶ Restrictions on the press

Freedom of the press has been, in theory at least, a cornerstone of civil liberties in England for centuries. One of the most important results of this is that English Law does not require publishers to obtain a government licence, as is the case in some other countries. This means that in theory, anyone may publish a newspaper or magazine, though in practice economic considerations mean that our biggest and most widely-read publications are concentrated in the hands of a small number of companies.

Fears of a movement towards monopoly conditions in sectors of the press led, after an inquiry by a royal commission, to the enactment in what is now the Fair Trading Act 1973, ss. 57–62, of provisions to ensure that newspaper mergers above a certain scale do not take place in a manner contrary to the public interest.

The aim of the provisions is to prevent any one newspaper from obtaining a monopoly over areas of the press by means of mergers between papers. Where the combined circulation of two newspapers is more than 500,000, any proposed merger between them requires the consent of the Secretary of State for Trade and Industry. Before consent is given, the proposed merger will usually be investigated by the Monopolies and Mergers Commission, which considers 'whether the transfer in question may be expected to operate against the public interest, taking into account all matters which appear in the circumstances to be relevant and, in particular, the need for accurate presentation of news and free expression of opinion'.

Even so, when Rupert Murdoch, owner of the *Sun* and the *News of the World*, acquired *The Times* and *Sunday Times* in 1981, the purchase was not referred, even though it gave him 30 per cent of the national daily circulation and 36 per cent of the national Sunday circulation. By 1987, three publishers between them owned 73 per cent of national daily circulation and 81 per cent of national Sunday circulation.

Complaints about the press, which usually concern invasion of privacy or unfair or inaccurate reporting, can be made to the Press Complaints Commission. The Commission is a non-statutory body, comprising a chairman and fifteen members, one-third of whom are not associated with the press. The Commission can request that newspapers publish corrections, apologies or statements about the complaint, but has no power to enforce this request. In recent years there has been growing concern that its powers are too weak, particularly in the area of invasion of privacy, and that a fully-fledged privacy law should be created (see p. 398).

▶ Restrictions on broadcasters

All broadcasting organizations are required to be licensed by the Government; it is an offence under the Wireless Telegraphy Act 1949 to broadcast radio or television signals without a licence. The BBC receives its licence from the Government under the Wireless and Telegraphy Acts, while the ITV companies are awarded theirs by the Independent Television Commission (ITC), whose members are appointed by the Home Secretary. The licences are periodically renewed, at which point commercial organizations bid against each other; provided that certain minimum quality thresholds laid down in the Act are met, including that the applicant 'is a fit and proper person to hold' a licence, the licences must be awarded to the highest bidder. There are restrictions on political or religious organizations and newspaper proprietors holding licences. Licences for commercial radio are awarded in the same way, but by the Radio Authority, which, like the ITC, was created under the 1990 Act.

The BBC

The BBC, which is funded by TV licence fees, is headed by a Board of Governors, with a chairman and deputy chairman who are appointed by the Crown on the advice of the Prime Minister. This structure has recently been criticized as having the potential for political bias, and there have been allegations that the BBC has been too ready to respond to Government pressure in withdrawing certain programmes which the Government preferred not to be broadcast.

The operation of the BBC is regulated by the terms of its licence and an agreement between the Home Secretary and the BBC's Board of Governors, which impose a number of duties. It must broadcast a daily account of the proceedings in Parliament, and any government minister can require announcements to be broadcast. Where such announcements concern issues of political controversy, the opposition in Parliament has a right of reply.

Perhaps more importantly for the purposes of freedom of expression, the minister responsible for broadcasting may require the BBC not to broadcast certain matters. Where it is told not to broadcast on a particular subject, or not to show a particular programme, the BBC may tell the public that such a ban is in place, but is not obliged to; as a result, there is no way of knowing how well used this power is, and in what areas. In recent years, it has been used to prevent direct broadcasting of statements made by members of certain organizations in Northern Ireland, among them Sinn Fein, a recognized political party with some electoral support.

The BBC is not allowed to use its broadcasts to express its own political views; it can issue political broadcasts on agreement with the main political parties in the country. In case of emergency, the Government has the right to take over the BBC for the duration. As the Government is responsible for both the organization and the financing of the BBC, some people have argued that the Government may have too much influence over it. This concern has been particularly pronounced in relation to broadcasting of the Gulf War. It is now becoming clear that the public were only given a sanitized version of what actually happened during the conflict.

Commercial broadcasters

Commercial broadcasters are financed by revenue from advertising. They are now regulated by ITC, under the provisions of the Broadcasting Act 1990. The commission is obliged to ensure that a wide range of services are provided and that there is fair and effective competition in the provision of services.

Important restrictions on what may be broadcast are contained in s. 6 of the 1990 Act, which parallels regulations guiding the BBC. This requires the ITC to be satisfied that nothing is included in the programmes which offends against good taste or decency or is likely to encourage or incite to crime or to lead to disorder or be offensive to public feeling; that all news is presented with due accuracy and impartiality; that due impartiality is preserved in respect of matters of political or industrial controversy or relating to current public policy; and that due responsibility is exercised with respect to the content of any religious programmes and in particular that any such programmes do not involve any improper exploitation of any susceptibilities of those watching the programmes. Section 10 of the Broadcasting Act 1990 grants the relevant minister of state powers to direct TV companies to broadcast announcements, or to refrain from including certain matters in programmes.

The 1990 Act also contains strict rules on advertising. Advertisements directed to political ends may not be shown; in other countries, it is common to see political parties advertising on television, but here this is not allowed. Restrictions also apply to advertisements concerning industrial disputes; the Government may place such advertisements, but nobody else is allowed to.

As with the BBC, the Government has been quick to oppose programmes which criticize its role in Northern Ireland, and particular controversy was caused by a 1988 documentary made by Thames Television. Called 'Death on the Rock', it investigated the shooting of three members of the IRA by members of the SAS in Gibraltar, and re-opened a previous debate about whether the security forces were operating a shoot-to-kill policy against suspected terrorists. The programme was fiercely criticized by the Government, and many believe it was no coincidence that when the time came to renew independent television licences, Thames lost theirs to another company.

Similar rules to the above apply to commercial radio, and are regulated by the Radio Authority.

The Broadcasting Complaints Commission

The Broadcasting Complaints Commission was created in 1980. It is appointed by the Home Secretary, and adjudicates upon complaints of unjust or unfair treatment in television or radio programmes, and of unwarranted intrusions of privacy (Broadcasting Act 1990, s. 143).

The Broadcasting Standards Council

The Broadcasting Standards Council was established as a consumer watchdog in 1988 to monitor standards of programming with respect to violence, sex, taste and decency. It accepts complaints about these issues direct from the public, provided there is no legal remedy available (Broadcasting Act 1990, s. 154), and produces a code of conduct for broadcasters.

▶ Theatres

As recently as 1968, all stage performances and plays were subject to direct censorship; they could be lawfully performed only with permission from the Lord Chamberlain (an officer of the royal household), and it was a criminal offence to stage a play without such a licence. Plays dealing with controversial topics, such as homosexuality, or featuring nudity or bad language were likely to be censored.

A Private Members' Bill was introduced to abolish the Lord Chamberlain's censorship powers; it became the Theatres Act 1968. Premises still require a local authority licence if they are to be used for the public performance of a play, but this is simply in regard to such matters as public health and safety, and may not be used to impose restrictions on shows or plays to be performed (although displays of hypnotism may be subject to restrictions).

▶ Cinema and video

Film has the highest level of direct censorship of any media in this country, and is subject to a two-stage process. First, all films for general release are certified by the British Board of Film Classification (BBFC), a body set up and run by the film industry. It classifies films as 'U', which stands for universal exhibition, and means the film is suitable for any age; 'PG', which stands for parental guidance, and means that although no age restriction is imposed, some scenes may be unsuitable for young children; '12', which means not to be shown to children under twelve; '15', not to be shown to under-fifteens; '18', not to be shown to under-eighteens; and 18R, which means restricted distribution and over-eighteens only – this category would cover the kind of films shown in sex cinemas. The Board may also refuse a film a certificate altogether, or grant one only if certain parts of the film are cut. Although these classifications have no statutory authority, and failure to receive a certificate does not mean a film cannot be shown, widespread acceptance of the system means that in practice it has a strong effect. This is partly linked to the second stage of the censorship process; local authority licences. All cinemas have to be licensed, and in granting the licences, local authorities may impose conditions; one of these is commonly that films without BBFC certificates should not be shown without the express permission of the licensing authority, which in practice makes a BBFC certificate almost essential if a film is to be seen in any numbers. However, even where a film has a BBFC certificate, it can still be banned by a local authority from being shown in local cinemas.

The Departmental Committee on Obscenity and Film Censorship recommended in 1979 that a statutory body for censoring films should be created, but that recommendation has not been acted upon. However, concerns about 'video nasties' being too easily available to children led to the BBFC being given a statutory responsibility, under the Video Recordings Act 1984, to classify all videos which are available for sale or hire, with the exception of those which are educational, or concerned with music, sport or religion. It is an offence under the Act to supply an unclassified video outside the terms of the statute.

▶ Provisions applying to all media

The Official Secrets Acts

There are quite severe restrictions on the publication, in any form, of information concerned with areas of government such as defence, the security services and foreign relations, and these are contained in the Official Secrets Acts 1911, 1920, 1939 and 1989.

The latest Official Secrets Act was passed after longstanding criticism of s. 2 of the 1911 Act, a widely-drawn section which made it an offence for any Government servant to reveal, without authorization, any information about, or gained in, their job. There was no requirement for the information to be secret, or potentially damaging to the Government; revealing the number of cups of tea drunk in the Department of Health canteen, or the brand of vacuum cleaner used on Ministry of Defence floors, for example, would technically come within the scope of the old s. 2.

The section had been criticized in several trials, and its abolition was recommended by the Franks Committee in 1972. The Committee suggested that criminal sanctions should be restricted to areas of major significance, such as wrongful disclosure of information relating to the defence, security, foreign relations and reserves, Cabinet documents and the use of official information for private gain or information supplied about particular individuals, but these recommendations were ignored until two controversial trials created yet more opposition to the section.

The first of these arose after Sarah Tisdall, a civil service clerk, discovered that ministers intended to lie about the date on which cruise missiles were to arrive at Greenham Common, so as to avoid any demonstration against that arrival. Tisdall passed this information to a newspaper, and was caught when the newspaper was forced by the courts to hand back documents which allowed their source to be traced. Despite the fact that the courts agreed that the information leaked was no threat to national security – and the fact that she had exposed wrongdoing in the Government – she was sentenced to six months imprisonment.

The second controversial trial was that of Clive Ponting, an assistant secretary in the Ministry of Defence. Ponting discovered that the Government had misled the House of Commons over an incident during the Falklands War, the sinking of the Argentinian battleship the *General Belgrano*. Under the Official Secrets Act as it stood at the time, Ponting would be banned from making such a disclosure, unless it was to someone 'to whom it is his duty in the interests of state to communicate [the information]'. Ponting admitted that he had leaked the information, but argued that he was justified in doing so, because Parliament was part of the state, and therefore it was in the interests of the state that such information be disclosed to an MP. This argument was flatly rejected by the judge, who stated that the interests of the state simply meant the interests of the government of the day, and directed the jury that they should not allow Ponting's defence. Nevertheless, the jury acquitted Ponting, to the enormous embarrassment of the Government.

The controversy over these two cases led to pressure to reform s. 2, and this was eventually done in the OSA 1989. In the new s. 2, blanket secrecy on all Government information is replaced by six categories of information. In two of these, covering the work of the security services, and information obtained under or concerning activities under Interception of Communications Act (1985) and what was to become the Security Services Act, any disclosure is an offence. The other four categories are international relations, information obtained in confidence from other governments, information relating to defence, and information impeding the prevention or detection of offences. In all these cases, only disclosures which are defined as harmful are offences, but the tests of harm are not difficult for the prosecution to satisfy.

The then Home Secretary called the 1989 reforms 'an essay in openness unparalleled since the Second World War', but it is difficult to see how this praise can be justified. The range of protected information may be narrower, but in practice it covers all the kinds of information ever likely to be – or to need to be – leaked. All the prosecutions brought over the last 30 years would have fitted these categories. In addition, civil service disciplinary codes were redrawn to cover information not covered by the new OSA, so the commitment to openness mentioned by the Home Secretary is hard to spot.

The 1989 Act does not include a public interest defence, even in the limited form highlighted by Ponting's defence. This means that even where a civil servant discovers major wrongdoing, it should not be disclosed; official secrecy is given a higher priority than good government. The Government argued that a public interest defence would amount to a licence to leak, but this claim ignores the fact that the individual concerned would have no guarantee that a jury would accept the defence in a particular case; even if they did, and the individual was acquitted, he or she would have destroyed any chance of a successful career in the civil service. Given all this, civil servants are unlikely to leak information unless they believe there are very good reasons for doing so. In addition, where real wrongdoing has gone on, it can be argued that the public has a right to know.

A further problem with the draconian nature of official secrets provisions is the climate of secrecy they create, which may make newspapers and broadcasters reluctant to touch stories concerning official wrongdoing. Just after the Ponting trial, Channel 4 withdrew a television programme in which another civil servant, Cathy Massiter, revealed that the security services were targeting members of trade unions for surveillance. The programme was eventually shown much later, but there is no way of knowing how many such stories are abandoned for fear of the OSA.

The OSA also creates wide search and seizure powers against the media. The potential breadth of these powers was seen in 1986, when the investigative journalist Duncan Campbell produced a film for the BBC, as part of a series entitled 'Secret Society'. The programme revealed the cost and extent of a secret Defence Ministry project to put a spy satellite into orbit, and once the Government discovered this, it was banned. Using search powers derived from both PACE and the OSA, police raided Campbell's home and office, and the Glasgow offices of the BBC, removing substantial numbers of documents, even though Campbell had already published the story in the *New Statesman* before the injunction had been granted. The BBC eventually broadcast an agreed version of the programme.

'D' Notices

The 'D' Notice system is a little-known but powerful means of censoring broadcasters and the press. The Defence, Press and Broadcasting Committee is made up of Government representatives, permanent civil servants, and representatives of the press and broadcasters. The 'D' notices it issues are requests from the Government to the media, asking them not to publish particular material on the grounds that it would have an adverse effect on national defence or security and would therefore not be in the public interest. Refusal to comply with a 'D' Notice is not an offence (though depending on the nature of the information, publication may be a breach of the Official Secrets Acts), but broadcasters and publishers who do refuse to go along with the system may find it more difficult to get access to confidential information. In addition, the arrangement is somewhat one-sided, in that gaining the Committee's approval for an item to be published does not guarantee that the publisher will not be prosecuted under the Official Secrets Act. A BBC radio series, 'My Country Right or Wrong', which included interviews with former intelligence service employees, was cleared with the secretary to the Committee during its planning, yet when the BBC attempted to broadcast it, the Attorney-General secured an injunction to prevent its transmission. The series was later broadcast unamended.

In 1979–80, the 'D' notice system was reviewed by the Defence Select Committee, which heard evidence that the system was not working effectively. Chapman Pincher, an investigative journalist, pointed out that in the past, there had been an unspoken agreement that if broadcasters or journalists asked whether a story was the subject of a 'D' Notice before publication, and were told it was not, publication of such stories would not lead to prosecution. Once that arrangement ceased to exist, media confidence in the system had declined, and the press and broadcasters were less willing to submit to it. In addition, the growing influence of the international press was making it more difficult to keep stories within the national boundaries of the United Kingdom.

The Select Committee was divided on the issue of whether the 'D' notice system should be reformed, but agreed that some form of control over press and broadcasting activities in these areas should remain. The Government have suggested that they may re-examine the workings of the Committee at a later date.

Contempt of court

Contempt of court provisions punish conduct which tends to obstruct, prejudice or abuse the administration of justice, either in a particular case or generally. It creates two restrictions on freedom of expression; first, in preventing publication of any material which creates a substantial risk that the result of a trial will be prejudiced; and secondly, in requiring journalists, in certain circumstances, to disclose the sources of their information.

Publications prejudicial to a trial

Here a balance needs to be struck between protecting the right to a free trial, and allowing the media to publish information which it is in the public interest to know. The possible conflicts between the two can be seen in the case of **Sunday Times *v* United Kingdom** (1979), which concerned the thalidomide tragedy described on p. 441. During the thalidomide parents' struggle for compensation, the *Sunday Times* published an article about the situation, which, among other things, urged Distillers to make a generous settlement to thalidomide victims. The newspaper was planning to run a second feature dealing with the background to thalidomide's launch, but the House of Lords granted Distillers an injunction, preventing publication of this second piece, on the grounds that it was contempt of court to publish an article prejudging an issue which was the subject of litigation, where such publication created a real risk of prejudice to the trial. It was also contempt, the House of Lords said, to pressurize litigants to settle on terms to which they did not wish to agree, or criticize then for exercising their rights in the courts.

The *Sunday Times* took the case to the European Court of Human Rights, which said that the injunction infringed art. 10 of the European Convention on Human Rights, concerning free expression. The ban could only be justified if the reason for it was 'a social need sufficiently pressing to outweigh the public interest in freedom of expression', and since the thalidomide issue was one of great public concern, the press had a duty to inform the public about it.

Partly as a result of this case, the 1981 Contempt of Court Act was passed, and in this respect at least, has proved a liberalizing measure. Publication of material related to a trial is now contempt only if it 'creates a substantial risk that the course of justice in the proceedings in question will be seriously impeded or prejudiced'. The difference between this approach and that of the *Sunday Times* case can be seen in the Court of Appeal's refusal to prevent the *News of the World* from publishing allegations about the cricketer Ian Botham that were the subject of a libel action with another newspaper. The Court agreed that the publication would create a risk of prejudice to the libel trial, but decided that since that trial was ten months away, the risk was not substantial.

This approach recognizes that for members of a jury, actually sitting and listening to a trial is a powerful experience, which tends to drive out other influences, especially things heard and seen many months before. The courts have also recognized that where juries are not involved, there is even less need for protection against the influence of published material. In **Re Lonrho Plc** (1990), the Trade and Industry Secretary had appointed inspectors to assess the affairs of Lonrho, a large company, but then refused to publish the resulting report. Lonrho applied for judicial review of the Secretary of State's decision, and in the meantime, got hold of a copy of the report. The *Observer* newspaper agreed to publish it, and issues were sent to some of the Law Lords who were to hear appeals on Lonrho's application for judicial review. However, the court held that there was no risk of prejudice, stating that it was 'difficult to visualise circumstances in which any court in the UK exercising appellate jurisdiction would be in the least likely to be influenced by public discussion of the merits of a decision appealed against'.

Provisions against prejudicial publications apply only where court proceedings are active: criminal proceedings become active for this purpose when the suspect is arrested or charged, or an arrest warrant is issued; civil actions, when the action is set down for trial.

The Act offers three defences against a charge of prejudicial publication:

Innocent publication. Here the publishers must prove that despite taking all possible care, they did not know the proceedings were active.

Fair and accurate report. Publishers are allowed to publish a contemporary report of legal proceedings held in public, if fair, accurate and produced in good faith. The court may delay such reports where necessary to prevent substantial risk of prejudice to the administration of justice.

Prejudice merely incidental. This defence applies where a good faith discussion on public affairs contains material which is merely incidentally prejudicial to a trial. An example occurred in the case of **Attorney-General *v* English** (1983), which concerned an article published by the *Daily Mail*, on a pro-life election candidate. The candidate's election manifesto referred to the practice of hospitals allowing newborn babies with very severe handicaps to die, and

argued that this should be banned. The article was published
during the trial of a doctor accused of allowing a baby to die in
those circumstances. The House of Lords agreed that the article
was capable of prejudicing the jury, but said that to prevent it
would mean that all discussion of the subject was banned from the
time that the doctor was charged, until the end of his trial, ten
months later, and such a ban would prevent the election candidate
from publicizing her policy.

By contrast, the journalist Sir John Junor was fined for
contempt, after publishing a personal attack on the doctor which
made no attempt to set the issue in a wider context.

In the United States, court proceedings are fully open to publication
(and of course are shown on TV). Restrictions on publication are allowed
only if defendants can prove there is a real danger they will not receive
a fair trial.

Contempt of court powers were apparently extended by the Court of
Appeal in **Attorney-General *v* Newspaper Publishing plc** (1987), which
concerned the *Spycatcher* saga discussed p. 392. As part of a long series of
litigation, the Government had obtained injunctions against the *Guardian*
and *Observer* newspapers in relation to the writings of former MI5 officer,
Peter Wright. When three other papers, who were not parties to this
injunction, published details of Wright's revelations, it was held that they
were guilty of contempt. The result is that where an injunction is placed
on one publication, others who publish the relevant material will be in
contempt, if they knew of the injunctions binding the other newspapers
and, by publication, destroyed the subject matter of those court orders
with intent to impede or prejudice the administration of justice.

Contempt in the face of the court

The charge of contempt in the face of the court is the kind of contempt often referred to in TV dramas, where witnesses or the defendant
are told they will be in contempt if they do not stop shouting or making
impolite or inappropriate remarks, especially to the judge. However, it
also covers refusal of a witness to answer questions, and it is in this
context that journalists who refuse to disclose their sources may find
themselves in contempt. This has implications for freedom of expression,
in that those who disclose wrongdoing to journalists are often putting
their own position at risk by doing so, and will only make such revelations
if the journalist promises to keep the source secret. An example might be
a civil servant who discloses wrongdoing among ministers, or an employee
who spills the beans on mismanagement or corruption in their firm; both
would be likely to lose their job, and quite possibly be unable to find
alternative employment in a similar area if it was discovered that they
had leaked such information. Civil servants might also find themselves

prosecuted under the Official Secrets Act. Clearly people in this position will be much less likely to divulge wrongdoing if they know that the courts can demand that journalists reveal their sources.

Before the Contempt of Court Act 1981, there was very little recognition of any right of journalists to keep such sources secret. In **Attorney-General *v* Mulholland and Foster** (1963), journalists who had helped expose a spy scandal refused to disclose their sources to a tribunal enquiring into the affair. The High Court said that journalists had no legal privilege to refuse to divulge sources where the information was relevant and necessary to trial.

The 1981 Act's provisions on disclosure of sources appeared to liberalize this area of the law, recognizing that there was a public interest in keeping such sources confidential which must be balanced against other interests. Unfortunately, subsequent judicial interpretation of the Act has weakened this approach considerably.

The Act provides that a court can no longer order disclosure of sources unless it is satisfied that such disclosure is necessary in the interest of justice, national security, or the prevention of disorder or crime. But by giving each of the categories so far litigated a very wide interpretation, the courts have ensured that there are in practice very few cases in which disclosure would not be ordered.

The issue of when disclosure is necessary in the interests of national security was tested in **Secretary of State for Defence *v* Guardian Newspapers** (1985), the case involving civil servant Sarah Tisdall, who leaked documents showing that the Government intended to mislead the public about the date on which Cruise missiles would arrive at Greenham Common. The court agreed that the revelation itself posed no threat to national security, but held that the threat was not what Ms Tisdall had revealed, but what she could have revealed; the fact that someone in her position could disclose any information was itself a threat to national security.

A similarly wide interpretation was given to disclosures in the interests of preventing crime, in **Re An Inquiry Under the Company Securities Act** (1985). Here a journalist had published articles disclosing that information useful for insider dealing was being leaked. Inspectors investigating into insider dealing wanted the sources disclosed, and argued that it was necessary for 'prevention of crime'. The journalist argued that this meant prevention of a specific crime which would otherwise happen; since the leaks he had referred to had stopped, disclosing his source would not do this. The court, however, agreed with the inspectors, that prevention of crime meant prevention of crime in general, and information about one case of insider dealing might help prevent others.

Finally, disclosure in the interests of justice was examined in **X Ltd *v* Morgan-Grampian** (1990). In this case, an employee of X Ltd stole a business plan, which showed that the company, which had been boasting of its success, was potentially in financial difficulties. The employee leaked the plan to a young journalist, Bill Goodwin, who was employed by Morgan-Grampian. When his magazine attempted to publish a story based on the plan, X Ltd obtained an injunction against publication, and sought disclosure of Goodwin's source, arguing that this was 'in the interests of justice' because they intended to prosecute the thief.

Morgan-Grampian argued that the court was required to strike a balance between the interests of justice and those of free expression, and in doing so, it was not the court's job to put right breaches of X Ltd's own security, nor to order disclosure just because otherwise X Ltd would have had no remedy. They pointed out that having promised his source confidentiality, Goodwin had a moral obligation to honour that promise.

The Court of Appeal agreed that X Ltd's lack of an alternative remedy was insufficient in itself to require disclosure in the interests of justice, and that the interests of justice had to be balanced against the public interest in protecting press sources. However, they stated that in this case, there was no particular public interest in publishing the story, as there might have been if the company had been a public one with shareholders who could have been deprived of useful information otherwise – a conclusion which seems to ignore the employees, customers and clients who might well have had an interest in knowing the company's true position. Neither was the court impressed with arguments about a moral obligation, stating that it could not override a legal duty.

The case was taken to the European Court of Human Rights, where the Commission found that there was a clear violation of art. 10, commenting that 'Protection of the sources from which journalists derive information is an essential means of enabling the press to perform its important function of public watchdog in a democratic society. If journalists could be compelled to reveal their sources this would make it difficult for them to obtain information and inform the public about matters of public interest.' The verdict of the Court was awaited as this book went to press.

Breach of confidence

The doctrine of confidentiality of information comes from private law, and was originally designed to prevent industrial espionage. In recent years it has been widened, and can now be used to stop revelation of any information which has been imparted under an obligation of confidence; such an obligation is implied in a contract of employment, consultancy or confidential relationship. In **Duke of Argyll v Duchess of Argyll** (1967), it was used to prevent the revelations by the Duchess about her marriage being published in a newspaper, and then in **Attorney-General v Jonathan Cape Ltd** (1976), the Government attempted to prevent the publication of the diaries of an ex-minister, Richard Crossman. In fact the court held that publication could not be prevented because the events discussed in the diaries had taken place too long ago, making the information stale, but it accepted that Cabinet discussions could be regarded as giving rise to an obligation of confidentiality.

This doctrine has proved to be of enormous value for those who wish to suppress information, and as far as the Government is concerned, provides a more satisfactory alternative in many cases to prosecution under the Official Secrets Act. First, it allows them to seek an interim injunction, preventing publication, without having actually to prove their case in a full hearing. Since the actual trial may take a long time to come to court, in many cases the issue will have become so stale by then that there is no point in publication, so the person seeking to prevent publication gets what they want even if their case was weak. In addition, they may exploit the courts' power to order discovery of evidence at this stage to vet articles and programmes before publication. When the Government objected to the BBC radio series 'My Country Right or Wrong', the courts granted an interim injunction with discovery, which allowed the Government to preview and vet the programmes. Finally, the civil law has a lower standard of proof than that required for criminal prosecutions, and there are no juries, who may be inclined, as in the Ponting trial, to acquit those whose revelations seem to be in the public interest.

The threat which the doctrine of confidentiality can pose for freedom of expression was shown in what has come to be known as the *Spycatcher* saga. *Spycatcher* was a book written by Peter Wright, an ex-member of the security services, which contained allegations that MI5 had tried to destabilize the Government when Harold Wilson was Prime Minister, and Wright and others had 'bugged and burgled our way across London at the State's behest, while pompous, bowler-hatted civil servants in Whitehall pretended to look the other way'. (Peter Wright, *Spycatcher* (1987) p. 54).

Despite the fact that most of the allegations had been published by other writers, in some cases years before, the British Government was determined to prevent publication of the book. Wright had emigrated to Australia before writing the book, and it was due to be published there, putting it out of reach of the Official Secrets Act. Unable therefore to bring any criminal prosecution against Wright, in 1985 the Attorney-General started civil proceedings in Australia, seeking an injunction to prevent publication of the book. This action failed, and after an unsuccessful appeal, the book was duly published in Australia.

While the Australian litigation was in progress, the *Observer* and *Guardian* newspapers published a summary of the key allegations in the book, and the Attorney-General then applied for, and got, interim injunctions preventing them from printing further information from either the books or the Australian court hearings, on the basis that Wright was disclosing information obtained under a duty of confidentiality. As mentioned above, the *Independent*, the *London Evening Standard*, and the *Daily Mail* later published reports of the Australian hearings, and were found in contempt of the injunction on the *Observer* and the *Guardian*. In the meantime, not only were reports of the hearings, and the book's allegations, being published around the world, but the book itself had been published in the USA, where the First Amendment commitment to freedom of speech meant there was no point in the UK Government even trying to prevent publication, and copies were being imported from there into the UK, becoming fairly freely available to anyone who could be bothered to seek them out. The result was that newspapers in the UK were banned from publishing reports of court proceedings which were open to the public and the media and reported in other countries, and which revealed information that was freely available in the UK anyway.

When the full hearing eventually came to court, the House of Lords decided to lift the injunction, stating that, as the newspapers pointed out, even if Wright's disclosures were covered by confidentiality, by now they were all in the public domain, and further publication could not be harmful. This alone was enough to lift the injunction, but the court also considered the question of public interest, and concluded that wherever Government sought to suppress official information, the courts were required to balance the alleged need for such suppression against the interest in freedom of expression, and the Government would have to give reasons for suppression which outweighed those in favour of disclosure. The absolute protection of official information which the Government wanted the court to grant 'could not be achieved this side of the Iron curtain'.

Though the courts eventually came down on the side of disclosure, the fact that they allowed the interim injunction in the first place – a decision which was appealed right up to the House of Lords – has been much criticized. It contrasts sharply with the approach of US judges in the Pentagon Papers case, where American newspapers published extracts from a record of top-secret policy discussions about Vietnam. The US Government tried to restrain further publication of the information, but the Supreme Court held that they could not do so, unless they could prove that publication would cause 'grave and irreparable damage to the public interest' (**New York Times Co** *v* **United States** (1971)). The European Court of Human Rights held that the UK courts' refusal to lift the injunction after *Spycatcher* was published in the USA violated art. 10.

Copyright

The *Spycatcher* case highlighted a further possibility open to a government interested in preventing publication. The House of Lords accepted that neither the publishers nor the author had copyright in the book as copyright vested with the Crown, which suggests that in a similar future case, the Crown could sue for breach of copyright, which would allow it to seek damages. Since publishers are unlikely to want to publish anything where the potential profits are at risk of being claimed by the Government this may prove a useful course of action.

Treason

The offence of treason is committed if one owes allegiance to the monarch and conspires or incites others to kill or overthrow her, or to levy war against her. Treason is still punishable by the death penalty.

Treason felony overlaps with treason and consists of inciting rebellion against the Government of the UK, or conspiring to deprive the monarch of her sovereignty in any of her dominions (Treason Felony Act 1858). It is punishable with life imprisonment.

Incitement to disaffection

Incitement to disaffection concerns attempts to persuade Government servants, such as police officers or members of the armed forces, to disobedience of their orders. The Police Act 1964 s. 53 prohibits conduct calculated to cause disaffection among police officers or to induce them to withhold their services or commit breaches of discipline, while under the Incitement to Disaffection Act 1934, it is an offence maliciously and advisedly to endeavour to seduce a member of the armed forces from his duty or allegiance. It is also an offence for any person, with intent to commit or to aid, counsel or procure commission of the main offence, to possess or control any document whose distribution among members of the forces would constitute that offence. The Act allows the suppression of pacifist literature, and was used in the 1970s against campaigners for the withdrawal of British troops from Northern Ireland.

Sedition

Sedition is a common law offence, committed where a person tries to bring the monarch, the Government or the constitution of the UK, or the administration of justice, into hatred or contempt, or incites another to use unlawful means to try to bring about changes in the state or the church, to promote feelings of hostility between UK subjects, or promote discontent among them. In practice its scope is not as wide as it sounds; it is not a criminal offence to criticize the Queen, or the Government, or the courts, for example, nor to try to bring about changes in church or state by lawful means. Cases in this century have stressed a need to prove an intention to promote violence and disorder.

In **R *v* Chief Metropolitan Stipendiary Magistrate ex parte Choudhury** (1991), an attempt was made to bring a private prosecution against Salman Rushdie, author of *The Satanic Verses*, on the grounds that the book was seditious because it had created widespread discontent and disaffection among UK subjects – publication of the book, which some Muslims claimed was blasphemous, created hostility between British Muslims who were deeply offended by it, and those who defended the book on the grounds of freedom of expression, and was said to have damaged international relations between the UK and Islamic countries. The magistrate refused to issue a summons, and this decision was supported by the Divisional Court, which stated that it was not sufficient simply to create ill-will between subjects; seditious conduct must be aimed at disturbing established authority, by violent means.

Because of the overlap between sedition and other offences, such as incitement to violence and incitement to disaffection, the Law Commission in 1977 suggested the abolition of sedition; this has not been done, but the offence is rarely prosecuted.

Blasphemy

At common law it is a criminal offence to criticize the Christian religion in a manner that is likely to outrage the feelings of a Christian. This offence had fallen into disuse during the 60 years leading up to 1978, but was revived in **Whitehouse *v* Gay News Ltd and Lemmon** (1978). In a case brought by the well-known anti-porn campaigner Mary Whitehouse, the publishers of *Gay News* were convicted of blasphemy by a jury after publishing a poem linking homosexual practices with the life and crucifixion of Christ. The conviction was upheld by the House of Lords, who stated that so long as there was proof that the defendants intended to publish the offending words, there was no need to prove an intention to blaspheme, nor that the publication was likely to cause a breach of the peace.

In **ex parte Choudhury** (discussed above), the High Court confirmed that the offence is limited to criticism of Christianity and does not extend to other religions. This decision was criticized on the grounds that a multi-religious society should protect all faiths or none at all, though given the existence of many small cults and sects, it might be difficult to define a religion for this purpose.

In 1985 the Law Commission recommended that the crime of blasphemy should be abolished, but in June 1989 the Government announced that it had no plans to change the law.

Defamation

Defamation is both a civil and a criminal wrong and we will consider each briefly in turn.

Civil liability

In civil law liability for defamation can take one of two forms: libel or slander. Libel covers statements made in some permanent form – this usually means printed or written, though it includes statues, films and the performance of plays. Slander applies to defamation made in a transitory form, such as spoken words or gestures. The main significance of this distinction is that for slander some damage must usually be proved to have resulted from the slander while this is not necessary for libel; the mere fact that a libellous comment was made is sufficient to give rise to civil liability.

In order for liability for defamation to lie in civil law plaintiffs must prove that the defendant made a false, defamatory statement that appeared to refer to him. A statement is defamatory if it lowers the plaintiff's reputation in the minds of right-minded people. An insult which does not affect a person's reputation is not sufficient. A statement need not directly criticize the plaintiff; it may do so by implication, known as an 'innuendo'. In **Tolley** v **J S Fry & Sons Ltd** (1931) the plaintiff was an amateur golfer, and his amateur status meant that he was not allowed to accept money to advertise people's products. Without his knowledge the defendants published an advertisement containing a cartoon of him, with a rhyme praising the chocolate. He succeeded in proving that the advertisement amounted to a defamatory statement by way of innuendo, because readers seeing the advertisement were likely to assume that Tolley had been paid to lend his name to it and therefore compromised his amateur status.

The requirement that the plaintiff be 'lowered in the estimation of right-thinking members of society generally' is illustrated by **Byrne** v **Dearne** (1937). After the police raided a golf club and removed an illegal gambling machine, a verse appeared on the club notice board which included the words 'but he who gave the game away may he byrn in hell and rue the day', thereby hinting that Byrne was the person who had informed the police about the existence of the machine. The plaintiff sued the club, alleging that the statement was defamatory. It was held that although the statement might lower him in the estimation of the club members, it would not do so in the estimation of right-thinking members of society, who would not disapprove of conduct designed to prevent crime. The action failed.

It is not possible to defame a dead person. Nor is it usually possible to defame a class of people. So, for example, if a newspaper said that all politicians were useless, no individual politician could sue. However, where the class mentioned is very small, the statement may be taken to refer to each and every member of it, and any or all of them may sue. If, for example, a defamatory statement was applied to 'all female football managers', when in fact there were only three or four in the country, any of them could sue. A remark about football managers in general would not usually allow any of them to sue because the class referred to would be too big. This law was laid down in **Knuppfer** v **London Express Express Newspapers Ltd** (1944). The defendants had published an article stating that an émigré Russian group was a fascist organization. The group had approximately 2,000 members, of which 24 were based in the United Kingdom. The plaintiff was a Russian immigrant living in London and he brought an action for defamation. His action was rejected by the House of Lords on the basis that the accusation of fascism was aimed at the class of people and there was nothing that singled him out.

The statement must be published. Communication of the defamation to anyone other than the plaintiff, or the defendant's wife, can amount to publication – it does not have to be printed in a newspaper or broadcast on television or radio to satisfy this requirement.

A range of potential defences are available of which we will mention the three most important. First, if a defamatory statement is true, the defendant will have a defence of justification. Secondly, a defendant will have a defence if it can be proved that the statement made was fair comment on a matter of public interest. Finally, certain statements, such as those made by Members of Parliament in the House and those made during judicial proceedings enjoy a defence of 'absolute privilege'.

Criminal liability

Criminal liability is imposed under s. 5 of the Libel Act 1843 and applies only to libels and not slander. Unlike civil libel, criminal libel may apply to a class of persons or a dead person. Under the Act it is a defence to prove that the publication was both true and in the public interest.

A prosecution for criminal libel against a newspaper proprietor, publisher or editor can only be brought with leave of a judge. Leave was given for a private prosecution in 1976 by Sir James Goldsmith against the publishers of *Private Eye*. The prosecution related allegations that Goldsmith was the ringleader of a conspiracy to obstruct the course of justice. The High Court judge said that the press was not free to publish scandalous or scurrilous matter which was wholly without foundation.

Defamatory words published in the course of a performance of a play amount to criminal libel under ss. 4 and 6 of the Theatres Act 1968.

It has been argued that defamation is not an area in which the criminal law should be involved, and in 1982, the Law Commission recommended that criminal libel at common law should be abolished and replaced by a narrower statutory offence, directed at a person who, knowing or believing it to be untrue, publishes a deliberately defamatory statement which is likely to cause the victim significant harm.

Obscenity

The Obscene Publications Act 1959 creates the statutory offence of publishing obscene material, which can be used against the authors, photographers, artists, publishers, booksellers and other distributors of such material. The Criminal Law Act 1977 extended the provisions of the 1959 Act to films, and the Broadcasting Act 1990 to television and radio.

An article is obscene under s. 1 of the 1959 Act if it tends to deprave or corrupt a person likely to read, see or hear it; a few words or sentences are not enough. Although the Act is mainly used against pornography, it is not only concerned with sex; for example, a book which described the pleasures of drug-taking has been held to fall within the scope of 'deprave and corrupt'.

The prosecution must prove that a significant proportion of the people likely to come into contact with the material would have their morals adversely affected, but there is no need to prove an intention to deprave and corrupt. It is a defence that the defendant had not examined the offending material and had no reasonable cause to believe that publication or possession would be an offence, or that publication was for the public good in the interests of science, literature, art or learning, or other objects of public concern.

Other restrictions on indecent material include the Protection of Children Act 1978, which prohibits indecent photographs of children under sixteen, and the Theatre Act 1968, which makes it an offence to present or direct the performance of a play which is obscene. The controls discussed above on films, broadcasting and the theatre can also be used to control obscenity.

Other restrictions on speech or writing

A great number of criminal offences and torts can be committed purely by the use of spoken words or writing. For example, it is an offence to blackmail or to incite another to commit a crime, and intimidating words accompanied by threatening behaviour may be an assault although there is no physical contact with the person put in fear. Several offences under the Public Order Act 1986 have implications for freedom of expression: threatening behaviour (s. 4); disorderly conduct (s. 5); and incitement to racial hatred (ss. 17–23). These are discussed in the section on freedom of assembly and public order at p. 365.

Fraudulent misrepresentation and deceit are torts which can be committed by speech alone.

▶ A right to privacy?

Just as there is no positive right to freedom of expression in this country, there is no right to privacy either. Those whose privacy is invaded have no remedy, unless a specific crime or tort has been committed.

Concerns over intrusive press reporting has led to much debate about whether a right to privacy ought to be made law. After a spate of stories about the private lives of royalty and politicians, the case of **Kaye** *v* **Robertson** (1991) highlighted the lengths to which some papers would go to get their story. The actor Gorden Kaye had been involved in a serious car accident, and was recovering from the resulting surgery in hospital. A newspaper photographer managed to sneak into Kaye's hospital room, and photographs of Kaye in his hospital bed, taken without his consent, were then published in the newspaper. The Court of Appeal granted an injunction on the basis of a malicious falsehood, but affirmed that there was no general right to privacy in English law.

As a result of concerns over this type of reporting, the Calcutt Committee was set up to consider whether there should be statutory powers to control media invasions of privacy. Its first report, in 1990, rejected this idea, in favour of a self-regulatory system, the Press Complaints Commission. But in his second report in 1993, Calcutt concluded that the Press Complaints Commission 'has not proved itself to be an effective regulator' and recommended tighter controls. The Committee recommended a new statutory Press Complaints Commission, to investigate allegations of unjust or unfair treatment by newspapers or magazines, with new powers to impose fines, award costs and require the printing of an apology, correction or reply. It also suggested there should be criminal offences to cover physical intrusion, such as the use of surveillance devices on private property, a tort of infringement of privacy, tightening up of the laws under the Data Protection Act 1984, and legal restrictions on press reporting empowering any court to restrict the publication of the name and address of any person by whom an offence has been alleged to have been committed. The Government's response has not been in favour of a statutory tribunal, but consideration is being given to the other recommendations of the Calcutt Report.

These issues were also considered by the National Heritage Committee in 1993. It recommended that there should be a strengthening of both civil and criminal law on privacy. A tort of infringement of privacy should be created, and the criminal law could be applied to offences resulting from the unauthorized use of invasive technology and harassment. The Committee favoured the retention of some form of Press Complaints Commission, but with powers to order publication of apologies and in suitable cases the award of compensation. An ombudsman to be appointed by the Lord Chancellor and funded by the Treasury would supervise adjudications of disputes.

As far as newspapers are concerned, the reports, with their threat of privacy laws, have changed nothing. Bitter competition between rival titles have made newspapers even keener to expose sensational stories, using whatever means may be necessary, and it seems likely that they may eventually go far enough to persuade the Government into introducing laws of privacy. While this would protect both public figures and private individuals from unwarranted intrusions, the danger is that it could also be used to prevent genuine investigative journalism from uncovering facts that the public ought to know. A privacy law with a public interest defence might be one way round this problem.

▶ A right to information?

While individual citizens have little legal protection for their privacy, the UK Government remains one of the most secretive in the world, giving the public only very limited access to information. As we have seen, Government information is protected by Official Secrets legislation, by 'D' Notices, and by the doctrine of confidentiality; state papers (often called public records) are made available to public scrutiny only after a lapse of 30 years, or longer in some cases.

The Government have made some moves towards more open government, but on the whole these have been reluctant or of limited value. The Data Protection Act (1984) was forced on them by international obligations, while the Access to Medical Reports Act (1988) and Access to Personal Files Act (1987) originated in Private Members' Bills, and were much weakened by Government amendments along the way. The Citizens' Charter provides for publication of information such as performance targets and league tables of performance, there is now a minister with responsibility for Open Government, and a 1994 Code of Practice commits Government departments to publishing the facts and analyses considered relevant in framing major policy proposals, giving reasons for administrative decisions and meeting reasonable requests for information. However, none of these provisions give a legal right to information – the Code of Practice, for example, is policed by the Parliamentary Ombudsman, who can only recommend disclosure; there are no powers to enforce it, and the Government rejected the idea of a tribunal for this purpose.

By contrast, in most modern democracies freedom of information (FOI) legislation establishes a basic right of public access to official information. In the USA, for example, FOI laws start with the assumption that access to information is a right, not a privilege; it is for the government to justify secrecy. Citizens have a right of access to government documents, subject to exempted categories, and if denied access, can appeal to a court or tribunal. Where official information kept on a person proves inaccurate, there is a right to get it amended. The legislation also aims to open up the decision-making of government agencies to public scrutiny, and incorporates a 'whistleblowers' charter', protecting public servants who disclose evidence of illegality, mismanagement, gross waste of funds, abuse of authority, or substantial danger to public health and safety.

Such legislation is not entirely without its problems. For a start, it is expensive – Canada and Australia spend the equivelant of £6.6m a year on it. However, when compared with the £200m that is spent annually on publicizing information the British Government wants released, the cost seems comparatively low. There are also complaints that the system has ended up being used mainly by 'data brokers' who gain information in order to sell it to those with an interest, and by businesses seeking commercial information; clearly taxpayers should not have to foot the bill for this.

However, the beneficial results of FOI legislation seem to outweigh these drawbacks; over the past few years, investigations made possible by FOI legislation have revealed radioactive contamination of water supplies, abnormal rates of cancer in nuclear plant employees, the health risks of silicone breast implants, and potentially corrupt connections between public servants and big business, to name but a few.

In 1984 a Campaign for Freedom of Information was launched in the UK, with support from some major political groups. The Campaign accepts that information related to national security and certain other sensitive issues should be kept confidential, but points out that there is an enormous amount of other official information which could and should be made available to the public.

REMEDIES FOR INFRINGEMENT OF CIVIL RIGHTS

Rights are only worthwhile if there are adequate remedies for their enforcement. The fact that we do not have a Bill of Rights, but only a collection of laws detailing what we may not do, has inevitably meant that remedies are similarly scattered. Some of the main remedies available in English law for unlawful infringement of basic rights are the subject of this section.

▶ Judicial review

Where a public body – such as a local authority, the police, or a Government department – acts illegally, the result will often be an infringement of an individual's rights, and in some cases the remedy for this is a procedure known as judicial review. This is discussed in chapter 14.

▶ Habeas corpus

Personal liberty is regarded as the most fundamental of all freedoms, and where individuals are wrongfully deprived of their liberty, the fact that, on release, they can sue their captor for damages under the ordinary civil law is not regarded as a sufficient remedy. *Habeas corpus* is an ancient remedy which allows a person detained to challenge the legality of detention, and if successful, get themselves quickly released. *Habeas corpus* does not punish the person responsible for the detention, but once the detained person is set free, they can still pursue any other available remedies for compensation or punishment – for example, unlawful detention is the tort of false imprisonment, and so a person released on *habeas corpus* will normally be entitled to recover damages in tort against the persons responsible for the detention.

Habeas corpus may be sought by, among others, convicted prisoners; those detained in custody pending trial or held by the police during criminal investigations; those awaiting extradition; mental patients; and those with excessive bail conditions imposed on them. Application is made to a Divisional Court of the Queen's Bench Division, and has virtually absolute priority over all other court business.

In **X** *v* **United Kingdom** (1981), which concerned the right of mental health patients to challenge their detention, the European Court of Human Rights stated that the scope of *habeas corpus* was too narrow; it imposed a duty on the UK to make a remedy available to test the legality of any contested detention. The role of *habeas corpus* has diminished in recent years, but it still provides an important element of supervision over the detention powers of the executive.

▶ Civil action

Where a public body breaches a person's rights in such a way as to amount to a tort, that body may be sued in the same way as a private citizen would be; since the Crown Proceedings Act 1947, this includes the Crown.

As far as civil rights are concerned, this remedy is of particular importance in relation to illegal behaviour by the police; possible actions include assault, malicious prosecution, false imprisonment, wrongful arrest and trespass to property or goods. Exemplary damages may be awarded against the police even where there has been no oppressive behaviour or other aggravating circumstances.

In practice most actions against the police are settled out of court, possibly because of a desire on the part of the police to keep them out of the public eye. In 1984, for example, the Metropolitan Police settled 107 of the 181 civil claims made against them, paying damages of £178,603, while the South Yorkshire police is reported to have paid a total of £425,000 to 39 former striking miners, who sued for assault, wrongful arrest, malicious prosecution and false imprisonment, after clashes between police and demonstrators at Orgreave coking plant in June 1984.

▶ Criminal proceedings

Criminal proceedings may be brought for false imprisonment or assault, if necessary by means of a private prosecution.

▶ The European Court of Human Rights

A person whose rights have been breached may find that they have an eventual remedy in the European Court of Human Rights (see p. 345).

▶ The Police Complaints Authority

Under the Police and Criminal Evidence Act, complaints made by a member of the public about the conduct of a police officer are submitted to the chief officer of the force concerned, who should take steps to obtain or preserve relevant evidence. Complaints about officers above the rank of chief superintendent are then handled by the local police authority; complaints about other ranks by the chief officer. Minor complaints are dealt with informally, but where the problem is more serious, there may be disciplinary proceedings or a criminal prosecution. The most serious complaints must be referred to the Police Complaints Authority, which supervises the investigation itself.

Over 5,000 cases are referred to the Authority each year to determine whether an investigation should be supervised; supervision is actually undertaken in only a few hundred of these. These investigations have included high profile cases such as the policing of the miners' strike of 1984/85; policing certain student demonstrations; police conduct during the picketing outside the Wapping printing works in 1987; police behaviour surrounding the Broadwater Farm riots in 1985 and the conduct of the West Midlands Serious Crime Squad between 1986 and 1989.

▶ The admissibility of evidence

Where police officers commit serious infringements of a suspect's rights during investigation of an offence, the courts may hold that evidence obtained as a result of such misbehaviour is inadmissible in court, the idea being to remove any incentive for the police to break the rules.

Under s. 76(2) of PACE, confession evidence is inadmissible where it was obtained by oppression or in circumstances likely to render it unreliable, and if the defence alleges that this is the case, the onus is on the prosecution to establish otherwise (s. 76(1)). Oppression is defined as including 'torture, inhuman or degrading treatment, and the use or threat of violence (whether or not amounting to torture)'. (s. 76(8)). In **R** *v* **Fulling** (1987) the court said that 'oppression' should be given its ordinary meaning, that is to say, the exercise of authority or power in a burdensome, harsh or wrongful manner or giving rise to unjust or cruel treatment. In that case it was held that there was no oppression where a confession had been made by a woman after being told by police of her lover's affair with another woman. However, much of the potential protection offered by this section is lost by s. 76(4), which provides that the exclusion of a confession does not affect the admissibility in evidence of any facts discovered as a result of the confession, or 'where the confession is relevant as showing that the accused speaks, writes or expresses himself in a particular way, of so much of the confession as is necessary to show that he does so'. This means that the police can use oppressive treatment to secure a confession which will help them find other evidence.

Section 78 provides that in any proceedings the court may refuse to allow evidence on which the prosecution proposes to rely 'if it appears to the court that, having regard to all the circumstances, including the circumstances in which the evidence was obtained, the admission of the evidence would have such an adverse effect on the fairness of the proceedings that the court ought not to admit it'. This provision covers all types of evidence, not just confessions. It is generally invoked only if the police have committed serious breaches of PACE, such as refusing a suspect access to legal advice over a long period.

▶ The right to exercise self defence

Any citizen may use reasonable force to prevent unlawful interference with their person or property, or to protect others from such interference. This can affect both civil and criminal liability.

▶ Parliamentary controls

One of the basic functions of Parliament is to act as a watchdog over the rights of citizens, protecting them from undue interference by Government. A numbers of methods are available, from questions directed to ministers in Parliament, to committees designed to scrutinize legislation. However, this function has suffered as a result of the strength of party discipline, which means that many MPs appear to put loyalty to their party above loyalty to the citizens they represent. The result is that even measures which clearly restrict fundamental rights can be voted through if the Government has a clear majority.

▶ The Ombudsman

The Parliamentary Commissioner for Administration, known as the Ombudsman, has a role in protecting individual rights, and is discussed in chapter 15.

. . . .
ANSWERING QUESTIONS

1 'British history has . . . no statute of liberty, no Bill of Rights . . . Instead of a set of basic principles . . . we have a vast array of disparate statutes and decided cases from which, as often as not, no satisfactory principle can be derived.' (G. Robertson, *Freedom, the Individual and the Law*).
(a) Explain this comment by reference to any freedom(s) (15 marks).
(b) Consider how the protection of freedom(s) might be improved (10 marks).
AEB

(a) The first thing to note here is that you are asked to answer the question with reference to a specific freedom or freedoms. This means that although you obviously need to explain the general approach of English law to basic freedoms (namely the idea of residual rights as opposed to rights-based systems) you need to do this by showing how this approach works with reference to one or more specific freedoms. A good one to choose would be freedom of assembly, where there is a good deal of case and statute law to which you can refer. Highlight the fact that there is no statement of English law of a right of assembly, merely a collection of statutes and cases which show what freedom of assembly is left when the restrictions on it are taken away, and explain the effect this situation has, and particularly the problems it causes for those who wish to use or protect freedom of assembly, citing cases to prove your point.

Part (b): Here you can address some of the ways in which the problems you have highlighted might be addressed, talking first about any piecemeal reforms which could be used to create rights – an example might be the idea that when assessing whether a march or assembly should be banned, the banning authority should take into account a public interest in freedom of assembly. Then go on to discuss more fundamental reforms, in particular the creation of a Bill of Rights, explaining how, if at all, this would improve protection of rights.

20

Law and rules

Before looking at specific laws, and the way in which our legal system operates, it is useful to consider what law actually is. What do we mean when we say that something is 'the law'? One answer is that a law is a type of rule, but clearly there are many rules which are not law: rules of etiquette, school or club rules, and moral rules, for example. One way to understand more about what law is, is to look at what distinguishes legal rules from other types of rule.

▶ What is a rule?

A good starting point is the definition of a rule given by Twining and Miers in their book *How to Do Things With Rules*: 'a general norm mandating or guiding conduct or action in a given type of situation'. This definition contains several important statements about rules. Rules are general – they tend to apply to people in general or a specific class, rather than singling out individuals. They are normative, meaning that they set a standard of how things ought to be, rather than how they are – for example, 'cars should be driven on the road' is a normative statement, a rule stating how things ought to be, in contrast to 'cars are driven on the road', which is simply a factual statement. All rules – whether they are legal, moral or just customary – lay down standards of behaviour to which the rules say we ought to conform if the rule affects us.

Rules may mandate action, meaning that they say something must or must not be done – and there may be a penalty for disobedience; or they may guide behaviour, by saying what ought or ought not to be done. They tend to cover situations which have arisen in the past, and are likely to arise again; if we do not know that a particular situation could arise, there will be no rules to guide behaviour in that situation. Rules may be written down, or simply known among those whom they affect.

Rules can be distinguished from principles, which may take a similar form to rules, but tend to be more general, and usually have to be translated into rules before they can be put into practice. For example, the principle that if all motorists going in a particular direction drive on the

same side of the road, there will be fewer crashes, can be put into practice as the legal rule that all cars should drive on the left.

Rules can also be contrasted with policies. Policies are broad goals at
which law may aim – in our example of driving on the left, the policy
behind the law is that the risk of accidents should be minimized as far as
possible. Other policy aims include increasing racial harmony or sexual
equality, and again, they have to be translated into rules in order to be put
into effect – the policy of increasing racial harmony has been translated
into legislation against racial discrimination, for example.

Legal rules clearly fit into the definition of rules, and are different
from legal principles and from policy. But what makes them different
from other types of rule?

▶ Austin: the command theory

The seventeenth-century writer John Austin, in his book *The Province of
Jurisprudence*, argued that law differed from other rules because it was the
command of a sovereign body, which the State could enforce by means
of punishment. The relevant sovereign body would vary in different countries; in Britain it would be the Queen in Parliament, but in other countries it might be the monarch alone, or an emperor or president.

Austin's definition has fairly clear application to some areas of law,
most obviously criminal law, where we are told we must do or not do
certain things, with penalties for disobedience. But there are large areas
which fall outside it. Contract law, for example, details the sanctions
which can be imposed when contracts are broken, but it does not command us to make contracts in the first place. The law concerning marriage does not command anyone to marry; it simply sets out the conditions
under which people may do so if they wish, the procedure they should
follow in order to make the marriage legally valid, and the legal consequences of being married. The rules about marriage and contracts
could be described as rules giving power, in contrast to the rules imposing duties which comprise criminal law; they have different functions, but
both types are legal rules.

As Hart and others have pointed out, there are an enormous number
of legal rules which neither make commands, nor impose sanctions. The
complexity and variety of legal rules make it impossible to cover them all
with the proposition that laws are commands.

▶ Hart: primary and secondary rules

In his influential book *The Concept of Law*, Professor Hart attempted to link
types of rule with types of legal system. He divided legal rules into primary

rules and secondary rules, and argued that the existence of secondary rules was a mark of a developed legal system.

Hart described primary rules as those which any society needs in order to survive. These rules forbid the most socially destructive types of behaviour – typically murder, theft and fraud – and also cover areas of civil law, such as tort. According to Hart, simple societies, which generally have a high degree of social cohesion, can survive with only these basic rules, but as a society becomes more complex, it will require what he described as secondary rules.

Secondary rules confer power rather than impose duties, and can be divided into three types: rules of adjudication, rules of change and rules of recognition.

Rules of adjudication

In simple societies, the primary rules can be applied and enforced by means of informal social pressures within the group; this works because the community is close-knit, and individuals rely on each other. As societies become bigger and more complex, these bonds are broken, and social pressures will not be enough to shape behaviour. Therefore the community needs some means of giving authority to its rules, and the secondary rules of adjudication are designed to provide this. These rules will provide for officials (usually judges) to decide disputes, and will define the procedures to be followed in cases of dispute, and the sanctions which can be applied when rules are broken. Examples of secondary rules in our society are those which lay down what kind of issues can be decided by courts, who is qualified to be a judge, and rules on sentencing in criminal cases; there are many more.

Rules of change

The second type of secondary rule is concerned with making new rules, both primary and secondary. A developed society which is changing over time will need to respond to new situations with new rules – perhaps the clearest example in our society is the huge number of laws introduced over the last century or so as a result of the invention of motorized transport. Rules of change lay down the procedure to be followed in making new rules or changing old ones. In our system, the main rules of change are those concerning how legislation is made, and how judicial decisions become part of the common law.

There are also rules of change concerning the power of individuals to produce changes in the legal relationships they have with others.

Rules of recognition

The fact that in simple forms of society rules are enforced by social pressure means that rules are only binding if the community as a whole accepts them, and within a small-scale, close-knit community it will generally be obvious to all what the accepted rules are. In a more complex society, this is not the case; there may be many rules, some of them complex, and individuals cannot be expected simply to know them all. To minimize uncertainty, the developed society, according to Hart, develops rules of recognition, which spell out which of the many rules that govern society actually have legal force. As Hart explains, 'in the simpler form of society we must wait and see whether a rule gets accepted as a rule or not; in a system with a basic rule of recognition we can say before a rule is actually made that it will be valid if it conforms to the requirements of the rule of recognition'.

Hart described the UK as having a single rule of recognition: 'what the Queen in Parliament enacts is law'. This leaves out the issue of judge-made law (see the section on case law in chapter 1), the difficulties in pinpointing exactly how precedent works mean that a rule of recognition is more difficult to specify here, but we certainly cannot say that **only** 'what the Queen in Parliament enacts is law'.

▶ Dworkin: legal principles

Professor Dworkin rejects Hart's analysis of law as consisting purely of rules. He argues that the 'rich fabric' of law contains not just rules, but a set of principles on which all legal rules are based. Dworkin defines rules as operating in an all or nothing manner, stating a particular answer to a particular question. Legal principles, on the other hand, are guidelines, stating a reason that argues in one direction, but does not dictate a decision. Take, for example, a hypothetical murder of a father by his son. One of the legal principles Dworkin advances is that no one should benefit from their own wrong, and this should clearly be taken into account in deciding this dispute. But it does not dictate a particular answer; there may be other aspects to the dispute which make other principles a stronger influence (perhaps the son killed in self-defence, for example). By contrast, a rule that no-one can inherit property from a person they have murdered is clear-cut and straightforward in application; the son cannot inherit from his father.

Other differences between principles and rules, according to Dworkin, are that principles have a dimension of weight or importance – a suggestion of morality – that rules lack. Conflicts between principles can be weighed up by a judge, and the background guidance they give means that even in 'hard cases' they should provide a fairly clear answer; if rules clash, a further rule will be needed to establish which should prevail (for example, the rule that if law and equity conflict, equity prevails). Finally, the strength of a principle can become eroded over time, whereas rules stand until they are removed.

▶ The natural law theory

The theories of Austin and Hart attempt to define what law is, without examining what it says; in a sense, they could be said to look at the outside appearance of law, rather than defining it by its content. This approach is called positivism. Another school of thought, natural law theory, defines law by its content; only laws which conform to a particular moral code, seen as a higher form of law, can genuinely be called law. The natural law theory is discussed on p. 421.

▶ The function of law

Some writers have taken the view that law is best understood by looking at the role it plays in society; what is it for? The following are some of the key theories in this area.

Social cohesion

The nineteenth-century French sociologist, Emile Durkheim, looked at the issue of social cohesion – what it is that keeps a society together – and concluded that law played an important role in this area. Durkheim looked at the role of law in two contrasting types of society; the first a relatively simple, technologically undeveloped society; the second highly developed in terms of technology and social structure.

Durkheim argued that in the first type of society, the whole group would have clearly identifiable common aims, and would work together to achieve them; the interests of any individual within the group would be exactly the same as those of the group as a whole. A moral and legal code based on these aims would be recognized and accepted by all, and would keep the group working together; Durkheim called this 'mechanical solidarity'. An individual who deviated from this code would be punished, and this punishment would reflect the group's disapproval of the wrongdoing, and so reinforce the code.

As social groups become larger and more complex, and develop links with other social groups, the interests of individual members become less closely linked to those of the group as a whole, argues Durkheim. To take a simple example, members of a forest tribe might hunt together to provide food for everyone, whereas in a developed society, individuals and families look after their own interests. However, social solidarity does not disappear, but becomes based on increasing interdependence, which in turn is based on the division of labour. Whereas in the small-scale society, each family would make its own bread, for example, in the developed society this task is shared between, farmer, flour mill, bakery and retailer, all dependent on each other and the consumer. This interdependence, argues Durkheim, means that the individual has social importance in his or her own right, rather than occupying a social position simply as one member of the group.

Durkheim argued that these changes would be accompanied by a corresponding change in the type of law present in the society. Penal law would become less important, and would increasingly be replaced by compensatory law, where the object is not to punish, but to resolve grievances by restoring the injured party to the position they were in before the dispute arose. There would be less need for resolution of disputes between the individual and society, and more for those between individuals.

Durkheim's analysis has been criticized for overestimating the extent to which criminal law would decline and give way to compensatory law in an industrialized society; if anything, industrialized societies have increased the application of criminal law, and indeed industrialization has created new crimes, such as computer fraud and pollution. Anthropological studies have shown that Durkheim also underestimated the degree to which compensatory or civil law already exists in simple societies.

Survival

Professor Hart argues that the main function of law is simply to allow human beings to survive in a community. He suggests that there are certain truths about human existence which, without rules guiding our behaviour, would make life excessively dangerous. We know we are all vulnerable to attack by others; we all have roughly equal physical and intellectual powers, limited concern for others, and limited will power; and we live in a world of limited resources. Given that we know all this, and we want to survive, Professor Hart argues that human beings in any society will recognize a need for rules imposing self-restraint, on the basis that without such rules, we may be tempted to take someone else's property, or even their life, when they are in a weak position, conveniently forgetting that one day we too might be weak and vulnerable to the same treatment. The resulting conflict would eventually make it impossible for the group to stay together, yet individual members might be even less safe if they have to face the world alone.

The realization that we are not safe in the world alone, and can only be safe in a community if there are rules of self-restraint leads to the development of such rules, protecting the property and person of others, and to acceptance of the idea that observance of the rules must be guaranteed by some kind of penalty directed against the rule-breaker. Hart maintains that such rules are the minimum necessary content of law in any society.

The maintainence of order

The German sociologist Max Weber argues that the primary role of law is to maintain order in society. Law makes individuals accept the legitimacy of their rules, and gives them the power to make law, and coerce individuals into obeying it. Without this coercive power, argues Weber, order could not be maintained.

This idea has enjoyed much political support, and political parties from either side of the spectrum are keen to present themselves as promoting 'law and order'. But Weber's view can be criticized as overestimating the role of law in keeping order. If Weber is to be believed, a relaxation of law would result in immediate degeneration of society into chaos and disorder, but to suggest this is to ignore the many other factors which make our society relatively orderly. In many cases, we obey the law not because it is the law, but because of social or moral pressures – we do not steal, for example, because we have been brought up to think stealing is wrong, not because we might be caught and punished for it. Similarly, we may obey moral or social rules as strictly as we would legal ones – we are unlikely to find ourselves in court for swearing at the vicar, for example, but few of us would do it, because of strong social and moral pressures.

Critics argue that what Weber's theory fails to allow for is the fact that societies are not just a loose group of independent individuals; they have clear patterns of behaviour, relationships and beliefs, which differ from society to society. These are what hold society together, and while law is one aspect of them, it is not the only force for social cohesion. Other social institutions which promote cohesion include the family and schools, which transmit social standards to new generations; political institutions (Parliament, political parties); economic and commercial institutions (trade unions, manufacturers' associations, patterns of production and trade, and so on), religious institutions, and cultural institutions (such as literature and the arts, the press, television and radio). All of these play a part in establishing social rules.

The importance of these social rules can be seen if we compare a human society to a group of animals. Like animals, we have instincts to eat, sleep and mate. But whereas animals do all these things in response only to instinct and opportunity, our behaviour is controlled, directly and indirectly, through moral standards, religious doctrines, social traditions and legal rules. For example, like animals we are born with a mating instinct, but unlike animals, human societies attempt to channel this instinct into a form of relationship which has traditionally been seen as offering benefits for society: heterosexual marriage. As we have said, there are no legal rules commanding people to marry, but there are a great many social and moral pressures upholding heterosexual marriage as the desired form of relationship; the predominant religion in our history upholds it, and alternatives, such as homesexual relationships or hetoro-sexual couples living together without marriage have traditionally been seen as immoral and socially unacceptable. It can be argued that these pressures have operated just as strongly as laws do in other areas, though they now appear to be breaking down.

Balancing different interests

The American jurist, Pound, saw law as a social institution, created and designed to satisfy human wants, both individual and social. Pound identi-fied different interests in society: **individual**, including personal, domestic and property interests; **social**, including general morals, social institu-tions, security and order; and **public**, the public interest of the state in guarding social interests. Pound argued that law's main aim was to secure and balance these different interests.

Where interests on a different level conflicted – such as individual against social – they could not be weighted against each other, but where there is a conflict between interests on the same level, they must be weighed against one another with the aim of ensuring that as many as possible are satisfied.

'Law jobs'

Karl Llewellyn was a member of the American realist school of thought which, like the positivists, is concerned with what law is, rather than what it ought to be. Working with Hoebel, an anthropologist, Llewellyn stud-ied American Indian groups, and from this research, constructed a theory of 'law jobs' to explain the social functions of law.

Llewellyn's theory is that every social group has certain jobs which need to be done for it to survive, and law is one of the main ways in which these jobs are done. The jobs include preventing disruptive dis-putes within the group; providing a means of resolving disputes which do arise; allocating authority within the group; and providing mechanisms for constructing relationships between people, including ways of adjust-ing to change. Although these jobs are common to all societies, the ways in which the jobs are done will vary from society to society. For example, the allocation of authority in a simple society might be done by simple rules on electing or appointing a chief, while in a more complex society, this job can be done by a constitution.

Robert Summers has also looked at law in terms of the various jobs it

does for society, and identified five main uses of law: putting right grievances among members of a society; prohibiting and prosecuting forbidden behaviour; promoting certain defined activities; conferring of
social and governmental benefits, such as education and welfare policies;
and giving effect to private arrangements, such as contracts. Although
their theses are different, both Llewellyn and Summers look at law in its
social context, in contrast to writers such as Austin who believe rules,
including legal rules, can be analysed without reference to their settings.

Exploitation

A radical alternative to the views of writers such as Durkheim and Weber
is put forward by Karl Marx. Durkheim and Weber disagreed about the
precise functions of law, but they accepted the idea that law must in some
way be of benefit to society as a whole. Marx, however, rejected the idea
that there was a common interest in society which law could serve. He
argued that society was composed of classes whose interests were fundamentally opposed to each other. Law, Marx maintained, was not made in
the interests of society as a whole, but in the interests of the small group
which rules society; through law (and other social institutions, such as
religion), this group is able to exploit the working class, which Marx
called the proletariat.

Later Marxist writers, such as Althusser and Gramsci, have developed
this thesis. They argue that the ruling class controls the ideology of society – the beliefs and ideas which shape it. This ideology is expressed
through social institutions such as the school, the family, religion and the
law. By shaping the way in which people see the world around them, the
ruling class is able to ensure that the working class see their exploitation
as natural, as the only way things could be, rather than as the oppressive
state of affairs that Marxists see. This minimizes their resistance.

Law is seen as an important part of this process. Because, for example,
the law protects private property, we come to view private property and
all its implications as natural and inevitable. Take the acceptance of profit
for example. If you pay £100 for a set of raw materials, and pay me £100
to turn those materials into goods worth £400, it is quite acceptable in
our society for you to keep the profit, because you purchased both the
raw materials and my labour; they were your property. Clearly an acceptance of this theory is fundamental to acceptance of the capitalist system as a whole, and the legal doctrine of private property is the basis of
this acceptance. But Marxists point out that the situation can be looked
at in another way, as the employer stealing from the worker the added
value his or her labour gives to the raw materials. The fact that we would
not usually think to see it this way is, Marxists say, because we see it
through a capitalist ideology, and law plays a fundamental role in upholding this ideology.

Marx believed that law was only needed because of the fundamental clash of interests between those of the ruling class and those of the proletariat; once society was transformed by communism, these divisions would no longer exist, and law would wither away.

▶ Why are laws obeyed?

Austin thought laws were obeyed because of the threat of sanction and out of a 'habit of obedience' to the state. Hart rejects this explanation, arguing that acceptance of a rule is more important than possible sanctions. As well as the external aspect of obedience – recognition of the validity of the rule, and a potential sanction – Hart argues that there is an internal process, which inclines us to obey because we consider it 'right and proper' to do so. Hart suggests that if a law is not internalized, an individual will feel no obligation to obey it. In our system there are many examples of laws which for some reason widely fail this internalization test; parking offences, speeding, and tax evasion are obvious examples of laws which large numbers of people apparently feel no real compulsion to keep. Hart suggests that in order for law to promote social cohesion in a simple society, with only primary rules, members must not only obey those rules, but also consciously see them as common standards of behaviour, breaches of which can legitimately be criticized; in other words, they internalize all the rules, keeping them not just because they are rules, but because they consider it right to do so. But in a more developed legal system like ours, Hart believes individuals need not internalize every rule. It is clearly desirable for individuals to internalize as many as possible, but failing this, the necessary functions can be served by officials internalizing the rules, and thereby becoming committed to their maintenance.

Fear and internalization

If we obey laws because we internalize them, what makes us internalize some rules and not others? One theory, put forward by Professor Olivecrona, suggests that fear is a strong motivation. He points out that we are all aware from childhood of the consequences of breaking rules, and as a result, we experience a tension between temptation to break rules, and fear of punishment. Olivercrona suggests that the human mind cannot accommodate such tension indefinitely, and so we gradually adjust psychologically to accept conformity to rules as a means of getting rid of the fear of punishment, so that eventually we do not believe we are acting out of fear at all; we have just become used to keeping the rules.

Perhaps because of the efficacy of this process, many writers have suggested that law can be used to shape moral and social ideas. Aristotle suggested that law could be used to educate citizens, commenting that 'Legislators make citizens good by forming their habits'. More recently, Lord Simon of Glaisdale has observed that law still has an educative function, which it exercises when certain conduct becomes stigmatized by becoming illegal.

On the other hand, social pressures can often bring about changes in conduct which legal rules have been unable to do. A recent example is that of drink-driving. At one time this offence was seen as being in a similar category to speeding or parking offences; it was against the law, but people still saw it as acceptable. Now, as a result of social pressures, partly driven by public information campaigns, it is viewed as highly anti-social behaviour, and the law is apparently more widely obeyed.

•
ANSWERING QUESTIONS

(a) Distinguish between rules, principles and policy as they apply to law. *(10 marks)*

(b) Assess the contribution of principles and policy to the development of rules of law *(15 marks) AEB*

Part (a): this part of the question is fairly straightforward. You need to explain what rules, principles and policy are, highlighting the separate meanings each of them have in the context of law. Give examples of each – you might give an example of a legal rule, such as that all cars drive on the left, the principle behind it (that if all cars drive on the same direction on each side of the road, there will be fewer crashes), and the policy behind it (that accidents should be prevented as far as possible).

Part (b): Now take some areas of law which you have studied, and taking some specific rules of law, discuss how far, and in what way, principles and policies have contributed to their development. Discuss each separately – on the subject of principles, for example, the principle of no liability without fault could be explained through rules of criminal and/or civil law. Then move on to policy – you might look at the policy behind legislation, such as consumer protection or race discrimination, or the policy behind the judicial decisions which have led to the development of the law of negligence.

Whatever areas of law you choose to discuss, you should give detailed examples of the rules you are discussing, and analyse the contribution of principles and policy to them.

21 Law and morals

M orals are beliefs and values which are shared by a society, or a section of a society; they tell those who share them what is right or wrong. In our society, moral values have been heavily influenced by the dominant religion, Christianity, though this is not our only source of moral values.

Debate about moral values often centres around sexual issues, such as sex outside marriage, homosexuality and pornography. But moral values also shape attitudes towards money and property, gender roles, friendship, behaviour at work – in fact it is difficult to think of any area of our lives where morality has no application. Mary Warnock, an academic who has been involved in enquiries into issues of moral concern, says 'I do not believe that there is a neat way of marking off moral issues from all others; some people, at some time, may regard things as matters of moral right or wrong, which at another time or in another place are thought to be matters of taste, or indeed to be matters of no importance at all.' However, she points out that 'in any society, at any time, questions relating to birth and death and to the establishing of families are regarded as morally significant.' These can perhaps be regarded as core moral issues.

As Warnock points out, moral attitudes tend to change over time. It is only within the last couple of decades, for example, that the idea of couples living together without marriage has become widely accepted; even now acceptance is not total, but 30 years ago it would have been unthinkable. Similar shifts have taken place with regard to homosexuality and women's liberation.

The French sociologist, Durkheim, has highlighted the fact that in a modern, developed society, it is difficult to pinpoint a set of moral values shared by all. In less developed societies, such as small tribal groups, Durkheim argued that all the members of the group are likely to share a moral code, but in a technologically advanced society such as our own, where individuals differ widely in social status, income, occupation, ethnic background and so on, members of society are unlikely to share identical moral values, even if they largely agree on some basic points. For example, most people in our society agree that it is usually wrong to kill or steal, but there is much less agreement on whether it is wrong to take drugs, have abortions, experiment on animals or help a terminally ill person to die. Even on the basic crimes of theft and murder, some people will see these as always wrong, while others will believe there are situations in which they may be justified; within this second group, there will be disagreement as to what those situations are.

Criminologist Jock Young has pointed out that much depends on the standpoint of the observer, and how they see the norms of society. Looking at attitudes to illegal drug use, Young pointed out that to those who see society's rules as based on a moral consensus, drug-taking was against that moral consensus, and those who indulged in it were therefore maladjusted and sick. But if society's rules on deviant behaviour are seen simply as a yardstick of what that particular society considers normal, drug-taking is neither necessarily deviant nor necessarily a social problem; it is merely deviant to groups who condemn it and a problem to those who wish to eliminate it. What is being made is simply a value judgment, and values vary between people and over time.

▶ Law and morality

Both law and morals are normative; they specify what ought to be done, and aim to mark the boundaries between acceptable and unacceptable conduct. While moral rules tend not to be backed by the obvious sanctions which make some legal rules enforceable, they are often reinforced by pressures which in some cases may be as strong, if not stronger: the disapproval of family and friends, loss of status, and being shunned by the community are powerful disincentives against immoral conduct. Of course many types of undesirable behaviour offend against both moral and legal rules – serious crimes are obvious examples.

Both law and morals are often presented as if they were the only possible responses to social or political problems and crises, yet both vary widely between societies. For example, in our society, private property is such a basic doctrine that we readily condemn any infringement of our rights – legal and moral – to acquire, possess and enjoy our personal property. Stealing is seen as immoral as well as illegal. But in a society where property is held communally, any attempt by one individual to treat property as their own private procession would be regarded as every bit as immoral as we would consider stealing. The idea of private property is not a basic part of human nature, as it is often presented, but a socially-constructed value. Our society has for centuries been based on trade, and this requires a basis of private property.

Some areas of law are explicitly presented as raising moral issues, and when these areas arise in Parliament, MPs are allowed to vote according to their own beliefs, rather than party policy; this is called a vote of conscience, and has been used, for example, when the issue of capital punishment was debated. However, the kinds of issue on which a vote of conscience would be allowed are not the only ones to which moral values apply; when MPs vote on tax changes, the welfare state, employment or any number of issues before Parliament in every session, they are voting on moral issues, because they are voting on the way a government treats its citizens, and the way in which citizens are allowed to treat each other.

Similarly, some areas of law which you will study, such as crime, have obvious moral implications, but these are also present in areas where morality is less obvious. Tort law, for example, and especially negligence, is built around the principle that those who harm others should compensate for the damage done; that, as Lord Atkin noted out in the famous case of **Donoghue** *v* **Stevenson** (1932), the biblical principle of 'love thy neighbour' must include 'do not harm your neighbour'. Similarly contract, as Atiyah has pointed out, is based around the principle that promises should be kept. Even land law, which seems to consist of technicalities which are far removed from great questions of morality, has enormous moral importance because it is upholding the whole notion of property and ownership. Take the question of squatting, for example: it is essentially a question of property rights; the property owner has all the rights to begin with, but if the squatting continues for long enough and in the right circumstances, the squatter may gain some rights. Is it moral that the property owner should lose rights to someone acting illegally? But on the other hand, is it moral that some should be homeless while others have property they can afford to leave empty?

▶ Changes in law and morality

As we have said, the moral values of a society tend to change over time; the same applies to its laws. In our own society, legal changes have tended to lag behind moral ones, coming only when the process of moral acceptance is well advanced. For example, the law was changed in 1991 to make rape within marriage a crime, the House of Lords stating that the change was necessary because marriages were now seen as equal partnerships, in which the husband could no longer enforce rights to sex. This shift in attitude had taken place long before 1991, but the time lag between moral change and legal change was fairly typical. Often it is the possession of effective political power which finally determines which and whose definition of morality is reflected in the law.

On the other hand, law can sometimes bring about changes in social morality. Duster (*The Legislation of Morality*) has traced the history of drug use and its legal control in America, from the end of the nineteenth century. At that time, drug addiction was commonly restricted to the middle and upper classes, who had become addicted to morphine through the use of patent medicines; despite the fact that these contained morphine, it was perfectly legal to buy and sell them. At this time addiction carried no social stigma. However, when certain drugs were made illegal under the 1914 Harrison Act, such drugs began to be supplied by the criminal underworld, and drug addiction began to be associated with this underworld, and with the lower classes who had most contact with it. This in turn led to social stigma. Interestingly, this stigma, which was in a sense created by legal controls, was partly responsible for the calls for greater legal controls on drug-taking which have been heard over the last two decades, as more and more young people take drugs.

Academics from the Scandinavian realist standpoint, such as Olivercrona, argue that our morality is created by the law, rather than the law emerging from our morality. Olivercrona suggests that law has an influence on us from our earliest days, helping to mould our moral views. From the start, parents and teachers tell us what we must and must not do, and we quickly learn the consequences of disobedience.

▶ Differences between law and morality

Although law and morality are clearly closely linked, they have points of divergence. There are many types of behaviour which may be widely considered immoral, yet we would be very surprised to find laws against them: telling lies, for example. Equally, there are some types of behaviour which are illegal, but which it is hard to see as immoral, such as parking on a yellow line. Then there are areas where the law shares morality's disapproval, but not so far as to prohibit the relevant behaviour. Adultery, for example, is not illegal in this country, but it has long been grounds for divorce, an important legal step for individuals.

The problem for the law in deciding whether to respond to appeals to morality is that there are very often conflicting moral views in a given situation. We can see this in the case of **Gillick *v* West Norfolk and Wisbech Area Health Authority** (1986). In this case, the plaintiff, Mrs Victoria Gillick, was a Roman Catholic, who objected to advice from the Department of Health and Social Security (DHSS) to doctors, that in exceptional cases they could offer contraceptive advice and treatment to girls under sixteen, without parental consent. Mrs Gillick sought a declaration that this advice was illegal, because it encouraged under-age sex.

Mrs Gillick lost at first instance, won in the Court of Appeal and lost by a majority in the House of Lords. The House held that the guidelines were legal, because they concerned what were essentially medical matters, and in such matters girls under sixteen had the legal capacity to consent to medical examination and treatment, including contraceptive treatment, as long as they were sufficiently mature and intelligent to understand the nature and implications of the proposed treatment. The majority, in reaching this conclusion, stressed that they were merely applying the law as it stood, and not taking a moral standpoint; the minority referred to the kind of moral arguments Mrs Gillick had advanced. However, this does not mean that in rejecting Mrs Gillick's view the majority ignored morality, even though they claimed to be making an objective decision. It could be argued that if teenage girls were likely to have sex anyway, preventing doctors from giving contraceptive help would simply increase the chances of unwanted pregnancies, and it would therefore be moral to protect girls from that. Neither view is objectively wrong or right; in this, as in many areas, there are opposing moral views.

▶ Should law and morality be separate?

The view taken by Mrs Gillick would seem to suggest that if something is immoral, it should also be illegal, and to the person who holds strong moral opinions, this may seem a natural conclusion. But there are problems with it. First, moral opinions, however strongly held, are just that; moral **opinions**. Mrs Gillick believes under-age girls should not be given contraception and many people agree with her, but many others disagree. Which group's moral opinions should be adopted by the law?

Even if there were complete consensus, the logistics of enforcing as legal rules all the moral rules of our society would present enormous problems. How would we pay for the necessary manpower, both for policing and prosecutions? What sanctions would be severe enough to compel obedience, yet not too severe for the nature of the offences? Making every immoral act also illegal seems both impossible and undesirable, yet law with no connection to morality might find it difficult to command much respect. There is still much debate as to how far law should reflect morality; the following are some of the key suggestions.

Natural law

Natural law theorists argue that law should strongly reflect morality. Though their specific theories differ, their basic premise is that there is a kind of higher law, known as the natural law, to which we can turn for a basic moral code; some, such as St Thomas Aquinas, see this higher law as coming from God, others see it as simply the basics of human society. The principles in this higher law should be reflected in the laws societies make for themselves; laws which do not reflect these principles cannot really be called law at all, and in some cases need not be obeyed. The campaign against payment of the poll tax on the grounds that it was unfair might be seen as an example of this kind of disobedience.

Different natural law theorists disagree as to the actual content of natural law, but it is usually felt to embody basic human rights which governments should respect. Bills of Rights, like that in the US Constitution, could be seen as embodying natural law principles.

Professor Lon Fuller, in *The Morality of Law*, talked about law's 'inner morality' which he formulated in terms of eight procedural requirements of a legal system:

1   Generality; there should be rules, not *ad hoc* judgments.
2   Promulgation; the rules should be made known to all those affected by them.
3   Non-retroactivity; rules should not have retrospective effect.
4   Clarity; rules should be understandable.
5   Consistency; rules should not conflict.
6   Realism; rules should not require people to do the impossible.
7   Constancy; rules should not be changed so frequently that people cannot use them to guide their behaviour.
8   Congruence; the rules as announced should coincide with the actual administration of those rules.

Fuller claims that a legal system which fails in any one of these areas is not just a bad system; it is not a legal system at all. As an example, he gives the legal system of Nazi Germany; although laws were made by recognized methods, in Fuller's view the system's failure to meet the above criteria meant that those laws were not really law at all.

Utilitarianism

During the nineteenth century, the rise of science, and the beginning of the decline in social importance of religion meant that natural law theories declined, and in their place, the theory of utilitarianism grew up, apparently offering a rational and scientific theory of law. One of the best-known exponents of this theory is John Stuart Mill, and as part of his theory, Mill argued that rather than society imposing morality on individuals, individuals should be free to choose their own conduct, so long as in doing so they did not harm others, or if they did, that the harm done did not outweigh the harm which would be done by interfering with individual liberty.

The view that people should be left alone to do what they like so long as they do not harm others remains influential today, but it is open to criticism. First, the fact that someone's actions do not cause another direct and physical harm, in the way Mill envisaged, does not necessarily mean they do no harm at all. For example, opponents of pornography claim that while looking at pornography may not directly inspire individual users to rape, the fact that pornography is available and, to a degree, accepted, promotes the view that women are sexual objects, and this in turn promotes sexual violence against women.

Secondly, who counts as 'another'? This issue is clearly at the heart of debates over abortion and experimentation on embryos; does harming an unborn child count as harming another person, and from what point? For example, the fact that abortion is legal up until a certain stage in pregnancy suggests that the law sees this as the point at which the foetus becomes 'another'; many people believe that point is reached earlier in pregnancy, and those opposed to abortion believe it is at the moment of conception. On the other hand, many people who support the law on abortion nevertheless disapprove of experiments on embryos, even though their views of abortion might suggest that the embryo is not 'another' at this point.

Crimes without victims

Modern theories which subscribe, at least partly, to Mill's view of individual liberty have tended to focus on what are often called 'victimless crimes'. Using the examples of drug use, homosexuality and abortion, all of which were illegal at the time in which he was writing, Schur states (*Crimes without Victims*) that the common characteristics of such crimes are that they involve no harm to anyone except the participants; they occur through the willing participation of those involved; and as a result, there is no victim to make a complaint and so the law is difficult to enforce. Schur argued that there was a social demand for these activities, which continued to be met despite illegality, in the form of back street abortions, and black market drug supply, for example, and there was no proof that prohibition brought greater social benefits than decriminalization; therefore, he said, there was no good reason to prohibit them.

As with Mill, the main criticism of Schur's theory is his assertion that these activities harm no one who has not willingly taken part in them. Anti-abortionists would certainly dispute this as far as abortion is concerned. A further criticism is that of the participants joining in of their own free will; in the case of drug-taking, for example, that may be so at first, but can we really say that drug addicts take drugs of their own free will?

The Hart–Devlin Debate

The issue of whether or not law should follow morality was hotly debated during the late 1950s, when there was public concern about what was perceived to be a decline in sexual morality. The Government set up a commission to look at whether the laws on homosexuality and prostitution should be changed, and much debate was triggered by publication of the commission's findings, known as the Wolfenden Report. Central to this debate were the writings of the leading judge, Lord Devlin, who opposed the report's findings, and Professor Hart, who attacked Lord Devlin's position.

The Wolfenden Committee recommended that homosexuality and prostitution should be legalized, with some restrictions. Their reasoning was based on the notion that some areas of behaviour had to be left to individual morality, rather than being supervised by the law. The purpose of the criminal law, said the Report, was:

> to preserve public order and decency, to protect the citizen from
> what is offensive and injurious and to provide sufficient safeguards
> against exploitation and corruption of others especially the
> vulnerable, that is the young, weak in body or mind, inexperienced
> or those in a state of physical, official or economic dependence.
> The law should not intervene in the private lives of citizens or seek
> to enforce any particular pattern of behaviour further than
> necessary to carry out the above purposes.

The reasoning is very like that of Mill; leave people to make their own choices, so long as they do not harm others. So for example, the Committee recommended that prostitution itself should not be an offence, since the individual should be allowed to choose whether to take part in it, but activities associated with prostitution which could cause offence to others (such as soliciting in the street) were still to be regulated by the law.

Lord Devlin was opposed to this approach. He argued that some form of common morality, with basic agreement on good and evil, was necessary to keep society together. This being the case, the law had every right – and in fact a duty – to uphold that common morality. Lord Devlin compared contravention of public morality to treason, in the sense that it was something society had to protect itself against. How are we to know what this public morality consists of? Devlin argued that we can judge immorality by the standard of 'the right-minded man', who could perhaps be thought of as 'the man in the jury box'. Opinions should be reached after informed and educated discussion of all relevant points of view, and if there is still debate, the majority view should prevail, as it does in the ordinary legislative process.

In addition, said Devlin, there was a set of basic principles which should be followed by the legislature. First, individuals should be allowed the maximum of freedom consistent with the integrity of society, and privacy should be respected as much as possible. Secondly, punishment should be reserved for that which creates disgust among 'right-minded' people, and society has the right to eradicate any practice which is 'so abominable that its very presence is an offence'. Law-makers should be slow to change laws which protect morality. Thirdly, the law should set down a minimum standard of morality; society's standards should be higher.

Reaction to Devlin's thesis was mixed. Those who felt the Wolfenden

Report had gone too far agreed with him, and there were many of them – the commission's recommendations seem rather tame now, but at the time they were ground-breaking. Others felt that Devlin's approach was out of step with the times; Hart, who was influenced by Mill and therefore approved of the commission's approach, led this opposition. Hart argued that using law to enforce moral values was unnecessary, undesirable and morally unacceptable: unnecessary because society was capable of containing many moral standpoints without disintegrating; undesirable because it would freeze morality at a particular point; and morally unacceptable because it infringes the liberty of the individual. Devlin's response was that individual liberty could only flourish in a stable society; disintegration of our society through lack of shared morality would therefore threaten individual freedom.

Hart also pointed out that the standard of 'the right-minded man' is a tenuous one. When people object to unusual behaviour, the response is not always prompted by rational moral objections, but often by prejudice, ignorance or misunderstanding.

Hart gives four basic reasons why moral censure should not necessarily lead to legal sanctions. First, punishing the offender involves doing some harm to them, when they may have done no harm to others. Secondly, the exercise of free choice by individuals is a moral value in itself, with which it is wrong to interfere. Thirdly, this exercise of free choice can be valuable in that it allows individuals to experiment and learn. Fourthly, as far as sexual morality is concerned, 'the suppression of sexual impulses' is generally 'something which affects the development or balance of the individual's emotional life, happiness and personality', and thus causes them harm. He objects strongly to the idea that the law should punish behaviour which does not harm others, but merely causes them distress or disgust by its very existence, even out of their sight: 'recognition of individual liberty as a value involves, as a minimum, acceptance of the principle that the individual may do what he wants, even if others are distressed when they learn what it is that he does, unless, of course, there are other good grounds for forbidding it'.

Judicial support for Devlin's view – and perhaps reaction against liberalizing legislation – can be seen in some of the more high-profile cases which arose in its aftermath. In **Shaw** *v* **Director of Public Prosecutions** (1961), Shaw had published a booklet entitled *The Ladies' Directory*, which contained advertisements by prostitutes, featuring photographs and descriptions of the sexual practices they offered. He was convicted of the offence of conspiring to corrupt public morals, an offence which had not been prosecuted since the eighteenth century. The House of Lords upheld the conviction, and defending the court's power to uphold the recognition of such an antiquated offence, Viscount Simonds said: 'In the sphere of criminal law I entertain no doubt that there remains in the courts of law a residual power to enforce the supreme and fundamental purpose of the law, to conserve not only the safety and order but also the moral welfare of the State.'

As an example of offences against this moral welfare, Viscount Simonds said 'Let it be supposed that at some future, perhaps early, date homosexual practices between consenting adult males are no longer a crime. Would it not be an offence if, even without obscenity, such practices were publicly advocated and encouraged by pamphlet and advertisement?' This proved to be an uncannily accurate prediction; in 1967 the Sexual Offences Act was passed, which stated that homosexual acts between consenting adult males in private were no longer a criminal offence, and in the case of **Knuller *v* Director of Public Prosecutions** (1972) the defendants were prosecuted for having published, in their magazine *International Times*, advertisements placed by readers inviting others to contact them for homosexual purposes.

Once again, the charge was conspiracy to corrupt public morals, and it was upheld. Lord Reid (who had dissented from the majority decision in Shaw's case, but felt that Shaw should still apply to avoid inconsistency) recognized that the 1967 Act legalized homosexual acts, but said: 'I find nothing in that Act to indicate that Parliament thought or intended to lay down that indulgence in these practices is not corrupting. I read the Act as saying that, even though it may be corrupting, if people choose to corrupt themselves in this way that is their affair and the law will not interfere. But no licence is given to others to encourage the practice.'

More recent decisions still show support for the Devlin viewpoint that some acts are intrinsically immoral, regardless of whether they harm others. In **R *v* Gibson** (1991), an artist exhibited earrings made from freeze-dried foetuses of three to four months gestation; a conviction for the common law offence of outraging public decency was upheld.

In **R *v* Brown** (1992), the appellants were homosexual men who had willingly participated in the commission of acts of sado-masochistic violence against each other, involving the use of, among other things, heated wires, map-pins, stinging nettles, nails, sandpaper and safety-pins. Evidence showed that all the men involved had consented; although the activities were videotaped by the participants, this was not for any profit or gain; none of the injuries were permanent and no medical attention had been sought; the activities were carried out in private; and none of the victims had complained to the police. They were convicted of a variety of assaults against the person, and appealed to the House of Lords, arguing that since all the participants had consented and the activities took place in private, the law had no reason to intervene. Their convictions were upheld; by a majority, the House of Lords held that public policy demanded such acts be treated as criminal offences. The judgment has been heavily criticized and is currently being appealed to the European Court of Human Rights for breach of the Convention.

The Warnock Committee

Despite the debate between Devlin and Hart, their two views are not always as opposed as they may seem, and in practice both are influential; a recent Government commission, the Warnock Committee, incorporates features of both approaches in its reasoning.

The Committee was set up by the Government to consider issues relating to scientific advances concerning conception and pregnancy. With the advent of *in vitro* fertilization (the technique used to create test-tube babies) and other technological advances, new scientific possibilities have arisen. These include the possibility of creating embryos for use in medical experiments, sperm, egg and embryo donation by fertile men or women to those who are infertile, and the use of surrogate mothers – women who bear a child for another couple, using their own egg and the father's sperm. These practices raised a number of moral issues, including that of payment for surrogacy, and the parentage of children born from donated eggs and sperm.

The Committee's report, published in 1984, advised the setting up of an independent statutory body to monitor, regulate and license infertility services and embryo experiments. On the specific issues before them, they recommended that experiments on embryos up to fourteen days old should be lawful; and that sperm, egg and embryo donation should be facilitated in that the babies born could be registered as the legitimate children of the non-contributing parent(s) on the birth certificate, and donors should be relieved of parental rights and duties in law. But surrogacy arrangements met with disapproval by the majority, who recommended that surrogacy agencies should be criminally prohibited, and private surrogacy arrangements between individuals should be illegal and unenforceable in the courts – although no criminal sanction would be imposed as it would be against the child's interests to be born into a family threatened by imprisonment). Many of the Committee's conclusions became law in the Human Fertilisation and Embryology Act 1990.

If we look at the reasoning behind the Committee's findings, we can see aspects of both Hart's utilitarian approach, and Devlin's upholding of common morality. In its conclusions on embryo research, it points out:

> We do not want to see a situation in which human embryos are frivolously or unnecessarily used in research but we are bound to take account of the fact that the advances in the treatment of infertility, which we have discussed in the earlier part of this report, could not have taken place without such research; and that continued research is essential, if advances in treatment and medical knowledge are to continue. A majority of us therefore agreed that research on human embryos should continue.

But this utilitarian approach is balanced against issues of morality.

A strict utilitarian would suppose that, given procedures, it would be possible to calculate their benefits and their costs. Future advantages, therapeutic or scientific, should be weighed against present and future harm. However, even if such a calculation were possible, it could not provide a final or verifiable answer to the question whether it is right that such procedures should be carried out. There would still remain the possibility that they were unacceptable, whatever their long-term benefits were supposed to be. Moral questions, such as those with which we have been concerned are, by definition, questions that involve not only a calculation of consequences, but also strong sentiments with regard to the nature of the proposed activities themselves.

As the report shows, issues of law and morality cannot easily be separated into theoretical approaches like those of Hart and Devlin; legislators in practice have to tread an uneasy path between the two.

ANSWERING QUESTIONS

1 **To what extent are moral views significant in the development of law?**
AEB

A good start to this essay would be to define the meaning of morality – you could do this by contrasting moral rules with rules of law. Point out that although morality is often talked of in connection with sexual issues, it is actually a much broader issue, covering many areas of law.

If you give morality this broad definition, you can argue that moral values have influenced most, if not all, areas of law, illustrating this point with areas of law you have studied in detail. For example, if you have studied contract law, you might consider the moral view which holds that some promises should be binding and others not; in criminal law, you could discuss the idea of *mens rea* as being indicative of moral fault, and the values behind some of the defences. You need to make this part of the essay quite detailed, giving specific examples from case and statute law which back up your points.

You might then go on to make the point that some areas of law seem to have an overtly moral content, but that here again, morals are not absolute – the *Gillick* case is an example of a situation where the two sides each believed that their view represented morality.

Finally, you could discuss how far morality should influence the law, using the theoretical arguments of Devlin and Hart, and relating them to cases which you know.

22 Law and justice

Doing justice is often seen as one of the most basic aims of a legal system. When areas of that system go wrong, the result is often described as injustice; for example, when people are convicted of crimes they have not committed, as in the recent cases of the Tottenham Three and the Birmingham Six, we say that a miscarriage of justice has occurred. But what is justice, and what is its relationship with law? These questions have been addressed by writers throughout the centuries, and we will look at some of the most important views in this chapter.

▶ Aristotle

The Greek philosopher Aristotle is responsible for some of the earliest thinking on justice, and his work is still influential today. Aristotle considered that a just law was one which would allow individuals to fulfil themselves in society, and distinguished between distributive justice and corrective justice.

Distributive justice was concerned with the allocation of assets such as wealth and honour between members of the community. Here the aim of justice was to achieve proportion, but this did not mean equal shares; Aristotle held that individuals should receive benefits in proportion to their claim on those benefits.

Corrective justice, on the other hand, applies when a situation that is distributively just, is disturbed – for example by wrongdoing. A judge should discover what damage has been done, and then try to restore equality by imposing penalties to confiscate any gain made by the offence, and compensate for damage done.

▶ Natural law theories

Natural law theories assume that there is a higher order of law, and if the laws of society follow this order they will be just. Aristotle supported this view, and believed that the higher law could be discovered from nature;

others, such as the medieval scholar St Aquinas, thought that that higher law came from God.

For Aquinas, there were two ways in which law could be unjust. First, a law which was contrary to human good, whether in its form or in its result, was, according to Aquinas, not true law at all. However, such laws might still be obeyed if to do so would avoid causing social disorder. Secondly, a law which was against God's will, and therefore a violation of the natural law, should be disregarded.

▶ Utilitarianism

The utilitarian movement, which includes such writers as Mill and Bentham, is based on the idea that society should work towards the greatest happiness for the greatest number, even if this means that some individuals lose out. Utilitarians assess the justice of rules (and therefore law) by looking at their consequences; in their view, if a rule maximized happiness or well-being or some other desirable effect, for the majority, it was just. A law could therefore be just even if it created social inequalities, or benefitted some at the expense of others, so long as the benefits to the many exceeded the loss to the minority.

The utilitarian approach can be criticized as focusing only on justice for the community as a whole, and leaving out justice for individuals.

▶ The economic analysis of law

This approach has developed mainly in the United States, and attempts to offer a more sophisticated alternative to utilitarianism. While the goal of utilitarianism was to promote the greatest happiness of the greatest number, it offered no reliable way of calculating the effect of a law or policy on this goal, or measuring the relative benefits.

The economic analysis takes the view that a thing has value for a person when that person values it; its value can therefore be measured by how much the person is prepared to pay for it, or what would be required to make them give it up. As we have seen, a conflict exists between the concerns of utilitarianism, and individual justice, and the same conflict exists here. Take the example of an NHS doctor with a limited budget, faced with one person who needs a life-saving operation costing £100,000, and ten others who each need more minor operations costing £10,000 each. On the face of it, doing the ten operations clearly seems to produce benefit for a greater number at the same cost, and in this sense may be the best way to spend public money. But can we say that this solution offers the first man justice?

A common criticism of the economic analysis of law is that it favours a particular ideology, that of market capitalism. This is based on the idea that the prices at which goods and services are bought and sold are the direct result of the value placed on them by buyer and seller, and therefore the result of free will; it presumes that sellers cannot exploit buyers, because nobody would pay more for something than it was worth to them. Critics of this view point out that in practice, power in the marketplace is frequently unequal; a seller may have the monopoly on particular goods, or sellers may collude to keep prices high. Equally, the idea that a thing has value because a person wants it ignores the question of where the desire for that thing originates; expensive advertising campaigns may produce the desire for what they sell, but can we objectively say that that gives them value? In the same way, people may take low paid jobs, not because they agree with that valuation of their labour, but because there are no other jobs and they have no power in the labour market.

▶ Rawls: A Theory of Justice

Professor John Rawls first presented his ideas in *A Theory of Justice*, published in 1971, and amended them slightly in his latest book, *Political Liberalism*. He approaches the idea of justice through an imaginary situation in which the members of a society are to decide on a set of principles designed to make their society just, and advance the good of all its members. He describes this initial debate as 'the original position'. The individuals involved will hold their discussions without knowing what their own position in the society is to be – whether they will be rich or poor, of high or low social status, old or young, and what will be the economic or political situation in the society. This 'veil of ignorance' is designed to ensure that the ideas put forward really are the best for all members of society, since nobody will be willing to disadvantage a section of society if they might find themselves a member of it.

Rawls believes that the principles which would result from such a discussion would include an equal distribution of what he calls 'social primary goods': these are the things which individuals are assumed to want in order to get the most out of their own lives, including rights, powers and freedoms, and, in Rawls's later work, self-respect. In addition to this, there would be two basic principles. The first involves liberty: a set of basic liberties – including freedom of thought, conscience, speech and assembly – would be available to all, and each person's freedom would be restricted only where the restriction on them was balanced out by greater liberty for the community as a whole. So, for example, the liberty of a person suspected of crime could be restricted by police powers of arrest, since these would increase the freedom from crime of society as a whole.

The second basic principle is based on equality. This covers both equality of opportunity – offices and positions within society should be open to all equally – and equality of distribution. Rawls envisages an equal distribution of wealth, with inequalities allowed only where necessary to help the most disadvantaged.

If a social order is just, or nearly just, according to these principles, Rawls argues that those who accept its benefits are bound to accept its rules as well, even if they may disapprove of some of them, provided that those rules do not impose heavy burdens unequally, nor violate the basic principles. Professor Rawls would support limited disobedience, where the basic principles are violated, other means of obtaining redress fail, and no harm is done to others.

Rawls's theory has been extensively criticized. The clearest problem is simply its artificiality, particularly that of the 'veil of ignorance'. As Dworkin has pointed out, even if we accept the scenario Rawls creates, the fact that individuals accept certain principles when they do not know what their position in society will be does not necessarily mean that they will continue to live by them if they find themselves in a position to maximize their own advantage at the expense of others. Rawls's theory appears to view human beings as rather more perfect than they have in fact shown themselves to be.

▶ Nozick and the minimal state

Robert Nozick's provocative essay 'Anarchy, State and Utopia', argues that for a truly just society, the state should have the minimum possible right to interfere in the affairs of individuals; its functions should be limited to the basic needs, such as protecting the individual against force, theft and fraud, and enforcing contracts. Written in 1974, the essay revives a claim traditionally associated with the seventeenth-century writer John Locke, and has strong links with eighteenth-century individualism, and nineteenth-century *laissez-faire* capitalism.

Nozick's theory emphasizes the importance of individual rights, and in particular rights to property. He argues that the right to hold property is based on the way in which that property is obtained, either by just acquisition (such as inheritance) or just transfer (such as purchase from another), or by rectification of an unjust acquisition (such as returning stolen property to its owner). Provided individuals have obtained their property in a just manner, the distribution of property throughout society is just, according to Nozick; attempts to redistribute wealth are unjust because they interfere with the individual's right to hold justly obtained property. The state should therefore have no role in adjusting the distribution of wealth. In fact Nozick rejects the idea that there are any goods belonging to society; goods belong only to individuals and the state has no right to interfere with them. Nozick's theories have been criticized, but they do reflect a growing disenchantment in Western society with the idea of redistributing wealth – in Britain we can see this in the emphasis placed by Government on lowering taxes and expecting individuals to look after themselves, rather than taking taxes from the rich to help the poor.

Karl Marx

Marx held that it was impossible for a capitalist society to be just; such a society was organized with the aim of upholding the interests of the ruling class, rather than securing justice for all. For Marx, a just society would distribute wealth on the basis 'from each according to his capacity, to each according to his needs'; individuals should contribute what they can to society, and receive what they need in return. Marx's views are still influential, but the main criticism made of them is that so far no country has been able to practice them with sufficient success to bring about the fair society Marx envisaged.

Kelsen and positivism

For positivists, law can be separated from what is just or morally right. Parts of law may be based on or incorporate ideas of morality or justice, but this is not a necessary component of law; a law is still a law and should be obeyed even if it is completely immoral.

One of the best-known positivists is Kelsen, whose theories were first published in 1911, and further developed in his *General Theory of Law and State*, published in 1945. Kelsen tried to develop a pure theory of law, to explain what law is rather than suggesting what it ought to be. He saw justice as simply the expression of individual preferences and values, and as such, as an irrational ideal. Therefore, argued Kelsen, it is not possible to scientifically define justice.

Justice in our legal system

One of the most important aspects of the British legal system is parliamentary supremacy, which essentially means that Parliament is the ultimate law-maker, and can make or unmake any law it wishes (this has been qualified by membership of the European Union, but that does not affect the point being made here). In most other developed countries, a written constitution sets down basic principles with which law should conform, and judges can strike down any legislation which conflicts with them. In this country that is not the case; our constitution is unwritten, and judges must apply the law that Parliament makes, even if they believe it is unjust. If Parliament wanted to make laws condemning all blonde women to death, banning old men from keeping pet dogs, or obliging parents to sell their eldest child into slavery, there would probably be political obstacles to doing so, but there would be no legal ones, and judges would be obliged to apply the laws.

Clearly this situation conflicts with the natural law approach we discussed earlier, where unjust laws were considered not to be true law, and in some circumstances, not to require application by the courts or obedience by the citizen. Arguments for a Bill of Rights, a statement of basic principles against which courts could measure legislation and strike down any in conflict with them, have something in common with the natural law approach, since they assume that some values are basic, and those given the power to make law in a society should be bound to follow them, rather than being free to make any law they like.

Like most developed legal systems, ours is based on the idea that to achieve justice, like cases must be treated alike – so, for example, if two people commit a crime in identical circumstances, they should be punished in a similar way. This aim requires fixed rules, so that decision makers base their verdicts on the application of those rules to the case before them, and not on arbitrary factors such as their own mood or what they personally think of the defendant. However, the other side of this situation is that fixed rules can make it difficult to do justice in individual cases. Take the crime of murder, for example. To commit a murder, a defendant must have intended to kill; if this intention is present, the motive for killing is largely irrelevant. While this promotes the idea of like cases being treated alike, allowing judges to opt out of assessing the pros and cons of different motives, which must of necessity involve personal views, it presents problems in individual cases – can we say it is just for someone who kills a terminally ill relative to spare them from pain to be treated in the same way as someone who kills another so they can rob them? They both have intention but are they equally blameworthy? Fixed rules can sometimes promote justice in the majority of cases at the expense of justice in the individual, out of the ordinary one.

The problem of fixed rules preventing justice in individual cases was one which our legal system faced early on in its life, when the common law was first becoming established. Then the answer was to develop a special branch of law, equity, with the specific aim of providing justice in cases where the ordinary rules of law failed to do so. Equity is no longer a separate branch of law, but equitable principles are still important in some areas of the civil law, and allow the courts to use their discretion in order to do justice in individual cases. In the criminal law (though not for the offence of murder) discretion over sentencing can fulfil a similar role. The challenge is to maintain a balance between too much discretion, leading to the possibility of arbitrary decisions, and too little, leading to harsh results in individual cases.

. . . .
ANSWERING QUESTIONS

1 **(a) To what extent should a legal system be concerned to promote 'justice'?** *(10 marks)*
(b) How far do you believe that the English legal system does promote 'justice'? *(15 marks)* *AEB*

Part (a): a good way to start this question is to define justice, so that you can then assess the importance it should have for a legal system. We have seen that there are various theories on the nature of justice, and you could mention some of these, pointing out that they sometimes conflict. As a result, you might point out, how far a system should be concerned to promote justice will depend on what you think justice is. Probably everybody would agree, for example, that a basic view of justice as fairness, is something a legal system should promote, but the meaning given to fairness often depends on a person or society's political stance, so that issues such as distributive justice may be desirable or undesirable depending on the political views of a society. You can discuss the different types of justice in this way, pointing those which you feel a legal system should be concerned to promote. Note that this question is asking to what extent the legal system **should** be concerned to promote justice, so you need to do more than just describe how concerned it **is** with that issue for that part.

Part (b): This is an opportunity to apply the theories you have just discussed to areas of law which you have studied in detail. The choice of area is up to you – the important thing is that you have a detailed knowledge of both the operation of that area of law, and its background values. For example, you could talk about contract law and the capitalist values it upholds, which is linked with the kind of justice supported by Robert Nozick, and could be contrasted with the theory of distributive justice. You could also refer to any issues of law or the legal system which you feel show justice or injustice in the system – you might talk about the miscarriages of justice and their implications for the criminal justice system for example. Make sure you can make your answer detailed, mentioning specific cases or research that prove your point – it is better to choose a few areas of law you know well than to skim over the surface of everything you have learned.

23

Legal rights and duties

One of the functions of a legal system is to define the rights owed to individuals within it, and the duties imposed upon them. The individual's relationship with the state, for example, creates a mass of both rights and duties, including rights to social security benefits, and the duty to pay tax. Rights and duties will also apply between individuals: for example, if Anne runs Peter over in her car, she may have a duty to pay him compensation, arising from his right to claim that compensation. Similarly, parties to a contract have a duty to perform according to their agreement, and each party has a right to claim such performance.

When you study substantive branches of law – criminal, tort or contract for example – you will learn the specific rights and duties which they create, and look at how they apply to individuals. But in this chapter, we are considering a more fundamental question: what exactly do we mean when we speak of a legal right or a legal duty?

An obvious answer might be that a claim is a legal right if it can be enforced; equally a legal duty might be one which you can be made to perform. But as Hart suggests, there may be many occasions where someone is physically unable to prevent their property being taken by another without authorization; the fact they could not enforce the law by preventing the property being taken would not mean they had no legal right to the property.

As well as a physical inability to enforce a legal right, there may be legal barriers to doing so. Claims in contract and tort, for example, must be brought within a certain period (usually six years); once this has expired, a court will not hear the claim. So if Barry owes Susan money, and Susan fails to bring an action within the specified period, Susan's right to a remedy is no longer available. She still has a legal right to the money, but cannot enforce that right in court.

▶ Hohfield's analysis of rights and duties

Clearly rights are less easy to define than they seem to be at first sight. The American legal writer, Wesley Hohfield, has pointed out that this is because the term 'rights' actually applies to a wide range of different legal situations and relationships. It is difficult to find one meaning of rights which covers all of these.

In his book *Fundamental Legal Conceptions*, published in 1913, Hohfield sought to clarify the different kinds of legal relationships in which rights and duties could apply. He showed that the sentence 'X has a right to R' has four different possible meanings.

The claim-right

Hohfield's scheme started with the kind of relationship which he described as correlative; where a right gives rise to a corresponding duty. Here the sentence 'X has a right to R' may mean that Y (or indeed everyone) has a duty to let X do R, so that X has a claim against Y. A contract is a good example of this situation: if Y has agreed to sell a CD to X for £10, and X has paid the money, X has a right to claim the CD and Y a duty to give it to X. This kind of right can be described as a claim-right.

The idea of a claim in fact presupposes a correlative duty, because there must be something to claim. The phrase 'X has a claim' is meaningless, but the statement 'X has a claim to the CD she has paid for' clearly has a meaning that derives from Y's duty to give X the CD. The right and the duty in this case could be described as opposite sides of the same coin.

However, not all rights have corresponding duties, and nor does every duty imply a correlative claim. This area was studied by, among others, the influential nineteenth-century writer Austin. He distinguished between relative duties, which, as in our example of the sale of a CD, involve corresponding rights, and absolute duties, which are imposed by law without implying any corresponding rights. Austin's primary examples of absolute duties were those imposed by the criminal law. Clearly we are all under legal duties not to commit crimes, but it is hard to see who could gain rights against us from the creation of those duties. The same can be said of some duties created by statute; as those of you who study tort will see, these only occasionally give rise to specific correlative rights for individuals.

The function of these kinds of legal duties is primarily to regulate conduct so as to avoid what is seen as harm to society – that is why crimes are prosecuted by the state, rather than being seen as an issue of rights and duties between individuals. In theory, it would be possible for the law to impose only duties, without creating corresponding rights, so that all breaches of duty were prosecuted by the state as crimes are, rather than individuals suing each other on the basis of their rights in tort or contract, for example. In practice, such a situation would demand enormous and expensive state machinery, and legal systems usually include a mixture of the kind of absolute duties discussed by Austin, where no individual correlating rights are created, and duties which do create correlating rights for individuals, and must therefore be enforced by individuals rather than the state in the event of their breach. While in some cases it will be clear which side of the line a duty falls – serious crimes such as murder, for example, will usually be dealt with by the state – other duties may be dealt with by public prosecution in one legal system, and by private legal action in another. The distinction between duties which do give rise to individual rights and those which do not can therefore be quite arbitrary, suggesting again that there is no reason why duties should necessarily give rise to rights.

The liberty/privilege-right

Hohfield's second analysis of the sentence 'X has a right to do R' states that it may, and usually does, mean that X is free to do or not do R. It is not a statement of what Y must do (or not do) but of what X may do. Hohfield called this type of 'right' a 'privilege'; others have preferred the term 'liberty'. Privilege can mean a special position, and encompasses situations where someone has a right to do something which would normally be a breach of legal duty; examples include the rights of judges to make slanderous remarks while acting judicially, without incurring legal responsibility, or the right to perform abortions granted to doctors in specified circumstances by the Abortion Act 1967.

Of more widespread application is the idea of a right in the sense of a liberty. What we mean here is a freedom to do something, in the sense that no one can prevent you from doing it, rather than an enforceable claim to do it. For example, when the term 'right to work' is used in our society, it refers to the fact that someone, usually trade unions, cannot prevent someone working in a particular trade by, for example, denying employment to anyone who is not a member of the union. It does not mean that we all have an enforceable claim to a job. Nor does it necessarily mean that our freedom to work is unlimited – many employment contracts include terms restricting an employee's area of work on leaving that employer, by stating, for example, that they may not join a similar firm or set up a similar business within a specified distance of the previous employer. An employer can make a legal claim against any ex-employee breaking such a term. In this case the employee's liberty-right is qualified by the employer's claim-right.

Hohfield's concept of a liberty-right includes freedom not to do something; having the right to wear a red dress by implication means also having the right to choose not to wear a red dress. The liberty-right is therefore the opposite of a duty; a duty to wear a red dress by implication means there is no liberty-right not to wear it. In the case of a liberty-right, 'X has a right' can be expressed as 'X may...'.

The power-right

Hohfield's third category of right is described as power. X has a power when X has the ability to alter a particular legal relationship by doing or not doing a particular thing. An example would be the right to foreclose on a mortgage, or to sell property.

Powers are usually based on claim-rights and privileges: for example, the owner of property has the power to sell it because of the claim-rights involved in having title to it; a police officer has the power to enter and search premises in some circumstances because of the privilege-rights granted to the police by law. But powers can exist independently of other types of right: for example, if someone offers to sell you their property, you have a power-right to accept that offer, and thereby create a binding contract between you. Such a contract will change the seller's legal relationship with you.

Just as claim-rights give rise to correlating duties, power-rights may create correlating liabilities. In the case of a contract of sale, for example, the person offering to sell is generally free to withdraw that offer at any time before it is accepted; if the offer is withdrawn within this time, the power to accept it, and the seller's liability to sell, both cease to exist. But if the seller makes a binding agreement to keep the offer for sale open for a specified period, then he has a duty to do so, and if the offer is withdrawn before this period has expired, the potential buyer will have a claim against the seller for breach of their agreement.

In the case of a power-right, 'X has a right' can be expressed as 'X can'.

The immunity-right

Hohfield's fourth, and final type of right is an immunity. Where Y has no power to change X's legal relations, we can say that X has an immunity. An example of such an immunity occurs where a landowner gives another permission to use the land, under a licence which the law deems irrevocable. The user of the land – called the licensee – is immune from any withdrawal of the licence. The correlative of an immunity is a disability; in this example, the owner of the land is under a legal disability because he cannot withdraw the licence. Such an arrangement creates two types of right for the land user: an immunity-right preventing withdrawal of the licence, and a claim/right to use the land in accordance with the licence. The immunity-disability relationship is the basis of the claim-duty relationship.

Where an immunity-right exists, 'X has a right' can be expressed as 'You cannot do R to X'.

▶ The nature of rights

There are two main theories about the nature of rights: one emphasizes will or choice; the other interest or benefit. The will theory, expounded by Hart, among others, is based on the view that the purpose of law is to secure for individuals the greatest possible means of self-expression and self-assertion. This theory is closely related to ideas of moral individualism, in which individuals are seen as the best judge of their own interests, as opposed to society making decisions in the interests of us all, and the effect of individuals all acting in their own best interests is assumed, by the working of the market, to produce the best outcome for society. The will theory defines the bearer of a right by the power he or she has over the duty created by that right: the power to choose whether to enforce it or not, to waive it or even extinguish it completely. The discretion allowed to the individual is the most important feature of this concept of rights.

By contrast, the interest (or benefit) theory argues that the purpose of rights is not to protect individual free will, but to protect interests or benefits. Originating in the work of Bentham, and expounded by modern writers such as MacCormick, this theory sees rights as benefits secured by rules which regulate relationships. The exact nature of such rights varies between different versions of the theory. One states that X has a right whenever X is in a position to benefit from the performance of a duty; another, put forward by MacCormick, argues that X can have a right whenever X's interests are recognized as being a reason for imposing obligations, whether those obligations are actually imposed or not. The latter position has the advantage of allowing us to identify where rights may lie, without needing to determine what the correlating duty may be, or on whom it should fall.

· ·
ANSWERING QUESTIONS

1 Examining the various approaches to their analysis, discuss the importance attached to rights and duties in English law. *AEB*

As you can see from this chapter, the terms rights and duties are capable of bearing a number of different meanings, as explained by Hohfield. A good way to approach this answer might be to start by explaining this, and then go on to discuss each different meaning as analysed by Hohfield, relating it to areas of law which you have studied. So, for example, claim-rights and their correlative duties are obviously central to the whole notion of contract law, while absolute duties are the basis of criminal law, and liberty/privilege rights are important in the area of civil liberties. As you go through each category, you should give detailed examples of cases and other legal authority to support your points about the importance of different types of right to different areas of the law.

24 Legal personality

As far as the law is concerned, it is not only human beings who can be counted as persons. In some cases, the law creates artificial persons, such as companies and corporations, which are dealt with legally as if they are people; this is called having legal personality. On the other hand, some human beings do not have full 'legal personality'. Only when an entity has legal personality can it have legal rights and duties.

▶ Human beings

A human being has legal personality from the beginning to the end of their life, but this is not as simple as it sounds. There is, for example, much debate over when life begins: is it at birth, at conception, or at some stage in between? Among the cases where this issue has arisen is the litigation surrounding the thalidomide tragedy during the 1960s and 1970s. Thalidomide was a drug prescribed to pregnant women for morning sickness, which was later discovered to cause severe deformities in their unborn children. When the parents tried to sue for compensation, the issue arose of whether the drug manufacturers, Distillers, could owe a duty of care to an unborn child – in other words, whether the child could have legal personality before it was born. In the event, the litigation was settled out of court, leaving the issue undecided. Later legislation, in the form of the Congenital Disabilities (Civil Liability) Act 1976, provided that if negligence caused a pre-natal injury to the mother, affecting the parents' ability to have a healthy child, then the disabled child could sue in tort after their birth for the damage caused to his or her self, but here the child's rights derived from the parent rather than from their own possession of legal personality before birth.

Later cases have confirmed the view that an unborn child does not have legal personality of its own. In **Paton v British Pregnancy Advisory Service** (1979), a husband attempted to prevent his wife from having an abortion. Dismissing the case, the judge stated that 'a foetus cannot in English law have any right of its own at least until it is born.' Similarly, in **Berkshire County Council** *v* **Director of Public Prosecutions** (1986), a mother addicted to drugs gave birth to a child who had severe withdrawal symptoms. Legislation allowed a child to be taken into care if its health was being avoidably impaired, and defined a child as a person under the age of fourteen. The court decided that an unborn baby could not fall within that definition, and so impairment to the baby's health before it was born could not justify a care order; on the other hand impairment which happened after birth but resulted from the mother's conduct while pregnant could.

Once a child has been born, it has a legal personality, but some legal rights and duties may be restricted during childhood. Mental incapacity can also limit a person's legal rights and duties. Until the last century, married women lacked legal personality; a married couple was legally seen as one person, and that person was the man. Women could neither hold property nor make contracts.

A human being ceases to have legal personality when they die, but like the beginning of life, the end is not as straightforward as you might expect. Life support technology and the transplanting of living organs have opened up possibilities with profound moral, social and legal implications, as can be seen in the case of Tony Bland, the football supporter injured in the Hillsborough disaster.

Although legal personality ends at death, the law still has an interest in the form of wills and inheritance, which in a sense give legal life after death, allowing the deceased to have their wishes carried out.

▶ Corporate personality

As well as individuals, groups of people – such as companies, schools, councils – can have legal personality. They are broadly called corporations, and they allow the law to treat the group as separate from the individuals who operate or own it. There are two basic types of corporation.

Corporations sole

The corporation sole is a device which makes it possible to continue the official capacity of an individual beyond their lifetime, or tenure of office. The Crown is a corporation sole; its legal personality continues while individual monarchs come and go. The same can apply to holders of positions such as bishop, or vicar, or any office which continues to exist even though each individual only holds it for a limited time. The device of the corporation sole allows a particular occupant to acquire property or make contracts for the benefit of successors, or sue in tort for injuries to relevant property while it was in the hands of a predecessor.

Corporations aggregate

This terms covers groups of people with a single legal personality, such as companies. A corporation aggregate can be created by royal charter (universities, for example), by statute (local authorities, for example), or most commonly, by registration under the Companies Act 1985 s. 1.

Incorporation allows investors in a company to limit their liability if the company does not succeed. If a corporation has debts, no individual member has to pay any more than the amount outstanding, if any, on the value of their shares. By contrast, a firm which is set up as a partnership rather than a corporation has no legal personality separate from that of its individual members, and the debts of the firm are therefore the debts of the individual members, payable in full. So if you and two friends each invest £100 in a partnership which later incurs debts of £10,000, the three of you will be liable for the whole £10,000. But if you set up your business as a company with limited liability, your liability will be limited to the value of your shares in the company: £100. The company might go bankrupt but you would not. If, on the other hand, the company turned out to be very profitable, those profits can be paid out to shareholders in dividends. If, for example, the company's annual profits were double the money invested in it, it could pay out a £2.00 dividend for each £1.00 share, so for your initial £100 investment you would receive £200. The value of your shares would also increase as the high dividends attracted others to invest. Of course, if you were running the company as a partnership you would also receive profits, but you would be running the risk of losses as well.

This is of course a rather simplified account, but what you should see is that the concept of legal personality is used here to encourage investment, and so oil the wheels of commerce. Without it, investors would only put their money in the lowest-risk investments, and economic development would be slowed down.

Incorporation can also be used by individual traders, allowing them to keep business debts separate from their personal finances. This can lead to some rather bizarre, and some might say unjust distinctions, as the case of **Salomon** *v* **Salomon** (1897) shows. Mr Salomon formed a company called Salomon & Co, in which himself, his wife and their five children were the only shareholders. He had already been running a business, and sold this to the newly-formed company at an exorbitant price. This new company went bankrupt shortly afterwards, still owing £10,000 of the purchase price to Saloman, and £7,000 to other creditors. Its assets only totalled £6,000, and Saloman was what is called a secured creditor, giving him prior claim to the assets over the other, unsecured, creditors.

The creditors argued that Saloman was disqualified from claiming against those assets, because he was the company and the sale was a sham.

The trial judge and the Court of Appeal agreed, and gave the creditors prior claim to the assets, but the House of Lords unanimously reversed this, holding that the company was in law a person distinct from Salomon and that, therefore, Salomon was preferentially entitled to the assets as secured creditor and so was entitled to be paid.

An additional reason for corporate legal personality is that it allows individuals to act in the name of the company, so that, for example, companies can make contracts and be sued. You will read more about this if you are studying contract law.

. . . .
ANSWERING QUESTIONS

(a) Using appropriate examples, explain what is meant by legal personality.
(13 marks)
(b) To what extent does the notion of legal personality indicate the capacity of the law to adapt to change (for instance, economic or technological)? *(12 marks) AEB*

Part (a): here you need to distinguish between natural (human) legal personality and artificial (corporate) legal personality, and deal with each in turn. As far as natural legal personality is concerned, you should consider examples of human legal personality – for example, unborn children, newly born children (especially those who are handicapped) and comatose patients. For artificial personality, you need to distinguish between corporations and other forms of business organizations, discussing the consequences for liability of different types of corporate personality.

You should note that the examiners' report for this question points out that it was not intended to raise issues of *status* capacity (regarding children and women for example). However, the examiners say that where such discussion is combined with other more relevant material the student might gain a few extra marks.

Part (b): Again, it would be sensible to deal with natural personality and artificial in turn. With regard to natural personality, obvious issues to discuss might be the treatment of people in comas, mentioning the Anthony Bland case, and the rights of unborn children. Although there is room to explain your own views in a question like this, an emotional outpouring about the rights or wrongs of abortion (or anything else) will not score high marks – you must anchor your points in clear legal examples.

As far as corporate personality is concerned, you could discuss the social and economic aspects of different types of corporate personality, including, for example, the growth of the limited company as a way of encouraging investment and growth.

Appendix

ANSWERING EXAMINATION QUESTIONS

At the end of each chapter in this book, you will find detailed guide-lines for answering exam questions on the topics covered. Many of the questions are taken from actual A Level past papers, but they are equally relevant for candidates of all law examinations, as these questions are typical of the type of questions that examiners ask in this field.

In this section, we aim to give some general guidelines for answering questions on the English legal system.

Citation of authorities

One of the most important requirements for answering questions on the law is that you must be able to back the points you make with authority, usually either a case or a statute. It is not good enough to state that the law is such and such, without stating the case or statute which says that that is the law. Some examiners are starting to suggest that the case name is not essential as long as you can remember and understand the general principle that the case laid down. However, such examiners remain in the minority and the reality is that even they are likely to give higher marks where the candidate has cited authorities; quite simply, it helps give the impression that you know your material thoroughly, rather than half-remembering something you heard once in class.

This means that you must be prepared to learn fairly long lists of cases by heart, which can be a daunting prospect. What you need to memorize is the name of the case, a brief description of the facts, and the legal principle which the case established. Once you have revised a topic well, you should find that a surprisingly high number of cases on that topic begin to stick in your mind anyway, but there will probably be some that you have trouble recalling. A good way to memorize these is to try to create a picture in your mind which links the facts, the name and the legal principle. For example, if you wanted to remember the contract law case of **Redgrave** v **Hurd**, you might picture the actress Vanessa Redgrave and the politician Douglas Hurd, in the situation described in the facts

445

of the case, and imagine one of them telling the other the principle established in the case.

Knowing the names of cases makes you look more knowledgeable, and also saves writing time in the exam, but if you do forget a name, referring briefly to the facts will identify it. It is not necessary to learn the dates of cases though it is useful if you know whether it is a recent or an old case. Dates are usually required for statutes. Unless you are making a detailed comparison of the facts of a case and the facts of a problem question, in order to argue that the case should or could be distinguished, you should generally make only brief reference to facts, if at all – long descriptions of facts waste time and earn few marks.

When reading the 'Answering questions' sections at the end of each chapter in this book, bear in mind that for reasons of space, we have not highlighted every case which you should cite. The skeleton arguments outlined in those sections **must** be backed up with authority from cases and statute law.

When discussing the English legal system, as well as citing relevant cases and statutes it is particularly important to cite relevant research and reports in the field being discussed. If there are important statistics in an area, being able to quote some of them will give your answers authority.

There is no right answer

In law exams, there is not usually a right or a wrong answer. What matters is that you show you know what type of issues you are being asked about. Essay questions are likely to ask you to 'discuss', 'criticize', or 'evaluate', and you simply need to produce a good range of factual and critical material in order to do this. The answer you produce might look completely different from your friend's but both answers could be worth 'A' grades.

Breadth and depth of content

Where a question seems to raise a number of different issues – as most do – you will achieve better marks by addressing all or most of these issues than by writing at great length on just one or two. By all means spend more time on issues which you know well, but be sure to at least mention other issues which you can see are relevant, even if you can only produce a paragraph or so about them.

Civil or criminal

In some cases, a question on the English legal system will require you to confine your answer to either the civil or criminal system. This may be stated in the question – for example, 'Discuss the system of civil appeals'.

Alternatively, it may be something you are required to work out for yourself, as is often the case with problem questions. For example, a question might state:

'Jane has been charged with criminal damage.
a) How may she obtain legal aid and advice? and
b) If convicted, to which courts may she appeal?'

This question only requires you to discuss the legal aid and advice available in criminal cases, and the criminal appeals system; giving details of civil legal aid and the civil appeals system will waste time and gain you no marks, as would bringing the criminal appeals system into the previous question. Equally, where a question does not limit itself to either civil or criminal legal systems, you will lose marks if you only discuss one.

Because of this danger, it is a good idea to make a point of asking yourself before you answer any legal system question whether it covers just the civil legal system, just the criminal, or both.

The structure of the question

If a question is specifically divided into parts, for example (a), (b) and (c) then stick to those divisions and do not merge your answer into one long piece of writing.

Law examinations tend to contain a mixture of essay questions and what are known as 'problem questions'. Tackling each of these questions involves slightly different skills so we consider each in turn.

▶ Essay questions

Answer the question asked

Over and over again, examiners complain that candidates do not answer the question they are asked – so if you can develop this skill, you will stand out from the crowd. You will get very few marks for simply writing all you know about a topic, with no attempt to address the issues raised in the question, but if you can adapt the material that you have learnt on the subject to take into account the particular emphasis given to it by the question, you will do well.

Even if you have memorized an essay which does raise the issues in the question (perhaps because those issues tend to be raised year after year), you must fit your material to the words of the question you are actually being asked. For example, suppose during your course, you wrote an essay on the advantages and disadvantages of the jury system, and then in the exam, you find yourself faced with the question 'Should juries be abolished?' The material in your coursework essay is ideally suited for the exam question, but if you begin the main part of your answer with the words 'The advantages of juries include . . .', or something similar, this is a dead giveaway to the examiner that you are merely writing down an essay you have memorized. It takes very little effort to change the words to 'Abolition of the jury system would ignore certain advantages that the current system has . . .', but it will create a much better impression, especially if you finish with a conclusion which, based on points you have made, states that abolition is a good or bad idea, the choice depending on the arguments you have made during your answer.

During your essay, you should keep referring to the words used in the question – if this seems to become repetitive, use synonyms for those words. This makes it clear to the examiner that you are keeping the question in mind as you work.

Plan your answer

Under pressure of time, it is tempting to start writing immediately, but five minutes spent planning each essay question is well worth spending – it may mean that you write less overall, but the quality of your answer will almost certainly be better. The plan need not be elaborate: just jot down everything you feel is relevant to the answer, including case names, and then organize the material into a logical order appropriate to the question asked. To put it in order, rather than wasting time copying it all out again, simply put a number next to each point according to which ones you intend to make first, second and so forth.

Provide analysis and fact

Very few essay questions require merely factual descriptions of what the law is; you will almost always be required to analyse the factual content in some way, usually highlighting any problems or gaps in the law, and suggesting possible reforms. If a question asks you to analyse whether lay magistrates should be replaced by professional judges you should not write everything you know about magistrates and judges and finish with one sentence saying magistrates should/should not be kept. Instead you should select your relevant material and your whole answer should be targeted at answering whether or not magistrates should be kept.

Where a question uses the word 'critically', as in 'critically describe' or 'critically evaluate', the examiners are merely drawing your attention to the fact that your approach should be analytical and not merely descriptive; you are not obliged to criticize every provision you describe. Having said that, even if you do not agree with particular criticisms which you have read, you should still discuss them and say why you do not think they are valid; there is very little mileage in an essay that simply describes the law and says it is perfectly satisfactory.

Structure

However good your material, you will only gain really good marks if you structure it well. Making a plan for each answer will help in this, and you should also try to learn your material in a logical order – this will make it easier to remember as well. The exact construction of your essay will obviously depend on the question, but you should aim to have an introduction, then the main discussion, and a conclusion. Where a question is divided into two or more parts, you should reflect that structure in your answer.

A word about conclusions: it is not good enough just to repeat the question, turning it into a statement, for the conclusion. So, for example, if the question is 'Is the criminal justice system satisfactory', a conclusion which simply states that the system is or is not satisfactory will gain you very little credit. Your conclusion will often summarize the arguments that you have developed during the course of your essay.

▶ Problem questions

In problem questions, the exam paper will describe an imaginary situation, and then ask what the legal implications of the facts are – for example, 'Jane had suffered physical violence at the hands of her husband for many years. One days she lashes out and kills him. She is arrested by the police and later charged with murder. In which court will Jane be tried? If she is convicted to what court may she appeal?'

Read the question thoroughly

The first priority is to read the question thoroughly, at least a couple of times. Never start writing until you have done this, as you may well get halfway through and discover that what is said at the end makes half of what you have written irrelevant – or at worst, that the question raises issues you have no knowledge of at all.

Answer the question asked

This means paying close attention to the words printed immediately after the situation is described. In the example given above you are asked to advise about the courts and appeal procedure, so do not start discussing sentencing powers as this is not relevant to the particular question asked. Similarly, if a question asks you to advise one or other of the parties, make sure you advise the right one – the realization as you discuss the exam with your friends afterwards that you have advised the wrong party and thus rendered most of your answer irrelevant is not an experience you will enjoy.

Spot the issues

In answering a problem question in an examination you will often be short of time. One of the skills of doing well is spotting which issues are particularly relevant to the facts of the problem and spending most time on those, while skimming over more quickly those matters which are not really an issue on the facts, but which you clearly need to mention.

Apply the law to the facts

What a problem question requires you to do is to spot the issues raised by the situation, and to consider the law as it applies to those facts. It is not enough simply to describe the law without applying it to the facts. So in the example given above it is not enough to write about the appeal procedure in general for civil and criminal cases; you must apply the rules of criminal appeal to the particular case of Jane. She has committed an indictable offence that would have been tried by the Crown Court so you are primarily concerned with appeals from the Crown Court to the Court of Appeal. Nor should you start your answer by copying out all the facts. This is a complete waste of time, and will gain you no marks.

Unlike essay questions, problem questions are not usually seeking a critical analysis of the law. If you have time, it may be worth making the point that a particular area of the law you are discussing is problematic, and briefly stating why, but if you are addressing all the issues raised in the problem you are unlikely to have much time for this. What the examiner is looking for is essentially an understanding of the law and an ability to apply it to the particular facts given.

Use authority

As always, you must back up your points with authority from case or statute law.

Structure

The introduction and conclusion are much less important for problem questions than for essay questions. Your introduction can be limited to pointing out the issues raised by the question, or, where you are asked to 'advise' a person mentioned in the problem, what outcome that person will be looking for. You can also say in what order you intend to deal with the issues. Your conclusion might simply summarize the conclusions reached during the main part of the answer, for example that Jane will be tried in the Crown Court and her main route of appeal will be to the Court of Appeal.

There is no set order in which the main part of the answer must be discussed. Sometimes it will be appropriate to deal with the problem chronologically, in which case it will usually be a matter of looking at the question line by line, while in other cases it may be appropriate to group particular issues together. Problem questions on the English legal system are often broken down into clear parts – a, b, c and so on – so the answer can be broken down into the same parts. Thus with the example about Jane the question was clearly broken into two parts, and so your question should deal with first the trial court and then with the issue of appeal.

Whichever order you choose, try to deal with one issue at a time – for example, finish talking about the trial court before looking at the issue of appeal. Jumping backwards and forwards gives the impression that you have not thought about your answer. If you work through your material in a structured way, you are also less likely to leave anything out.

Select Bibliography

Abel, R. (1988) *The Legal Profession In England and Wales*, Oxford: Basil Blackwell.

Aquinas, St. T. (1942) *Summa Theologica*, London: Burns Oates & Washbourne.

Austin, J. (1954) *The Province of Jurisprudence Determined*, London: Weidenfeld and Nicolson.

Bailey, S. and Gunn, M. (1991) *Smith and Bailey on the Modern English Legal System*, London: Sweet and Maxwell.

Baldwin, J. (1992) *The Role of Legal Representatives at the Police Station*, (Royal Commission on Criminal Justice Research Study No. 2), London: H.M.S.O.

Baldwin, J. and McConville, M. (1979) *Jury Trials*, Oxford: Clarendon Press.

Baldwin, J. and Moloney, T. (1992) *Supervision of police investigations in serious criminal cases*, (Royal Commission of Criminal Justice Research Study No. 4), London: H.M.S.O.

Bennion, F.A.R. (1990) *Statutory Interpretation*, London: Butterworth.

Bond, R.A. and Lemon, N.F. (1979) 'Changes in Magistrates: Attitudes During the First Year on the Bench' in Farrington, D.P. et al. (eds) (1979) *Psychology, Law and Legal Processes*, London: Macmillan.

Bottoms, A.E. and Preston, R.H. (eds) (1980) *The Coming Penal Crisis: A Criminological and Theoretical Exploration*, Edinburgh: Scottish Academic Press.

Brown, D et al. (1992) *Changing the Code: Police Detention Under the Revised PACE Codes of Practice*, (Home Office Research Study No. 129), London: H.M.S.O.

Burney, E. (1979) *Magistrates, Court and Community*, London: Hutchinson.

Carlen, P. (1983) *Women's Imprisonment: A Study in Social Control*, London: Routledge.

Consumer Council (1970) *Justice Out of Reach: A case for small claims courts: A Consumer Council Study*, London: H.M.S.O.

Bell, J. and Engle, Sir G. (eds) (1995) *Statutory Interpretation*, London: Butterworths.

Denning, A. (1982) *What Next in the Law?*, London: Butterworth.

Devlin, P. (1965) *The Enforcement of Morals*, Oxford: Oxford University Press.

Devlin, P. (1979) *The Judge*, Oxford: Oxford University Press.

Dicey, A. (1982) *Introduction to the Study of the Law of the Constitution*, Indianapolis: Liberty Classics.

Dickens, L. (1985) *Dismissed: A Study of Unfair Dimissal and the Industrial System*, Oxford: Blackwell.

Duster, T. (1970) *The Legislation of Morality*, New York: Free Press.

Dworkin, R. (1977) *Taking Rights Seriously*, London: Duckworth.

—— (1986) *Law's Empire*, London: Fontana Press.

Enright, S. (1993) 'Cost effective criminal justice', *New Law Journal*.

Evans, R. (1993) *The conduct of police interviews with juveniles*, London: H.M.S.O.

Fuller, L. (1969) *The Morality of Law*, London: Yale University Press.

Genn, H. (1982) *Meeting Legal Needs?: An Evaluation of a Scheme for Personal Injury Victims*, Oxford: S.S.R.C. Centre for Socio-Legal Studies.

Genn, H. (1987) *Hard Bargaining: Out of Court Settlement in Personal Injury Actions*, Oxford: Clarendon Press.

Griffith, J.A.G. (1985) *Politics of the Judiciary*, London: Fontana Press.

Gudjonsson, G.H. (1992) *The Psychology of Interrogations, Confessions and Testimony*, Chichester: Wiley.

Hale, Sir M. (1979) *The History of the Common Law of England*, Chicago: University of Chicago Press.

Hart, H.L.A. (1963) *Law, Liberty and Morality*, Oxford: Oxford University Press.

—— (1994) *Concept of Law*, Oxford: Clarendon Press.

Hayek, F. (1982) *Law Legislation and Liberty: A New Statement of the Liberal Principles of Justice and Political Economy*, London: Routledge.

Hedderman, C. and Moxon, D. (1992) *Magistrates' Court or Crown Court? Mode of Trial Decisions and Sentencing*, London: H.M.S.O.

Hohfield, W.N. and Cook, W.W. (1919) *Fundamental Legal Concepts as Applied in Judicial Reasoning*, London: Greenwood Press.

Ingman, T. (1987) *English Legal Process*, London: Blackstone.

Jackson, R.M. (1989), *The Machinery of Justice in England*, Cambridge: Cambridge University Press.

Joseph, M. (1981) *The Conveyancing Fraud*, London: Woolwich.

Joseph, M. (1985) *Lawyers Can Seriously Damage Your Health*, London: Michael Joseph.

Kelsen, H. (1949) *General Theory of Law and State*, Cambridge, Massa: Harvard University Press.

Kennedy, H. (1992) *Eve was Framed: Women and British Justice*, London: Chatto.

King, M. and May, C. (1985) *Black Magistrates: A Study of Selection and Appointment*, London: Cobden Trust.

Lee, S. (1986) *Law and Morals*, Oxford: Oxford University Press.

Leigh, L. and Zedner, L. (1992) *A Report on the Administration of Criminal Justice in the Pre-trial Phase in London, France and Germany*, London: H.M.S.O.

Leng, R. (1993) *The Right to Silence in Police Interrogation*. (Royal Commission on Criminal Justice Research Study No. 10), London: H.M.S.O.

Levi, M. (1992) *The Investigation, Prosecution and Trial of Serious Fraud*, London: H.M.S.O.

Locke, J. (1967) *Two Treatises of Government*, London: Cambridge University Press.

Maine, Sir H. (1917) *Ancient Law*, London: Dent.

Malleson, K. (1993) *A Review of the Appeal Process* (Royal Commission on Criminal Justice Research Series No. 17), London: H.M.S.O.

Mansfield, M. (1993) *Presumed Guilty: The British Legal System Exposed*, London: Heinemann.

Markus, K. (1992) 'The Politics of Legal Aid' in *The Critical Lawyer's Handbook*, London: Pluto Press.

McConville, M. and Hodgson, J. (1993) *Custodial Legal Advice and the Right to Silence*, (Royal Commission on Criminal Justice Research Study No. 16), London: H.M.S.O.

McConville, M. and Baldwin, J. (1977) *Negotiated Justice: Pressures to Plead Guilty*, Oxford: Martin Robertson.

McConville, M. and Baldwin, J. (1981) *Courts, Prosecution and Conviction*, Oxford: Oxford University Press.

McConville, M., Sanders, A. and Leng, P. (1993) *The Case for the Prosecution: Police Suspects and the Construction of Criminality,* London: Routledge.

McConville, M. (1992) 'Videotaping Interrogations: Police Behaviour On and Off Camera', *Criminal Law Review.*

Mitchell, B. (1983) 'Confessions and Police Interrogation of Suspects', *Criminal Law Review.*

Montesquieu, C. (1989) *The Spirit of the Laws,* Cambridge: Cambridge University Press.

Moxon, D. (1985) *Managing Criminal Justice: A Collection of Papers,* London: H.M.S.O.

Moxon, D. and Crisp, D. (1994) *Case Screening by the Crown Prosecution Service: How and Why Cases are Terminated,* London: H.M.S.O.

Mullin, C. (1990) *Error of Judgement: The Truth About the Birmingham Bombings,* Dublin: Poolbeg Press.

Nozick, R. (1975) *Anarchy, State and Utopia,* Oxford: Blackwell.

Olivercrona, K. (1971) *Law as Fact,* London: Stevens.

Owens, A. (1995) 'Not Completely Appealing', *New Law Journal.*

Pannick, D. (1987) *Judges,* Oxford: Oxford University Press.

Paterson, A. (1982) *The Law Lords,* London: Macmillan.

Pickles, J. (1988) *Straight from the Bench,* London: Coronet.

Plotnikoff, J. and Wilson, R. (1993) *Information and Advice for Prisoners about Grounds for Appeal and the Appeal Process* (Royal Commission on Criminal Justice Research Study No. 18), London: H.M.S.O.

Pound, R. (1968) *Social Control Through Law,* Hamden: Archon Books.

Rawls, J. (1972) *A Theory of Justice,* Oxford: Oxford University Press.

Rawls, J. (1972) *Political Liberalism, John Dewey Essays in Philosophy,* New York: Columbia University Press.

Robertson, G. (1993) *Freedom, The Individual and The Law,* London: Penguin.

Sanders, A. (1993) 'Controlling the Discretion of the Individual Officer' in Reiner, R. and Spencer, S. (eds) *Accountable Policing.*

Sanders, A. and Bridge, L. (1982) 'Access to Legal Advice' in Walker, C. and Sturner, K. (eds) *Justice in Error.*

Schur, E. (1965) *Crimes Without Victims: Deviant Behaviour and Public Policy, Abortion, Homosexuality, Drug Addiction,* New York: Prentice Hall.

Smith, D. and Gray, J. (1983) *Police and People in London* (The Policy Studies Institute), Aldershot: Gower.

Smith, J.C. and Hogan, B. (1992) *Criminal Law,* London: Butterworths.

Stern, V. (1987) *Bricks of Shame: Britain's Prisons,* London: Penguin.

Summers, R. (1992) *Essays on the Nature of Law and Legal Reasoning,* Berlin: Duncker & Humblot.

Thomas, D. (1970) *Principles of Sentencing: The Sectencing Policy of the Court of Appeal Criminal Division,* London: Heinemann.

Twining, W. and Miers, D. (1991) *How To Do Things With Rules,* London: Weidenfeld & Nicolson.

Vennard, J. (1985) 'The Outcome of Contested Trials' in Moxon, D. (ed) *Managing Criminal Justice,* London: H.M.S.O.

Vennard, J. and Riley, D. (1988) *Triable Either Way Cases: Crown Court or Magistrates' Court?,* London: H.M.S.O.

Waldron, J. (1989) *The Law,* London: Routledge.

Weber, M. (1979) *Economy and Society,* Berkeley: University of California Press.

Woolf, Lord Justice H. (1995) *Access to Justice: Interim Report to the Lord Chancellor on the Civil Justice System in England and Wales*, London: Lord Chancellor's Department.
Young, J. (1971) *The Drugtakers: The Social Meaning of Drug Use*, London: Paladin.
Zander, M. (1988) *A Matter of Justice*, Oxford: Oxford University Press.
—— (1994) *The Law Making Process*, London: Butterworth.
Zander, M. and Henderson, P. (1993) *Crown Court Study*, London: H.M.S.O.

Glossary

Administrative law. The body of law which deals with the rights and duties of the State and the limits of its powers over individuals.

Arraignment. The process whereby the accused is called to the Bar of the court to plead guilty or not guilty to the charges against him.

Bill of Rights. A statement of the basic rights which a citizen can expect to enjoy.

Case stated. Under the proceedings, a person who was a party to a proceeding before the magistrates (or the Crown Court when it is hearing an appeal from the magistrates) may question the proceeding of the court on the ground that there was an error of law or the court had acted outside its jurisdiction. The party asks the court to state a case for the opinion of the High Court on the question of law or jurisdiction.

Caution. 1. A warning to an accused person administered on arrest or before police questioning. Since the abolition, by the Criminal Justice and Public Order Act 1994, of the right of silence, the correct wording is: 'You do not have to say anything. But it may harm your defence if you do not mention when questioned something which you later rely on in court. Anything you do say may be given in evidence'.

2. A formal warning given to an offender about what he has done, designed to make him see that he has done wrong and deter him from further offending. This process is used instead of proceeding with the prosecution.

Certiorari. An order quashing an *ultra vires* decision.

Chambers. The offices of a barrister.

Community sentence. This means a sentence of one or more community orders (which include probation orders, community service orders, combination orders, curfew orders, supervision orders and attendance centre orders).

Community service order. This order requires an offender to perform, over a period of 12 months, a specified number of hours of unpaid work for the benefit of the community, and to keep in touch with the probation officer and notify him of any change of address.

Constitution. A set of rules and customs which detail a country's system of government; in most cases it will be a written document but in some countries, including Britain, the constitution cannot be found written down in one document and is known as an unwritten constitution.

Contingency fee. A fee payable to a lawyer (who has taken on a case on a 'no win, no fee' basis) in the event of him winning the case.

Convention. 1. A long established tradition which tends to be followed although it does not have the force of law.
2. A treaty with a foreign power.

Corporation aggregate. This term covers groups of people with a single legal personality (e.g. a company, university or local authority).

Corporation sole. This is a device which makes it possible to continue the official capacity of an individual beyond their lifetime or tenure of office; e.g. the Crown is a corporation sole; its legal personality continues while individual monarchs come and go.

Counsel's opinion. A barrister's advice.

Custom. 'Such usage as has obtained the force of law' (**Tanistry Case, 1608**).

Delay defeats equities. Where a plaintiff takes an unreasonably long time to bring an action, equitable remedies will not be available.

Discovery of documents. The procedure whereby one party to an action provides the other party with a list of documents relating to the action which are or have been in his possession. The other party can then ask to see some or all of the documents.

Ejusdem generis rule. General words which follow specific ones are taken to include only things of the same kind.

Equity. In law it is a term which applies to a specific set of legal principles which were developed by the Chancery Court and add to those provided in the common law.

Expressio unius est exclusio alterius. Express mention of one thing implies the exclusion of another.

Green Form Scheme. The legal advice and assistance scheme known as such because the application form is green.

Habeas corpus. This is an ancient remedy which allows people detained to challenge the legality of their detention and, if successful, to get themselves quickly released.

He who comes to equity must come with clean hands. This means that a plaintiff who has been in the wrong in some way will not be granted an equitable remedy.

He who seeks equity must do equity.   Anyone who seeks equitable relief must be prepared to act fairly towards their opponent.

Indictable offences.   These are the more serious offences, such as rape and murder. They can only be heard by the Crown Court. The indictment is a formal document containing the alleged offences against the accused, supported by brief facts.

Law Officers.   They are the Attorney-General and the Solicitor-General.

Lawyer.   This is a general term which covers both branches of the legal profession, namely barristers and solicitors, as well as many people with a legal qualification.

Leapfrog procedure.   This is the procedure provided for in the Administration of Justice Act 1969, whereby an appeal can go directly from the High Court to the House of Lords, missing out the Court of Appeal.

McKenzie friend.   A litigant in person may take with him to the court or tribunal someone to advise him (a McKenzie friend), but that person may not usually address the court.

Mandamus.   An order requiring a particular thing to be done.

Natural law.   A kind of higher law, to which we can turn for a basic moral code. Some, such as Thomas Aquinas, see this higher law as coming from God, others see it simply as the basis of human society.

Noscitur a sociis.   The meaning of a doubtful word may be ascertained by reference to the meaning of words associated with it.

Obiter dicta.   Words in a judgment which are said 'by the way' and were not the basis on which the decision was made. They do not form part of the *ratio decidendi* and are not binding on future cases, but merely persuasive.

Parliament.   Consists of the House of Commons, the House of Lords and the Monarch.

Per incuriam.   Where a previous decision has been made in ignorance of a relevant law it is said to have been made *per incuriam.*

Plea bargaining.   This is the name given to negotiations between the prosecution and defence lawyers over the outcome of a case; e.g. where a defendant is choosing to plead not guilty, the prosecution may offer to reduce the charge to a similar offence with a smaller maximum sentence in return for the defendant pleading guilty to that offence.

Practice direction.   An official announcement by the court laying down rules as to how it should function.

Prohibition.   An order prohibiting a body from acting unlawfully in the future; e.g. it can prohibit an inferior court or tribunal from starting or continuing proceedings which are, or threaten to be, outside their jurisdiction, or in breach of natural justice.

Puisne judges. High Court judges are also known as puisne judges (pronounced puny) meaning junior judges.

Ratio decidendi. The legal principle on which a decision is based.

Relator action. A proceeding whereby a party, who has failed to prove *locus standi*, can choose to permit the action to be brought in the name of the Attorney-General.

Small Claims Court. This is not actually a separate court but a procedure used by the county courts to deal with claims under £3,000.

Sovereignty of Parliament. This has traditionally meant that the law which Parliament makes takes precedence over that from any other source, but this principle has been qualified by membership of the European Union.

Stare decisis. Abiding by precedent; i.e. in deciding a case a judge must follow any decision that has been made by a higher court in a case with similar facts. As well as being bound by decisions of courts above them, some courts must follow their own previous decisions.

Summary offences. These are most minor crimes and are only triable summarily in the magistrates' courts. 'Summary' refers to the process of ordering the defendant to attend court by summons, a written order usually delivered by post, which is the most frequent procedure adopted in the magistrates' court.

Ultra vires. Outside their powers.

Wednesbury principle. This principle, which was laid down in **Associated Picture Houses Ltd** *v* **Wednesbury Corporation**, is that a decision will be held to be outside a public body's power if it is so unreasonable that no reasonable public body could have reached it.

Youth court. Young offenders are usually tried in youth courts (formerly called juvenile courts), which are a branch of the magistrates' court. Youth courts must sit in a separate court room, where no ordinary court proceedings have been held for at least one hour. Strict restrictions are imposed as to who may attend the sittings of the court.

Index